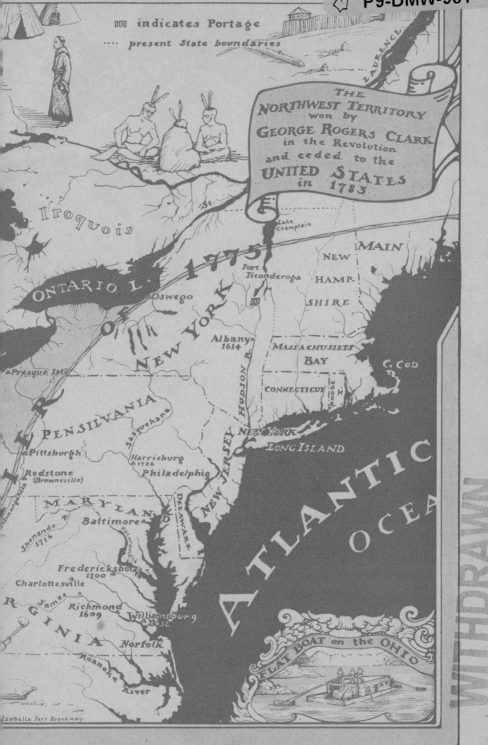

...ⅅ in 1783 by JOHN WALLIS, London. The SPELLING FOLLOWS the OLD MAP.

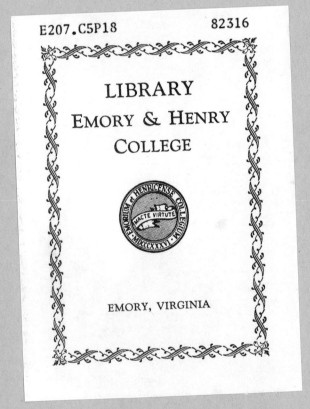

CLARK OF THE OHIO

GEORGE ROGERS CLARK. FROM A PAINTING IN MIDDLE AGE BY
MATTHEW JOUETT, IN POSSESSION OF THE FILSON CLUB OF
LOUISVILLE. THERE IS NO PORTRAIT OF CLARK IN HIS YOUTH

CLARK
OF THE OHIO

A Life of
George Rogers Clark
by
FREDERICK PALMER

With Illustrations

New York
DODD, MEAD & COMPANY
1929

PRINTED IN THE UNITED STATES OF AMERICA
BY THE VAIL-BALLOU PRESS, INC., BINGHAMTON, N. Y.

PREFACE

In a period when a new outlook, coursing familiar waters, is recharting great reputations and often finding that their achievement is not altogether worthy of their fame, a voyage of discovery may reveal men whose reputations are far below their achievement.

Why should we know young Paul Jones and young Alexander Hamilton so well and so little of a youth who should mean as much to us in our origins and character as Clive or Drake to England, La Salle to France or Cortez to Spain?

Except in one section of the United States the historical association of the name of Clark is with William Clark of the Lewis and Clark expedition. He was the Clark of the Northwest of his time and as it is known today, a competent army officer to whom fame was assured when, through the recommendation of his elder brother, George Rogers Clark, he was assigned, by President Thomas Jefferson, with Meriweather Lewis, Jefferson's private secretary, to explore the unknown northern portion of the new Louisiana Purchase.

George Rogers Clark was the genius of that enterprising Clark family. He was the Clark of another Northwest who won all the area from Pittsburgh to the source of the Mississippi which was once officially "The Territory of the U. S. N. W. of the River Ohio." Its seal is on the cover of this book.

But for him the borders of Canada might be on the Ohio and Allegheny rivers, and there might even have been a British corridor east of the Mississippi to the Gulf of Mexico, which would have made the Louisiana Purchase rather an impracticable accession, not to mention that it might have deprived younger brother William of his pioneering journey to the unexplored Rocky mountains. This makes

v

interesting speculation when one is looking out of the car window on the way to the Pacific coast; but its value, for my purpose in this preface, is the suggestion of results which were gained through sheer personality by Clark before he was thirty years of age.

One of the dramatic moments of the Revolution was when harassed George Washington received word of the capture of Vincennes by the young leader of forlorn hopes. Historians who differ in manner as much as Theodore Roosevelt and Albert Bushnell Hart have fallen under the spell of Clark's career; and yet he has not come into his own. Is the reason that his uncanny skill in action against superior numbers won almost bloodless victories? that he had some of the failings of genius which often go with its force and the prodigality with which it is spent? that he lacked the proper popular heroic pose in his later years? that he was ahead of his own time? that he did not think that to kill an Indian was the only way to make him a "good" Indian?

His swift movements, his blithe conquest of obstacles and distances, without funds or support when for a year he had no word from his chief, while he won an empire in the wilderness, would have the incredibility of a legend if documentation did not attest the fidelity of his own records which were long hidden from the world in family garrets.

I have written something of the social and economic background from which he sprang, and of which he was the product, as every leader is no less than of his own times. He grew to manhood in a period of the searching of minds and of agitation which culminated in a people's revolutionary action. It found in him the instrument and the spirit of an advance more formative, hazardous and picturesque than its offspring of the covered wagon and cowboy epoch of the trans-Mississippi plains. He was romance, American romance, which we may now the better appreciate in human discrimination as we re-examine the influences that have made us what we are. He dealt with forest Indians who had thickets for ambush and many waterways for their swiftly paddled canoes.

The readers will at once perceive where, in the lapses of documentation, especially in military action, I have interpreted him out of my own observation of marches and sieges and the making and unmaking of nations. After having seen armies of millions of men in the World War and the play of politics behind the lines I find a family intimacy in his direction of a handful of soldiers and the reflection, in his ruler's part when he was so much more than a soldier, of all the human elements on a huge stage. He was his own cabinet "thinking of things in general" and working out policies "agreeable to human nature," this young patriarch of fractious settlers' families, this counsellor with Indian chiefs who came many hundreds of miles to see him in awe of the exploits of the White Brother of the Great Spirit.

One can not help relishing in juvenile fervor his successful boyish stratagems which I have often seen characterized as masterly conceptions by the commanders of large armies and by eminent statesmen of our time. His foibles give his shortcomings a more sympathetic note when he makes holiday with Indian chiefs to study the origin of Indian mounds; and his disappointment is shared when, later, the rivalry of the realtors of his day prevented the execution of his plan to make the city he had founded a "city beautiful" with a great esplanade on the banks of his beloved river, connected with a park system and civic center.

In considering a moot point, my inclination is to think that the written confirms the circumstantial evidence of his love for Terese De Leyba, the sister of the Spanish governor of St. Louis.

FREDERICK PALMER

BIBLIOGRAPHY

The basic and indispensable material for a life of Clark, aside from his Memoir and his Letter to Mason, is in the Draper manuscripts in the archives of the State Historical Society of Wisconsin to which reference is made in the body of the text. Without the indefatigable and prolonged research by Lyman Draper no comprehensive understanding of the man or narrative of his career would be possible.

Invaluable, as an adjunct to the Draper manuscripts, are Clark's letters and vouchers, and other papers relating to him, in the Virginia archives, which are also a storehouse of vital background material. Among the many courtesies the author has received in his work, he holds in pleasant memory the kindly assistance of Dr. McIlwaine of the Virginia State Library, and of Miss Nunns and Miss Kellogg of the State Historical Society of Wisconsin.

The Memoir is printed in full in W. H. English's *Conquest of The Country Northwest of the River Ohio,* and also, with Hamilton's report included, in Milo M. Quaife's *The Capture of Old Vincennes* which is accompanied by valuable notes.

Sources of fundamental value are Francis Parkman's *La Salle and the History of the Great West, The Old Régime in Canada* and *Frontenac and New France and Louis XIV;* and Justin Winsor's *The Mississippi Basin, The Westward Movement and Narrative and Critical History of America.*

In later research and publication grateful acknowledgment is due to Frederick Turner's *The Frontier in American History;* to Clarence C. Alvord's *The Mississippi Valley in British Politics, The Illinois Country, 1673–1818,* and his services in the *Illinois Centennial History;* to Reuben G. Thwaites' own history of Clark and his editorship of *The Early Western Travel Series;* to Miss Louise Kellogg's *Frontier Advance on the Upper Ohio* and her other works; to Louis Houck's *The Spanish Régime in Missouri;* to E. J. Benton's *The Wabash Trade;* to James Alton James' masterly research in the history of the Mississippi valley which he has made so distinctively his field, and to his life of Clark which is so full about Clark's later career and so valuable about Spanish relations with the States during the Revolution; and to the life of Clark by Temple Bodley who has so intimate a knowledge of Kentucky history, and whose legal training has illuminated his researches into the part of the land companies in frontier history and into the Wilkinson plot.

Among other sources, including manuscripts, are Theodore Roosevelt's classic *Winning of the West; The American State Papers and Archives; The Journals of the Continental Congress;* the writings of Washington, Jefferson and Franklin; The Letters of James Madison; Pollock Papers; A. S. Withers' *Chronicles of Border Warfare; Ohio Valley Historical Series; Journal of Nicholas Cresswell; Filson Club Publications;* J. P. Dunn's *Indiana;* Burke's *Old Northwest;* Henderson's *Conquest of the Old Southwest;* Pope's *Tour of the Western and Southern Territories, 1790–1;* Comans' *Industrial History of the United States; Mississippi Valley Historical Association Review;* Harper's *Colonial Men and Times;* Semple's *American History and its Geographic Conditions;* Tyler's *Patrick Henry;* Wilkinson's *Memoirs of My Own Times;* Beveridge's *Life of John Marshall; Journal of William Maclay; Michigan Pioneer and Historical Collections;* Morse's *Life of Jefferson;* Letter Book of Benjamin Harrison; Letter Book of Thomas Jefferson; *American Historical Review; Chicago Historical Society Collections;* Letters of Henry Knox; and George B. Park's recent *Richard Hakluyt and His Voyages,* an achievement in literary style as well as research, which is invaluable to understanding the origins of the British overseas movement which challenged Spanish power on the American continent.

CONTENTS

The Background

xi

ILLUSTRATIONS

LIST OF MAPS

xv

THE BACKGROUND

I

RIVERS OF DESTINY

OUR pioneers followed the rivers when bad roads ran into Indian trails which disappeared into the forest. On the rivers' banks they made their clearings, built their cabins and towns. The current, which soon took a boat out of sight beyond a bend, assured quick retreat from Indian attacks; it carried products to port.

The ancestral Clarks were among the pioneer Virginians who moved up the James. Early generations were aided by the flood of the tide. Later generations kept on until they were at headwaters. There, at the foot of the Blue Ridge, they formed another new frontier county, Albemarle.

Young George Washington, not yet twenty, was setting out as a surveyor in the wilderness when John Clark and Ann Rogers were married. It had been barely thirty years since royal Governor Spotswood and his exploring party, in 1716, had climbed the Blue Ridge and looked down upon a very pleasant river. The Shenandoah seemed to be seeking the sea by a route at right angles to the habit of Virginian rivers; but, as tributary of the Potomac, its waters finally kept Virginian faith by flowing eastward into the Atlantic.

What lay beyond the green wall on the other side of the Shenandoah? The answer to that inquiry which concerned the valley of the Monongahela, whose waters went to the Gulf of Mexico, was to be left to another generation, young Washington's; and the winning of the great Ohio valley beyond that was to be the part of a son of John and Ann.

The Clarks were not of the tidewater aristocracy whose

3

immense plantations were tilled by indentured white labor, in addition to gangs of slaves, to meet the demand for the rapidly spreading European use of the "smoke weed" which America had given to the world. It was this oligarchy, in the flush period of a monopoly of the field of production, which enthroned the first group of American "kings." For tobacco kings preceded cotton and oil kings.

So rapidly had the slaves been augmented by drafts from Africa that the blacks outnumbered whites in Virginia when Governor Spotswood's report started the stampede to the "West" of the fertile lands of the Shenandoah valley, more than one hundred years after the founding of Jamestown. The call was heard over the Virginian border in Maryland and Pennsylvania, and then in the British Isles, particularly by the Scotch-Irish. It brought families which owned no slaves, and soon the whites again outnumbered the blacks in Virginia.

The Clarks had a few slaves. They were "gentry" who did not disdain work with their hands. In their middle strata they were in touch with both the tidewater aristocracy and the farmers who had no slaves.

Originally Clark was written Clerk. In America, after we began calling the man who served us across the counter a clerk, the family name of Clark was spelled as originally pronounced.

John, then Jonathan and then John again, the eldest Clark son of succeeding generations was christened. If the object were to keep the spirit of Junior, or I, II, and III and avoid confusion, the custom was not wholly successful. Jonathan Clark, father of John who married Ann Rogers, had made his "mark" in signing his will. Yet he disposed of two farms and other property. His daughters received twenty shillings more than his sons, John and Benjamin, while his wife's life interest included all his negroes.

It was the sturdy small planter class whose sons were

spurred toward the blue haze where mountain rim melted into the sky. They married young. They had many children who in turn could make new homes on new land.

Son John received the four hundred acres, under the shadow of the Blue Ridge on the Rivanna river, to which his father had taken out patents. This was his marriage portion for his start in life with his bride Ann Rogers, his patrimony for founding another family. He married rather old for the time. He was twenty-three.

But Ann Rogers, who was his second cousin, was young to marry even for those days. She was so young that present day canons would have broken a scandal about John's head for having robbed the cradle; and doctors would have subscribed to shocked elders' prophecies of physical catastrophe for both Ann and her offspring. She was fifteen. Pathology, as well as psychology, is different in different epochs. In early America, apparently, those who survived childhood's ills were strong.

The fact that Ann's mother was a Byrd is as irrelevant as are the forbears of her own husband in view of this pair's own achievement in ancestry. Ann bore ten children which was slightly above the average of the period, while brother-in-law Benjamin's thirty one children—by two wives, let it be said—was unusual even in those days.

I know of no record of a woman who did more than Ann toward officering the future Continental Army. Of her six sons, the first two were generals, the third a captain and the fourth and fifth both lieutenants in the Revolution. William, the sixth, was too young to be allowed to serve even as a drummer boy against King George.

Ann's eldest son, in keeping up the family custom, had been named Jonathan after his grandfather Jonathan. The second son, born November 19th, 1752, was called George Rogers—and always to be George Rogers, his mother's family name included in full. Virginians were much given then, as they still are, to keeping up family names, which is the habit of people rooted in the soil.

When visitors arrived on horseback and wanted to see the new baby, it was noted that he had red hair and luminous black eyes, which is not the combination of philosophers. It may give birth to dreams which, instead of disappearing up the chimney with the firelight's glow, are the summons to action.

Both parents were devout Episcopalians. As soon as each child, in turn, was old enough to go, another was added to the row of Clark heads in the family pew. When Ann was absent from church it meant that another little Clark was coming.

The father, a methodical man, kept strictly to the business of winning support for his increasing family out of his four hundred acres. His account book and his letters show that he had a modest primary education. He left public affairs to neighbor Peter Jefferson whose Shadwell estate adjoined his own.

Peter was very well educated for the time. He was a burgess, a master surveyor, who was called in as arbitrator in the frequent boundary disputes. His hand was on everything going on in the county. Important business often called him to Williamsburg, Richmond and Fredericksburg.

He was wealthy for his time in a plantation of nearly two thousand acres; but his environment in the "back country" had made him a Whig, although he had married a Tory in Miss Randolph of one of the old colonial families. In the growing feud, which was soon to come to a head, he was one of the spokesmen for economic justice to the small planters against the tidewater aristocracy which had the royal governor's ear.

His pride was in his son Thomas who was nine when George Rogers was born. Already, he not only rode well and danced well and played the violin; but he was so remarkably precocious at his lessons that his father was determined that he should have the highest education available.

Thomas Jefferson's future championship of democracy, nurtured in the small planter's protest against privilege, was long to continue to be the attitude of the West against the East. The later settled portions of the country were always asking credit from the older settled portions which had the capital to lend. The seaboard was debtor to London long after the bond with the mother country was broken, until the World War made us a creditor nation with Europe in debt to us.

Aside from writing the Declaration of Independence and being twice President of the United States, Tom was to found a new university "out West" in Albemarle County where the Jeffersons and Clarks had been neighbors when neighbors were few and widely separated. The friendship of the two families was not to be forgotten in troublous times to come when the philosophical statesman was to appreciate the character of the red haired Clark son which was so different from his own.

In that year 1752 when George Rogers Clark was born, George II was on the British throne; Louis XV on the French, and Frederick the Great on the Prussian throne. John Wesley's eloquence was winning a vast following for his new Methodism in England, and Samuel Johnson, who so despised the Americans, had nearly finished his new dictionary. Voltaire and his patron, Frederick the Great, were wearying of each other at Potsdam.

Busy Benjamin Franklin, lately elected to the General Assembly of Philadelphia, was preparing to reform the Colonial postal service. John Adams and John Hancock were students at Harvard College. Patrick Henry, after having made a poor job of his books, was clerking in a store and considering the study of law. George Washington had accompanied his tubercular half-brother Lawrence in the vain hope of a cure in the West Indies, where George himself came down with smallpox which pitted him for life.

Half of the two million population in the thirteen colonies were in Massachusetts, New York and Pennsylvania. Half of the immigrants from the British Isles were voluntary or forced indentured labor. The voluntary were the very poor who thus paid the price of a passage to America. Forced indenture included paupers as well as criminals who escaped the home penalty when there were three hundred crimes on the British calendar. Fourteen years indenture was in place of the death penalty and seven years of branding and whipping. The custom of binding poor children out for their "keep" which prevailed to a much later period was a survival of the indenture system.

Boston and Philadelphia were growing towns approaching twenty thousand inhabitants. Richmond had less than ten thousand. Charleston had four thousand and all South Carolina thirty thousand. Ten years ago Miss Elizabeth Lucas had planted an indigo seed on the Lucas plantation near Charleston. Now South Carolina produced 200,000 pounds of indigo which was to rise to 1,000,000 before the Revolution.

"This country carries on a great trade with the other parts of the world," wrote Peter Kahm of Philadelphia, "yet, none but English ships are allowed to come to this port. But all the money which is got must inevitably be sent to England in payment for goods which are got from thence, and yet these sums are insufficient to pay our debts."

So much for the world of Europe and the British Colonial world of America east of the Alleghenies. What was going on west of the Alleghenies? It was in 1752 that Squire Boone settled on the Upper Yadkin river. He had a son as promising in his father's chosen line as young Tom Jefferson. Daniel Boone, aged eleven, was practicing with his rifle on live game, not far from the Cumberland Gap into

LA SALLE, THE FRENCH EXPLORER. FROM A PAINTING
AS HE APPEARED AT COURT

Kentucky which he was to make the field of his future marksmanship and his service under George Rogers.

North of the Yadkin, of the Santee and the Savannah rivers was the Roanoke, then the James and then the Potomac, all rising in the Appalachians and flowing eastward, channels for westward migration. But where the Atlantic coast line bent eastward from the Susquehanna's mouth to the Penobscot, the rivers flowed generally southward and the settlers were advancing northward up their valleys until they too approached headwaters and began making homes in the laps of the watershed hills. The New Englanders were tilling stony slopes when they did not know of the fertile soil of western New York and the Ohio Reserve which could be reached only by crossing streams and was to wait on development until man made a water route in the Erie Canal.

A great river was the Hudson, to Hendrick Hudson who sailed his Half Moon up its broad reaches and gave it his name, and great to the Dutch and to the British who came after them to Manhattan; great the Potomac to John Smith and to those who came after him; and great the Connecticut to those who followed its course. The Hudson was as great as the Rhine; the Susquehanna as the Rhone; and the James as the Thames.

When the destiny of America was being shaped by its navigable streams the average settler of the Eastern seaboard had heard vaguely of rivers far mightier than the Hudson or Potomac in the distant wilderness. These were better known in Paris than in Richmond or Philadelphia.

Not with the British colonists but with the French were the honors of bold inland pioneering. The French *voyageurs* did not wait on economic pressure to push them out to learn what lay beyond the frontier. Theirs was the spirit of adventure and exploration.

René La Salle had set the pace in 1669. He and Duluth

and Joliet and Father Marquette wove a spell over French youth. Where Columbus set out for a passage to India and discovered America, La Salle set out to find the river of Indian report which he thought emptied into the Pacific and would make a short cut to China and so discovered the Ohio. Duluth, if he had not had to turn back to help La Salle, might have gone as far as the Dakotas before being rebuffed by the inhospitable plains in his effort to reach the Pacific, which he thought was so much nearer than it was, and was not to be reached by that route until nearly a century and a half later by Lewis and Clark. They, after crossing the plains, had to surmount the Rockies whose existence was apparently unknown to Duluth.

La Salle was the first man to float down the Mississippi. He knew only that the broadening stream must lead him to the sea. His ear keen for the roar of falls ahead, his eye keen against ambush by savages, he knew not what misadventure might leave his experience a mystery instead of a tale which he would proudly bear to the court of Versailles. Alas, the only portrait of him left to posterity is of a dandy in ornate uniform rather than in the rough garb of his travels. He would have been a poor servant of the *Grand Monarque* if he had not considered the grand monarch of rivers and all the rivers which flowed into it as henceforth French.

Such was the vast prospect of empire which he opened to the vanity of Louis XIV and such the prospect of souls to be saved by the churchmen of His Catholic Majesty. These incredibly majestic rivers were to be Louis XIV's rivers; and his the lakes as large as the North Sea across which La Salle and other *voyageurs* sailed the ships they built, lakes of clear fresh water in a chain which made an inland Mediterranean to be Louis' own sea.

Louis, too, relieved home pressure of criminals and paupers by deportation to America. Quebec was the pioneer settlement. The Gulf of St. Lawrence was directly across the Atlantic. It drew the tide of French migration. The Gulf of Mexico was far away athwart the sea routes of jealous Spain. La Salle was to perish in the grim extinction of that colony which he founded in Texas after, on his voyage from France, in the confusion of the deltas on the hot lowlands, he failed to find the mouth of the Mississippi through which he had once passed.

Further royal action, after this fiasco by the father of the great dream, waited until the British threats of occupation on one hand and Spanish pressure on the other endangered the French sovereignty of the lower Mississippi valley. Then Louis gave his sanction to a grandiose scheme of planting settlements by a grant to a land company. This led to the mad speculation in its shares and the bursting of the "Mississippi Bubble" of which nothing was left but a few survivors eking out a bare existence between New Orleans and Mobile.

But the French throne had a stake to defend against European rivals. Government patronage took the place of private enterprise in a fresh effort. France had learned her lesson at the price of blood and failure which leaves the bones of one set of pioneers to pave the pathway to success by a later one.

At the time of George Rogers' birth the French had made the Mississippi an inlet of empire no less dependable than the St. Lawrence. These two great arteries and their tributaries were the thoroughfare of their at once bureaucratic and venturesome but scanty colonization, as were the rivers of the eastern seaboard of the sturdier British colonization.

When his ministers could draw the attention of Louis XV, successor of Louis XIV, away from his pleasures and his mistresses to the map of the North American continent, he might survey the extent of his colonial domain. He was

not in the unhappy case of the English king across the
British channel in having to share ownership with a Parliament.

Over all that region drained by the Father of Waters
that La Salle and Duluth had traversed, north and south
from the Lakes to the Gulf and east and west from the
Appalachians to where Spain had set her missions on the
Pacific coast, the French *voyageurs* had set the *fleur de
lis* of the Bourbon flag. Rival Britain, her home population
then half of that of France, had only a slice of land on the
Atlantic coast.

II

IN THE GREAT VALLEY

PORTAGES between rivers were the links in the chain of destiny of empire. That from the St. Lawrence to Lake Champlain and the headwaters of the Hudson, a link between the British and French colonial worlds, was to entice Burgoyne to disaster at Saratoga in his effort to cut the loosely integrated rebellious British colonies in two.

When La Salle first passed around Niagara under the direction of Indian guides, he heard its roar in the distance, but was too intent on his mission to make any side trips to the wonder of that mighty volume of water which was still better known in Paris than in London drawing rooms and market places in 1752.

Beyond the Niagara portage were other portages, the bridges of La Salle's travels which later were the bridges between his dreams and reality. There was a portage from the headwaters of the Maumee which flowed into Lake Erie to the headwaters of the Wabash; another from Lake Michigan to the headwaters of the Illinois; and another from the headwaters of the Fox River into the Wisconsin.

Down the Wabash into the Ohio and down the Illinois and the Wisconsin into the Mississippi! French America was cut in its depth and breadth, for a distance farther than from Paris to Russia, by the two waterways, both French, which flowed into the sea three thousand miles apart. These were figures which had caught the imagination of the great Louis XIV if they had become stale to novelty-loving little Louis XV who took all possessions for granted as appurtenances of the world's most splendid king in the most splendid court.

Once over the lake portages and downstream Quebec met New Orleans at Vincennes or St. Louis. Priests and *voyageurs*, who had last seen each other in France, exchanged tales of the ice-bound ports and tropical ports where they had disembarked after their voyage by sailing ship.

Had the steam railroad not come, the Erie Canal would have been the precursor of other canals joining the Lakes and the Gulf. Boats were the covered wagons of the seventeenth and eighteenth centuries; boats called dugouts because hollowed out of a log; rafts and boats of planks that carried families and freight; boats of all sizes for all streams. The pioneer who passed over a portage and came to a headwater at the forest's edge needed only an adze to provide transportation. The pilgrims of the gold rush of 1898, whipsawing lumber for their boats on the shore of Lake Lindeman to float them down to the Klondike gold fields, brought the method back to life.

For three quarters of a century, then, this movement had been spreading the French frontier in the great valleys by thousands of miles when George Rogers Clark was born on a farm one hundred and fifty miles from the site of Jamestown, one hundred and forty-six years after the first settlement in Virginia.

Indians brought to the French posts reports of new tribes which had not yet heard the gospel; of new streams and portages and regions where furs were plentiful. The priests had in the individual examples of the *voyageurs'* highhandedness and the trappers' cunning and cupidity, undermining spiritual labors, the same ground of complaint as the missionaries of our day against the worldly ways of the foreign traders in the Chinese ports on the South Sea Islands.

The profit of the great valley to the French was mainly in furs, although at first, they had dreamed of gold; of finding such Eldorados as the Spanish *conquistadores* had found in Mexico and Peru. Their only mine was some lead deposits at St. Genevieve south of St. Louis.

No nugget picked up on a river bar was ever to set the early pathfinder in the great valley aflame at the prospect of a bonanza fortune. If the word of a strike on the Mississippi had gone forth to London and Paris in the seventeenth century history would have been much speeded in the making.

The advancing settlers from the eastern seaboard did not carry a pan to pan for "colors" in the habit of the prospecting pioneers until after gold was found in California. The wealth they won east of the Alleghenies was not in gold. It was of the slow producing mine of rich surface soil, its dividends increasing long after Spain had spent her gold of Peru and Mexico.

Paris had heard of another great river which flowed into the Mississippi where the principal French settlement, St. Louis, had risen at the joining of the waters. Little was known except by hearsay of the country the Missouri drained. The bold who dared its expanses brought back confirmation of treeless plains, wicked heat in summer, fierce cold winds in winter, with no furs of account except of the buffalo (bison) which was then plentiful east of the Mississippi. The farther west the traveler went the worse the prospect. He came to bare mountains and deserts where there was neither food nor water.

In 1752 the matins of the Spanish missions at Santa Barbara and Santa Fé were as far away from those in the French mission at St. Louis as Tangiers from Luxor and across a land which seemed as forbidding as the reaches of the Sahara. Yet, if the great valley had remained French, if the spirit of La Salle had carried on, a *voyageur*, or perhaps a Jesuit missionary, might have discovered Pike's Peak long before Zebulon Pike.

In the coming French and Indian War, a victorious

France, which had absorbed the Spanish possessions instead
of yielding the lower valley to ally Spain to save it from
being more spoils of the British triumph, might have found
gold in California earlier than 1849. Such the *voyageur*
spirit, such the Jesuit thirst to find new souls to save.

Both as pathfinders and as settlers the French had a
gift with the Indians, or better a system in which a pontifical church and an autocratic state co-ordinated. In the
early days the whispered word of a cardinal in the royal
ear was often more powerful than a governor's petition
for colonial expansion. The early priest in the great valley
was no pale townsman hugging village comforts. He shared
the hardships of the trail, took an oar under the hot sun
in rowing upstream, carried a pack over the portages.

The worship of the Great Spirit was blended into the
Catholic ritual, making conversion inductive. A tithe of
all products from tilled fields to fur hunters' traps went
to the church by law. At the church door they were col-
lected and there the syndic presided over the assembly of
the people to consider communal matters. Indian passions
and white man's passions were measurably restrained from
conflict, racial antagonisms softened by religious paternalism, in a period when French tractability to ecclesiastical
and governmental direction was a habit.

Life in St. Louis, Kaskaskia or Vincennes, or any other
French settlement, in 1752, was much like that to-day in
French Canada where the traditions of the Middle Ages,
transplanted before the French Revolution, have been little
changed. There were rows of whitewashed, one-story and
story-and-a-half wooden houses set in flower gardens surrounded by a picket fence. Dancing was frequent on the
"puncheon" floors of log slabs. Coming out of distances
where for days he had not met a human being, there sometimes appeared in the doorway at a dance, the lean, fur-
hunting *coureur de bois*. The twinkle of lights at night, the

LOUIS XIV

spots of whitewash against the green fields by day, were
town and holiday to him.

Back of the houses were the strips of land assigned by
the syndic to the farmers. There were no isolated farm
houses. All farmers lived in the settlements and went back
and forth to their fields. Wine was made from the plentiful
wild grapes. The priests tried to keep strong drink away
from the Indians, but not altogether successfully when the
coureurs de bois, themselves drinking to excess in town
after prolonged absences on the trail, found that firewater
was cheap exchange for furs from the natives.

There were two types of *coureurs de bois*. One still held
with his race. He might have a white wife in the settlement.
The other was a "squaw man," more Indian than French.
But neither might indulge in "shooting up the town" on
a drunken spree. There was a curb on individual license
in the military garrison which stood for the final authority
of church and state. For the France of the Bourbons was
stern for order.

The comings and goings of the *coureurs de bois* broke
the village monotony. Traveling priests, visiting Indians
from the distances, also had tales to tell. So had an occasional young blade of the gentry of old France who was
still a *voyageur* for adventure's sake in the spirit of the
past.

Otherwise, the day's round flowed as serenely as in the
village under the shadow of the *seigneur's* château in the
homeland. Carpenters who built new houses fashioned fur-
niture of Louis Quinze models for them. They made *charrettes* which were drawn by two horses tandem over the
narrow trails for the well-to-do who asserted social superiority by not always traveling on horseback to points which
could not be reached by boat.

A *charrette* was shaped like a sedan chair: but in the
Illinois country, where men would not serve as porters, it

was put on wheels. The evolution was the same that built the first railroad coaches in the form of stage coaches. The best horses were the same breed as the cowboys' wiry cayuses of later times. They came from the Pawnee Indians far out in the region which is now Nebraska.

No one worked very hard. Farmers did not need to grub with New England energy which farther eastward was piling stones from the hillsides in walls to enclose new fields. Expanses of virgin lowland waited only on indifferent cultivation to yield bountiful crops.

Apple, peach and pear trees in the gardens and succulent wild plums provided fruit. Game was plentiful. Hogs as well as turkeys ran wild. Salted venison and buffalo meat and great quantities of wheat in addition to furs were in the cargoes that took two weeks to float downstream to New Orleans.

In the Spring and the late Fall the settlers were looking forward to one of the two red letter days of the year. Then all the population would be at the river bank just as that of Dawson one hundred and fifty years later, under the shadow of the Arctic Circle, was for the first boat down the Yukon in the Spring. *Coureurs de bois* would make it a point to be in town, too.

The bi-annual convoy would soon be arriving after two or three months' push against the Mississippi's current from New Orleans. Twenty blacks were at the oars of each of the dozen or more boats, averaging forty feet in length with a nine-foot beam, which kept together as protection from Indian marauders and white pirates.

They brought immigrants, wives of men who had gone ahead to prepare the way, perhaps a new governor, new priests and those people who were returning from a visit to France. They brought letters six months old and news of the French court and of European wars and politics; goods in answer to orders which had been made a year ago; drafts showing how much consignments of pelts or tallow or wheat had sold for in the New Orleans market; and ruffled shirts and silver buckles and brocades for men's coats and women's gowns and all manner of luxuries.

Freight costs doubled Paris prices. Some of the well-to-do colonists who lived in the few stone houses had solid silver plate on their sideboards, and they also had billiard tables which had been rowed all the way up the Mississippi. Usually the rich men had made their money out of the fur trade.

In the great valley, then, there was one breed of men, one pattern of manners, one faith, with life a replica of that in France and all the formative impulse from the top. But in the little valleys, east of the Appalachians, each a world of itself, there were several breeds of men of differing manners and faiths, the impulse in themselves. Yet the very qualities, which geographical separation and varying climatic influences would tend to intensify in estrangement, had one common factor which was eventually to draw them together in the strength of many strands woven into one.

III

IN THE LITTLE VALLEYS

JOHN CLARK, in caring for his large family, did not go back and forth from a house in the village to till his fields. Town was where you went to market to buy and sell, where the court sat and fairs and public meetings were held. The syndic did not assign you a strip of land. You took out patents for the one you had prospected on the frontier.

So it was from Georgia to the Maine border. Very early the Virginians had broken free from the system of the communal stockade at Jamestown and the Pilgrims from the communal row of huts at Plymouth.

"A man's house is his castle" fell oftener from English speaking lips in the seventeenth and eighteenth centuries than in the nineteenth, after the American and French revolutions, when it had become a principle so well established that it was taken for granted. The pioneer went forth to build his own castle; to be a lord in his own right in a new land when that privilege was restricted to the few in the old land, as he made a clearing and raised a house farther upstream or over the divide.

At dawn, when he started for his day's labor, he stepped from his doorsill into his own kingdom. Isolation he did not fear, even when he liked company for social diversion. He depended on his self-reliance for defense against the depredations of wild animals and Indian prowlers. An Indian uprising, with its inflicted individual tragedies, roused the neighbors who went on the warpath with an Indian ferocity which made retribution so severe that it would be borne in mind by the offenders.

It was not the spirit of La Salle and later of Wolfe at

Quebec nor for adventure's sake, not glory nor to add to the domain of king and church, which brought the mass of sea-board colonists to America when many sought freedom to worship in faiths apostate to the English state church. They were loyal subjects, yes, but they saw kings with the faults of men. The spirit that had made the barons brave King John, that had brought the British Parliament into being, was pervading a lower stratum against the exactions of caste and the corruption of the time under the rotten borough system and the accepted dispensation that the gentry were born to rule.

The simple faith in the divine right of kings which kept Louis after Louis on the throne of France had been weakened in England by civil wars, the rebellion of Cromwell, the change of dynasties, the low tone of morals under Anne, the importation of William of Orange and the Hanoverian Georges. And the leaven, largely "non-conformist," kept working under favorable environment in America. There men might speak aloud what they might only whisper in England; there men felt in self-dependence their own strength independent of paternalism.

Both in the seventeenth and eighteenth centuries, the ruling element of the migration, which was so much more mixed than the old historians confess, was in the serious and ambitious. They prevailed by force of character, position and wealth over the other elements, Puritan elder over the ungodly, the land-owning class of Virginia over the irresponsible and lawless. They had ever fresh reminder of the motherland's attitude in the worthless sons whom guardians exiled to America, and the town indigent, scapegraces and criminals for whom passage was provided under the plea of good riddance and economy in poor rates and prison maintenance.

The sprig of the gentry who came to see the strange wilderness and the rough barbarian manners of the colonists was the butt of "old timers" long before the cowboy forced the "tenderfoot" to dance to the music of shots from a six shooter in a western barroom.

Any addition which the colonists made to the royal domain was in the course of each making domain for himself. What each won out of the wilderness by the sweat of his brow was his own. The battle was with nature, not against the armies of kings in war against their own king. Contribution for the defense of the king's realm was already a far cry from Europe's quarrels in young Hartford on the Connecticut and young Fredericksburg on the Rappahannock and still farther from the headwaters of the James, the Delaware or the Hudson.

While every stroke of the axe, every furrow, every new cabin, every new shop in town, New England's fledgling shipyards and factories meant an increase of British domain, it was becoming more an American domain in the nascence of the evolution of a new civilization. People of the Clark type had been generations in America. They had ceased to think of England as "home." Home was in Virginia as it was for the others in the colony where they lived.

It was not His Majesty's American Colony. It was His Majesty's American Colonies, and they were already a troublesome litter. The very difference between the colonies, which time was seeming to intensify, gave a false assurance to royal governors that only the cement of royal rule could hold them together. If they showed signs of striking hands astute royal politicians might aggravate their jealousies. But in the middle of the eighteenth century no two colonies were so different in life and outlook from each other as any one was from the mother country.

The various religious denominations did not try to blend the Indian's spirit into their rituals when only the Church of England of the Protestant denominations could be said to have a ritual. The devout Clarks or other good Episcopa-

LOUIS XV.
LXV. Roy de France.

LOUIS XV

lians did not hold the Archbishop of Canterbury in the pontifical awe of the English villager touching the cowlick to the Dean, or the Lord of the Manor, in the shadow of York or Winchester Cathedral. A bare wooden "nonconformist" church interior, with long sermons and long prayers, had no colorful appeal to savage emotions.

Missions to the Indians were supported by the subscriptions of those who chose to give, which hardly included those who lived on the frontier in danger of Indian raids. Conversion by the evangelists was not by the scenic route but that of stern faith and salvation. An Indian who appeared in church was given a seat; but there is no record that Indians often went to church.

It was in 1699 that a Puritan clergyman, the Reverend John Eliot, published his primer for the religious instruction of the Indian. His translation of the Lord's Prayer into the Indian language began: "Nooshun kefukgut wunneetuptaamunuch koowefank. Payaumooutch kukkeitaffootamoonk." His efforts were hampered by the chiefs and medicine men who threatened the lives of converts.

Generally, Puritans, who were thinking in terms of religious freedom for their sect, left it to the Indians more consistently than to some of their fellow colonists. The plodding, surefooted, trading Dutch of Manhattan were not given to "evangelistic drives" among the natives; and the industrious Quakers, as partisans of peace, kept it without the Indians often joining their sect.

There were as many views about how to deal with the Indians as on other subjects among the colonists. In that self-reliant world of mutual competition and individual war on nature men sharpened their wits in the discussion of public matters while they hardened their muscles at labor and on the trail and gained fortitude in the survival of the fittest. They learned to turn a hand at all manner of trades. Every frontiersman was an architect and carpenter who knew how to "raise" a cabin. Do not forget that the women spun yarn that they wove into cloth and made into garments.

All developed quickness in improvisation to get out of pinches and a general adaptability in meeting emergencies. This quality, of early seaboard origin, the product of pioneering, often appeared in our soldiers in the World War in proof that it was not yet relegated to tradition when no more virgin soil called the pioneer. Meanwhile, people in the old world were pegs whittled in youth—a method transplanted to America in the French and Spanish colonial plans—to fit in certain holes in which they were set for life.

In all the complaints to royal governors, in all the petitions sent to London, mainly about economic rights, which were one day to culminate in the Revolution, there was yet no hint of rebellion against the king. The suggestion in 1752 that the dark eyed, red haired Clark child would one day lead a band of frontiersmen in immortal marches to capture British garrisons and be the American La Salle would have been as preposterous as in 1890 that we should have two million soldiers in France in 1918.

At that time the republican system existed only in neutral Switzerland which kept the key of the mountain lock by default when all the other kings would have instantly gone to war against a king who tried to purloin the key.

Nations must have kings as surely as they must have coinage, courts, forts and excise; bad kings had to be endured with good, no less than the changes of weather, as one of the inflictions of variable human nature upon human nature. All the kings of Europe seemed solidly settled on their thrones. Indeed, the king situation was never more comfortable with George II seeming to have a firm hold in England. It was England's persistent outlawry which had worried royal minds in the past.

As England saw in France the breeding ground of revolution in the closing years of the eighteenth century and the first three quarters of the nineteenth, so France looked on England in the seventeenth and nearly to the close of the eighteenth. England had sent a king to the block. That France would ever send one to the guillotine was as inconceivable as that one day men would fly.

The French of the great valley in 1752—when the Bourbon dynasty seemed as eternal a fixture as the college of cardinals—saw the English with the racial prejudice that has outlasted many dynasties. They saw the England of regicide; of much married, wife killing Henry the Eighth, the heretic who had set up a state church; England of a rowdy Parliament; of brutal beef eaters and ruthless buccaneers.

Spawned by this England, which held so light a hand over them, were the seaboard colonists in their lawless individualism, a people so unsocial that farmers would not live in villages together. They were given to hard drink and their young people allowed to practice the indecent custom of "bundling." Yet, in their bigotry, they hanged witches, allowed no one to play on Sunday and thought it wicked to dance. Neighbor to Quakers who practiced non-resistance were rough frontiersmen who exterminated the natives. There was no logic in the seaboard people and danger in their lawless energy. From their northern contacts the French, to whom the method of the Puritan and Cavalier was the same, spoke of them as the "Bostonnais," an earlier characterization than that of the Virginians as "The Big Knives."

France not only built forts on her home frontier facing her ancient Teutonic enemy, but forts to defend her colonial empire in the West. Back of forts, commanding the sea approaches, were rims of forts commanding the lake and river portage routes. Back of Quebec's heights of Abraham, whose guns had a plunging fire on the bottleneck of the St. Lawrence, was a fort at Presque Isle, the site of the present city of Erie.

There was also a fort at Detroit commanding the entrance to Lake Huron, Fort Michillimackinac at the entrance to Lake Michigan, Fort St. Joseph near the site of Chicago, Fort Miami on the Maumee and Fort Vincennes on the Wabash—strong points up and down the great valley, with a final rallying central point at Fort Chartres defending Kaskaskia below the present St. Louis, in the heart of the great valley where the Ohio and Missouri joined the Mississippi.

But there was one danger as yet unprovided for; one river undefended against the approach of an army whose skirmish line, armed with squirrel rifles and hunting knives and knowing no military drill, was already in sight. The magnitude of that threat was emphasized in the extent of territory that France had to protect in relation to her meager colonial population from which to recruit militia with which to strengthen her regular garrisons against attack.

The *voyageur* spirit had died out under Louis XV who did not encourage emigration when the spirit to leave their own country was as alien to the French as it is to-day. Against the authority of "scraps of paper" registered in European chancelleries establishing France's legal claim to the great valley, there were, between Detroit and New Orleans, only five or six thousand French representing the authority of tenure by settlement in the area of the vast inland sea and majestic rivers. Already in 1740, Virginia promoters had organized a land company to exploit the next valley, that of the Monongahela, beyond the Shenandoah; and the Monongahela flows into the Ohio.

Virginian settlers in numbers were already over the Atlantic watershed by 1752, the year of George Rogers Clark's birth. Bold Pennsylvanians were making over the divide from the branches of the Susquehanna. They and the Virginians had the shortest distance of our colonials to go to the French frontier. The Virginians had the easier approach of the two with the Monongahela's current to bear their boats. Therefore, at first the Virginians' part was that of settlers and the Pennsylvanians' that of traders.

Indians were bringing word to the French posts of the flash of steel in the thickets of the immemorial mountain wall of their hunting grounds. The Big Knives were feeling their way down the slopes of the Ohio as the Bostonnais had advanced up the New England valleys toward Canada.

They were no adventurers far from their base but the restless scouts of the main body of two million people who had been advancing cabin by cabin in new clearings, with village after village rising farther and farther upstream. Each forward step was rooted in self-reliance and in the tenure of established economic interest.

In addition to the large families of children reinforcing that unique army were the increasing number of immigrants from the motherland. These had not, as the French had, to make a long journey by river and boat at the end of their ocean voyage. They landed at a port at a river's mouth. They might tarry if opportunity met them there or they might move on farther upstream until they found it. George II need not encourage emigration. As we have seen, the kind His Majesty's government promoted was not the kind desired.

Ambition's impulse was now sending over the sturdiest of British manhood and womanhood who expected no government subsidy, paid their own way and knew that they would have to earn their own way in America. There was never a great formative movement in the history of peoples so strictly the product of self-initiative; never a movement in which judgment of a man was so little on his past and so much on his achievement, as this from an old world into a new land to make a new world.

The indentured laborer, whether, in order to reach America, he sold his brawn for a term of years, or he was working out a penalty, often faced westward to begin life afresh when his term expired. Sometimes those who had been sent over for crime reverted to lawlessness. They might become "border ruffians."

Once over the Atlantic watershed the scouts of the army began beckoning to the main body. The strength and experience which had been gained toiling uphill and upstream now quickened the momentum downstream into the great valley with the current of a mighty river whose rich bottom lands spread up many long navigable tributaries.

This movement, which had banked up on one side of a watershed and then passed over to the other side, rather than the rivalry of kings vain of power, the play of diplomacy, or the strategy of generals, brought on the war between two colonial civilizations which we call the French and Indian War. The inevitable was precipitated in 1752, the year of Clark's birth, when Marquis du Quesne built the fort which bore his name where the Monongahela and the Allegheny join to form the Ohio.

This was on soil claimed by Virginia, and Virginia's vague pretension to all the Ohio country as a part of her domain now became the conviction of a legal claim. Royal Governor Dinwiddie of Virginia chose a legate who knew the rivers and the trails of the wilderness for a winter journey to warn off Duquesne. Young George Washington, then twenty-one, brought home the word that Duquesne was determined to hold the Ohio for the French. Duquesne could not do otherwise. The Ohio was a Rubicon.

The anger of Virginia was communicated to London fur merchants who were seeing the peltries of the great valley further alienated from the London market and schemes for land companies balked. It was an influence in royal councils

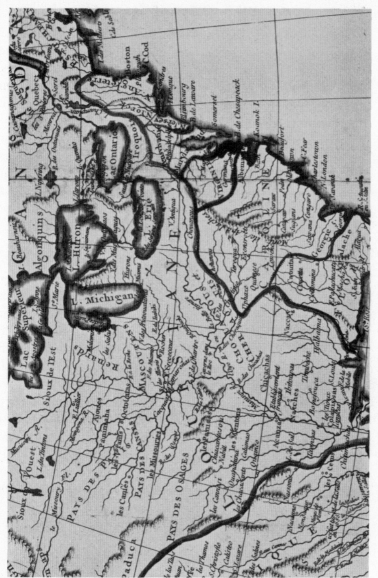

ROBERT DE VAUGONDY'S MAP OF THE FRENCH POSSESSIONS IN AMERICA, IN 1750

when opinion in France and England was ripe for another clash at arms to settle many differences which had recently become acute.

Not by the size of the British and French garrisons in America, not by the number or the strength of forts, not by Wolfe's victory at Quebec was the sovereignty of that rich region of the temperate zone where white men flourish to be decided.

If, in the gay distractions and profligate grandeur of the court of Louis XV, the substance behind them under Louis XIV was weakening, French national instinct still realized that the defense of the national life was on the Rhine. So in Britain, when under the Hanoverian George the corrupt politics of a Newcastle was weakening the vigor of the Britain of Elizabeth and Cromwell, British national instinct, in the persistence of that first principle of self-preservation, realized in face of the Channel moat that the defense of the national life was by sea. One people thought of the guard at the gate as a soldier, the other of him as a seaman even as they do to-day.

And France, if she had not a king of the Charlemagne tradition, had a soldier in the Turenne tradition, in Sieur Beaujeu-Villemonde, so worthy of a great king, who marched his one hundred and thirty-two soldiers, after Wolfe's victory, from Michillimackinac at Lake Huron's entrance through the wilderness to Fort-Chartres in Southern Illinois. He would keep his king's flag flying to the death when there could be no succor for him with Britain holding the Atlantic bridge secure. If France had held this bridge Wolfe's victory would have been of no avail with the sea clear for French transports to bring a fresh French army against him.

Sea power, which earlier or later decided the destiny of India, Egypt, and Cape Colony, was now to decide the destiny of the great valley—but only for a brief time. The final decision was with Ann Rogers Clark's second son who was to make such a march as Beaujeu-Villemonde had made and not for his king, but leading the advance of that army of settlers who needed no sea bridge to protect their gains.

FORMATIVE YEARS

IV

A PLANTER'S SCHOOLING

JOHN CLARK, being able to "read, write and cipher" and, therefore, better educated than his father, responded to the American parental impulse for further improvement in the next generation. He sold his Albemarle County farm for a good price and moved to a farm which his uncle had bequeathed him in Caroline County where his children would be near good schools.

There were now four little Clarks. George Rogers was five. It was two years since the outbreak of the French and Indian War which lasted twice as long as the Civil War or the World War. Britain lost in the first encounters as usual.

The dawn of George Rogers' boyhood memory was in the period of sinister reports from the "back country" of Braddock's disaster and the general repulse of British regulars and bands of hastily raised, undrilled frontiersmen. French propaganda had roused the Indians to fight as allies against the lawless and godless Bostonnais and Big Knives who would destroy their game and exterminate their race. No atrocity call in any war had a nearer appeal than that in answer, picturing the horror of women and children tomahawked or led away into captivity over the dead body of a settler defending his isolated cabin.

George Rogers Clark was eleven when the war was over. His hero, the hero of every Virginia boy, was young Colonel George Washington. To Mother England there was Wolfe; but to Mother Virginia there was also Washington, her own son. The glamour of his name had spread from remote villages at the headwaters of the Roanoke to those of the Con-

necticut before he was of the age of the average college
senior to-day.

His was the one great reputation that a Colonial had made
in the war; and the recollection of it brought the common
agreement, in the midst of inter-colonial jealousies, which
later summoned him to the command of the Continental
Army at Cambridge. If he were the indispensable man to the
success of the Revolution, then his fame in the French and
Indian War was indispensable in giving him opportunity to
become "the father of his country."

Returning veterans who had served under him revealed a
Washington as different from the Washington of legend—
the Washington in his twenties—as that of the historians
who, in their humanizing process and rereading of source
material, leave him still unreal by not stressing Washington
in his formative years.

He was the daring blade of the tidewater aristocracy, the
glory of his class. When others had remained at home to
enjoy their privileges he had been forth at seventeen to risk
his life on wilderness trails. To the frontiersmen he was a
man among men whose endurance was equal to theirs. He was
seeking new land for development and realizing on his
knowledge in the promotion of land companies.

Quick of movement and thought, a giant for strength,
cool in a pinch, passionate in action, he was seen as the
Washington whose agility and resource at stupid Braddock's
elbow had saved a remnant of the proud British regulars
who had marched into ambush; the Washington who held
his prestige and the faith in his personality after his capitulation at Fort Necessity which might have ended the
career of the average commander; the Washington who had
defended a frontier of three hundred and fifty miles with
seven hundred men.

He did not wait on the crises of the Revolution to attain
that moral stature which impressed on his fellows the con-

viction that what Washington could not do could not be done. Had he fallen in action in the French and Indian War he would have been immortalized and his influence upon the young America of the seventeen sixties and seventies would hardly have been less vital. For this reason I dwell on him as he appeared to the youth of his time.

The qualities that he had shown with Braddock in the company of British regulars touched our pride in the American being a natural soldier which was one of the things that his drill-master von Steuben had to combat when Washington of the later years had to form raw material into a disciplined army.

Home from the wars and looking after his private affairs, the great planter did not capitalize his military renown by an active part in politics. He left politics to the lawyers. But he had a quiet commanding influence in all political thought, this first citizen of Virginia from 1753 until 1775 before the outbreak of the Revolution.

To gay and dashing young Virginia, he had the appeal of a sporting country squire and generous host. He rode to hounds, he was a good judge of Madeira, he drove a thrifty but not a mean bargain, knew a good horse and lost and won at cards or at the races in a becoming manner. The small planters, in their intensifying feud with the large planters, felt that this richest of landholders was in a class by himself, a man apart in his physical and mental endowment, having already that dignity of person which was to grow upon him with responsibilities and honors as his physical vigor slowed with age.

This dignity was a Virginian characteristic which led other Colonials to think that the Virginians sometimes thought too well of themselves. Back-country men as well as the tidewater aristocracy had it. George Rogers Clark had it and the strain was to carry on to Robert E. Lee whose model in his boyhood, no less than Clark's, was Washington.

To Virginians it was only Virginia that could produce a Washington. It was said that Clark looked like Washington. Their pictures do suggest the likeness, but we have no picture of Clark in youth. Probably the suggestion of resemblance sprang from the Clark of Kaskaskia and Vincennes carrying out so brilliantly the tradition of young Washington as a frontier fighter.

Washington's career having been set by his inheritance as a planter, it was not the custom in Virginia, as it was in New England, that he should be as well educated as John Hancock or John Adams or the young Virginians who went to William and Mary. Many Virginian boys must have found in the Washington example an excuse for not trying to excel in their books. The rare ones who went to college looked toward the law or the church. Some sons of the tidewater aristocracy went to Oxford and Cambridge often less for an education than for the name of it; but fewer were going abroad after the French and Indian War than previously.

More were going to William and Mary, or north to Princeton, in the course of the growing sense of colonial independence. The thought of young Washington at Oxford instead of surveying the wilderness destroys the figure of him in history no less than the thought of a young Lincoln rolling barrels for a New York merchant on a New York wharf instead of splitting rails destroys the Lincoln of history. Either was the product of his times and environment as were other leaders of their periods; and the environment and the opportunity which produced George Rogers Clark and other leaders of his period was the bridge between the periods of the two.

One hundred and fifty years ago in Virginia, and no less for the most part in the rest of the colonies, taxpayers whether large or small planters would have scorned the suggestion that they help pay for the education of other people's children. The concept of freedom did not contemplate a de-

WASHINGTON ON HIS MISSION TO MARQUIS DU QUESNE
ON THE OHIO. FROM AN OLD ENGRAVING

mocracy of manhood suffrage which must be literate through a public school system.

Education was a private affair, and you paid for it as you paid for the luxury of silver buckles or food, clothes, and shelter. Many of the best Virginian schoolmasters were Scotch, a product of the canny tradition of much thorough learning on little oatmeal. They meant that the parent should get his money's worth. If his child were not in earnest he had better save his money by not sending him to school.

The suggestion of vocational training courses belonged to a remote future. The place to learn farming or business was on the farm or in the office. Pupils had few elective opportunities. No fads disturbed the set curriculum of Greek, Latin and mathematics.

Donald Robertson, who made a high reputation for his school, had married a relative of Ann Rogers. To him were sent elder son Jonathan and second son George Rogers. With them, on the benches facing Donald, were James Madison, a future President, and John Tyler, the father of a future President of the undreamed-of United States.

According to all accessible evidence, George was not as good a pupil as brother Jonathan, not to mention being as good as Madison, son of a rich planter, who was to go to Princeton. George had some ability in mathematics, but when he came to recite Greek and Latin his mind was out of doors coursing the woods for deer and wild turkeys. He could outwrestle and outrun the prize wrestlers with the ancient languages among his fellows; he was a master hand at settling disputes among them.

The quick interest in history and geography of the boy who liked to roam in the woods was to make history and change maps but was of no purpose in gaining marks under Donald Robertson. Geography? There was Scotland, and then there were England and Europe, the Colonies and the heathen world. History? If you were so minded to learn

more than was in Cæsar, the Anabasis and the Bible you
might have it by reading books. In a modern elective course
George might have shone. He would surely, by all we may
learn about his youth, have had an A in natural history
through his knowledge of wild life. In this Donald might
have gone to school to him.

Details are lacking, but evidently Donald concluded it was
a waste of parental money to try to pound Greek and Latin
into Ann's second son. Only a few were chosen to be scholars
in Colonial days; and George Rogers, in that Scotch process
of elimination, was back on the farm at the end of the school
year.

At twelve, then, his formal education was finished. At
least he could write and spell better than his own father who
had a father who made "his mark" in signing his will. His
power of expression in his letters and his Memoir suggests
that he had a good foundation at twelve or that he made up
for his laggardness under Donald by application in later
days and from listening to George Mason.

On a small farm, small for Virginia of the period, with a
few slaves, no tidewater aristocracy life of ease awaited him.
If he were to be a planter it were better that he should know
how to break a colt than to read Homer at sight. John Clark
determined that his son should be equipped for his future
when he should leave the parental roof to set up for himself
on a farm of his own.

In the father's methodical account book, George, when he
was fifteen, was debited with the cost of his clothes and all
articles bought for him and credited with the proceeds of a
crop of tobacco he had grown. At sixteen he sold his corn
and tobacco for thirty pounds or one hundred and fifty
dollars in the currency of the future United States, equal to
six or seven hundred to-day.

Staking a boy in this fashion was not common to Virginia

alone. It held throughout the Colonies where at sixteen a boy
was doing a man's work and younger sons joined the migration to make more new homes and villages farther up the
valley. The principle was the same as that which sets the son,
when he is out of college to-day, at the bottom round in his
father's factory, on a minimum wage, to learn the business
from the ground up.

So, at sixteen, George Rogers could feel he was something
of a capitalist, already a planter among planters, at the
fairs at Richmond and Fredericksburg, where buyers and
sellers met and lost and won at the horse races. Either town
was about thirty miles away from the Clark farm across
country which was to be the cockpit of the Civil War. The
roads were not so good in the seventeen sixties as when
Grant's and Lee's men cursed the hot and heavy dust of
summer and the deep chill mud of winter in the eighteen
sixties.

Fredericksburg could boast that it was more progressive
than Richmond. It was the first to abolish wooden chimneys.
Its taxpayers, grumbling at the cost, recognized the economic value of laying timbers in the streets as a pavement
when wagons sank up to their axles in the mud. Down the
James and the Rappahannock rivers went the crops from the
towns on their banks which had grown as the area of tilled
grounds around them spread; and up the rivers came the
manufactured goods from England. Above the rows of shops
were the "shingles" of lawyers and surveyors. Some men
combined the two professions in profit of litigation which was
long to flourish through "line fence" disputes.

Fall was the busy season for the storekeepers. Then the
farmers paid their bills and made purchases from the sale of
their crops. Among the wives who came to do their shopping
must have been Ann Rogers to provide winter clothing for
the little Clarks and thinking of Christmas presents when

the stockings were hung up before the fireplace and resisting personal temptations in millinery displays when so large a family had to be provided for.

Going to town meant meeting old friends and relatives who were scattered by the movement in making new plantations and new "co't houses" at new crossroads. It was a small world in which the succeeding generations of many children of the founding families had intermarried and every Virginian of the old stock had many cousins. Small worlds also were those of New York, Philadelphia, Charleston, Baltimore, Boston, Hartford and New Haven.

Through all the small worlds only two names of Colonials, Washington and Benjamin Franklin, were well known. Robert Morris was known in financial circles. Franklin was the Ben of "Poor Richard"; odd wise Ben, paragraphist and inventor who caught the lightning with his kite; excellent business man who had made a fortune; father of all manner of public improvements, many of which seemed whims at the time; delegate to the Albany convention which was the formal beginning of Colonial unity.

He had found time to study to make up for lack of early education. He had learned to read three foreign languages. Now he was in England again as delegate hobnobbing with scholars and writers and trying to prevent the passage of that "Mother of Mischief," as he called the Stamp Act, and to bring home to the mother land a sense of the growing indignation in the new land which was chafing in swaddling clothes. Thomas Jefferson, Patrick Henry and John Adams and John Hancock were rising young men with local reputations.

The rich men of America were still the great planters of Virginia. The son of a planter who counted his acres by thousands and his slaves by hundreds, when he rode into Fredericksburg or Richmond was followed by a body servant. Indeed, he could not move at all without this faithful black, so soft voiced and soft footed in anticipation of his "Massa's" wants and always ready to grin in flattering unction at "Massa's" quips.

The servants' mother might have been the "Mammy" who had brought up young "Massa" in that "old Virginia," which the struggle in that nearby cockpit between those who had slaves and those who had not was to make forever a memory enriched by the achievements of the sons of such mothers, north and south, as Ann Rogers Clark. And the Anns of Virginia, in having slave nurses to "mammy" their children had an easier lot than the equally prolific mothers of the north who had to do all the housework and nursing in person when they had not the aid of a "hired" girl, who was so distinctly "help" and not a servant—as she would be called in England—and who was only waiting until her man had established himself to move on up the valley to a home of her own.

There were occasions when the southern body servant played the part of human crutch in assisting a "Massa," young or old, to mount his horse or even to get to his lodgings and ease him, with the skill of experienced tact on such occasions in the midst of the object's incoherent complaints, out of his clothes. Otherwise "Massa" might go to bed with them on, which was not the habit of the Virginia gentry although night shirts were not general among the poorer classes.

For the taverns were almost as numerous as the shops in Fredericksburg and Richmond. In them card playing proceeded from early until late by men who were in town to make both a day and a night of it. There were taverns, which were frequented only by the gentry, through the grades to those of the rougher sort which a gentleman entered only in the sportive curiosity which took the younger set of the eighteen nineties "slumming" or takes those of the present day to a very devilish night club which "racketeers" are said to frequent.

The question was not whether one drank at all or not, but how much one drank and how well he could carry his liquor. A Virginian was not altogether without excuse for taking strong drink after long rides across country in winter when there was no heat in a house except the open wood fires, before the new stove, which was called the Franklin after the versatile Ben who had invented it, had been widely introduced.

But the Virginian had not so great an excuse as the New England elder—in his case it might have been reason in his sometimes adjustable Puritan logic—who could not see the snowbanks outside for the frost on the window pane as he broke the ice in the bedroom pitcher and then warmed his "innards" by a "tot" of rum before, in the wake of the steam from his breath with the thermometer below zero, he went downstairs to build the kitchen fire.

These reasons and excuses of the Eighteenth Century America have passed, now that we may turn a button and the fluid fire that the insatiable curiosity of Franklin caught with his kite will warm us.

When men in their cups got into an argument in Virginia taverns, or enemies flushed with liquor met in the streets, they had a care as to the language they used. Among the gentry a loss of temper might mean a call for seconds and shots might ring out at dawn on the bank of the river where lovers had been boating the previous evening.

In the rougher taverns disputants, who did not possess silver-mounted dueling pistols from the best London makers, did not wait on etiquette for action. The one who drew first won even as in later days when the movement from the little valleys over the watershed and across the great valley reached the cattle ranges.

Wherever men gathered there was one subject that never became stale. Any doubt on this scale is resolved in comparing the conversational resources of "horsey" people of to-day with those who discuss the make of motor cars. Every Virginian could ride soon after he was out of the creeping stage. Everyone had a horse; everyone knew a horse and was never quite willing to admit in his heart that anyone else knew a horse as well as he.

It was back to the horse after talk about the tobacco market, which held the place of the stock market to-day, after exhausting politics and the latest news about land sales and new developments in the back country and flings of resentment at the Stamp Act.

A likely colt was the apple of the eye of a planter as he surveyed his pasture. Horses not only did the farm work but drew or packed goods and carried people wherever they went away from the river. Care of horses and keenness for improvement of the breed had ever been characteristic of great peoples in their progress from the days of legend and mythology. Poor spirited the Virginian who did not hope that one day he would be the owner of a winner at the races. Lesser souls liked to own a winning bird when cockfighting was common among a certain class.

Youth's surplus energy found vent according to the customs of the time and resources of the region. Life was not dull when there were plenty of horses in a hospitable planter's world and people who lived by the soil had free days in winter when the soil slept. It was into the saddle and away, perhaps twenty or thirty miles, to dance far into the night and then back sleepy eyed and nodding over the pommel the next day.

One did not telephone or telegraph to a friend asking if he could be put up for the night. Ride up to the door—if not that of a friend it might be of a family who knew your family at least by reputation—and a black took your horse which he would have ready groomed for you at the curb when you went away. There was hot toddy before the fire for the chilled rider, always food enough and an extra bed for the visitor who would be so happy to return the favor when you came his way.

Diaries often mentioned the name of the host where a traveler "layed" for the night. The more isolated the plantation the more welcome the guest as he was sure to bring some news when conversation itself was more of an art and a diversion than in these days of radio and the telephone and the daily arrival of newspapers and magazines by the rural free delivery. The hospitality of the townsmen was returned by the planter in the hunting season when no one need bother about game preserve privileges in virgin forests. Although each man's house was his castle there was no end of goings and comings between castles in a land where everybody kept open house. The merits of the host's hounds as well as of his horses had to be appraised.

In a world where personal acquaintances and friendships were so numerous, owing to the common interdependence of hospitality, youth was more in touch with elders of light and leading than in a later period. Sixteen and sixty sat around the big wood fires after the day in the open.

The Clark and Mason families were ever riding over to see each other. George Mason kept open house at his country seat, Gunston Hall. He was the fourth of that name in the family line which was descended from a royalist partisan who fled from England after the execution of Charles I. John Clark consulted with friend Mason when he needed legal advice. Only George Wythe could be said to share Mason's leadership of the Virginian bar.

Mason was more than an able lawyer, he was a first citizen type, wise, human and scholarly, aloof from political turmoil, but his counsel much sought. He was very fond of young George Rogers. Perhaps his shrewd insight saw the

GUNSTON HALL, THE HOME OF GEORGE MASON, CLARK'S PATRON AND TEACHER

possibilities in the boy which others did not see; saw him as a high spirited colt who would travel fast and far and in the right direction if trained right; recognized in the chemistry of his nature explosive elements which were bound to make some kind of a noise in the world.

It was a case of disciple and master well met. If Donald Robertson had given George his "prep" course Mason gave him his college course. The curriculum of Mason's talks included history and geography and world affairs. Here was advice from one in whom youth had faith. It was after he had won the Northwest in 1779, when he was in the full tide of his success, that George Rogers wrote to Mason this tribute, which was sweet reward to the preceptor for the pains he had taken with a pupil:

"Continue to favor me with your valuable lessons; continue your reprimands as though I were your son."

Probably young George danced as late as other young men; probably he had his fling in Richmond and Fredericksburg. He must have been conspicuous as he passed under the "shingles" of the lawyers and surveyors in the streets in giant vigor of his six feet two inches with his red hair and his deep set eyes—not a type with whom the canny would pick a quarrel.

V

THE FRONTIER'S CALL

But his bent was not toward town or the ways of town. Not the guest who "layed" at the Clarks and brought the latest gossip around the royal governor at Williamsburg or from Europe interested him. It was the tales of the man fresh from the back country he wanted to hear. A figure in buckskin shirt and moccasins rather than lace ruffles excited his emulation.

Appearing at the door of planter hospitality and holding forth to groups were lean men with a hunter's watchful eyes which had the fixed gleam of rare and remote experience out of weather-beaten wrinkles. They had a gait formed on distant trails. Their shoulders were calloused by pack bearing, yet their new store clothes seemed to chafe them. They were the returning scouts of the army advancing over the watershed.

Since 1763 the French at Fort Duquesne no longer barred the way down the Ohio. A royal British proclamation in 1763 had anticipated the migration which should begin with the end of the French and Indian War. It prohibited the purchase of land or settlement without a special license beyond the headwaters of the Atlantic. London feared that settlement might interfere with the fur trade which was a part of the spoils of the victory won from the French merchants.

Development should be under royal guidance patterning after the paternalism of French colonization. Special licenses should go to those in royal favor and to royal governors who came to America as Cæsar went to Gaul, to retrieve their fortunes, or to make fortunes which should settle them in titled leisure on English estates. After the reaction from the strain and waste of war British interest in the future of America was acutely economic; but so also was the interest of the Colonials. Lord Dunmore, then Governor of Virginia, had his own stake in land schemes. So his own ox was being gored when he wrote to the British Colonial Secretary:

"I have learnt from experience that the established authority of any government in America and at home are both insufficient to restrain the Americans; and that they do and will remove as their avidity and restlessness excite them. They acquire no attachment to place; but wandering about seems engrafted in their nature; they do not conceive that Government has any right to forbid their taking possession of a vast tract of country either uninhabited or which serves only as a shelter to a few scattered tribes of Indians."

The complaint still holds that Americans, ever tearing down and rebuilding, never keep long settled in a home. Its modern instance is in the spring and summer migration of city apartment dwellers, all in that eternal desire to better themselves. And observe that Lord Dunmore—pardonably petulant at the wrecking, by those lean leather faced men in buckskins, of his dream of a competence for the future in land rents drawn from America—speaks of the seaboard colonists as Americans, recognizing that they had already become a distinctive type among peoples.

There was truth in his letter which was expressive of two view-points as far apart as buckskin shirts and court uniforms and the Falls of Ohio and London town on the Thames. The king's attitude was natural enough from the outlook of Whitehall, the Foreign, and the War and Admiralty offices, and also of the British taxpayer. Were not British arms protecting these ungrateful and fractious colonials? Had not Wolfe fallen at Quebec and British regulars endured hardships and British seamen fought to clear the

French out of America and make it a British possession?
England had footed the bill. All loyal subjects would consider the "royal will and pleasure" of that proclamation
which prevented settlement over the divide.

The frontiersmen, and all the colonial merchants and
financiers interested in profits from lands, furs and expansion, were thinking in terms of their own will and pleasure.
Their answer to the post bellum question of "Who won the
war?" envisaged frontiersmen driven from their homes by
Indian attacks and forming the militia under Colonel
Washington who had held the frontier while Wolfe was
winning glory in Quebec which was a long way from the
Monongahela.

They had kept the British flag flying on the watershed;
they had built something for England to fight for. What
had made the Atlantic seaboard worth while to England as
a market? Their toil and sweat transforming the wilderness with towns in place of Indian tepees. Their right to
advance over the watershed was as clear as it had been
to advance up the seaboard valleys and for the same reason.

So clear was it—and, anyway, they were going—that
they only grinned and crooked a finger at this proclamation
which was so ill advised a bit of politics as a further influence in estranging the colonists from the mother land.
It was like ordering the rivers of destiny to stop their flow.

Special licenses by royal grant! The pioneer took out
his own when he came to a stretch of ground which his
knowing eye favored near a spring or stream which would
supply water for his family and his beasts. He blazed trees
enclosing the acreage of his future farm, and then confirmed
this "tomahawk" claim by the "corn" title of clearing and
planting. His was the right of eminent individual domain
which was conferred by his labor and enterprise and confirmed by something stronger than royal power, a frontier
public opinion supported by flintlock rifles. King, or royal

governor, who disputed it must deal with him on the spot far from garrison towns. The police power of the distant British Isles could not stretch so far.

To have enforced the royal proclamation of 1763, which preceded the first Stamp Act by two years, would have required a British army far larger than had ever been in the Colonies or Marlborough had at Blenheim, the building of roads, of a line of block houses with the intervals between them patrolled; and that all pioneers caught slipping through the cordon be put in concentration camps in the fashion of the pacification of the Boers in South Africa or of the Filipinos of Batangas province.

And this would have been only a temptation for the restless to keep pushing around the ends of the line until it would have had to extend from the St. Lawrence to the Savannah. The same sense of the right of eminent individual domain born of the "every man's house is his castle" tradition, still persists in the Kentucky and Tennessee mountaineers—descendants of the pioneers who halted in the passes instead of following the movement to the river bottoms—against revenue officers who would interfere with their doing what they wish with their own corn by making it into "moonshine."

As the Virginians and the Carolinians had the easiest access to the Ohio valley they felt most intimately its spell and also the stupid injustice of the royal proclamation as a fresh illustration of royal policy, while the New Englanders busy in manufacturing development felt most keenly British trade restrictions.

So it was that the sparks of rebellion first took flame in the extreme ends in both distance and manners and customs of the colonies. The movement from the ends toward the middle promoted unity of action when the Stamp Act of universal application aroused widespread indignation.

Young George Rogers lived in a back county near the

"back country" in the thoroughfare of the movement over
the watershed. He was in the dawn of the realization of the
promise of the new land which kept growing with his stature.
Each year brought reports from men who had gone still
farther down the Ohio finding still richer land.

Prosperous people, already established on paying plantations or doing a good business in town or having a profitable
clientele in their professions and being near church, schools,
markets, relatives and friends, were content to remain "as
is." They saw the frontiersmen as aliens to their own routine
world, yet they thrilled in common pride in their boldness
and hardihood, and took a chance on "shares" in grubstak-
ing them and paying their land entry fees. "Daring do"
was ever for youth which in the seventeen sixties and seventies need not ask the way. Only the young and the trail-
hardened could bear the hardships.

The great valley was being "discovered" again a hundred
years after La Salle. The new country must be surveyed
not only by counties and townships but in small sections
that would register "corn" titles at the courthouse. This
would make work for young surveyors beyond the area of
competition with the old.

Surveying was as valuable a professional training to the
planter as the law of contracts to a business man to-day; a
profitable side line in winter when the crops were in. Young
George Washington had understood this, and learned surveying before he set out for the wilderness. His example
might have glutted the market if demand had not so rapidly
increased with the opening up of the "West" after the
French and Indian War.

At nineteen George Rogers was back in the books, this
time under his namesake George Rogers, his mother's
brother. Entered in his father's account book we find an
item for surveying instruments, and also for "Euclid's
Elements" which would have probably reminded Scotch

Donald Robertson that he now had to make up for neglect of mathematics in school. Thus he was prepared and staked for his venture when he was at the age of the average college sophomore whose mother, if he is an only son, is still worrying lest he shall get his feet wet.

Ann Clark had heard of the savagery of Indians seeking scalps from ambush; of the finding of the bones of pioneers who had lost their way in the forest; of men breaking down from "scald" feet on the trail; of sickness on a bed of boughs far from a doctor; of the hard drinking of the frontier; of the rough ways of those who had fled from the law to find refuge in the back country where all the murders were not done by the Indians; of that terrible animal the panther, or "painter," who leapt from limbs of trees to sink his claws into the throats of his victims; of canoes wrecked in rapids and of venomous snakes; of the many men who had disappeared over the Blue Ridge never to be heard of again.

It was not war. George did not have to go with other sons to fight for his country. He was doing well, as it was, and might soon marry and settle on land near the homestead. But he was not the only son. There were now six children with a daughter who would soon be old enough to marry.

The tie of those days was weakened by the apron string being split into many strands. The very psychology of large families, as well as the movement of the times, reconciled parents to the risks for which children were prepared in self-reliance. There was a Spartan strain in colonial mothers born of pioneering courage.

Ann might have wished that it was Jonathan who was going, Jonathan who was so steady while George was so hot tempered. Father John, in man knowledge of his sons took the reassuring view. George was quick as a cat. He would always land on his feet. He would never get lost in the woods. He would see an Indian or panther first—and he was the son who could shoot straight.

And if George had made up his mind to go, there was no stopping him, he was so headstrong. And it was Springtime. George would be traveling in fair summer weather and back safe and sound in the Fall, having had his fling.

In all that I found about Ann in the Draper Mss. three words describing her in old age shine as the flame for which all the rest was fuel. "She was a majestic woman," this Ann who had married at fifteen. She had enough children to know the hearts of children, and that youth's quick pulse can not be slowed to the pace of that of elders. She must have been majestic when she said good-by to the tall son who was to be seen as a majestic man, even when the shortcoming of his declining years was heaviest upon him.

Maternal fears aside, she knew it was time for him to leave the parental roof. There must be a weaning time for all sons and daughters. Such weanings had been the making of America, spreading the clearings and villages toward the watershed. And the weaning of the colonial children which the motherhood did not understand was very near. Stamp Acts and other harassing measures were only incidents in a movement which gave action its battle cries.

Year by year the record shows a further spread of the cleavage, but no year was conscious of its part, not even the first years of the eighteen seventies when the writing on the wall is now so clear to the historian.

INTO HIS OWN

VI

OVER THE WATERSHED

Richmond and Philadelphia were capitals of an old world. All was old world, now, back of the watershed. The thirty houses of Fort Pitt, which was not yet called Pittsburgh, stood at the river gateway to a new world. In the distance beyond the little garrison the white man must protect his own life and property.

"I left Fort Pitt, June 9th, 1771," the Reverend David Jones, later chaplain in the Continental Army, writes in his journal, "in the company of George Rogers Clark a young gentleman of Virginia who, with several others, was inclined to make tour of the new world."

Fort Pitt had long been a trading post. But the influx of furs at Fort Pitt had not been as great as anticipated after the end of the French and Indian War. The direction of the river's flow had been against it. The peltry of the great valley was still mainly gathered by French trappers. Disappointed London merchants still saw it going down the Mississippi to New Orleans and to the Paris market.

But in the summer of 1772, the occupants of the thirty houses might feel a "Watch our city grow!" expansion of business in the waxing tide of westward migration. Never had so many settlers come down the Monongahela. At the river's junction they broke their journey. Here those who had come overland might be provided with boats; all might replenish their stores; and they might learn from the old-timers, who had come up the Ohio, the mood of the Indians, hints about navigation and where land prospects were best.

In June traffic was at its height past Fort Pitt, as the emigrants set out from their starting points in early Spring to make the most of the warm weather. There was no spare room in their boats for tentage or elaborate camp equipment. A pot or two, a skillet and a few cups, were sufficient. Seed grain and salt for curing meat were more important cargo.

When it looked safe they could beach their boats for the night on a sand spit which would be their bed on the southern bank of the river. They shunned the northern bank where the Indians were unfriendly. Always the rifle was at hand primed for alarm.

There was no worry about shelter for the winter. The saw, axe and auger and long knife would care for that on the edge of virgin forest when the use of pegs in place of nails kept down the sales of hardware merchants. Before frost the new settlers would have rowed and poled their way up one of the southern tributaries and blazed their "tomahawk" claims on likely bottom land. They would have "raised" their cabins, jerked buffalo and elk meat for their winter store in case fresh meat should become scarce.

In the Spring they would sow their seed grain; and with autumn harvest would be independently established. Often they grew a crop of corn the year of their arrival. If they heard of a richer valley beyond they might move on if they could dispose of their "improved" frontier land to some later arrival who traveled with some cash.

Looking back to the seventeen seventies, youth, with all the modern facilities for thrills at command, may take thought that in nothing more than adventure are human emotions subject to the relative values of time and place. The first man to ascend Mount Washington rejoiced in his triumph no less than the first to ascend Mount McKinley. There was no less thrill in the first ride in an automobile than in the first flight by plane.

Youth, ever loving movement, and especially being the author of movement, youth roughing it in Canadian wilds and packing over portages and running swirling rapids in a canoe, may consider the thrill of the young gentlemen of Virginia as they shot their boat from the banks at Fort Pitt into the Ohio stream which the French had called *la belle rivière*. How small the James and the Rappahannock seemed beside this mighty river! It was the river of legend flowing into the land of the travelers' dreams with their guide their own volition and sagacity.

Big game shooting in Africa to-day offers no such alluring prospect as was theirs if they struck into the forest from either bank. They had been learning to shoot as soon as they were old enough to have a rifle in their hands, practice being on game. The scatter of birdshot or buckshot was not at their service. When powder and ball had to be rammed home from the muzzle no miss could be quickly retrieved by another cartridge slipped in the breach or automatic reloading from the chamber. Proof of markmanship was to hit a wild turkey with a bullet.

Youth might see trout flash in streams that had never been fished. If the fierce reputation of the panther were not up to the reality of the African lion there was another danger. While you stalked a wild animal you might be being stalked, yourself, as game by savage man. A shot out of a thicket might drop a member of your party forward into the campfire. Around the next bend Indians in war paint might be waiting in their canoes.

Temptation must have been strong to youths loving risk to keep on going; to make the river's destination their own. They had only to allow the current to bear them, their volition absorbed in its flow. Its volume would keep on growing with the addition of other rivers as large as the James and Shenandoah until its own waters were merged in a river which drained an area greater than that of the Danube, the Elbe, the Rhine, the Seine and the Rhone combined.

But George Rogers Clark was not forth for adventure

for adventure's sake; or exploration for exploration's sake. His purpose in the spirit of the seaboard colonists, was to better himself. Promises that limited his tour had doubtless been exacted by the practical father and the solicitous mother. He was looking for likely virgin land to develop beyond the area in which it had already been occupied, when every year blazed "tomahawk" claims farther afield. He would raise his own cabin on a likely site for a new settlement which would require the services of a surveyor.

Meeting only one white man on the way he and his party had passed the site of Wheeling and had gone one hundred and twenty miles from Fort Pitt when they turned up the Kanawha. He was no longer going downstream in a broadening vista but upstream in a narrowing vista, his planter's eyes judging the quality of the bottom lands that each bend revealed. Where Fish Creek empties into the Kanawha he came to a location bordered by fine hardwoods where he set his journey's end by blazing a claim.

Now he started homeward, but not by the route by which he had come. This would be against the current of the Ohio and then of the Monongahela. He chose to work his way along the faint trail through the forests over the mountain ridge, cutting distance by the base of the angle which the rivers formed with Fort Pitt as its point.

We do not know what became of his companions. Those who returned to Virginia must have been the lions of local parties; the elders yielding the floor and listening to their tales.

Our concern is with the enthusiasm that burst in at the door of the Clark house in Caroline County when the absent son, neither with "scald" feet nor having been clawed by a panther, but bronzed, trail hardened—when he could send no letter or telegram ahead to prepare his parents for his coming—appeared by surprise much earlier than expected.

He had changed. Something very definite had happened

to him. The spell of the distances was in his eyes. He had been on the edge of an undeveloped empire which called him back. There was time to return and prospect still farther for still fairer spots during the Autumn.

John Clark's own planter spirit responded to his son's glowing narratives, but doubtless with the qualification that George was a gifted talker with most winning ways. The father did not think of himself as an old man yet. He could still hold his own with youngsters on the trail. The schemes of the son's fertile mind seemed worth backing if the picture were as good as he painted it. This meant capital for land entry fees, tools and labor. An influence in the parental decision was doubtless to check off youth's optimism with mature personal observation.

So father accompanied son back to Fish Creek. With them went two blacks as labor for clearing and planting. Unwearied, George was down the Ohio for a prospecting trip of another hundred and seventy miles before the Winter set in. His father returned with the evident conviction that the Kentucky frontier was the place for George "to grow up with the country," but not for him or Jonathan, not yet. George should have such backing from his means as he had to spare from so large a family and the rest George must do for himself.

In the Spring of 1773, once his seed corn was in the ground, George was afield again, this time to the interior of Kentucky. Then he was home for a brief time to see the family and probably to learn the situation in the raging disputes about land titles, to safeguard his own and to enlist further support for his enterprises and encourage emigration.

The more settlers the more rapidly land values would rise. He was becoming an expert on where the best lands were located and establishing claims at other points than in the Kanawha Valley. On his return from Virginia to Fish

Creek, we know that he was accompanied by Colonel Muse and William Higgens who presumably were willing to match some capital with his experience.

So rapid was the movement westward that his Fish Creek plantation was now classed as "improved" land. He wrote to his brother Jonathan that he had a good offer for his place; he was driving ahead with further clearing. In some parts of the frontier, corn was selling for seven shillings sixpence (nearly two dollars) a bushel; but he had plenty. His first crop had been bountiful.

As he ranged the trail and met boats coming down the Ohio, he was enlisting a following, already a leader at twenty-two. In the Spring of 1774 he had gathered ninety men at the mouth of the Little Kanawha to go down the Ohio. They would form a settlement on rich land that he knew; and he would be the surveyor to run the lines between their farms.

But this plan was checked by something more alarming than shots from ambush by roaming Indians. In the sudden transition of frontier life Clark was to lead his band as soldiers. Through the Winter reports had been coming into Fort Pitt that the Indians north of the Ohio had been exchanging their furs for powder and bullets at Detroit. In the Spring of 1774 the storm broke.

Fair Kentucky was now on the way to get the name of "the dark and bloody ground." To the Indians it had been a happy hunting ground. There was a sort of understanding, obeyed in spirit regardless of how exact the letter, that an area so rich in game should be left to the wild animals as a preserve shared by all the neighboring tribes.

Here herds of buffalo and elk fed on the lush "blue" grass. The hoofs of buffalo were the original roadmakers of Kentucky. As they passed through the woods from pasture to pasture of the rich meadows they beat trails which became highways for the pioneers. Where there were buffalo and elk there was plenty of fresh meat and the grass that fed them would feed the white man's cattle which took their place, and grow rich crops.

The French had kept the faith of the Indian tradition. They had never molested the native game preserve. Now the Indians realized that the French warnings of numbers and the ruthless ways of the Big Knives from over the watershed were coming true. Now, when the red men crossed the river or descended from the southern mountains to hunt, they found the paleface ploughing the buffalo pastures and the elk and buffalo in retreat from the frequent sound of the rifle. Not only were the Virginians coming down the Ohio but the Carolinians were coming through the Cumberland Gap. For gaps as well as rivers and portages had their part in the destiny of colonization.

In the early seventeen seventies eastern Tennessee had been occupied; the Watauga Association of an independent self-governing community had been organized; the settlers on the Holston river were selling their improved land and beginning a fresh migration in answer to the same downstream call of virgin soil as the Virginians. Following the course of the Kentucky river, James Harrod, with forty or fifty followers, had just formed the settlement of Harrodstown—across the valley from the present site of Lexington—of the same order as the one which George Rogers was planning.

Most redoubtable of the Indian tribes north of the Ohio were the Shawnees. They had never been really off the warpath in casual guerilla action against the settlers. Young Shawnee bucks were not long bound by the latest treaty of amity when royal governors were always making treaties with the tribes. They waited on no declaration of war or the beat of drums. A paleface's lock was particularly a trophy of prowess which would certify to the veteran bucks that they had proved their manhood. It was the fear of the

Shawnees for the most part that kept the settlers' boats from the north bank; and the fact that the south bank was neutral ground which had prevented more frequent scalp quests by canoe trips across the Ohio.

Indeed, the appearance of the white man, if it had not been for his reprisals, might have helped conserve the native population. Before he came the young Indian buck could qualify as a brave who had won his "varsity letter" only by taking the scalps of the members of another tribe. Through all ages before the white man came tribes rose under strong chiefs and fell under weak ones. They were split into factions that became new tribes. From time to time tribes were extinguished or their remnants absorbed into the ranks of the victors in the endless warfare.

When one wonders why no strong aboriginal leader in the present United States had ever spread his dominion over a larger area, as in Mexico and Central America and Peru, one ready answer is that he had not attained this stage of evolution or else had receded from it. Such conquest has often afforded the security, prosperity and constructive prevision which were the genesis of a civilization. Absence of prevision in other things means lack of military prevision, which in turn, is often the sternest teacher of racial and individual prevision.

The Indian warrior never had a supply train. On the warpath he got his rations by hunting. Regular meals were not his habit. He could travel for long distances without food after a gorge, but eventually he must have another gorge. Where game was absent he was without commissariat.

His tribal customs led him to seek scalps rather than territorial conquest; individual renown rather than tribal expansion. He spent his accumulated energy in a burst of swift loping movement on the trail. He was vain of the distance he could cover in a single day; it enabled him to surprise and baffle his enemy. He was a great *poseur*, a great egoist. A savage child, he soon wearied of action and his war passion died out, when hunger gnawed his vitals after he had a certain number of scalps and had revenged tribal wrongs.

As a rule it was not in him, when he already had scalps at his belt, to follow up a retreating foe who was as swift as he and as artful in slipping into forest recesses. When he ravaged an enemy camp he must not wander too far in pursuit of enemy survivors lest he might return to find some other tribe had killed his women and children and ravaged his own camp. A reserve force to guard his base was not in his tactical conception when all able-bodied braves were in the front line.

The social requirements of a youth to qualifiy in scalps, which was a primitive expression of the custom which created European aristocracy on the battlefields, never wanted causes of war after a period of peace in which a fresh generation of arrow and tomahawk fodder had grown up. Each Indian was a general, his own strategist.

Surprise is a first principle of strategy. Without due notice by a declaration of war the civilized world regards it as murder and treachery. The Indian was an expert in ambush. Leaping upon his enemy from a thicket, firing at him after he had adopted the paleface's rifle, was in keeping with the stealth and the swift strokes of the predatory animals whose ways in the forest he knew so well.

Indians took the names of animals, sometimes names which seemed out of keeping with martial character. But anyone who knows a bucking bronco or has seen an unbroken two year old colt let fly with his hoofs will understand that to be called "Crazy Horse" is a promise of trouble for all who would tame him. Beware "Sitting Bull" when he lowers his horns for a charge; and have no doubt "The Owl" is a wise old man.

A young buck with no lock yet in his belt was a poor

strategist, in the prospect of the disgrace of facing the Great Spirit scalpless, if he lost his own scalp before he had won a single scalp. The first was the vital one, the initiation fee to the order of braves; and all could not have a first or all the bucks would have been killed. Keeping on guard and watching to catch an enemy off guard on the trail skilled the Indian in unsurpassed sublety of wood craft; the survival of the fittest in a harsh climate gave him an unsurpassed physical endurance. Temptation was hard, to resist by a young buck at sight of another tribesman's inviting scalplock when it might be his for a treacherous blow, and especially so when he was approaching twenty-five in the doldrums of peace which his impatience to attain manhood rank saw as promising to last forever.

By his blow he had done the youth of both tribes a service. Now the warriors of the fallen buck's tribe marshaled for the war dance in their war paint. The war drums were beaten in the ritual of blooding the courage of the men going to the front, which takes different forms among savages and among civilized peoples whether the object be scalps or spoil or saving civilization. The advantages that the civilized men had over the savage were prevision, organization, commissariat, numbers and the will that sustains the conflict.

Another cause for a tribe taking to the warpath, which was of the same order as the infraction of frontiers among civilized peoples, was the invasion of a tribe's hunting grounds by another tribe. This was a blow at an economic right; at the only and very vital economic right the Indian had, as precious to him as England's defense of the sea routes by which she receives her rations of daily bread. Combine it with a treacherous scalping of one of your own young bucks who had to face the Great Spirit scalpless, and the medicine men could distill a most poisonous brew to intoxicate braves with the martial ardor of death or victory.

The Indians who were slipping north to Detroit for ammunition, as they met others on the trail and spoke in the sign language, pointed southward to that game preserve which had been an all-animal land, a no man's land for residence and every man's land for hunting. Where the Indian had never set up his camps, the white man was raising his cabins. Where one cabin rose many would rise around it. Such was the Big Knives' way. Without taking one another's scalps here was a supply of scalps sufficient for all young bucks.

These settlers were not like the trappers, used to frontier ways. They would be easy victims. So the Shawnees were winning other tribesmen to their view by their pictures of the paleface threat. It was a threat appealing to the instincts of self preservation which held a vision of the future of the Indian race. Westward, step by step, clear as the geologic strata of a cleft rock wall, it was to happen that when the pioneer came the buffalo went—and when the settler came the beaver and otter went—both the source of food to prevent starvation and of fur to trade to the paleface for rifles and ammunition.

Greatest of savages, the Indian, thoroughbred, pure savage, temperate zone, carnivorous savage, whom all "he men" admirers should recognize as the supreme prototype. Other native races, hypnotized by the glamour of uniform and welded by the formal unity of drill and the display of parade, might be taught to serve as auxiliary soldiers, but never the red men. The British might make legionaries of the East Indians and the African blacks, but they, before our regulars tried the experiment, gave up their effort to train the American Indian into squads and platoons. One Indian would turn right face in answer to the command of about face; another left face; and another not turn at all. As allies, the Indians must be allowed to fight in their own way.

French and Spanish priests might teach tillage and trades

to the Mexicans and Peruvians and the Cubans and Filipinos and adapt them to the communal life of the European pattern, but not to the Red Indians. No old family was ever more set in its traditions than the primitive American family.

The northern Indian was like the old Roman senator who would not rise from his seat when the barbarians swept into the forum. He might take blankets and rations on the reservation, but he would not submit to the routine of white-man's labor or cease to be an Indian.

In action he was no Fuzzy Wuzzy fanatic asking paradise by a mass charge. No Shawnee brave would have recognized any likeness to his tactics in the merry-go-round ride of the Indians in a motion picture Indian attack.

The method of the Ohio country forest Indian was that of the tiger stalking his kill. He could melt into the forest background like the branch of a tree; he could be as still as its trunk; he could move without making a twig crackle and detect movement and identify it where a white man saw nothing.

His was an indifferent remoteness in misfortune without servility; and possibly all this explains that his character touches our spirit of chivalry and that one does not conceal the possession of Indian blood in a land where the color line has been sharply drawn. He was the greatest individual fighter of all savages, a genius among savages as a guerilla. In this coming war rage, when all bucks were thinking only of white scalps in the Ohio valley, he was against the most individualistic of pioneer civilizations as King Philip was when he took the warpath against the New Englanders. The last outburst, the last savage protest of this kind against fate, came from plains Indians more than one hundred years later on the threshold of the twentieth century.

When it was known that the Indians were gathering to cross the Ohio, Daniel Boone, who had sold his place on the Upper Yadkin and come to Kentucky, was the courier who traveled eight hundred miles carrying the alarm from settlement to settlement and cabin to cabin on the extreme frontier. No one knew where the Indians might strike. They were past masters in concealing their objectives; the speed of their flying columns the marathonic envy of light infantry. The same party of braves might appear at one settlement one day and thirty or forty miles away at another the next day. They made hurricane work of attack, often killing the women and children as well as the men, but first submitting them to horrible torture when it pleased their mood and they had the leisure.

Retreat, when such foes were close at hand, was out of the question. They would slip past the refugees to ambush them on the trail. Settlers, with families to protect, were in flight not only from Kentucky but the valleys of the Kanawha, in what is now West Virginia. Even those of the Monongahela valley, which was now comparatively well populated, were joining the exodus to the security of beyond the old barrier of the Atlantic watershed.

One hundred families, with their children and their household goods on pack horses, and driving their cattle before them, were reported to have passed Braddock's Road in one day. The sight of the refugees in the World War was hardly so pitiable and in no wise so fraught with danger; for these pioneers knew that to be taken meant death.

It was the Virginians whom the Indians saw as the enemy. They were the land hunters, the settlers, the game destroyers. Classed with them in the Indian mind were the Carolinians and the few Pennsylvania settlers. Generally the Pennsylvanians were still traders and buyers of furs. The thing was to take the scalp of any Virginian and it was allowable to rob a Pennsylvanian.

The sight of those footsore refugees, blood of their blood, land seekers born of a planter's world, banking up at their door for food and shelter, was a further irritation against royal ways for the home Virginians. A certain Dr. Connolly enjoyed one of those perquisites which it was the pleasure of the royal governors to bestow at the time. He had received from Lord Dunmore the monopoly of the trading privileges on the Virginia frontier which then included the region of Fort Pitt. It appears clearly that he encouraged the Indian outbreak to stem the tide of settlers who were interfering with his profits in furs and the sale of rum.

Connolly might trade; but the settlers meant to have back the lands where they had established corn titles by their hard labor after their hard journeys. There was a glitter in the eye of these fathers and brothers once they had their families safe. They waited on no call to arms. Again the scattered pioneers grouped in common cause against the Indian. They did not have to wait for a supply of arms; they had their muskets. They did not have to go to a training camp to learn the manual of arms when they knew how to shoot. They elected their own captains; they would pit Indian tactics against Indian tactics. The Virginia militia was summoned to their assistance.

As the rivers gather volume from the tributaries, the bands grew by additions in the upper Ohio valley. Three thousand were on the march. Lord Dunmore, when the spark of rebellion was already beginning to flame in Virginia and the shots at Lexington and Concord were less than a year away, may have welcomed a punitive war against the savages to divert public indignation in which that against Connolly was only a contributing incident.

Young George Rogers Clark had placed his following at the mouth of the Little Kanawha at the disposition of Colonel Cresap, a veteran Indian fighter. Clark's own plan it would seem—and this was in keeping with the spirit of his coming campaigns—was to take the offensive by crossing the Ohio and overrunning the Scioto valley. Then the Indians would fall back to the succor of their villages. Had the plan been carried out it would have probably scotched the outbreak, then and there.

But Cresap was against this; he was for trying for peace. As a pacifist he was to be the subject of grim historical satire in one of the wickedest libels in frontier history. To so-called "Indian lovers" of the eastern communities, whose living generations had never known intimate relations with scalping parties, Cresap became the arch type of frontiersmen's barbarity of which Logan, Chief of the Mingos, arch type of the "noble red man," was the victim.

Logan's mother had been a captive French woman. He was tall and powerful with mien and form to be the model in stone on a western state capitol of the "vanishing race." His was the plight of the mixed blood of enemies in feud, when bred an Indian. Through the heritage of past generations both bloods spoke in him. Countering tribal traditions he restrained young Mingo bucks who wanted a scalp for the scalp's sake; he risked the loss of authority with his own people to be friendly to the whites.

In such a time he was more than a pawn, a knight, in the game for peace. And Cresap was evidently planning council with him when the tragedy occurred. Logan's brother, sister and wife, all his family, had crossed the river on a friendly visit to buy some rum from the whites. After having been made drunk they were murdered with the exception of a baby in arms.

Logan believed that Cresap was the murderer and it was years before the truth was publicly known. Now Logan became all Indian and savage Indian. The Mingo bucks were given the rein. Logan swore that he would not lower his hatchet until he had killed ten for one. In the glut of revenge he was said to have taken, single handed, thirty scalps in the Summer of 1774.

The real murderer was one Greathouse who kept the trading post where Logan's family bought the rum. When he

saw how his deed was regarded, he was prompt to shift the
blame. He was of the border ruffian type. Lord Dunmore
must have this type in mind as characterizing the whole
when he wrote in his letter to the Colonial Secretary which
I have already quoted: "Nor can they (the Americans) be
easily brought to entertain any belief of the permanent obli-
gation of Treaties made with those people whom they consider as but little removed from the brute creation."

The Colonial forces were in two parts. One, which included
the majority of the militia, had been mobilized at Fort
Pitt. It had reached the new Fort Fincastle (now Wheeling)
on the way down the Ohio to join the frontiersmen from
the more westerly settlements, under Colonel Lewis, who
was at Point Pleasant across the river from the forming
Indian army. Clark had been summoned up the river. We
find him under Dunmore with a captain's commission in
the Virginia militia.

Cornstalk, Chief of the Shawnees, and generalissimo of
the Allied Indians, proved to be the type of native military
genius which our regulars were to admire in Chief Joseph
of the Nez Percés a century later. He could depend upon
a superior intelligence service. The Indians always had that
against the whites. Cornstalk's swift soft padding scouts
advised him of the division of the enemy forces. He would
beat them in detail, strike Lewis before Dunmore could join
him.

It was the bravest savage show the Ohio had ever seen
when Cornstalk's braves in their war paint shot across the
river in their flotilla of canoes. The first notice Lewis had
of the Indians' approach was when they killed two of his
men who were out hunting. There were a thousand Indians,
according to accounts, a very large number considering
Indian resources in men in relation to Indian character.
The war drums had been beaten in high vengeance and the
"propaganda" of medicine men had stirred the native soul

JOHN Earl of DUNMORE, Viscount Fincastle, Baron Murray of Blair, of Monlin and of Tillinet, Lieutenant and Governour General of his Majesty's Colony and Dominion of Virginia, and Vice Admiral of the same:

To George Rogers Clark Esqr

BY Virtue of the Power and Authority to me given, as his Majesty's Lieutenant and Governour General, and Commander in Chief in and over this Colony and Dominion of VIRGINIA, with full Power and Authority to appoint all Officers, both civil and military, within the same, I, reposing especial Trust in your Loyalty, Courage, and good Conduct, do, by these Presents, appoint you, the said George Rogers Clark Esqr of the Militia in the County of Philip & Natl Jefferson, whereof Charles Lewis Esquire, is Lieutenant and chief Commander: You are therefore to act as Captain by duly exercising the Officers and Soldiers under your Command, taking particular Care that they be provided with Arms and Ammunition, as the Laws of the Colony direct; and you are to observe and follow such Orders and Directions, from Time to Time, as you shall receive from me, or any other superiour Officers, according to the Rules and Discipline of War, in Pursuance of the Trust reposed in you

Given at Williamsburg, under my Hand, and the Seal of the Colony, this 9.
Day of May and in the Fourteenth Year of his Majesty's Reign, Annoque Domini 1774.

Dunmore

CLARK'S COMMISSION AS A CAPTAIN OF MILITIA SIGNED BY THE EARL OF DUNMORE, THE LAST ROYAL GOVERNOR OF VIRGINIA. *Draper manuscript*

deeply with the crisis in racial defense to get so many to act together.

The meagerness of the Indian population is always a surprise to those who are not informed. Probably Indian numbers were on the decrease when Columbus came. The Indians applied the Malthusian theory in practice if not in the systematic purpose of birth control. Justin Winsor estimated that in all the area east of the Mississippi there were not twenty thousand warriors.

Lewis had thirteen hundred men. They had plenty of ammunition while the Indians might run short; they had better rifles than the Indians who usually got an inferior type from traders when comparative merits of different makes of rifles was as much discussed as different makes of cars among their descendants.

So effectually had Cornstalk, with the largest Indian force ever mobilized, taken the frontiersmen by surprise, that only the agility of their undisciplined groups saved them from being overcome. Finally, then, the gauge was set in two irregular lines in what is known as the battle of Point Pleasant, October 10th, 1774, each man choosing his cover behind rocks, tree trunks, knolls and fallen logs. So short was the range of the rifles that the foemen averaged twenty yards apart and white face could see red when it showed against the green, although not so readily as red saw white face.

There was no roar of battle, only a scattering slow fire in the thickets. Either antagonist wanted a clear target before he pulled the trigger, his barrel in rest, his eye glued to the sight ready to get the drop when foe flushed foe. Either was on the watch for any movement that indicated an enemy was creeping up on him, lest he be against a man with a loaded rifle while he was reloading his own. Then, if he escaped being shot and both their rifles were discharged, it might be close quarters. Knife against tomahawk, the knife had the advantage. But knife and tomahawk out of hand, the paleface met an agile and experienced wrestler in the red.

All attempts at rushes were held back. For hours the merciless sniping kept up, the Indian evidently having a shade the better of it. Indian warwhoops answered paleface yells. Indian derision challenged the palefaces to charge. Cornstalk, whose tall figure appeared directing his braves and seemed to have a charm against bullets, asked why the Big Knives were not tootling their fifes.

The whites were bound to have superior cohesion. In their advantage of numbers they seem to have had the prevision of a small reserve. At any rate, to break the stalemate, they tried the method by which lines are turned. Lewis moved a party to attack in flank. In the face of the sweep of crossfire, which puts even trained troops in confusion, Cornstalk prevented panic, and in marvelous control of so large a group of individual generals he held his army together.

However, he concluded that the flankers meant that Dunmore's army had come up. It was a superb feat of Indian generalship that he was able to make his retreat across the river carrying back every one of his dead and wounded. The whites had the heavier losses, a total of forty killed and eighty wounded, which was a greater tribute to their staying power than if they had been a drilled force.

When the united white forces crossed the river and moved on the Indian villages the inevitable disintegration began among braves. They had exhausted their war emotion; and defeat is always the penalty of that. They had to find game for food. There would be none at home with their villages being raided as the avenging whites marched up the valley of the Scioto.

Cornstalk was having the same trouble as an allied commander of a much more recent day. Braves of other tribes had wearied of serving under the Shawnee generalissimo.

They were sure that the Great Spirit could not approve
of this new kind of fighting. They had had to remove their
dead and wounded to keep them from being scalped and
had not secured as many scalps as in the style of warfare
which had been handed down by their fathers. Groups,
without bothering to consult Cornstalk, formed deputations
who went out to meet the whites for peace. Cornstalk had to
yield to their desire. Once more the pipe of peace was smoked;
again a treaty of peace was signed.

The Indians agreed to the Ohio River as their boundary
and not to molest the settlers' boats down the river or to
attack their settlements on the other side. This meant loss
of that good hunting ground. But the parties of the second
part made a mental reservation which is not uncommon in
the present era among civilized signatories. The reservation
related to the application of the treaty when any of its
terms became inconvenient. But Cornstalk himself remained
friendly to the whites. His fate was to be killed by a renegade Continental soldier.

Logan, however, held aloof. He would not attend the
peace parleys. As Clark, who greatly admired him, said,
"he was like a mad dog, his bristles had been up and were
not quite fallen."

Through an emissary, whom Dunmore sent to placate
him, Logan sent the message whose quotation has been so
frequent and is always warrantable. It won acclaim as De-
mosthenian from Thomas Jefferson. It is the supreme speech
of its kind in Indian history, with the dignity of Logan's
paternal race at its highest and the diamond cut logic of
the maternal race, in expression of outraged good faith
roused to arms.

"I appeal to any white man to say if he ever entered
Logan's cabin hungry, and he gave him not meat, if he
ever came cold and naked and he clothed him not. During
the last long and bloody war, Logan remained quiet in

his cabin, an advocate of peace. Such was my love for the whites that my countrymen as they passed, said, 'Logan is the friend of white men.' I had even thought to live with you but for the injuries of one man, Colonel Cresap, who, the last spring, in cold blood and unprovoked, murdered all the relations of Logan, not sparing even my women and children. There runs not a drop in my veins of any living creature. This called on me for revenge. I have sought it; I have killed many; I have fully glutted my vengeance. For my country, I rejoice at the beams of peace. But do not harbor a thought that mine is the joy of fear. Logan never felt fear. He will not turn on his heel to save his life. Who is there to mourn for Logan? Not one."

A great picture, that, when Clark and Logan met. Either was a superb type of the manhood of his kind, one a knight with errand to do, the other with errand done. Clark personified the invading race and the fate of Logan's. He was as tall as Logan, as hard as a brave from hard rations on the trail, with muscles exercised, attuned and toughened by swinging the axe in making clearings, bending to the oar and poling upstream and by long marches and exposure.

Dunmore's war, as it was called, had been a further special course in his postgraduate education after Donald Robertson's school. He had shared the lot of frontiersmen who for months had lived without bread. He knew their minds; he knew the Indian mind and the Indian way of fighting from the pursuit up the valley of the Scioto. He had made new attachments, steel bound by hardships shared, all the way from the humblest to the leaders who were to become his subordinates in his campaigns. His journeys back and forth to Virginia—two thousand miles of wilderness travel in three years—through all the stages of settlement, had kept him in touch with the temper and the events that formed their temper, all the way from the Kentucky River to the James.

VII

THE PROPHET RETURNS

Now the shuttle of events was humming fast in weaving the thirteen strands into one. His Majesty's American colonies were having practical lessons in how to act together.

While the battle with the Indians at Point Pleasant was being fought, the first Continental Congress was sitting in Philadelphia. George Washington was one of Virginia's seven delegates; Patrick Henry was another.

When youth was to the front all the honors in the Clark family were not with George Rogers. Brother Jonathan had become a man of importance at twenty-four. He was one of the delegates to the Virginia state convention that appointed the delegates to Philadelphia. Probably his influence in high quarters had something to do with his brother being made a captain of militia under Dunmore.

A happy and up and coming family, the Clarks, who were given to teamplay. But her husband complained in one of his letters that Ann had not been very well after the birth of her youngest child. This, considering her generosity to Colonial increase, seems hardly surprising.

George Rogers returned home in the fall of 1774, as a veteran of Indian warfare, to find people's minds so occupied with two other subjects that they had rarely to revert to horses as the stock reserve in conversational resource. The most indifferent were talking politics. "The Liberty men," as the loyalists called the radicals, were becoming noisier every day.

But in no colony were there fewer loyalists, when that meant supporting the king's measures, than in Virginia. Planter pride was a kind of baronial pride vested in land possession; the pride of the barons against King John. John Clark belonged to the sober element which was not making much noise. They were quiet talks that he and George Mason had while they were sharing the common suspense when from the Santee to the Penobscot trains of powder which had been laid were waiting only on the match.

The first explosion was bound to be in Virginia, the Carolinas or New England. When and how? The loyalists and the elders, disliking to have established routine disturbed, thought that the trouble would blow over. Patrick Henry's "If this be treason, make the most of it!" was behind him, but he had yet to say, "Give me liberty or give me death!" Jefferson and Henry were concerned that manhood suffrage should apply in the election of delegates to the state convention; but the majority, in their demand for liberty and taxation without representation, was against this quixotic suggestion that the ignorant and propertyless should have a say in how they were to be taxed and governed.

George Washington, as he surveyed the movement and measured its elements, was waiting on the event. So, too, was wise Ben Franklin. Washington, as a soldier, knew England's military strength. He realized how easy it was to take up arms in a passion and the ordeal untrained militia must go through before arms were grounded in success. Franklin knew England's wealth and resources; for he had been much in England.

Sober, far-seeing citizens of the Clark type had reason to go slow; to make sure that each step was on firm ground before they took another. They understood how the facile words of orators might have to be made good in action. Then such sons as Ann Clark bore would have to go to the front, and the strain of heavier taxes than King George had ever imposed might have to be borne. As the discussion raged the conservatives were saying "Hold your horses awhile!" in answer to the ugly reflections on their timidity.

The other subject which was stirring Mother Virginia was the one in which George Rogers could claim to be as much of an expert as George Mason about the proceedings of the Continental Congress.

Even on the march as militia against the Indians, the settlers were thinking in terms of land. And now the Indian menace was supposed to be over, the gate open, the trails free of danger. The refugees who had fled across the Monongahela were hastening back to their claims. This was proof to the home Virginians that their descriptions of the fertility of the new lands were not idle tales.

"What a Buzzel among the people about Kentucky!" wrote a clergyman who expressed alarm lest ministers should lose their congregations. However, his plaint had a .blithe and opportunist strain. "Ministers are movable goods," he observed, "as well as others and stand in need of good land . . . for they are poor farmers."

Those who had large land holdings at home and were not infected by the Kentucky craze were worried lest it should lower home land values. They remarked that there was still plenty of good land in Virginia itself if people would only work it properly; that rolling stones gathered no moss; and it was the way of the restless to think that the grass was sweeter in the next pasture.

Kentucky was as frequently on the tongue as California in 1849 and the Klondyke in 1898. It was the general name for all the wilderness beyond the Virginian watershed. Only a few of the daring, without families, were going to the extreme frontier. There were a dozen ways of spelling Kentucky varying with phonetic interpretations. It was Kantuck, Kintuck and Kaintuck, some of the versions beginning with a C and ending with a y, an ey and a double e and ett. No schoolboy could be without authority for his guess.

George Rogers was now a prophet, with honor in his own country, who might profit by the stampede. When he returned down the Ohio in the Spring of 1775, the son of the small planter had a position which was the envy of other youth who were about to try their fortunes in Kentucky. He had been appointed Colonel Hancock Lee's deputy. Lee was George Washington's successor as the surveyor of the Ohio Company.

We have a note about Clark while he was on his way to meet Lee. It is in the diary of Nicolas Cresswell, a young Englishman who was seeing the West and who fell into the company of Clark at Fort Fincastle (Wheeling). Clark took him for a visit to some Indian mounds and "showed me a root that the Indians call pocoon, good for the bite of a rattlesnake."

Cresswell is very wroth over the disloyalty of the "red hot liberty men" he meets, a reflection that the rebellious spirit is strong on the frontier. But as he found Clark "intelligent" and well behaved doubtless Clark considered his susceptibilities. Cresswell considered the "red hot liberty men to be a set of damned cowards" because of their apprehension over the Indian alarms—so soon after the treaty of peace won by the victory of Point Pleasant. (Cresswell had not yet encountered hostile Indians. Braddock had the same view before he was ambushed.)

The young deputy surveyor's salary was eighty pounds a year, four hundred dollars in the currency of the future United States and equal to at least two thousand to-day. At twenty-three he was not doing so badly when you consider that he had the privilege of taking up more land for himself in addition to the already large area to which he had made claim. Potentially he was land rich, and he was thinking in no terms except land promotion and development until the Revolution called him to defend the stake he had in Kentucky, and a far larger stake, by arms.

Here I make a digression, for we have come into the period of George Rogers' career when data about him are more plentiful. He is important enough to be mentioned in the first meager diaries and chronicles of Kentucky when there were already on the scene the founders of many western families. These included the one which meant "marrying up" for the descendant of a later and humbler immigrant, Abraham Lincoln, when he took Miss Mary Todd for his wife.

This period is also the point of departure for Clark's Letter and Memoir. They form the skeleton upon which to hang the flesh of any biography of him. The letter was written in the fall of 1779 to George Mason in response to a request for an account of Clark's conquest of the Northwest. The first words of this report from disciple to master I have already quoted. Dr. Draper found it among the papers of the Mason family after Clark's death. The Memoir was written in 1799 upon the urging of James Madison, his old schoolmate under Donald Robertson, when Clark had not at hand the Mason letter for comparison, and he had made no notes on his campaigns.

He was too strictly the man of action, too intent on the success of the event to spare the time, too unconscious that he was making history to have the inclination, to write down details when they were fresh in mind. (It has happened often that warriors who kept elaborate diaries needed many words to express failure in action. To the delight of all who would not live in a stuffy and pompous world, lack of interest in the diaries of little men, who deluded themselves that they were great men making history, has not always inflicted their publication upon a bored world.)

Writing was hard work for Clark; and at times he made hard work of it. But he gave us a convincing and restrained narrative which has the dignity of the style of the period of Franklin and Jefferson before that of the Fourth of July

rhetoric which flourished even after the last of the hoopskirts
was in the ashbarrel. One's regret is that Clark was so laconic
about very important actions, which were such a test of
judgment and decision, only to become quite elaborate about
some subject which interested him humanly or philosophi-
cally, such as his relations with Indian chiefs.

His own account, read in connection with other chronicles
which give the temper of the time, enables one who has known
campaigns of the same kind to see the living man, now
merry, now tempestuous, now cool, now persuasive, eyes
flashing their lightnings, eyes laughing, eyes imploring as
he rallied his followers—devil brother of the Great Spirit
to Indian braves. Pictures form between the lines and slip
into place on the margins of the pages. They join together
in the marches over a vast virgin landscape shaping the
destiny of states. They enable us of to-day, who see his vision
realized, to see it as he saw it when it was the rainbow of
youth's mad dream which spurred him forward on wilderness trails.

In a few unimportant points the Memoir and the Letter
do not jibe. The captious have made much of these differences; but to anyone, who has been on hazardous marches
when will was the spur of the last grain of fluttering vitality
and knows how tricky is the memory of swift action, the remarkable thing is how well the two agree and how little
variation in turn there is, for example, between Clark's account of the taking of Vincennes and Major Bowman's.

The two documents shine out with rare consistency in
comparison with many diaries and reports of the Civil and
World Wars, not to mention of political and diplomatic
conferences of a later day. Our generation may have had a
better education; but our eyes did not see more clearly than
the eyes of the leaders of that day; nor do our minds, which
have so much to keep in store, register more accurately than
theirs.

JAMES MADISON, A SCHOOLMATE OF CLARK'S, AT WHOSE
REQUEST CLARK WROTE THE MEMOIR

For a long time the question was bruited if the Memoir were written by Clark. This doubt has been set at rest and its value and accuracy have grown in respect under the check of later research.

There is something petty in the fourth grade pedagogy which has made a point of Clark's mistakes and inconsistencies of spelling and his disregard of the business of punctuation. Until I saw the original in the Wisconsin archives, I had seen only the copy of the Memoir in which spelling, punctuation and capitalization were corrected and modernized and from which I make my quotations for easier reading.

I was prepared, by accounts I had heard, to examine a manuscript which was illiterate and ill constructed, but the quality of the narrative left me sharing the conviction of greater experts in handwriting than myself, that the Memoir is in Clark's own hand. Moreover, if it had been written by an amanuensis the spelling would have been correct. Amanuenses of those days spelled correctly. Before the days of typewriters the test of their proficiency, even on the remote frontier, was a beautiful and legible hand. But, to be banal, amanuenses did not win empires. And this is the account of the winning of an empire in the anything but a legible old-fashioned hand of the man who won it. The Memoir is as precious a document to American archives as the letters of Wolfe or Clive to British archives.

Some of the pages, after the fading effect of nearly a century and a quarter, are much fainter than others. It was explained to me that Dr. Draper might have left these on a table in the sunlight. Perhaps he placed them on a chair, not impossibly on the floor in the connoting labor of his enthusiasm, this assiduous old-style librarian who would have been no partisan of the modern index system.

He would not be bothered by clerks, whom, anyhow, he could not afford, when he knew just where to turn for any paper for comparison. He did not hesitate to write his notes on the Memoir or other original documents. All were his if they concerned Clark, his hero. This absent-minded scholar was young in the heart of Clark's youth; he lived his own "daring do" in action of the man whom Donald Robertson had considered to be a poor scholar.

Yet he retained the true historian's sense in a period when scientific history had hardly invaded the realms of Fourth of July oratory. He was no disciple of Jared Sparks, who in editing the Washington diaries acted a censor's part in making them conform to Parson Weems' stuffed figure of the Father of his Country. Draper preserved the humanizing detail of faults and lapses which the propagandist of impeccability would have dropped in the wastebasket.

Dr. Lyman Draper was the Boswell of a man who was dead. A young professor who went West he fell under the spell of Clark's career. This set him his life's work. He sought out every source of material, traveled the roads where Clark had broken trail, delved in remote collections of Americana in the hope of a fresh item, interviewed relatives and traced tales that had been handed down to their origin in fact.

When he ran out of his own funds he borrowed money from interested men who would back him, and so kept on gathering material, never having enough, never getting beyond the period of garnering and gestation, even to arrangement. He died leaving the vast sheafage of documents and notes which were arranged under his sympathetic successor, Dr. Reuben G. Thwaites, who did "such yeoman work in Western history" and later put in volume form to fill long shelves—all about this one man. And Miss Louise Kellogg, collaborator of Dr. Thwaites and present guardian of the treasure, has carried on the spirit of her predecessors in the books she has written as the result of her thorough researches.

A very important possession they are to the Wisconsin State Library which has cannily gathered such a large collection of Americana, when perhaps but for Clark the flag would not be flying over the State Capitol at Madison; and just what would be on the present site of the University of Wisconsin, with its nine thousand students who go and come past the vault where the papers are so sacredly kept, may be left to conjecture.

Here is a bit from the Draper collection, which, with no connecting information and no mention of it in the Memoir, must have puzzled Dr. Draper. It is contributed by William Higgens, who, it will be remembered, accompanied George Rogers back to eastern Kentucky in the spring of 1774. He writes in a letter to Jonathan Clark, May 22nd, 1775:

"Your brother was in hilth the First of this instant he is gone down to Cantuck he had the misfortune to Loos almost all he had in this Part of the Country he lost his sarvant man by axident of getting his canoe upset."

What he lost in addition to the servant man, which must have concerned his land holdings in Fish Creek, is in doubt. There is no mention of it in George's letter to Jonathan who was the historian's friend. Brother Jonathan kept a letter file to pass on to posterity. From a letter to him from George Rogers a few weeks later we know that he and Lee had already laid out a town, which was called Leestown, or Leesburg, seventy miles up the Kentucky river not far from the present Lexington. George Rogers announced that he intended to live in Kentucky. He is sure that the new town will have fifty inhabitants by Christmas.

Colonel Harrod was back at Harrodstown with more followers. Other promoters were buying and selling and "swapping" land. Other towns were being founded. George Rogers was in his element.

Whatever the misfortunes of May—and they were only a

part of the gamble—he is again all youthful enthusiasm. He does not believe that "a richer or more beautiful country has been seen in America yet. My father talked of seeing this land in August. I shall not advise him whether to come or not, but I am convinced that if he once sees the country, he will never rest satisfied until he gets in it to live. I am engrossing all the land I possibly can, expecting him"— which was one way of putting the argument without formally advising father to come.

VIII

CLOUDED TITLES

GEORGE ROGERS was sure of his salary; of any fees that he
got in cash from the influx of settlers. But possession of
the land he was blithely engrossing was another matter
as his father may well have understood. This brought up
many questions in an extravagant situation for which he
was to supply the answer.

First, of what nation was this fair region of the Kentucky
Blue Grass a part? Spain now held that it was included in
the lower Mississippi valley by transfer from France. For
Madrid had been hearing that what seemed to be a worthless back lot of the vast Spanish colonial empire, which then
extended from St. Louis to the Andean slopes, had some
value. If Kentucky were not Spanish then it was British.
And whose among the Britons? Dismissing British claimants,
whose among the Americans? Kentucky was blanketed with
paper titles before Clark began his engrossing.

Lord Dunmore was not the only royal governor who was
concerned; or his the only British financial backers of a
western land scheme who had a stake and were busy plotting.
Sir William Johnson, the King's Superintendent of Indian
Affairs north of the Ohio, had been bribed by a gift of
shares in a London company. With the King's backing this
company claimed all the present states of Ohio, Indiana,
West Virginia and Kentucky through a grant negotiated
with the chiefs of the Iroquois Indians of New York State
by Sir William. The chiefs blandly told him that they had
a title in previous conquest when they had overrun all the
region to the Cumberland mountains. Sir William was
glad to accept this expanded tribal legend as truth without

much consideration for the land interests of Governor Dunmore of Virginia.

In exchange for wampum, trinkets, firearms, ammunition and rum an Indian chief seemed always agreeable to conveying the land of his fathers in perpetuity not only to the first but the second and the third applicants. The more delegates who appeared in this mission from the paleface rulers and capitalists the more prosperous the chiefs.

The finesse of the medicine men, who also profited, approved the policy. It became an excellent sport, especially in the period before the seaboard stampede began and the largess seemed to be secure "velvet." The supplies of the latest types of musket and abundant powder, which always were a part of the payment, strengthened the braves in their conviction that they could repel any of the claimants who tried to take possession of the grants.

There were rich pickings for the veteran frontier Indian trader who knew the Indian sign language as the medium of communication between the palefaces and the savages where settlement ended and the wilderness began. He became the frontline emissary of the land concession hunter. As one reads the annals of the time one can imagine the white go between and a sly old chief dropping an eyelid to each other in mutual understanding at the expense of the simple mindedness of the capitalists and royal governors.

And granted that the virgin region, broadly described as Kentucky, was British and not Spanish, to which one of the British seaboard colonies did it belong? It was under Virginian laws that Colonel Harrod had acted in establishing the first settlement in the valley of the Kentucky river in 1774. The interests of other colonies were quickening. Philadelphia had a land company. One of the promoters was William Franklin whose father, Benjamin, no less than the rising young statesmen of Virginia, had influence in the lobbies of the Continental Congress.

North Carolina, from which a trickle of pioneers had been flowing through the Cumberland Gap, was not indifferent to opportunity. Daniel Boone, who had been recently traversing the buffalo trails, had not gone to Kentucky merely out of an explorer's curiosity. He was scouting confidentially for Charles Henderson, who was both a colonel of militia and an associate judge of the highest court in North Carolina.

The character of the enterprise Henderson was undertaking fully reconciled the judicial conscience of the Colonel in face of any criticism of the propriety of his leaving the bench to become a concession hunter. Perhaps he was responding to the devout wish which Benjamin Franklin had expressed in a letter to George Wingfield, as far back as 1754 when at the Albany convention he had advocated the purchase of Indian lands and the planting of two colonies between the Ohio river and Lake Erie.

"I sometimes wish that you and I were jointly employed by the Crown to settle a colony on the Ohio. I imagine that we could do it effectually and without much expense; but I fear that we shall never be called upon for such service. What a glorious thing it would be to settle in that fine country a large strong body of religious and industrious people! What a security to other colonies, and advantage to Britain, by increasing her people, territory, strength and commerce! Might it not facilitate the introduction of pure religion among the heathen, if we could, by such a colony show them a better sample of Christians than they commonly see in our Indian traders—the most vicious and abandoned wretches of our nation."

This missionary fervor was not usual with Ben who was more of a philosopher than a religious devotee. It was still another proof of his versatility. Seekers after proprietary grants found it a model argument for their appeals, although probably the Indian traders did not linger long over it in bargaining with the chiefs to whom wampum and beads were more convincing. And it was not a proposal from Franklin or other Colonials which got the ear of King George when cabinet ministers and royal governors had an eye to the main chance.

Judge Henderson agreed with others that the priority of Indian tenure should be recognized, but negotiations should be with the rightful owners. While the Shawnees, Iroquois nations and other tribes north of the Ohio had been receiving a great deal of attention in granting titles, the Cherokees, in their stronghold in the Tennessee moutains, had been neglected. Obviously they had the real title to the region which Boone had glowingly described.

Having formed the Transylvania Company with six associates, Henderson summoned the Cherokee chiefs to a conference which he made a grand occasion to play upon the Indian fondness for ceremony. On March 17th, 1775, preliminary understanding became a formal contract. In return for ten thousand pounds, which was largely in firearms, gay clothing and ornaments which pleased the savage eye, he received title to all the land between the Kentucky and Cumberland rivers, about twenty million acres.

Just as the realtor of to-day breaks up suburban farms into town lots—which was the plan of all the proprietary companies—he would break up his domain into sections to sell to settlers. Kentucky should not be a part of the old colonies but independent under the name of Transylvania. He would be its patron, lord of the ducal estate, prince of the principality of his conception and fashioning, which was to be peopled by tractable men and women worthy to dwell in a land paradise. He would lay the lines of counties and townships, choose the sites of settlements which would become flourishing towns and recognize him as their benefactor. All would be order, thrift and content under wise and benevolent guidance.

BENJAMIN FRANKLIN, A FAVORITE PICTURE
OF HIM IN HIS MIDDLE AGE

As a lawyer he made sure of having the nine points of the law on his side by prompt possession. Before the Cherokee chiefs had signed his document Boone had gone ahead with an advance guard of sturdy men. They were to take care of any rough places in order to make good footing for pack horses over the path that the buffalo had beaten down in their migrations to the valleys of eastern Tennessee. This was to be the famous Wilderness Road, the future thoroughfare of the advance in that part of the watershed.

The speedy Boone found that the buffalo had been such good road-builders that he was soon on his way down the valley to carry out the next step in the Judge's instructions. But a minority exception, or perhaps a majority reaction, was filed to the terms of the treaty by young Cherokee bucks who were as prompt as Boone. They tested the accuracy of the rifles they had received from Henderson when they ambushed Boone and killed two of his men. However, Boone saved his baggage; and it was not in his bold spirit to retreat.

When he founded the settlement of Boonesboro not far from the present Lexington, he began building a "fort" at once. Harrod had taken the same precaution. A fort was a loopholed stockade where the settlers could take refuge from their cabins in case of Indian attack.

A strange activity had come into the valley of the Kentucky river. The strokes of the axe were ringing; corn was being sown on virgin meadows; the rifle was cracking as it brought down buffalo and elk.

Judge Henderson, "camping in the eye of rich land," was on the way to join Boone. The patron of Transylvania was traveling in force and in style worthy of his mission and his dream. He tells how he had a salute of forty guns from the "fort" when, at the head of a procession of forty men and boys with forty packhorses, he arrived at his future capital. The guns were not cannon. Boone, in appreciation of the occasion, had his men fire their rifles. The Judge found the prospect as fair as his legate had painted it.

"A description of the country," he wrote, "is a vain attempt, there being nothing else to compare with it, and therefore could be only known to those who visit it."

Both as Judge and Colonel he was conscious he was making history. Future narrators were not to regret in his case an omission which had characterized the founders of other states. He kept an elaborate diary. In one entry on the same date he spells Kentucky two ways, Caintuckee and Cantucky.

Immediately he established a store and land office, and planned building the first church in western Kentucky. Meanwhile "our Church, State House, Council Chambers" would be under a great elm "on a beautiful plain, surrounded by a turf of fine white clover, forming a green to the very stock. The trunk is about 4 feet through to the first branches, which are about 9 feet from the ground." The Judge speaks of having saved the elm from destruction for timber by the settlers, which was one credit mark for paternal rule.

He promptly "ran off" lots for the future farms and then, so there would be fair play, he held a drawing among his followers. After it was over he had a busy time making exchanges and new apportionments to satisfy the complaining.

The history of his Transylvania rapidly develops in the entries in his diary. "Captain John Floyd arrived . . . he was surveyor at Fincastle (Wheeling) under Colonel Preston who has exerted himself against us" . . . And "Mr. Dandridge and Mr. Todd, two gents of the law . . . and several other young gents of good families . . . 1000 acres to the principal gents . . . a certain Harrod and his men somewhere about fifty miles west of us."

Harrod was not the only man that he was "watching." When he sent out word among the settlements calling for a convention of eighteen delegates, they came from Harrodstown as well as from Boiling Spring and St. Asaph. Clark had not yet arrived to found Leesburg.

It was quite a moment when those delegates met under the Divine Tree, every man with his rifle ready, while Boone had sentries out to warn against Indian attack. It was the first legislative assembly west of the watershed and no one realized this better than the Judge. He had thought out his plan thoroughly as a steering committee of one and drafted the laws to be passed at the outset for the government of his fledgling principality.

There was provision for religious liberty and a judicial and military system. A cattle range was defined. Game was to be protected. He was on sure ground in arranging for the improvement of the breed of horses in that blue grass country.

"Everybody pleased," he writes after the convention. So they seemed for the moment. It is the way of frontiersmen to speak a proposition fair when its proponent speaks them fair. Afterward, when they get together and talk him over in clannish confidence, their real opinion begins to develop.

Game preservation was not in the Judge's control if in his prevision. When a rifle bullet was the price of meat frontiersmen were not used to taking out game permits. Moreover, how was the game to be kept in the preserve with Indians on the prowl? The new state now faced an economic problem of the kind, shortage of food, which had often overthrown the rulers of settled old states.

"Our game soon—nay, as soon as we got here—was drove very much," his diary tells us a month after the Judge's arrival. "Fifteen or 20 miles was as short a distance as good hunters thought of getting meat. Nay, sometimes they were obliged to go thirty, tho' by chance, once or twice a week buffalo were killed within 5 or 6 miles."

This disposed already of one, the most alluring, of the pictures that had excited migration. The buffalo and elk were not offering their steaks for a shot from the cabin door. They had learned the meaning of the activity that disturbed the peace of the valley. There was good pasturage farther away, farther and still farther. Their droves were still roving the western plains when the first transcontinental railroad was being built.

When good hunters, the old timers, had to go thirty miles for meat, the prospect was poor for the tenderfeet. And the meat had to be packed all the way back to the settlements in the planting season for those who had corn to sow as well as to build their cabins and help with the fort.

There is no mention of George Rogers in the Henderson diary. The Judge failed to see in the red-haired young Virginian, who could move as swiftly as Daniel Boone, the most important of the "young gents." But there is a reference to the Judge in George's letter to Jonathan.

"Colonel Henderson is here and claims all the country. If his claims should be good, land may be got good enough, as reasonable as any in the world."

If his claims should be good! The settlers, when they had to go thirty miles for meat, were not inclined to bend their backs and sweat to improve the land that they were told was theirs only to find that it was not. Rumors were as rife up and down the trails as in a gold mining community; and those "two gents of the law" doubtless also had something to say in the matter of titles. They could point out the joker in the conveyances. It was a quit rent system. The patron and his future subjects were getting better acquainted with each other.

Another entry from Henderson's diary. "Having many things on our hands have not had time to erect a pulpit, seats, etc., but hope by Sunday to perform divine service (under the elm) for the first time in a public manner, and that to a set of scoundrels who scarcely believe in a God or fear a Devil, if we were to judge from most of their looks, words and actions."

It was not for a worthy judge, taken out of his part by such a vision, not even for wise Ben Franklin, who was quite urban, to understand such "scoundrels" who were later to build their own churches and schools in their own way. Probably it was fortunate for Ben's versatility that it was not stretched by the fulfillment of his wish to found a colony under his personal supervision.

The looks, words and actions of the scoundrels expressed the tradition that had carried the clearings up the valley and over the watershed. This was no dainty task; and those who performed it had not the serenity of the judges in council, or the parliamentary decorum of even the fractious colonial assemblies which appeared as the foam on the boiling up of mob spirit—to royal governors. The skirmish line after march and battle, the engineers and workmen building bridges and developing mines in remote regions are never so presentable as on dress parade.

Many of the early seaboard colonists had been pawns of land grants. But the economic realism of the new world no less than its spirit had ended them. Indenture was going, too. Freedom of opportunity was no catch phrase; it was something fresh in the minds of men who had labored for it and the thirteen colonies were about to fight for it.

Under the spell of Boone's personality the settlers of Boonesboro, North Carolina men, might be held temporarily loyal, but not so those of Virginia who saw Henderson as pompous and exotic. His piety was a little overdone. His hands were soft. He was too unctious, too lawyerly and smooth spoken. It was easy to make prayers under the Divine Tree; but they had known trials which would make angels curse and they saw him as inflicting more.

So he had a treaty with the Cherokees whose bucks were

already on the warpath! An American had come, with forty men and packhorses, thinking that all he surveyed was his world, to impose a system of land proprietorship to escape which their ancestors had left the mother country. His Transylvania! Henderson was a Don Quixote tilting against a passive resistance more formidable than windmills.

And he was facing fire from flank and rear as well as in front. In flank, Lord Dunmore, who was still the voice of Virginia but near the end of his spokesmanship, denounced the Judge and his followers as disorderly persons operating contrary to the laws of Virginia. But Dunmore's was too bad a name on the frontier to carry much weight. The blow from the rear which carried more came from Governor Martin of North Carolina, Henderson's home colony. He proscribed the project of Transylvania as an "infamous undertaking" by an "infamous company of Land Pyrates."

Who were scoundrels now? The two "gents of the law" need make no further argument. They rested their case. Public indignation flamed; then it simmered into despair. In Henderson's diary of June 3rd we learn that the settlement at St. Asaph had "broken up, hid their tools, and on their way home." On the 6th, "abundance of people going away, and will not be detained." Still the exodus continued. What mattered a militia system on paper against the fact that on the 17th, when there was a muster at Boone's fort, only thirty-two men appeared under arms and "in bad order"?

Confusion was further aggravated by the news that arrived on June 7th when the sound of the shots at Lexington reached the valley of the Kentucky river in being heard around the world. Farthest away of Americans from the scene were these settlers at the extreme frontier, isolated from the action, waiting two months for the news of the event which held the future of their land titles and the future of their home colonies.

THE EARL OF DUNMORE, LIEUTENANT AND GOVERNOR GENERAL
OF HIS MAJESTY'S COLONY AND DOMINION OF
VIRGINIA. FROM A PAINTING

"Young gents" who had heard the call of frontier adventure were summoned to the supreme adventure of war. They were going home to join the regiments which Mother Virginia or Carolina was raising. Some of the "red hot liberty" men among the old timers probably were in time to join the one hundred and fifty frontiersmen, veterans of the war against Cornstalk, who marched six hundred miles across country under Colonel Cresap to Washington's army at Cambridge, while General Lewis and other frontiersmen drove Dunmore out of Virginia.

Henderson, himself, slipped back to North Carolina to look after his political fences. The fledgling settlements of western Kentucky were on the way to disintegrate in the fashion of a miner's rush after it was found that none of the claims except a few around "discovery" were panning out. But Clark was one "young gent" who did not start to the eastern front; and that would have been strange in him if he had not foreseen the part which was set for him.

"It was at this period that I first thought about concerning myself with the future of this country," he writes, and by this he meant not just as a land holder. He was out of the realm of private interest into that of public interest. "I saw clearly that the proprietors (The Transylvania Company) were working their own ruin . . . that their conduct would shortly exasperate the people and afford the opportunity to overthrow them."

For he understood the "scoundrels." He knew what it meant to those coming down the Ohio to have an "axident" in a canoe upset with all the stake they had in the world. He knew how after arrival they had to work their way inland to find the buffalo gone. He could sympathize with those who had had "scald" feet as they stumbled forward. Buffalo meat, which was brought from a distance, spoiled on the way for want of salt to preserve it.

Some of the settlers had brought no seed corn. Others had

seen it sprouted by rains on the trail. Those who were growing crops would have no harvest to share with those who had
not; or perhaps their crops would be ravaged by Indians.
As one travels in that fair valley to-day he may wonder that
men ever faced starvation there, but they did, backsore, lank,
eyes glazed with discouragement and uncertainty after a
dream was broken, men who were ill without medicines. They
were homesick for their womenfolk when not one white woman
was yet in the valley.

There were all kinds among them from the border ruffian
to the "young gents of good families"; from the "tenderfoot" who did not know how to tan a deerskin and make a
moccasin to the old timer who was used to a meat diet on
Indian campaigns. There was the "sooner," that restless
spirit who was ever used to passing on to new fields, ever
seeing another rainbow after one rainbow had dissipated;
the parasite who in later days was referred to as "supplying
the can opener and the experience while someone else supplied
the can"; and the well equipped upon whose bounty the
parasite would depend. And one outside of all, looking down
upon all, was the Indian trader, protected by his calling,
living like an Indian in his wanderings to gather the furs
which women wore in Paris and London.

Clark knew all the kinds; spoke the language of each. In
the phrase of to-day he was making "contacts." A tall young
man stopped to talk with men at work in the clearings and
on the trail. He could lend a hand to the inexperienced. He
could match old timer's tales with tales of his own.

Are you from Virginia? So am I. That young man was
never downhearted. He spread cheer; his dark eyes flashed
confidence. He was bidding the men who were of the right
kind to "stick it." And so was Daniel Boone, in his frontier
prestige, and so were lawyer Todd, and Floyd and Bowman
in pride against adversity. In common with Clark they had
come there to "live"; to stand or fall with the event.

The weak were being eliminated; another advance guard was putting its roots in the soil, two hundred miles from the main frontier. And they saw Clark as one who belonged to them and had friends at court back in Virginia. He was not asking the way out of their difficulties; but was going to make one when he started back to Virginia late in the Fall.

He took his commission from them while his young friends were taking theirs as officers from the Virginia legislature. And back of his fellowship and directing his irrepressible energy, there was a very practical mind. The narrative of achievement in the West during the Revolution becomes his biography. And, as he went over the trail back to the main body of seaboard colonization, he seems to have already had the vision of keeping the path free for advance of its skirmish line much farther than western Kentucky.

IX

EMPTY POWDER HORNS

The troubles which George Washington had foreseen out of his experience were beginning. He was breaking quarter-masters for stealing from patriot stores in the crisis after Bunker Hill. No Baron von Steuben was yet in sight to aid him in forming a disciplined army out of the individual ardor of a motley collection ranging from clerks out of Boston and Philadelphia shops and cod fishermen to frontiersmen in buckskin shirts.

Blows had been struck and blood shed, yet still the Colonies thought that the show of force would bring the king to his senses. It would take a month to carry the news of Lexington to England; another month to carry that of Bunker Hill; time for the king to consider the situation; then another month before his conclusion arrived in the American port whence it would have to travel by post riders through the country. The best colonial opinion was that the king might be stiff at first, but, when he saw the colonists were prepared to keep on fighting for their rights, he would yield.

Washington, himself, still hoped for a peaceful settlement. So did the Continental Congress and the provincial assemblies. Ann Rogers Clark might soon be welcoming back her sons who had hurried to the colors at the first call.

"I only desire what is good," was George III's maxim, "therefore, those who disagree with me are traitors."

The king's Hanoverian temper was up. He had no patience with demagogues like Burke and Pitt. There was only one thing to do with rebels, punish them.

He embarked an army under Lord Howe which he was

certain was large enough to overwhelm them if they refused to be overawed. And punish was no word to encourage prostration in loyalty by clerks in Boston or Richmond, by the Masons, Franklins or Hancocks, by frontiersmen or by the tidewater aristocracy. It was a case now of the rebels "hanging together" to escape "hanging separately."

In that seething Virginia to which George Rogers returned, the young men, his boyhood friends, were with Washington's army. Youth for action means that youth is unable to resist action and with quicker step passes the elders on the road. Alexander Hamilton, that other most interesting young man of the Revolution, fresh from Columbia, then King's College, at nineteen was captain of the artillery company he had raised and was soon to win Washington's attention by his courage, initiative and personal charm at the battle of Long Island.

It must have been hard for Clark to resist the call to the eastern front. But he was thinking of another front; he had plighted his faith to the vanguard of settlers at Harrodstown. The restless son of the up-country planter was seeking the advice of mentor George Mason, knocking at the doors of influence, busy in the lobby of the Virginia Assembly, which must have been cloying business to one of his high spirit.

"Diverse opinions were held about Henderson's claim," he wrote. "Many thought it good, while others doubted whether Virginia could with propriety advance any claims to the country. This was what I wanted to know."

His business was to mold one opinion out of the diverse opinions and spike the guns of James Hogg who was in Philadelphia representing Judge Henderson.

Clark did not go to Philadelphia. Neighbor Jefferson was there as a delegate. He was kept well informed of home matters by post riders. Hogg was asking the Continental Congress to validate Henderson's Cherokee Treaty. Then

Henderson would be sure of his titles against all comers unless the king put down the rebellion.

Business man John Hancock and lawyer John Adams looked over Hogg's documents, and they said that Henderson's quit rent system would reduce the settlers to vassalage. Whereon, they might well ask with New England literalness what the colonies were fighting for?

Other members found the new state of Transylvania, a thousand miles away in the wilderness, scarcely a pressing matter for other reasons. Jefferson and the Pennsylvanians hardly thought so when consulted about this scheme of a North Carolinian. Unity in great matters must not be disturbed by arousing feeling over minor and extraneous matters if prominent members were not to hang individually.

Clark had gained time at least. But were his people—just as much his people as the Bostonnais were Hancock's and Adams'—to be left exiles without sovereignty? Were they not to know whether or not the land they were improving was their own? Clark wanted a new county to be formed in place of the uncertainty as to whether or not Kentucky was a part of Fincastle County.

A very persistent, ambitious young giant, this Clark. When he was only just old enough to vote he spoke of Kentucky as if it were his pocket borough. Did he really represent public opinion in the distances from which he came? Or, was he a self-appointed emissary presuming on his asserted authority to further his own land interests?

He said that he would bring them an answer to that out of the distances. Doubtless the statesmen were glad to see him go so that they would hear no more for a time about his obsession, engaging youth that he was, and interesting as his frontier tales would be if things were going better with the Revolutionary cause in the field.

Word came to the settlements that their ambassador was on the way back. He asked that they have a convention at

Harrodstown on June 6th, 1776, when he would have something of interest to report. He was no less expert in human nature after dipping in home politics. No garbled news of his plan should be passed along the trails. All interested should get it at the source.

"My reason for withholding information," he wrote, "as to what I wished to be done was in part to insure a more general attendance, as everyone would wish to know what was to be done."

He desired an appointment as deputy with full authority for negotiation.

This time the fast wilderness traveler could not keep faith with his schedule. It was not until the evening of the appointed day that he arrived at Harrodstown. The settlers had turned out in numbers. They had a surprise for Clark. They had finished their meeting. It had been a protracted one in which every man who wished had had his say before "gents of the law" had put the articulate sense of the majority into writing. There was much to tell the returned ambassador in exchange for the latest news of the fighting in the east.

The Virginia party had won. Henderson's claim was repudiated. After agreeing that western Kentucky should be a new county of Virginia the settlers had taken a vote for two delegates who were to present the petition to the Virginia Assembly. As the settlers gathered around him Clark realized that the memory of him had held through the winter in all the little groups of cabins. They still saw him as their friend at court. He had been elected the first delegate and John Gabriel Jones the second.

It was not just the kind of authority he wanted, that of a suppliant's part asking for a favor; not giving him the whiphand in the seethe of politics in Virginia. But he was not at much pains to change their minds when he recognized their spirit which might strengthen paper authority as a card to play before the Assembly.

It was June. The cardinal birds were flitting through the branches of the trees. The crops of the men who had seed corn were green with promise. There were cattle grazing where the buffalo had grazed. Salt no longer had to be brought from Pittsburgh. At the licks, where the wild animals went for salt, the settlers were boiling the water and getting salt in the bottom of the kettles to preserve their meat.

The cabins in which the men had lived through the winter had become their homes. They were respecting the boundaries of one another's sections in the common public interest which was known as "miners' law" in the gold diggings of a later period. Rifles close by on a stump as they worked in their fields, they had a sense of security in knowing each other better. The grasshoppers had gone; the bees had hived. If the settlers had to rally in the stockade for defense the tenderfoot of last year had had a hardening which would make him cool in a pinch.

And they had had that thrill which is the brightest landmark in the progress of remote settlements and mining communities. They made the advent an occasion; they gathered around the cabin doors of their fortunate fellows in responsive gallantry and respect from the softer side of their natures. There were now women in the valley.

The forthright Boone had set the example by bringing in his family and two or three other men had followed. This was a good sign for permanency; that they were settlers actually settled. Ever in the advance of the seaboard colonization the man who made a clearing was preparing a place for a woman and a woman of his own breed. This was the future for which he labored. It held him to improving the plot of land he had chosen when tales of a better prospect farther on tempted his restlessness. It prevented his retreat from the back to the home country in admission of defeat.

When she came the cabin was not a camping place but home. Often she worked in the fields at his side in the pres-

sure of the harvest season. It was her presence, that woman
of his own breed, his wife, that struck the roots of tenacious
occupation deeper in the soil. It was she who guarded, in
rough surroundings, the transmission of the character of the
seaboard communities to the new in succeeding waves on-
ward to the Pacific.

The French women were more inclined to wait on the
establishment of garrison posts and settled villages; and
their Colonial propagation included more halfbreeds. The
Spanish, not pioneers but *conquistadores*, who were seekers
after gold, thinking in terms of return to Spain with their
fortunes, rarely brought women of their own kind. They
took, temporarily or permanently, native women and bred
the ancestry of that mixed population which makes the Rio
Grande—that so clearly demarked frontier in more than a
river or sign posts—the dividing line between the results of
the two systems.

A Spanish missionary, in the zeal of his idealism that rode
to the tune of saber's rattle, might see the Spanish as the
most Christian way in making a community of blood of all
peoples in the true faith; but that was not the way of the seaboard advance.

The bones of the white woman, who shared her husband's
lot in isolated settlements without garrison defense, as well as
of the white man, paved the way westward. Scattered north
and south and now far beyond that no longer mysterious
Missouri are descendants who have the same pride in ancestors who were in the vanguard into the great valley as
those of the Walloons of New Amsterdam or the Puritan
fathers, or of Lord Baltimore's or the Virginian or Charleston elect. They might find that these ancestors in the life had
not quite country club manners. A meeting with them would
be, therefore, not only the more instructive but might also be
salutary in the suggestion that the real right to pride is in
the ancestor himself rather than in the descendant whose con-

tribution to his community is limited to consciousness of his ancestors.

And that young Virginian, as he talked things over with Boone, Floyd, Bowman and Todd, must have been gripped the tighter by his obsession that here were his own people whose future was being welded into his when their leaders had chosen him instead of one of themselves to speak their cause before the Virginia Assembly when he was only twenty-three. Possibly the fact that the delegates had to pay their own expenses might have been an influence in their practical minds, but that would not have been a decisive factor when so much was at stake. They liked him because he was a blade, a keen flashing blade, temper of their temper.

Doubtless he and the other leaders had things to say to each other which had best be kept in confidence lest alarm should be spread. Redoubtable, a Boone, a Kenton, a Floyd or a Bowman, with a powder horn full against the Indians; but against Indians with full powder horns, when their own were empty, their scalps were tribute to the Great Spirit. Washington was requiring so much powder for his army that little was being brought over the watershed. The British had plenty which came by sea and then by lake to their post at Detroit. Between the Ohio and the Lakes there were six or seven thousand Indian warriors.

These isolated settlements which, as Clark foresaw, were the skirmish line of more than seaboard colonization now that the gauge of freedom was set in battle, must have enough powder for an emergency. This was another reason, aside from arriving in Virginia before the Assembly should adjourn for Clark and Jones to waste no time in taking the trail.

Usually, when settlers were traveling for any distance, they made up a party. A company of six or eight were going east in a few days by the Wilderness Road which Clark and Jones had chosen as their best route. Despite warnings the two did not wait on them. They set out with two horses and all their baggage in their saddle bags.

"We soon had cause to repent our rashness," says Clark. They were to have a reminder that rough trails and iron rations were only the static difficulties in the hardships of frontier travel in those days. Clark seemed to have a sixth sense about Indians; or perhaps one sense so highly developed that, as I heard an old army Indian fighter say of another, "he could smell an Indian" on the warpath. An average nose could detect an Indian village half a mile away if the wind were in the right direction, but not an Indian in the forest detached from communal odors.

On the second day out Clark discovered alarming signs of Indians. Then Jones' horse foundered. Heavy rain continued. Not daring to light a fire to dry their watersoaked socks they got "scald" feet. Perhaps they had no salt to put in the soles of their boots, which was a method of hardening the feet.

One of the two must always walk. The other could ride when the ascent to the pass was not too steep. They were hearing guns in the woods frequently. They were in plain sight on the road for an ambush. The natural precaution was to take to the woods. Then Clark was as likely to see an Indian first as an Indian was to see him first. This was an accomplishment which was not a matter of training. It was looked upon as a gift. Daniel Boone and Simon Kenton had it. But Clark and Jones, when every step was like pressing a boil on the sole of the foot, could not bear the torment of breaking trail through the thickets.

That same gift convinced Clark that the guns they were hearing were Indian guns; but he kept encouraging Jones that they were the guns of the white men of the settlement at Martin's Fort, who were out hunting. Martin's was only seven or eight miles away. If the pair could only keep stumbling on they would reach it. Then, with a little rest and treatment with oil and ousel made of oak bark, their feet would be cured. When they reached Martin's, they found the place abandoned. Evidently the last visitors had been Indians, for the only human tracks they saw were Indian.

"Our situation now appeared to be deplorable," Clark wrote. "The nearest inhabitants we knew were sixty miles away, we were unable to travel and the Indians appeared to be in full possession of the country. We sat still for a few moments looking at each other, and I found myself reduced to a state of perfect despair."

Clark's feet were in the worse condition, as probably he had ridden less as he was the stronger and hardier of the two. At length Jones asked him what they were to do. This roused Clark. He was never downhearted long. There must be action. He quickly canvassed the situation. Now he was in his element.

There was no use of hiding in the mountains in the rains. Their feet would only get worse. The party from Harrodstown would be up in a few days. Clark said he could establish a stronger defensive position against a larger number of Indians than Jones "had any idea of." If you made every bullet count in picking one off, the Indians were loth to storm across an open space at close quarters.

All the two had to do was to prepare to stand siege until relief arrived. In the meantime they had the oil and the ousel to cure their feet. They need not worry about provisions when there was corn in the cribs and some hogs were still around the cribs and there was a keg to fill with water. They were well armed with a rifle, a brace of pistols and two knives.

Clark picked out the best cabin for defense. He would burn the other cabins so the improvised fort would not catch fire from their flames if the Indians set fire to them. The enemy must therefore come to close quarters across the open. Jones became quartermaster and commissary; Clark engineer and chief of operations.

Jones killed a pig with a knife thrust through the heart so it would not squeal as an alarm and brought in water and corn. Clark climbed up the chimney and leveled it flush with the roof so he could drop into the house without a bad fall and more easily leave the cabin that way. Then he cut holes in the wall as embrasures for his rifle so he could cover all points of approach by the fire of his garrison. Then quartermaster Jones having the supplies inside, they barred the door. Their weapons were placed on the table ready for use, frontier fashion. Clark being the better shot, Jones was to load while Clark did the firing.

So they were all set to receive the enemy charge. Now they began cooking a meal and treating their feet. That is, they were all set except that they could not set fire to the other cabins without danger of igniting their own. In case it did catch fire, well, the chief of operations had provided for that, too. They must go up the chimney and slide down the roof and take their chances in the open on their "scald" feet.

The wind had died down and they were about to unbar the door to slip out to fire the other cabins when they heard in the distance the sound of a horse bell. It stopped and then was heard again coming nearer. This was curious and baffling. Either white men were advancing very carelessly in Indian country, or else a large party of Indians were on the warpath and confident of their numbers.

"We waited in suspense for some time," said Clark, "and then to our great joy" it was a white face that they first saw in the edge of the clearing. Some settlers from the Clinch river district had returned to get some tools that they had hidden at Martin's. The mystery about the horse bell announcing their movement was that it had become untied. They were on their way over the divide and Clark and Jones now traveled in their company. The experience had been only an incident of frontier travel in the seventeen seventies and therefore, because it was characteristic, worth the telling.

When Clark and Jones came to Botetourt County they learned that they were delegates with a petition to an Assembly which had already adjourned. Were they to go back to Kentucky and report that they were too late? Not Clark. After passing through hostile country he had a keener realization that he was on a mission of more immediate importance than presenting petitions.

Jones decided to go on to the Holston settlements where his own people were resisting Cherokee attacks, planning to meet Clark later in Virginia when the Assembly met for the autumn session. Probably Clark was not displeased that he had become a committee of one. He would not cool his heels waiting on the Assembly. There was a Governor in Virginia; there was also a Council; and his friends in Kentucky must have powder. If Virginia supplied it to them this was official commitment that Virginia regarded them as her own.

X

A POLITICAL SIEGE

Much had happened in the home country in George Rogers' absence. The results were written large in many changes. The first Fourth of July had been celebrated. Before the post riders had brought the news that set bells ringing in distant towns Lord Howe, on July 5th, 1776, had landed his army of more than twenty thousand men at Sandy Hook.

Washington had already withdrawn from Cambridge with his meager untrained battalions to cover New York. There was no longer any doubt of the king's determination to back up his anger with force. Colonial loyalists were taking heart. Moderates were not the only ones among the "rebels" who were secretly wondering if there would be much to celebrate on the second Fourth of July.

Virginia was no longer a royal colony. It was a state. However, the late royal governor, Lord Dunmore, who had retired to a British man-of-war to bombard Virginian coastal towns and to call on the negro slaves to rise against their masters, thought Virginia would soon be a royal colony again.

With his "Give me liberty or give me death!" well behind him, Patrick Henry, as the first governor under the new constitution which he had helped to form, George Mason having written the first draft, was concerned with the practical business of making liberty secure. If Dunmore returned to rule in Williamsburg it was quite clear that the other alternative of Henry's defiance would be his portion.

The author of that sounding phrase, which fired the spirit of rebellion and which was to be so definitely easy to remember for generations of school children, was no out-at-heels agitator, up from the alleys, leaping into fame as a mob leader. He was the son of a scholar. Although his name was Patrick his blood was Scotch on his father's side and Welsh on his mother's mixed with no Irish. The canniness in the strain was having its innings under responsibility.

Young Thomas Jefferson, whose star was rising to share the Virginian political zenith with Henry's, was now the wild man. He was the author of a sounding phrase which was the clarion headline of the supreme piece of war propaganda of all time; for such was its practical purpose. "All men are created free and equal" were only words which George Washington had to make good by arms. If he had failed the Declaration would be among the curiosities of history which would doubtless have had a considerable value at a collector's sale.

We should not quibble over that "all men" phrase being written by a slaveholder. It had not slaves for its audience. Not their morale had to be sustained as soldiers; they were not the objects of appeal of that bold recruiting poster which all the press of the day carried in a broadside and town criers repeated.

The members of the Continental Congress knew that Howe was mobilizing the forces of punishment at Halifax when they were considering the Declaration. In the lobbies, if not on the floor, the odds against Washington were frankly expressed. The political wisdom that fathered the Declaration only made it the more soundly and deliberately courageous.

It was a bold stroke in desperate case to separate the sheep from the goats, patriots from loyalists. Now there would be no intermingling between camps. Friend should know friend from foe. Every man must forthwith answer the question "Are you for us or against us?" The bridges were burned behind patriots. Sentries were placed at the fords to apprehend malingerers.

That "all men" phrase defied the king in the finality of

resolution. It challenged the attention, it was a summons to vision, as the introduction to the recital of all the wrongs that had been suffered. It played on every emotion to strengthen belligerency in the faltering. Translated in the public mood of the time, it was a notice served on all colonial loyalists that it was they who were now rebels against the state.

Equally clear was the warning to every man in arms, or known as a partisan against the king, that, in case the king won, home loyalists would be the recipients of rewards and favors and given the goad to harass the "rabble" which had fired on the king's uniform. The rabble! Such men as Washington, Mason, Morris, Jefferson, Laurens, Trumbull, the Adamses, Franklin and Carroll were of this proscribed rabble. Their words were the right and well considered words to strengthen the hands of Washington.

If, as some historians imply, the rebels were a minority of the people of the thirteen colonies, this is only more tribute to their strength—a very sturdy minority, indeed—when the majority, the loyalists, had on their side Howe's army and Burgoyne's, the royal navy and the might and gold of Britain.

In the Virginia Convention Patrick Henry had opposed the pronouncement of the Declaration of Independence as premature. His argument of policy was to postpone the bold stroke until the support of France and Spain were assured. Already he was embarked on his correspondence to win Spanish coöperation, acting as if he were a foreign minister for Virginia and all the states. But that was a way of governors in the loosely jointed federation.

Clark, seeking Henry at Williamsburg, learned that he was at his house in Hanover. When Clark rode up to the door he was told that the Governor was ill. But the Governor asked for him to be sent in. On his bed the pale Henry, never robust, saw young strength fresh from the trails and listened to his story of the mission which had sent Clark from the far away valley.

Henry may have wished that he were young too; that he was against Indians instead of all the problems in which he must set a precedent as the first native governor of Virginia. He took Clark's measure, found him a man after his own heart. Clark had won a mighty friend in the man who had dared "If that be treason make the most of it" to the astonishment of his colleagues of the Virginia Assembly amidst cries of "No! No!"

But Henry was taking care, lest, in the critical mood of the time, Virginia should complain that in putting him in the place of Dunmore the state had only changed autocrats. Moreover, as an owner of Kentucky land, his course might be open to misconstruction. It was not in his province to grant Clark's request. Authority was with the Council of Virginia.

Armed with Henry's favoring letter the destiny of the great valley went before Virginia's elect from the valleys of the little rivers. They were gentry ever conscious of the fact, everyone doubtless a land owner. They may have anticipated a stumbling and jumbled appeal from an uncouth illiterate frontiersman. Instead here was a youth of their own world with its manners and dignity, clad not in buckskin trousers, but in as scrupulous linen as they.

He had the flair of the returned explorer of a later time who had been over the roof of the world in Tibet as a change from routine business to men in the rut of home affairs. And there was more lore under that big forehead—a forehead too large for the rest of his face if not for his height and great shoulders and chest—than frontier tales. His flashing eyes of enthusiasm held the members' attention as they had those of the settlers. And he was so brilliant a talker, that doubtless these elders, who were used to hearing the petitions of

PATRICK HENRY, GOVERNOR OF VIRGINIA

the most eloquent of Virginian lawyers, were on their guard
even as father John had been when George came home with
his wonder tales of the richness of Kentucky land.

So this boy was concerned about the danger of western
Indian tribes all going on the warpath. Frontiersmen were
always piping this alarmist note. But the Council was convinced that there could be no immediate danger of a general
Indian attack. This was precluded by the treaty of amity
with the western tribes that had been recently concluded at
Pittsburgh.

Attacks by bad Indians and roving groups of young
bucks were always to be expected, however. And these
pioneers, busy in improving land, were without a soldier to
defend them. Of course they did not ask for soldiers. That
was not the way of the times. But powder for their rifles
against Indian rifles and to bring down game for their meat!

The members talked it over. They knew of Henderson's
claim. The question of making a new county in Kentucky
was one for the Assembly to decide when it met. There were
also the susceptibilities of the Continental Congress to be
considered. The settlers should have the powder, but strictly
as a loan to friends in distress. Clark must take its delivery
from the magazine's door; provide for its transportation,
and be responsible for it in case the Assembly should not
admit the Kentuckians as citizens of the state.

Clearly the members of the Council were aware of the
trap this young man was laying for them. There must not
be the slightest hint of commitment in recognition of
Kentucky as part of Virginia. And they insisted as they
gave him the order that even this was a "stretch of power."

"I had for twelve months past," he writes, "reflected so
much on the various situations of things respecting ourselves and the continent at large that my resolution was
formed before I left the Council Chamber."

As he saw it, a voice from the forest wilderness had been

crying out in vain in the wilderness of civilization. He had
no money with which to pay for the transport of the powder, no way to supply guards, as he told the Council. A
loan! How was he to pay it back? It was a gift in passing to
the waif left on the doorstep. How were "our people" to organize a government and militia for their defense, legalize
the claims to their farms, when they did not know to what
government they belonged?

So Virginia denied fellowship with the men who were defending Virginia! Clark loved his Mother Virginia, but he
was going to live in Kentucky. Virginia was only one of
many states fighting now as a nation since neighbor Thomas
Jefferson had written the Declaration of Independence.
These and all the new states to arise in the vast spaces over
the watershed, which made the seaboard spaces seem
cramped, would belong to the same family.

The Continental Congress was the assembly of the whole.
It would have powder. Already, in complaint that they
could not be governed from so distant a state capital as
Williamsburg or Philadelphia, the settlers in the region of
the present West Virginia had petitioned the Continental
Congress to set up a separate state to be called Westylvania.
Why not beyond that another state, a self-governing Transylvania of Henderson's dream without his proprietorship
and quit rents?

And these members of the Council in their little valley
spirit could not see the value of time when the country was
at war and that British post at Detroit was in touch with
all the Indian warriors between the Ohio and the Lakes. They
would see it and pay for the delay when refugees banked
up in the back country again. Young George Rogers was
very wroth at heart with that stuffy Virginia Council.
Doubtless if Mother Ann had been present she would have
told her red-headed son that he was losing his temper again.

"Our people" at Harrodstown and Boonesboro, just a

little band of frontiersmen, but such a mighty lot to him, must do for themselves, which meant that Clark was going to do for them. When there was no authority he would make authority, a way he had which sometimes took him over the hurdles and again tripped him. When declarations of independence were in the air the delegate with a petition did not wait for the approval of the absent colleague Jones, not to mention of another meeting of the Kentucky settlers.

In the part of a delegate with full power to act for "our people," as if he were the autocrat of a principality, he sent the order back to the Council stating that he was "sorry to find that we should have to seek protection elsewhere" which he did not doubt of getting and with the gingery further comment that "if a country were not worth protecting it was not worth claiming."

A very truculent young man, indeed. Members of the Council knew that frontiersmen had notoriously hot tempers, a result of the irritations of the lives they led, accumulating for the touch of the match of some incident. After a brimstone roar the outbursts usually subsided. The natural first impulse of the members must have been to read this obstreperous example of the younger generation a lesson in humility. However, the art of politics was well developed in Revolutionary Virginia.

The members were used to political threats. They were always assured of the distressing results if they failed to grant petitions. Obviously, if Clark had been just an average frontiersman, the conclusion would have been that he would be powerless to get the powder elsewhere and to pass over his letter as the conventional last resort of a petitioner.

This youth with an obsession, his eye so sharp set on a goal, who was a friend of Mason, and who had won Henry's favor, in his determined sincerity and self-reliant assertion! He might have a private stock of human powder to explode to get the powder he wanted for his settlers. There was something in reserve in his deep-set eyes which meant more than a flash in the pan.

He might go to the Continental Congress; he might make all kinds of trouble in his imperious and very Virginian way. He looked like the kind who, if he started what in later times was called a bluff, and found that it failed of its purpose, would carry it through. The thirteen colonies had made more or less of a bluff to the king which they now were carrying out.

And what if Clark were right? What if when the Assembly met it was found that settlers had been massacred because the Council had failed to supply them with powder? Promotion to the Governorship or the Continental Congress would hardly be in sight for members of the Council through the storm of public indignation. Better pacify this haughty young man.

The Council sent for him again. He met their mellow mood in kind. He had the floor for anything further he had to say. He won them and they won him to a "compromise." Five hundred pounds of powder was to be sent at the Council's expense under Virginian guard to Pittsburgh, the extreme point occupied by armed government forces.

Clark was content; he had the entering wedge. This time it was not a loan to friends in distress. Virginia had definitely recognized her responsibility to fellow Virginians. Now there would not be empty powder flasks in Kentucky.

This was on August 23rd, 1776, the day before Lord Howe crossed his army to Long Island. It was ten days before Lieutenant Governor Henry Hamilton of Detroit received royal authority in answer to his request to enlist the Indian tribes on the British side, and with it the assurance of money and supplies as bribes for the braves. But that order, carried from Quebec by a king's messenger, was secret and it would be months before it was known at Revolutionary headquarters. Naturally, Hamilton hoped that first news of it to the western frontier would come with the Indian attack planned for the coming Spring.

Clark sent a letter to Harrodstown to dispatch a party up the river for the powder. He knew Boone and Todd would be prompt to act in response. Meanwhile, he decided to remain for the opening of the Assembly six weeks later when he would face Judge Henderson in the battle for the rights of "our people" who were worrying lest he should never come back but should join Washington's army.

Now he might have a little time at home where Mother Ann had only one daughter and youngest son William with her. She could no longer have any doubt that the others must return with their shields or upon them. The hail for news met every man riding away from town. The news grew worse. Washington had had to withdraw from Long Island. He was in retreat up the Hudson with consummate adroitness while Howe in fabian delay lost his opportunity for a decision.

It must have been harder for hot blood to resist temptation to go to the eastern front than a year before now that the need had become so acute. Clark was between two appeals. The one that prevailed was to be seen on the roads leading from the Shenandoah and Monongahela valleys and the country beyond. It was in the cattle, hogs and grain which were going to supply Washington's army.

Future Fourth of July orators were to overlook the fact that the soldiers of the Revolution had to be fed, not to mention other vital economic factors. Washington might yet have to fall back to the Alleghenies. Then his granary would be in the back country where every crop in every clearing, every beef, hog and sheep and all the game that hunters could kill, would be required.

With that vision in mind Clark, Jones having rejoined him, brought his cause before the Virginia Assembly. The average member had never heard of St. Louis, Vincennes or

Kaskaskia. He did not know there was a Fort St. Joseph near the flats which are now covered by Chicago's "loop." All that region was something as remote and unassociated with prospective development as the wastes of Greenland to-day; and not without reason in the crisis of armed fortunes on the eastern seaboard.

The bill promptly introduced in the Assembly to make Kentucky a new county of Virginia was to meet strong and prolonged opposition in both houses. The Indiana Company muddied the waters by its claim to all the region west of the Alleghenies through its old treaty with the Iroquois. It protested that it was the real power to keep peace north of the Ohio. Colonel Arthur Campbell, old Indian fighter, once captive of the Indians, known as "Long Jaw," brought his prestige as a frontier expert to bear in favor of the inclusion of Kentucky in Fincastle County of which he was County Lieutenant.

Clark, with the influence of Mason and Henry on his side, faced veteran Campbell and the learned arguments of Judge Henderson while all sides were buttonholing members in the lobbies. Had not Henderson the treaty with the Cherokees? Was faith to be broken with them and set them on the warpath? But the Cherokee bucks were already ravaging the Tennessee settlements.

The Indiana Company and Henderson could assure members that friends interested in western lands would find that they would not be overlooked in the distribution of fertile sections. Clark, too, may have had an argument of that kind, but it could not have been so compelling when he was not representing a proprietary company with millions of acres as his fief. His appeal was for "our people," in the name of the old frontier individualism. Thus was the line drawn between two forces, between the two schools of economic thought of the time. Should a man be a tenant of a proprietor or own himself the land he improved?

Members were buffeted by the cross currents of many other affairs than the making of a new Kentucky county. They must have been taking an inordinate amount of snuff to soothe tired nerves. In the midst of debates on the floor and listening to arguments in the lobbies their ears were attuned to the echo of the hoofbeats of post riders.

News that Howe had full possession of Manhattan Island was followed by Washington's retreat from White Plains and of Howe's taking Fort Washington with three thousand prisoners, the heaviest blow of the Revolution. Washington was maneuvering in New Jersey to keep Howe out of Philadelphia.

There must have been hints from the opposition that young Clark better be at the front fighting. He might well have answered that he knew where there would be fighting enough for him. Word that the Indians north of the Ohio in spite of the treaty were becoming restless might have filtered in to Williamsburg from over the watershed; also of the forming of Burgoyne's army in Canada to cut off New England from Washington's army.

Early in the Revolution Washington had emphasized the importance of defending the frontier. The "winning ways" of the ubiquitous Clark in his boyish energy, so Virginian in his appeal to Virginians, finally won. On December 7th, 1776, the Virginia Assembly passed the bill making a new Virginian county of Kentucky. The last effort at proprietary government in the United States had failed. Clark was made a major of Virginia militia in charge of the defense of the new county.

Meanwhile, he had learned that his letter to Harrodstown about the powder had never been received. The powder was still at Pittsburgh when the horns of the Kentuckians might be empty. He and Jones must lose no time in making sure that it reached its destination. They hastened down the Monongahela to Pittsburgh.

XI

THE ROYAL BREAST

PITTSBURGH, which was the western garrison outpost of the Revolution, had disillusioning news which was soon to disillusion the Continental Congress. Clark arrived there to learn that the rumors which had been heard at Williamsburg were convincing reports brought in by settlers and traders fleeing from the storm.

The Pittsburgh commander was sending expresses asking for more troops. Now there could not be too many majors of militia who had a gift in fighting Indians. It was clear that all the negotiations with the chiefs, all the peace-pipe smoking, all the plans to prevent the outbreak had failed.

At the beginning of the Revolution the part of the Indians as Allies of the French had been still sharp in public recollection. The founding fathers realized that they faced the disembarkation of troops under the guns of the British Navy while savages were in their rear. What part would the savages play? Either side had to consider using them as allies.

"We need not be so delicate," said John Adams, "as to refuse the assistance of the Indians, provided we cannot keep them neutral."

Each colony was inclined to decide the question for itself. The Stockbridge Indians in Massachusetts were at first enlisted to act with the Minute Men. The Massachusetts Provincial Congress appealed to the Iroquois to "whet their hatchets and be prepared with the Colonists to defend their lives and liberty."

But border warfare had ceased in Massachusetts where the present generation was unfamiliar with Indian character;

the settlers had established themselves free of Indian dangers. The active frontier in that direction was beyond in the Mohawk Valley of New York State. Ethan Allen had appealed to the Northern chiefs, saying "my men fight as Indians do and I want your warriors to join with me like brothers and ambush the regulars."

He promised them presents dear to the Indian heart as the best proof of comradeship; but Ethan, trying to keep his men in patches rather than rags, had few presents to give. The Stockbridge Indians did not remain with the Minute Men: and the appeal of the Massachusetts legislature came to nothing.

The Virginia Assembly, and likewise the legislature of the Carolinas, knew the situation too well to authorize any vain attempt to play with two-bladed swords. To arm savages was surely to have the arms used against Virginians and Carolinians, who, the Indians, given to holding grudges, would not forget were the destroyers of their game preserves.

Virginian policy supported that of Colonel George Morgan, Commissioner of Indian affairs for the middle department, who was against employing savage scalping parties in a war between white men. He at once realized the acute danger in the Ohio valley. His aim was Indian neutrality to be secured through the old method of bribes; chiefs to bury the hatchet deep and remain spectators of a family quarrel between the whites.

The vengeful Lord Dunmore, last royal Governor of Virginia, had in mind not only a servile but a savage rebellion in his humiliation at the summary way the rebels had made him a prisoner at Williamsburg. One of his last official acts was to send his man, Dr. Connolly, whom he had favored with exclusive trading privileges in the Ohio valley, to arouse the Indians to action. The settlers got wind of Connolly's mission and made him prisoner of their man hunt.

Revolutionist peace delegations were sent to bring Cornstalk of the valorous Shawnees and other chiefs into conference. There were majestic "powwows" at Pittsburgh where the chiefs were honored with rifle salutes and fife and drum music and the colors and given money presents. A treaty of friendship was again made to endure until the sun stopped shining in the heavens and the waters ceased to run in the Ohio.

Twelve Indian chiefs were received by the Continental Congress, the first of the delegations which still attract attention when they call on the White Father at the White House. The chiefs made noble speeches of the type which were to win admiration for Indian eloquence through the generations. Noble speeches in kind were made in answer by our founding fathers.

"I have more than once heard addresses," as a French Jesuit missionary had written when French delegates met the Indians to win their support in the French and Indian War, "which would not be disavowed by the finest minds in France. An eloquence drawn wholly from nature does not cause anyone to regret the help of art."

He described also in contrast the orgies of yells and dances by the same chiefs, whose eloquence had had so impressive a repose, when they turned to the business of "blooding" themselves for the warpath. Even Logan, the half-breed, whose answer to Dunmore was the classic example, would switch from Ciceronian dignity to lunatic pantomime around the peeled post.

After all, the Indians, in their weather-vane changes of loyalty, were acting the part of self-preservation, according to the best counsel of their savage minds and to their resources, no less than civilized nations which are found in arms against other nations who were their bedfellows in alliance only a short time ago. "They have been taught by contending nations to be bought and sold," wrote George

Morgan. The great purchasing place was Detroit, the British post, where the Indians went to trade their furs for rum, ornaments, rifles and ammunition.

Morgan would have capitalized the friendly mood of the chiefs immediately after the treaty was signed in an unopposed passage for a force to capture Detroit. The project hung fire. Washington favored the taking of Detroit, but had more pressing things on his hands. St. Clair made plans for an expedition but lacked men and funds. The repulse of the invasion of Quebec was a deterrent from another adventure of the kind.

Each one of the states in that loosely jointed confederacy was defending its own frontier, while Patrick Henry was carrying on his negotiations with Spain. When the war went well, especially in the earlier period of the Revolution, each state became more independent; when the war went badly the states tightened the harness of coöperation and pulled together. The lesson of unity was to be learned by stages of costly examples.

Some renegade revolutionist, doubtless drunk at the time, made an end of Morgan's plan when he ruthlessly murdered the friendly Cornstalk. Such ruffians flourished under lax discipline far from Washington's headquarters; and he had many to contend with in his own army at the outset. It was useless to put a price on the renegade's head when he could not be hunted down. So the Shawnees' hatchet was not long buried deep; it was now raised to avenge their chief.

Perhaps canny Benjamin Franklin had been sound in his proposal on August 21, 1775, of an offensive and defensive alliance with the tribes of the Six Nations. Washington seemed to have come around to his view, when, on April 17, 1776, he suggested that it might be better to engage the Indians on the Revolutionist side as "they will be either for or against us."

On June 17, 1776, the Continental Congress had authorized Washington to employ the savages anywhere he deemed fit. On July 4, 1776, the Declaration of Independence decried against the inhumanity of their employment by the king. The inconsistency is a pointed example of the fluctuation of a legislative mood with that of a military situation. This change of view may have been owing to the frontier feeling in the matter which Clark shared and which governed his own policy. The fact was that Washington gave up his idea of employing Indians; and the final word of Congress in the Declaration became the permanent policy.

At Pittsburgh, while the commissioners were honoring the chiefs with salutes, they had shown the steel hand in the velvet glove. They warned the chiefs that the British could not fight in the American country "and you know that we can." If the chiefs took the British side they should be punished by the Revolutionists who could not fail to be victorious.

Lieutenant Colonel Henry Hamilton, British Lieutenant Governor at Detroit, was certain the treaty would not last long once he had consent to his own plan in face of the "haughty and violent disposition of the Virginians." King George wrote, "Every means of distressing America must meet with my concurrence." Lord Germaine, having in mind that "to bring the war to a speedy issue and restore those deluded people (the rebels) to their former state of happiness and prosperity, are the favorite wishes of the Royal Breast," directed Hamilton to engage all the Indians of the district he could and loose them on the frontier settlements, which would cripple Washington's source of supplies and detach soldiers from his main army for its defense.

So the Indians had no longer to bring furs to Detroit to barter for their needs. Here was bounty in place of bargaining over the counter. Sixteen gross of red-handled scalping knives as well as ornaments and rum, in addition to wampum,

KING GEORGE III

were among the supplies forwarded to Hamilton from Quebec. Vain were the salutes at Pittsburgh to win savage hearts in competition with such largess when the standard of depreciating American currency was in British gold; and vain the threats of Continental victory when Hamilton told of the flight of the rebel invading army from Canada and of the great British army forming under Burgoyne.

Those chiefs who had signed the Pittsburgh treaty were slipping north to powwows with Hamilton who could also turn out a guard—one in bright red coats, appealing to the savage eye—to fire salutes in their honor. Hamilton, his face painted black, Indian fashion, harangued the chiefs. Would they forget their ancient grudge? Would they any longer be made fools of by the Big Knives who killed any Indian who crossed the Ohio to his fathers' hunting grounds?

As Hamilton gave them the red-handled scalping knives and rifles and ammunition and amulets and strings of beads he bade them bring to him the proof of their valor. And the proofs would be scalps, of course. Hamilton could not visualize how the scalps would be taken. He did not see disemboweled women with child at a cabin door, only the token slashed from the crown of the head.

He was acting his part in the strategy of the coming British campaign of 1777 to bring the war to a speedy issue, the sooner to end its horrors—the old and ever-compelling argument—and to insure his earlier return to England away from frontier exile.

Burgoyne was to move down the Hudson valley driving a wedge through the colonies; Howe was to press Washington's army back into Pennsylvania. Hamilton's emissaries were also at work among the Cherokees, Joseph Brant and other emissaries among the Iroquois. Thus Washington's army, forced back to the mountain wall, would have the tomahawk in the rear with British regulars in front.

It was a plan that looked decisive on the map at Whitehall; one that exalted the Royal Breast as it was laid before King George. Regardless of compunctions and policy in employing the Indians, in the conflict of state interests and sentiment, here were the results. Britain had the savages from the borders of New York to the Carolinas blooded for the fray on her side.

The Indians wanted presents which the British had the factories and funds to supply. They wanted scalps as tribute to the Great Spirit. In the Indian system of fighting, scalps were more easily taken from isolated settlers than from British regulars who, whether in garrison or on the march, always had sentries out. Another argument was that the British never moved in force without cannon whose thunders, shaking the very earth itself, terrorized the braves. And every scalp taken from man or woman of the Big Knives avenged the ancient grudge.

The general Indian attack would wait on Spring to be concerted with the British army movement. But young bucks, eager to try out their new weapons, were not dissuaded by winter weather from following the frozen trails toward the Ohio. And powder horns at Harrodstown might be empty.

The youngster who typified the "haughty and violent disposition" of the Virginians, ambition in every heart-beat and his busy brain full of schemes, may have already foreseen Hamilton, whom he was to call the "Hairbuyer General," as his future antagonist. It seems likely that he had already scouted his plan of a stroke in the rear of the forces which were to harass Washington's rear.

However, the present business was to reach Harrodstown safely with the powder. Volunteers for any hazard, especially if it took them for a look at new land, were always forthcoming on that river bank in front of the row of cabins near the site of the great steel plants of to-day. With seven, who did not look afraid of labor at the oars and seemed to have the right fortitude and the eyes of good shots, Clark and Jones started to convoy the precious powder down the Ohio.

Soon Clark was aware that Indian bands were moving along the north bank. At length he became convinced that they were pursuing his party, watching for a chance to ambush him. They might even know the nature of his cargo. It was a prize to summon all the roving bands to a combined attack. There was a risk that, instead of filling the horns of his people, the precious powder might be sending bullets against them.

So, near Limestone, later Maysville, the party hid the powder in five or six different places, set their boat adrift and started for the settlements. Some tired legs were unable to keep up with Clark's pace. When they met four men who were out land prospecting, and who said John Todd was near by with a large party, they thought they could look after themselves.

Clark and two companions hurried on to bring further force from the settlements. The Todd party, reinforced by Jones and the others, thought they were strong enough to transport the powder which was much needed. On their way to get it they were ambushed and routed. Jones was killed and three others were either killed or taken prisoner.

Had Clark with his little force tried to take the powder through, they would have lost it and Clark might have lost his life. There was fear that the Indians might have forced the prisoners to reveal the location of the powder; but the party which was sent for it found all the kegs in their hiding places.

XII

AN INDIAN SIEGE

CLARK's own laconic comment was that his Christmas present of the powder was received with "universal joy." It seems to have been the first "Welcome Home to Our Hero" celebration in the Mississippi Valley. He was the rescuing knight; the leader come into his own with definite purpose in the uncertainty of divided councils of a beleagured people without any organized government.

John Todd, as the most articulate member of the community when he had a pen in hand, had expressed the situation by saying that he had not dared to leave his house lest some invader take possession of it. But why should he "preach politicks" when " 'tis a country failing? I am worried to death by this learned ignoramus set."

By "learned" he doubtless meant a sarcastic reference to each settler's stubborn conviction in following out his own ideas or whims, or talking in the air, without any sense of concerted action. Even at the expense of a fling at his own profession, Todd kept his sense of humor which was so requisite a saving grace in frontier troubles.

"And what is worse," he adds, "there are two lawyers and they can't agree!"

Clark, the settlers' friend at court, had resolved the doubts about government. He came bearing the birth certificate of the orphan as the legitimate offspring of Mother Virginia in full standing as a county. Kentucky was to have a sheriff; burgesses were to be elected to the Virginia Assembly. Justices of the peace were to sit in court. Any man with twenty-five acres of land on which he had raised a cabin, or

128

one hundred acres of unimproved land, was an elector. This excluded vagrant land prospectors, border ruffians who lived by the toil of others and passing hunters from voting.

A community of settlers was to be ruled strictly by settlers. Now a citizen could register his title with the clerk of the court. The property became his in perpetuity and, in turn, a provision for his heirs, when life insurance was not yet in vogue and any settler in that period of Indian warfare would surely have been very much of a war risk in modern actuarial reckoning.

Such was the assurance of the future, as the reward of the fortitude of the Kentucky pioneers, if they were now ready to fight for it. They must put their heads together and act together or the scalp locks of all their heads would be taken. In that respect they were in precisely the same position as the members of the Continental Congress and the generals of the Continental Army.

Clark's secret dream of an offensive stroke toward Detroit must wait on the present business of defense for this group, two hundred miles away from the nearest settlement, whose fortunes he had made his own. Major Clark of the Virginia militia would show the settlers how to use the powder which he had brought. The commander, no less than the powder, had come just in time.

After he had told them the good news he pressed home the bad news. The Indians would soon be upon them in earnest. His warning was fulfilled, two or three days after his arrival, by an attack on McClellan's Fort, one of the new settlements. Founder John McClellan and another man gave their lives in the fight; others were wounded.

Clark's word was that McClellan's must be abandoned. Concentration was the order against the coming storm. Clark's own Leestown, which he and Hancock Lee founded, had passed from consideration. Every able-bodied man must be in reach of a stockade to which he could retire and in numbers sufficient to protect the refuge for women and children.

"Good policy would seem to have required that the whole force be embodied in one place," Clark wrote, "but our dependence upon hunting for the greatest portion of our supplies forbade this."

In small as in large military operations the practical problem of commissariat interferes with theoretically logical military dispositions. Morale has also to be considered. The settler in fighting for his own saw it as the piece of land he was improving, the cabin he had built. He was naturally averse to abandoning both to the Indians and moving his tools, his household goods, his corn and any livestock he might have from his precious horse to his no less precious cow, sheep or hog, while he vacated his own land on which he would plant his crops in the Spring in sight of his home "fort" as a refuge.

The concentration was in Harrodstown, Boonesboro and Loganstown within an area about fifty miles across. This gave a satisfactory hunting range to each. Game had to be sought through forests where Indians lurked; and messengers and Clark as commander had to run the gamut of the roving bands in communication between the posts. Each fort had to care for its own local problems while Clark, his headquarters at Harrodstown, kept in touch with the other two.

Courage of itself was not lacking in the men Clark had for soldiers; but it was the most independent kind of courage to organize into teamplay. When their resourcefulness was rightly applied they were worth, against a given number of Indians, much superior numbers of veteran regulars who were pattern plates of drill and salutes.

Their concrete cause in the defense of their land and their rights to it and to rule themselves was after all the cause of the Continental Congress which they were to serve so well.

Man for man they were doing as much for the victory as the veterans of Washington's army.

Yet some may not have taken much interest in the war as a war. They may have seen it as having been stirred up by a lot of politicians and royal governors back East. They were too far detached to feel the passions of the eastern seaboard except when Henderson's proprietary system touched the quick. They lived in an age when even in Europe only a small proportion of the able-bodied men were ever engaged in a war. The world was far from the universal draft.

Telegraphic and press communication of later days, which was at first welcomed as promising international amity, only welded nations together as racial units for prompter and more unanimous action as a means of arousing their war ardor and a sense of a common stake.

Clark had to keep every day and hour of the day before the settlers the realization of the stealth and the lightning quick strokes of the foe; that there was no alternative in defeat except ravage and tortured women and tomahawked children. British agents were busy on the frontier promising rewards and safe passage to the British lines for Tory sympathizers.

"I frequently feared," Clark wrote, "the settlers would consider making peace with Detroit and suffer themselves and their families to be carried off."

His prestige as a leader among them would not be properly utilized if he did not apply discipline, and the regulation formula of military discipline was almost as offensive to them as to the Indians. After Braddock's disaster and the frontiersmen's victory at Mount Pleasant their contempt for the regulars was unbounded. Fighting was fighting; they knew how to fight. They could take care of themselves out on the trails. This attitude led to the American confidence that a million armed men would spring from the earth in an emergency, which was later confirmed by Jackson's exploit with his riflemen at New Orleans.

However, men who resent discipline by one kind of formula may be quite subordinate under another. These settlers would endure exactions from Clark, who had proved himself to them, which would have made them unruly under a regular officer applying the regular formula.

It was in the defense of the settlements that Clark first proved that he was a born soldier with a small force in the broad range of capacity which can not be trained or measured in garrisons or peace maneuvers. He had the power of command which is not delegated in commissions signed by rulers or taught in staff schools. He was blessed for this occasion even with the look that commands and the hot temper and the quick change to amiability and other characteristics which made him human in their kind to the frontiersmen.

"General actions with the enemy must be avoided," he wrote, "the loss of a single man at the time would be sensibly felt . . . as the enemy could easily retrieve their losses by recruits from the numerous tribes."

This was the formal way of putting it. In common with military reports it elucidates little. It meant that each man should fight when and how he was told to fight. Cresap and Lewis, both veteran frontier commanders, had not been able to exercise such control. Their groups would depart on private hunting trips or raids without asking an officer's leave.

Also Clark was determined that there should be no laggards. He called every able-bodied man into service under the Invasion Law. He had chosen his leaders, all older men than he, who were ready to obey that young major.

There is a record of "a court-martial of all the commanding officers of the country." "Present, George R. Clark, Daniel Boone, James Harrod, John Todd." In case any man called in under the Invasion Act left the service he was to be "looked upon as a deserter and the commanding officer is desired to advertise all such throughout the county as deserters in the most public manner."

Todd no longer had to complain about "politicks." Here was action. Now the two lawyers had to agree by doing what Clark ordered them to do or they might be proscribed. And whence could a malingerer desert? Out on the buffalo trails, taking a chance against the Indians and hoping to preserve his scalp until he reached a settlement two hundred miles away, or, by grace of savage favor, he might be taken prisoner to Detroit. The best military asset Clark had was in keeping deserters in hand.

He kept a diary in this period. Its scrawled words are now faint on time-stained stout linen paper before the days of the perishable product of wood pulp. It was not a day by day diary, but a vagarious schoolboy sort of diary. He wrote the briefest note of some point he thought worth recording, or which possibly it occurred to him he ought to record when the absent son was reminded that he had promised father, or mother, or the methodical elder brother Jonathan, to keep a diary.

There is the brief mention of the attack on McClellan's; that later McClellan died of wounds. "Moved to Harrodstown from McClellan's Fort" is all for that important decision in crisis.

"March 5th. Militia of the county embodied." This meant that his little army had been officially established under the Virginia law. "March 6th. Thomas Shores and William Ray killed near Shawnee Spring." "March 7th. The Indians attempted to cut off from the fort a small party of our men. A skirmish ensued. We had four men wounded and some cattle killed. We killed and scalped one Indian and wounded several."

And scalped! That gives us of to-day a cold chill. It was a form of frightfulness whose object a modern staff would describe as "depressing the enemy morale." Many settlers who had seen much bitter Indian warfare fell into the habit of it when the gauge was Indian method against Indian method. This is not saying that the practice was universal.

When the Indian was on the warpath his head, as a rule, was shaven except for the scalp lock in which a feather was often fastened. The lock was an offer to the enemy for a grip for one hand while the other severed the flesh that held the roots in a piece about the size of a monk's tonsure. The feather flaunted defiance to any enemy who would get a grip on the lock. Loss of his scalp lock being the final humiliation to an Indian, the sight of a fellow who had lost one made him cautious before the valor of the white man.

On March 8th there is an entry significant of Clark's prevision. Thus far the settlements had been harassed only by small parties of the advance guard. The heavy attacks would be coming when the trails were dry.

"Brought in corn from the different cribs until the 18th day." Corn when it was planting time! Corn in the stockades against siege! Corn which women would pound into flour and makes into cakes while the men manned the embrasures! The record goes on. "A small party of Indians killed and scalped Hugh Wilson." "Archibald McNiel died of wounds." "March 28th. A large party of Indians attacked the stragglers about the fort; killed and scalped Garret Pendergreet; killed or took prisoner Peter Flin."

Stragglers! Probably they were men off guard in the fields. Clark could point to them as examples of carelessness. In keeping up morale he must prevent over-confidence wasting life and at the same time not damp fighting spirit, when he was so miserly husbanding his forces. If he who had so much to tell had only kept as elaborate a diary as Judge Henderson; but then he and all "our people" might have lost their scalps.

"It is impossible to relate all the small actions that took

September

2 Neal Bowman & Co and
at this place. court held &c

8 27 Men set off for ye Sett.

9 Indians discov.d a shot
each nothing done

11 37 Men went to Fort Bowman
for Corn while shelling they
were fired on a Skirmish
ensued Ind. drew off leaving
2 dead on the spot & much
Blood
Eli Gerrard was killed on
the spot & others Wounded

12 Dan. Bryan died of his Wounds
rec. yesterday

17 Express sent to the Sett.
——— under son died

A PAGE FROM CLARK'S DIARY WHEN HE WAS DEFENDING THE
KENTUCKY SETTLEMENTS. *Draper manuscript*

place," he writes in his Memoir. "The whole of my time when
not thus employed was devoted to reflecting upon things in
general." It was his way of saying that he was thinking all
the way from Williamsburg to the Lakes.

Hard pressed as he was his dream was never out of mind.
That word Detroit was humming in his ears. Short of men
as he was, he spared two on the hazard of his great ambition
which seemed so quixotic in his present situation. It was like
detaching a battalion from a garrison of ten thousand in
siege or a shock division in the defense of Verdun. The two
were both young and agile, expert Indian fighters and trailsmen. They must be for the secret mission which Clark had
given them.

Also both were great hunters, which specially suited them
for their part. When Lieutenant Benjamin Linn and Lieutenant Samuel Moore slipped away from Harrodstown it
was given out that they were going to St. Louis to sell beaver
skins. They did not know the plan which was back of all
the questions which Clark would have their journey answer
for him.

St. Louis was on the other side of the Mississippi which
was Spanish. The east bank of the Mississippi was British.
Across from St. Louis on the little Kaskaskia river which
flowed into the Mississippi was the fort and settlement of
Kaskaskia, the outpost of the British area as distant Pittsburgh was of the American. On the Wabash river, between
the American frontier and the Mississippi, was Fort Sackville at Vincennes, a way station in promoting and supplying
Hamilton's Indian campaign.

What was the strength of the garrisons? How many can-
non in the forts? How were the forts best approached?
What was the attitude of the French colonists now under
British rule?

Linn and Moore had to go hundreds of miles ever watchful for ambush in every thicket, slipping past Indian camps,

speaking fair to any Indian who appeared friendly, but on guard against treachery, while they picked up any food they could in addition to the jerked buffalo meat in their bags. Their wits must serve them when flight or hiding failed.

To fire the bullets in their two rifles was not quite the last resort when resistance was their only hope; nor yet their loaded pistols, but their big knives whose tactical part in defense was that of both sword and dagger after the discharge of firearms. A sword was too clumsy for skinning animals and cutting meat and a dozen other practical purposes and the dagger too small.

Scouting in later days, farther west on the open plains of wide visibility, when the scout was astride a fleet cayuse which could show his heels against pursuers, hardly required more nerve than this jaunt of Linn and Moore through the forests who were making it without any reason known to them except that it was Major Clark's desire.

Buffalo Bill occupies his heroic place because he was of a period in touch with our times. Bill ended his career shooting glass balls in a Wild West show; but Linn, a devout man, who doubtless said his prayers every night before he went to sleep on the ground with one eye open, and who may have had the spiritual exaltation of his creed when he had to swim a stream, was to become a well-known pioneer Baptist preacher in Kentucky after the Revolution.

In face of the coming storm, after Linn and Moore had gone, Clark had at Harrodstown some eighty-four men fit for service, fourteen disabled men, twenty-four women, twelve children above ten years, fifty-eight children under ten—a fruitful race the pioneers. There were also seventeen blacks. Probably the population of the other stations was about equal to this number.

So, with such hostages to fortune, there was good reason for having the stockades strong. A grim or sour visaged commander would not have been in place. Clark made the defense a game.

As in all sieges both men and women made light of death to keep up their spirits. A public joke is better than a sigh on such occasions to keep fear out of the heart. "Why be downhearted?" was the rallying phrase in the darkest days in the Flanders trenches. The Indians got your neighbor to-day; they might get you to-morrow. But why dwell on the grim prospect which was in every mind?

The treble cries and laughter of children were heard behind the crack of rifles. Children did not play at being Indians but at being great Indian fighters like their fathers. Merriment took the edge off of danger.

No settlement was without its fiddler, so far as I have ever been able to learn. If he packed the fiddle the others would share their food with him. On evenings, after a day without attacks or alarms, or after an attack had been repulsed, couples did a reel on the hard earth inside the stockade or on a cabin's "puncheon" floor of big wooden slabs. Some adept had all for spectators as he danced a breakdown while loaded rifles rested against the walls ready for instant use.

Doubtless many a woman had a flutter when Major Clark asked her to be his partner. He was friendly with all, but even in his merriest moments he had a certain reserve. No one, I judge, was quite intimate with him, which is again often the characteristic of the natural leader.

There might be an interruption of the gayety when a sober face appeared in the doorway with the word that the "Injins" had got some man on the way to Boone's. An outcry came from a woman then, and women rushed to her side. Each tragedy was a common grief, each death brought home to all, when all knew one another.

Riflemen were on guard at the simple burials; and as the spade filled in the earth on the dead man the live men re-

solved afresh that the Indians should pay in kind. There
was no quarter in that warfare.

April 19th was a great occasion at Harrodstown. Clark's
diary reports important political and social items. It was
election day. John Todd and Richard Callaway were chosen
burgesses. James Barry was married to widow Wilson. It
was only six weeks since her former husband had been killed
by the Indians. There were so many lonely males at Harrodstown that a comely widow need not wait long for a new
alliance.

When every woman and her children acutely required a
man's protection an unattached woman was a challenge to
the gallantry of the community, an economic and social
solecism. One may presume that it was also a military dis-
advantage. Once the widow had made her decision among
the suitors distraction might not lead to their being ambushed and their minds would be on their work and defense.

"Which will win?" must have been a titillating question
of the gossip about the suitors' qualifications and their speed
and address in the contest. Although they had no daily or
even weekly paper the settlers lacked neither major issues
and excitements nor subjects for small talk.

Legends were to grow of the mighty feats of prowess of
those days by the mighty Indian fighters. Boone and Kenton
did not, or at least their friends did not, let their tales lag
for want of a leg in the glow of later reminiscence. The actual deeds of many of them, not only in the Summer of 1777,
but in the later border warfare, whether in eluding capture,
escaping from captivity, or hand to hand combat, make
those of the later frontier hero quite pale.

Again we are reminded to pay tribute to the Indian as
master savage. Truth was that only a few white men were
ever as good as the Indians at the Indian game. Boone and
Kenton were. It seems agreed that Clark also was as man to
man as well as commander; although in all we have from

him in his own words there is no hint of that kind of boasting on his own part or for others, when he was so preoccupied
with training and instilling the qualities of superiority in
his little force.

Through the summer months the bands from the main
Indian advance, who came to avenge the ancient grudge
against the isolated Kentucky forts and wipe out the stain
of previous defeats, kept appearing. They had new rifles and
plentiful ammunition supplied from Detroit. "Indians, 'tis
thought sustained much damage," says Clark moderately in
his entry of April 24th. Boone and Todd had been among
those wounded when the Indians tried to storm Boonesboro.

Storming having failed, they gathered their forces again
and tried a siege. All day and into the night they poured
Hamilton's ammunition at the stockade, and then all another day and until midnight. In vain they tried to burn
the stockade. Provision had been made against that old trick.

Two days was a long time for the Indians to keep up a
siege. Skillful as they were at taking cover, the riflemen from
the embrasures of the stockade had the advantage. After
the Indians had withdrawn they filled their stomachs again,
did more war dances to blood them for the fray, or fresh
bands, sent from Detroit, arrived to show those who had
failed what real fighting men could do against the forts.

But the defense must not be content to remain behind
walls. There must be sorties. In the lull between attacks
Clark had to hold back the too ardent who thought it was
safe to go abroad or who wanted to turn the tables. He, himself, led Indian hunts at propitious moments.

During the attacks the women loaded the rifles for the
men to fire. They cared for the wounded, and cooked the
meals. At intervals, parties sought to recover horses the Indians had stolen, and when they could take an Indian's horse
they did not ask if he were its original owner. All was fair
reprisal when your scalp or an Indian scalp was the stake.

Mounted men stole out from the settlements at night to get game and packed the meat back to replenish the larders.

Each man was a soldier one hour and a husbandman the next. In face of the harassing warfare, which was depleting the number of males, this self-sufficing community was growing crops of corn and vegetables, defending their cattle which gave milk for the children. The workers in the fields were the prize targets of Indian warfare. Their simple tactics were to keep a bullet's range between them and the woods; then stay the rush with the bullet in the barrel and fly for the refuge of the stockade whose open door which awaited them was instantly closed once they were inside.

The young commander of militia of the new county was chief of combat operations, intelligence and supply of that little force, which he molded for its test. He was having further experience and training for his venture over the Ohio, as he gave his spare time to "thinking on things in general" as he had done too often on the school bench under the eye of master Donald Robertson. He spared men for expresses to run the gamut with reports of his situation to General Hand at Pittsburgh.

An occasional express came through to him. One said that Washington had won a great victory over Lord Howe. In his diary Clark sprinkled a grain of salt on the report. "Joyful news if true," he remarks. And it was not true, far from it. Things were going badly with Washington as they were with General Hand whose offensive from Pittsburgh against the Indians had been driven back in rather humiliating fashion.

"June 22nd Ben Linn and Samuel Moore returned from the Illinois." This was all Clark had to say in his diary on the day that his scouts safely returned from their mission; all except, "Barney Stagner killed and beheaded one half mile from the fort (over-confidence again). A few guns (meaning rifles) fired at Boone's."

If the enemy captured Clark's diary they would not be apprised of his object in sending Linn and Moore to the Illinois country. They had had quite a highly successful trip "to sell beaver skins"; they had gained the information Clark wanted all the way to the walls of the British forts. What a conference that was between chief and the weather-beaten legates from the trails in some quiet corner where they would not be overheard, Clark masking his intense interest lest he arouse their suspicion of his purpose!

"I found by then," says the Memoir, "that the Illinois people had little expectation of a visit from us. They were kept in good order, however, the militia trained, etc., that they might be prepared in case of a visit. I learned that the greatest pains were taken to inflame the French inhabitants against the Americans notwithstanding which the spies had discovered trace of affection for us among some of the inhabitants; and that the Indians from that region were generally engaged in the war upon us."

He must have itched to set out at once to Williamsburg to get the authority, the means and the men for his expedition into the Illinois country. The scene was set for it; the time was now when his information was fresh. Beyond Vincennes was Detroit, and in Detroit was Hamilton who had provided the bullets imbedded in the walls of his stockades.

But present business was still there in the valley of the Kentucky where he was to live when the war was over among the settlers whom the ordeal through which they were passing made more than ever his own people. His departure might take the heart out of the defense. Public opinion would have seen the man who had drafted every able bodied man as himself a deserter.

How long could the settlements hold out? All depended upon how frequent and furious the Indian attacks which were gradually wearing them down. Should any large body of Indians appear, now, they might turn the scales. There might be the last desperate fight to the death and then a general massacre of the women and children.

Should they hold out until Winter when the game migrated, despite their little crops of corn, they might face starvation. Logan's would be the first to go. There the Indians, probably under the leadership of a white border ruffian in Hamilton's pay, were breaking precedent by maintaining a continual siege. Parties from Harrod's and Boone's could not relieve them without endangering their own women and children.

Clark had sent out expresses in the Spring telling of the precarious situation, but one never knew whether expresses would arrive. When they did not "probably killed by Indians" closed the record. But his appeal got through. Virginia heard it now from people who were a part of the state.

In the midst of Indian successes all along the frontier, the courageous stand of this far flung outpost, whose value was now realized, an indomitable human island staying savage waves, which otherwise would have broken on the main frontier, stirred Williamsburg and also the Holston in pride and admiration to the rescue, even when everywhere the cry was for men, more men to dam a flood of misfortunes. Clark had word that troops were being sent under Colonel John Bowman.

To Logan's, the sight of him on September second leading his file of one hundred Virginian riflemen with packhorses was as welcome relief as was later the sound of the bagpipes of the relieving column to the besieged of Lucknow. By this time most of the cattle had been stolen and the crops of corn burned before they could be harvested. There was little forage for the few horses that remained. At the end of September forty-eight mounted Tennesseeans who had ridden from the Yadkin arrived at Boone's. Soon after came another hundred expert Virginia riflemen.

Now Clark could go. His people might have a hard winter, but they would be safe. Had he been as good a writer as Henderson we should have a picture of the settlers as they gathered around him to say good-by; veteran men and women and children bound by their experience to the merry, cool-headed and inscrutable man who had brought them powder and succor and "seen it through" with them. Clark permits himself a little satisfaction in words.

"I plainly saw that every eye was turned toward me as if expecting some stroke in their favor." They were used to this from him by now. "Some of the settlers doubted my return, supposing I would join the army in Virginia. I left them with reluctance, promising (what I had predetermined) that I would certainly return to their assistance."

So he did, after many tribulations, with the best kind of assistance, that of carrying the war into the enemy's country.

XIII

THE GREAT VISION

CLARK would not have remained one among the settlers if he had not retained his interest in horses or if he had been above a horse trade; or so easily have held public respect if he had had the habit of getting worsted in a trade. In colonial days it was not only the New Englanders who were fond of barter, nor was all the shrewdness confined to Yankee smartness.

The tradition which was later personified in "David Harum" moved westward over the Blue Ridge at the same time it moved across the Hudson to the Mohawk valley. In lulls of the siege the Kentucky settlers enjoyed their passion for swapping.

For his journey Clark bought a horse for twelve pounds. Before his departure Isaac Shelby's eye became acquisitive as he looked over that horse. Shelby, who was afterward governor of Kentucky, had one which George Rogers thought as a man who knew horses would do just as well for the trail. On the trade George Rogers received ten pounds to boot which meant that he had mounted for the homeward trip for only two pounds.

He gave such items the same space in his diary as the repulse of Indian attacks. But it would not have been in line for him to have boasted of his bargain. A highly competent horsetrader, even as a highly competent diplomatist, never boasted of his triumphs except in the bosom of his family, or in the reminiscence of old age, or to the cronies of his own community when he had been victorious in an alien community.

There was a promise to be kept when Clark left Harrods-

town. It had been made to keep up the spirits of some of
the discouraged defenders who otherwise would have bolted
in one of the recesses between attacks. He had assured them
that they might go at the first opportunity after relief had
come. Then the desertion clause of that stiff Invasion Law
would no longer apply. Now that there were reinforcements
and the Indians were giving up their campaign, in answer to
the call of their villages and the Autumn's warning that they
must lay in a winter meat supply for the women and children, Clark would see the outgoing party safely on its way.

Inwardly he must have chafed at the slow progress of the
men, women and children who were carrying their tools, pots
and pans and blankets. They were also driving any cattle
they had left to be sure of a meat supply, for it was no
longer certain that they would be able to shoot any game.
However, luck was with them. They got three buffalo and
some deer, Clark records.

The crestfallen procession departing in disillusionment
met a procession going the other way into the dangers from
which the outgoing were fleeing. This meeting on the trails
had always been common from the beginning of the seaboard advance until it reached the Pacific coast. Nowadays,
trains carrying youth to the battle in the city pass trains
which are taking the vanquished back.

The incoming party had the freshness of illusion. They
had heard that the Indians had been well licked; the road
clear; government established and sound titles assured in
Kentucky where they wanted to be in time to get their share
of the fabulously rich land before it had all been taken. The
pessimism of experience could not dim the optimism of in-
experience. One thing the outgoing could not deny was the
fertility of the Kentucky valley. But what was the use of
raising crops for the Indians to burn and raising calves
for the Indians to steal?

The incoming were thinking that some people were not

meant to be pioneer settlers; that they would risk the Indians. Anyhow, they wanted a look at Kentucky of which they had heard so much, and a prospect of danger only whetted their curiosity.

Theirs was the bold conviction of adequacy to any trial which had repulsed the downhearted; theirs the frontier free agentry which made sport of paternalistic government. Some of the ingoing would in turn retreat; but some would remain to be the seed for further advance.

The Continental Congress had no way of holding back the fifty or any other party of the kind from risking their lives. Rather Revolutionary policy, after the lesson of the summer Indian campaign, now favored allowing them to go. Even if those fifty men had volunteered for Washington's army they would have been untrained recruits in the business of fighting British regulars. And they would not have volunteered.

For the service they were about to do every one of them was well trained. In fighting for their women and children and their land they were now seen in the developing situation as a definite and invaluable military asset. The war emotion of an Indian band spent against a distant settlement did not reach the main frontier.

The remote outpost threatened the rear of the Indians who passed it by. Its military position was that of a fort which an advancing army masks, but which must be contained by the detachment of sufficient troops to prevent sorties against communications. Thus, the back country proper with its more numerous farms was left secure to supply grain and meat for Washington's army. An army twice the size of Washington's stretched between blockhouses would not have been a sufficient screen to prevent penetration by Indian bands on that long frontier. And Clark's plan was the taking of the outposts of Vincennes

and Kaskaskia which were performing in Hamilton's campaign a similar service to that of the extreme American
settlements.

Once he had his convoy of returning settlers out of the
danger zone Clark was free of their slow progress and rode
rapidly ahead by himself. We hear no more of his traveling
with a servant. Such impedimenta were not in keeping with
frontier habit. When he stopped at small cabins for the
night, he paid his score and set down the amount. For food
and shelter for himself and food for his horse, the average
was about three shillings.

He came up with a Captain Campbell, "very agreeable
company," who was going his way, and they rode together
for a week. When they were over the divide and they rested
at a tavern for a day in a storm, Clark's share of the bill
was one pound four shillings.

Theodore Roosevelt, in his "Winning of the West," suggests there might have been a wine charge when men of a
kindred world were well met. This is not unlikely, considering that in those days the circuit preacher on his rounds
would have been too pinchbeck to make gospel popular if
he refused the beverages of current hospitality from the sin-
ners whom he would convert.

That tavern was at the outposts of what they called
"civilization" in Williamsburg and Richmond. Mine host
may have been of the discriminating kind who was pleased to
think that he knew a gentleman when he saw one; and, in
welcome to two leg-stiff riders from distant trails, he brought
up from the cellar, for palates which he judged would be
appreciative, two or three bottles of Madeira which he had
sedulously guarded.

Anyhow, it was a time for expansion of spirit by the
travelers who were about to part when they were now in
Virginia itself. The foliage was in autumnal glory. Ahead,

as Clark rode on alone were roads, bad roads, but still roads in place of trails, with eye at ease no longer having to be alert for signs of Indians.

He bought a new pair of shoes in place of his moccasins. He had no further use for his rifle at present, it had become an incubus, and he sold it for fifteen pounds. His own horse needed pasturage to fill out the sunken places between his ribs. A better one was becoming for the ride through Charlottesville. This time Clark paid seven pounds "boot" in a swap.

He was not yet twenty-five; he was without ache or pain. He had nothing to do but think of "things in general." He was bringing home the bacon, and his plan was glowing in his mind like the colors of the leaves in the sunlight. The world had been good to him and the best part of it was yet to come. Soon he would have his arms around his mother and his father and see how much little William had grown in his absence.

Black hat and frontiersman shirt, he was clad as he was when he left Harrodstown except for his new pair of shoes, a picture that must have been very wonderful to little brother William as glamorous big brother rode up to the parental door, his latest journey over. Some days he had gone only fifteen miles with the convoy. Again he had ridden as many as forty, having covered about the distance from Boston to Cleveland in the month since he had left Harrodstown.

He heard the family news. Brother Jonathan had distinguished himself at Brandywine and won promotion. The other brothers at the front were still alive. Mother Ann could hold her head still higher as a majestic woman now that tales of George Rogers' prowess at Harrodstown had reached the ears of the neighbors. None could say that the Clark family was not doing its part against King George.

Father John was keeping the plantation going with the

aid of the blacks, producing all he could for the maw of
the Continental Army, and getting his pay in Continental
script which rose a little at times but was, on the whole,
steadily going down, making business a gamble. Virginia
was being drained of its surplus supplies. Articles of luxury
were not coming in and, anyhow, no one could afford them.
People were making their old clothes and tools "do" when
there were no home manufactures.

But George Rogers was there before the wood fire again
with more strange tales to tell; the prodigal was getting the
fatted calf; he was sleeping in his own bed again—if only
for one night. He was still the same restless boy with his
tireless energy, his eyes on a goal in the distances of the
great valley.

Did he tell his father and mother of the project which
hastened him on to Williamsburg which was not a quiet
country village then, but so lively with politics as capital
of the new state? Very likely not. He told them only that
he would be about in the home country for awhile and then
away again. He had reason enough for making his home
visit brief in the prompt report he must make as commander
of the militia of the new county of Kentucky in order that
he might have his accounts audited.

Evidently he had been organizing defense of the settlement on credit, a habit of his in military crises which was
later to load him with debts incurred for the cause on his
personal responsibility.

However, this time he got cash for his vouchers, a total
of seven hundred and twenty pounds and six shillings. The
diary also records that he spent four pounds, fifteen shillings
for cloth for a "jackote" and three shillings for buttons and
mohair. This meant a new suit of clothes. He also bought
two new shirts.

Although his nature was not free from pose it was not
his way to appear before Virginia rulers in the frontiers-

man's garb which many returning heroes would have seen as effective. Probably he rejoiced in having all the appurtenances that went with his old world, no less than the explorer, who after he has long eaten out of a can, is captious about immaculate napery and polished silver and the best the kitchen affords as something very much due him in arrears.

He attended church and bought a lottery ticket. Virginian parishioners might talk lottery after church service much as they talk politics and markets to-day. Indeed, buying state lottery tickets had become a patriotic duty in kind with subscribing to welfare drives in the World War. Instead of the interest on Liberty Loans you had the incentive that you might multiply your investment many times. The profits of the lottery accrued to the state at a time when the state was in sore need of money.

George Rogers had learned the ways of legislatures as well as Indians. His judgment held his impatience. To present his project to so large a body as the Virginia Assembly was to draw a conflict of opinions. He might as well have told the settlers at Harrodstown why he had sent Linn and Moore into the Illinois country. Word would be bound to reach the British lines. Hamilton would be forewarned and prepared for his coming when surprise was his only hope of success. Clark always adhered strictly to the idea that the fewer people who shared a secret the safer it was; and the perfectly safe way was to limit it exclusively to one.

While he was waiting two weeks in Williamsburg to have his accounts audited and his new suit made, he remarks that he was "taking note of everything I saw or heard that shed light on the disposition of those in power."

And Williamsburg was exultant over great news, as compensation for the bad of Lord Howe's occupation of Philadelphia and the repulse of Washington's attack at Germantown. All the Summer and Autumn ears had been strained for the latest reports from the Hudson valley. With New York and New Jersey lost, would Burgoyne prevail, and, joining hands with Howe, cut New England off from the rest of the states?

One day the post riders' hoofbeats became glad music; again men riding out of town put spurs to their horses as they shouted the news in at doorways and across the fields, "We have Burgoyne! His whole army has surrendered at Saratoga." It was the most epochal thrill America ever had. Had Burgoyne won the war must have been lost. France would not have made alliance with an obviously collapsing rebellion.

Even with Williamsburg and the whole land rejoicing and the "powers" in a mellow mood, still Clark bided his time. Anyhow, he could not start his expedition until Spring, waiting on Summer for his contemplated rapid march. He was back at his home in Caroline County for a time, his mother doubtless preferring him in his new jackote to his frontier shirt. Probably she was wondering if he ever would marry and settle down.

Why should even the Council know of his plan? It is doubtful if at first he revealed it even to his beloved mentor, George Mason. All he asked was that the Governor supply him with funds and authorize him to raise men for the defense of Kentucky, and then, when he had his force down the Ohio in the Spring, leave the rest to him.

Again that young man who had asked Patrick Henry for powder was at the Governor's door. A reference to how he had used the powder might have been in order to open the conversation, the twinkle in Clark's eye getting a twinkle in response from Henry's. As he spread out the map of that western country, such an expanse of white with so few dots along river banks or between the rivers which webbed it, his was not untried youthful ambition. He had the prestige of military success; and in nothing does success succeed so convincingly as in war.

The cross below Pittsburgh, on the present site of Wheeling, which had been formerly called Fort Fincastle, was now Fort Henry, named after the Governor. This had been heavily attacked by Indians. General Hand's regulars and militia, eight hundred in all, had been unavailing. The Indians had massacred sorties from Fort Henry and relief parties sent to the assistance of the garrison, which was in extremities when the Indians changed their mood and suddenly raised the siege.

The Kanawha valley, just over the Monongahela watershed, was without a garrison for its protection. The American front had been pushed back not only in the east but in the west. Hamilton's plan had been a success the first season, encouraging him to bolder effort which might even endanger the settlements of the Monongahela valley the second.

And far down the Ohio from Pittsburgh, up the wiggly line on the white which was the Kentucky river, were the three little crosses of the forts that had held out under Clark. And up the Mississippi, five hundred miles across the white from Pittsburgh, was another cross, Kaskaskia and upstream on the Wabash river, with its portage to Detroit, was Vincennes, between Pittsburgh and Kaskaskia. And Clark, with a few companies of militia he would raise, proposed to go through that Indian country which had no American settlers, no succor, being all British territory, and capture those posts and their cannon and garrisons, after disposing of the opposition of any savages he might meet on the way.

This young man, who looked as if he had sold his crop of tobacco for a profit and was about town in his new jackote and ruffled shirt, seemed to make it all seem a kind of lark like a picnic in the dell. The same bold forehead and the same brilliant eyes under it that had asked for the powder, were making this a confidential enterprise which would be as successful as the first—just between the Governor of Virginia and Major Clark! Henry, who had horrified the Tories and shocked the moderates with his "If this be treason, make the most of it," could not help liking such audacity.

To youth all things are possible. Even this rash proposal might be possible to this boy. Probably Henry who was now forty wished that the boy was a little older.

He had to ask a statesman's questions. Would not the expedition invading their country arouse the anger of any Indian tribes which had been lukewarm to Hamilton? And Clark's answer was the expert's out of his knowledge of the Indian nature. Doubtful Indians would be overawed by the lightning stroke; those on the warpath would fall back to their villages. Hamilton would lose his prestige with them as a great medicine man and warrior.

Yet, in case Clark should be beaten? Beaten! Clark did not mean to be beaten. But even statesmen knew that good generals prepare to cover possible retreat. Clark replied that he would take refuge across the Mississippi in Spanish territory where the British might not follow him.

Those distances on the map—so far out in that wilderness! Risking men's lives in so wild a venture! Virginia, by this expedition, although it was nominally in the defense of Kentucky, would be put in the light of claiming the country north of the Ohio as a part of her state domain, when other states were regarding it as part of theirs and the Continental Congress had already mooted making it a separate territory under its direct jurisdiction. Again Henry was won by Clark's eloquence; but again he could not dare so much personal authority.

Certain "select gentlemen," as Clark called them, must

share the secret. One of those who, as a prominent member of the Continental Congress, had written the Declaration of Independence, was the Clarks' old neighbor at Shadwell, Thomas Jefferson. Another, soundest of Virginian lawyers, was Clark's mentor, George Mason. The third was George Wythe.

Son of a wealthy planter, Wythe was a graduate of William and Mary where he had excelled in the classics. In the prime of his powers he was now revising the state laws of British and Colonial enactment. He expended his fortune for the Revolutionary cause which profited so much by his wisdom. Jefferson had studied law in his office.

If the three thought well of Clark's plan, then, with their backing as well as Henry's, it should have to be shared by the Council. Clark answered their questions and won their favor.

There is extant a letter in which he put his plan in writing for the Council. It shows that he had worked out every detail, the surprise of the garrisons, winning the French inhabitants to his support and how he would deal with hostile Indians. To the legal minds of Jefferson, Mason and Wythe, and to such practical men as the members of the Council, it proved that here was no dashing adventurer who would trust to courage and leave the rest to chance, but one who counted all the hazards between him and success and how to bend them to his will.

The destiny of the rivers in the destiny of the great valley! His expedition when it had won its first objectives "would distress the garrisons at Detroit; it would fling the command of the two great rivers into our hands, which would enable us to get supplies of goods from the Spaniards and carry on trade with the Indians."

Clark's vision, born of thinking of things in general on the banks of the Ohio, as expressed to those who had had to think of things of detail in a circumscribed sphere, was

GEORGE WYTHE, ONE OF THE "SELECT GENTLEMEN" WHO
SUPPORTED CLARK'S DARING ENTERPRISE
ENGRAVED FROM A PAINTING

not alone for immediate war purposes but a summons to the national future. It was a vision of the economic unity of the little valleys and the great valley, in spite of the mountain wall between them, at the propitious moment when the closed seaports of the Atlantic coast turned thought westward.

Moreover, it touched close to Henry's interest in carrying on correspondence with the Spanish governor at New Orleans. The Mississippi would be free to the sea for powder and other munitions which could get past Britain's sea blockade by being arduously rowed all the way from New Orleans to Pittsburgh—but more of this later.

Early in the Revolution Sir Guy Carleton had said that trade follows the streams, his eye on the portages from the lakes to the great valley from which the French inhabitants sent grain to Detroit. The American complement of this British view was Washington's concern about the defense of the frontier at the outset of the Revolution.

Clark was certain that with five hundred men he could take more than the first objective. He could take Detroit. But he did not yet mention that to the Governor lest he be considered a visionary. In his own words, "it might lessen his esteem for me as it was the general opinion that it would take several thousand to approach that place."

The "select gentlemen" talked with the members of the Council. Still the project hung fire for some days. Time was beginning to count. Clark grew restless. The members of the Council found this matter a subject for thorough discussion. Very able men they were and fully conscious of their part in setting precedents in their experiment in a republican form of government.

By now the first elation of the victory at Saratoga had worn off. Many of the men who had helped to capture Burgoyne had gone empty of pocket back to farms where their hands had not been at the plow, to empty barns, to families on short rations. It was doubtful if they would re-enlist for the spring campaign.

From Pittsburgh General Hand had reported the certainty of the recrudescence of heavy Indian warfare in the spring. Washington was to send him reinforcements from his depleted army at Valley Forge, where his men were barefoot and ragged for want of means, while British sentries paced before Independence Hall in Philadelphia.

Yet Ben Franklin's presses, which had been removed with the Continental Congress from Philadelphia to York, were breaking previous records in printing Continental script. Young Alexander Hamilton, very much occupied on Washington's staff, was witnessing an example of inflation which must have had its influence upon him as the future proponent and resolute defender of a sound financial system for the Union.

With Virginia's man power depleted and resources drained, well might the Council of Virginia wonder how the men and funds in real money were to be forthcoming for this youngster's foray? The decision was that it could not be equipped and ordered without the consent of the Assembly which was very jealous of the Council's taking too much power to itself.

When Clark, about at the end of his patience, was again summoned before the Council he found that Henry and the influential ones had arranged for the Assembly to pass a bill for raising troops for the defense of Kentucky. Very few of the members even guessed at the real purpose of the bill.

"The instruction and necessary papers were ready for putting in the name of the person in command," Clark wrote in the Mason letter. He thought that they expected him to solicit the place. He would not, lest he be misunderstood. The plan was the thing. Then he was told that "the command of this little army was for me. I then got every request granted."

He was to have the men and the money, men on paper and paper money. He was authorized to raise seven companies of fifty men each, where he could and as best as he could, when county lieutenants were drumming up every possible recruit for Washington's army. His war chest for the expenses of mobilization, pay, supplies and moving his force down the Ohio and into the Illinois country, was twelve hundred pounds of the product of Ben Franklin's presses. At Detroit Hamilton was spending twice as much in gold in entertaining the Indians in a single powwow.

Jefferson, Mason and Wythe wrote a joint letter which held out a prospect of something more substantial than paper money to his soldiers once Clark was ready to begin the march into the Illinois country. The letter did not give away the secret. When that was divulged the "select gentlemen" would use their influence with the Assembly. The preamble of the letter was most discreet, when the operation was Virginian in defense of state rights, having regard to the susceptibilities of the sister states and the Continental Congress.

It is noteworthy that English habit still prevailed in referring to the subjects rather than citizens of the Commonwealth in an undertaking which was being financed in paper pounds. Citizens came into general use with dollars.

"As some Indian tribes to the westward have lately without any provocation massacred many of the inhabitants of the frontier of this Commonwealth in the most barbarous and cruel manner and it is intended to avenge the injury," the letter began . . . "If they (the soldiers participating in the expedition) are so fortunate as to succeed, we think it just and reasonable that each volunteer entering as a common soldier, should be allowed three hundred acres of land, and the officers in proportion out of the lands which may be conquered now in the possession of said Indians, not to interfere with the claims of any friendly Indians or any people willing to become subjects of this Commonwealth. And for this we think you may safely confide in the justice and generosity of the Virginia Assembly."

A governor of Virginia, too, did not forget to remind Clark that he was himself interested in lands. It was a habit of the time. Leaders who were impoverishing themselves for a cause considered the replenishment of their fortunes in case of victory.

Henry wrote a secret letter of instructions for Clark giving him a free hand in the distant world of his dreams. He was to treat British captives humanely. The white inhabitants, whom Henry boldly considered as living within Virginia's limits, if they took the test of loyalty prescribed by Virginian law, were to be treated as fellow citizens and "their persons and property duly secured." Otherwise, they must feel "the miseries of war," but always "under the direction of humanity."

It was long thought that, on the authority of this letter, the idea and the initiative of the expedition were Henry's. It was a skillful letter. It provided for full credit for Henry's prevision, repeating the details of Clark's own outline. Apparently, Clark had now told Henry of the ultimate goal he had in mind. For Henry proposed that Clark should proceed to take Detroit if all went well and Clark thought proper.

So, if there were failure the blame would be Clark's, and if success Henry would share the honors. This method of leaving the door wide open for escape by the statesman from responsibility, and setting up a pedestal to which he could mount to bask in the rays of the reflected glory of triumph, was not new in the seventeen seventies but as old as recorded history.

On paper, too, when paper promises were all that the heavily burdened rulers of Virginia had to give, were orders for boats and ammunition at Pittsburgh and recommending aid from all officials for the expedition going to the defense of the Kentucky settlers.

In their hearts the Governor, the Council and the "select gentlemen" must have seen the scheme as quixotic to madness. However, in that desperate situation, when the fortunes of the cause and their own hung on the valor of arms, any cast was in order. Twelve hundred pounds in paper money was worth investing in the potentiality of this fiery young man with his winning ways. As further proof of encouragement George Rogers had another piece of paper, his commission as a Lieutenant Colonel of the Virginia militia. This was no more on a gold basis than the Continental script. He would make it so when he had men to command.

HIGH ACTION

XIV

AS THE GODS DISPOSE

Final instructions and the paper money in hand on January 2nd fired the starting gun for the runner toeing the line for his long steeplechase. Happily it was not a prospect appealing to the soft. So the official blessing was unaccompanied by any suggestions from "select gentlemen" of the names of political favorites who would like to be attached to the expedition.

Clark was free to choose captains of his own spirit and kindred experience. In turn they might choose men in kind if these could be found. The place to find them was not at Williamsburg but in the back country.

The Carolinians and the Tennesseeans were the right sort. Clark dispatched one hundred and fifty pounds to Major William B. Smith, a veteran of Boonesboro, to raise recruits on the Holston which he was to march over the Wilderness Road down the valley of the Kentucky river to a rendezvous on the Ohio.

Captain Leonard Helm, of whom we are to hear much, was set to raise a company in Fauquier County. He and Clark had served together in Dunmore's war against the Indians. They saw eye to eye. By the same test of fellowship in action Captain Joseph Bowman was the man within reach of prompt call to raise a company in Frederick County.

Clark's appeal to each one was that of "Follow me!" and this the prospect which his captains, who had served with him, could hold out to the bold. He could not tell his captains of his plan; they could not offer the bait of land in the virgin Illinois country. But, no less, he expected speed from the men whose speed he knew on the trail. Helm and

163

Bowman were to have their companies ready and march them across country in time to be at Redstone on the Monongahela on February 1st.

Word from Helm brought the first disappointment. As he rode the countryside for volunteers to defend Kentucky he soon met with an active counter-propaganda from leading citizens of the region. They had heard nothing of any act of the Virginia Assembly calling for such service. By whose authority was this Helm acting in a fervor as if he were concerned with a matter of life and death?

Those fool Kentucky settlers had better come back to the main frontier. Every man was needed to defend that and put in the crops in the Spring. None could be spared for a wild goose chase led by some adventurer.

Clark and Helm had to appeal to Governor Henry, who was put in the position, as the good politician often is, when he must expend some of the capital of his popularity in behalf of a worthy but unpopular cause. Helm got Henry's assurance that he was acting by the Governor's orders.

This did not stop the opposition which fell back on the reflection that high-handedness in Williamsburg had not ended with Lord Dunmore. Henry might be interested in Kentucky land, but there were others who were not, although equally desirous of winning the war and doing their part by raising crops on farms which were nearer Washington's army than those surrounded by hostile Indians three hundred miles away.

By having Bowman and Helm at Redstone on February 1st Clark would be down the Ohio and ready to start north early in the Spring. But the two had to keep on knocking at the doors of cabins in a request that was proving to be fruitless except to those who had friends in Kentucky or were curious to see Kentucky. These were not always satisfactory types. Precious paper money might not be spent in giving them a free tour of the wilderness.

As the news of Clark's call for troops spread, the frontier became an uproar of disapproval. Again state interests were clashing with state and with Continental policy. Pittsburgh was no longer the thirty houses of a trading post on the river bank which Clark had first seen when he first went down the Ohio. Here Brigadier General Hand of the Continental Army was also summoning militia recruits to add to the nucleus sent to him from Valley Forge when the war was no longer a novelty to ardent youth.

Camp followers and supply merchants added to the motley population and discomfort in the raw winter months. Settlers, in retreat from Indian attacks, were coming out of the wilderness; others who had thought of going in were hanging about in idleness and uncertainty. Another civil commission had been trying to make another treaty of amity with the braves, much talk having evaporated without results. Loitering Indians, bringing in a few furs for sale, might be spies; and so might any white man in buckskins who gave lip service to the Revolutionary cause.

Over the trails from Detroit, Hamilton's emissaries were circulating verbal propaganda of the same sort that airplanes dropped behind the trench systems in the World War. Heavy penalties for anyone openly espousing the royalist cause lacked enforcement in some communities where the tory leanings were strong. In others the Revolutionists were hounding and hazing all tory suspects unmercifully in the bitterness of men of the same blood in arms against each other. Harassed royalists more than ever had reason for dissembling their views until they could reach the British lines where they could strike back at their persecutors in kind.

And more than ever Clark had reason for holding his tongue about his plan when, had the least suspicion of it got abroad, word would soon be swiftly padding in moccasined feet over frozen ground to Detroit. Of course he might not mention it to Hand. In the Pittsburgh region he found the strongest opposition to his request for volunteers, which was seen as another example of Virginian effrontery.

Who had started this Indian war that was raiding the frontiers, anyway? Who had ruined the fur business for the Pennsylvanian traders? These pushing Virginian settlers who were not content to work good land at home but had made trouble for themselves and for others by their folly.

A little group of them far down the river, where white men had no business to be, were now in a plight and howling for help. Some fool Pennsylvanian settlers had even joined them. Now they were calling for other Pennsylvanians to come to their aid. If any of these crazy Virginians wanted marching and fighting they would better join their fellow Virginian, George Washington, who thus far had not been making much of a success of this war. If he kept on retreating he would soon be back to Pittsburgh.

Not only were the Pennsylvanians in this mood but back in Virginia Clark's recruits were being encouraged to desert and deserters being harbored. And was not Brigadier General Hand in charge of the defense of the middle frontier which included Kentucky?

Before he resigned to settle in the Colonies Edward Hand had been a doctor who was a surgeon's mate in the British army. This pseudo-military experience might be easily capitalized by a man of address at the outset of the Revolution when so few leading colonists had had any training in arms. Another explanation for making him a brigadier was in the jealousy of preferments in the interstate play of politics which often prevented Washington from choosing his subordinates exclusively for military fitness. Resentment against discrimination in favor of leaders with political influence led that brilliant commander, if unprincipled character, Benedict Arnold, to turn traitor.

Hand, too, was dreaming of Detroit. His knowledge of

Virginia fct.

In council Williamsburg Jany 2: 1778

Lieut Colonel George Rogers Clark

You are to proceed with all convenient Speed to raise Seven Companies of Soldiers to consist of Fifty men each officered in the usual Manner and armed most properly for the Enterprize & with this force attack the British post at Kaskasky.

It is conjectured that there are many pieces of Cannon & military Stores to considerable amount at that place, the taking & preservation of which would be a valuable acquisition to the State.

OPENING PARAGRAPH OF THE AUTHORIZATION TO CLARK FOR AN
EXPEDITION INTO THE ILLINOIS COUNTRY

Indian fighting, until his severe lessons of the previous Summer, had been gained as one of Judge Henderson's party in smoking the pipe of peace with the Cherokee chiefs over the treaty which gave Henderson his proprietary grant in Kentucky.

For the capture of Detroit Hand wanted four or five thousand men and immense baggage trains. He had marshaled under a thousand men at Pittsburgh. More did not seem to be forthcoming. In February he set out with five hundred militia, including some regulars, to cross the Ohio in an expedition which would advance up the Scioto to take the British trading post at Sandusky. Later events left no doubt that Clark following his own plan of a stroke in the rear, with the same numbers, would have celebrated the Fourth of July in Detroit.

Clark's mistake was that, when he returned to Virginia in the Autumn of 1777, he did not, with Patrick Henry's approval, and bearing a letter from George Mason, start for Valley Forge as a suitor for the support of the whole instead of one of the parts for his enterprise. Mason lived in Washington's parish. They were close friends and neighbors. From no man would a word of approval have meant more to Washington.

Clark's appeal to the boyhood's hero whom he had emulated would have been to the understanding ears of Washington the young surveyor of the wilderness and of Braddock's campaign. That great commander, who had had to be so cautious in husbanding his forces and in waylaying maneuvers to avoid a decision against him, had shown his old intrepidity recently in his surprise of the Hessians at Trenton.

His questions to the young frontiersman would have a penetration that would make those of the "select gentlemen" seem amateurish. He, who had been quick to see the possibilities of the young artillery officer in the battle of Long Island, might have taken Clark's measure as a Hamilton for the frontier. Clark might have been down the Ohio early in the Spring commanding five hundred men.

But we return to General Hand. Spies could travel faster than his expedition with its impedimenta. So could the Indian bands. They left Hand to his own undoing in his midwinter madness. Apparently he must have been under the impression that the climate of Ohio in February was like that of the Carolinas. He overran some Indian villages. As these were deserted by all except a few women his offensive was called the "squaw campaign."

Beaten by the swollen icy rivers and the melting snow, his wasted, bedraggled survivors, in bronchial misery, returned to meet grins and derision as their welcome home to Pittsburgh. A year later Clark was to make his own midwinter march to the capture of Vincennes.

Hand's failure was manna for Hamilton at Detroit. It justified his contention that victory was with the British. He could cite it as a triumph of Indian tactics and make it an appeal to incite further ardor in the Indians to drive the settlers back forever from their hunting grounds. Discouragement at Pittsburgh spread along the frontier at the prospect of an Indian offensive which would be worse than that of the previous Summer.

There was a further call for help from Washington who must respond by more troops from his depleted force at Valley Forge. Hand asked to be relieved from command when there was a dark look for him in every face along the river bank. Congress, now fully alarmed about the frontier, decided that Detroit must be taken at any cost. When Washington had only about five thousand men fit for duty at Valley Forge Congress appropriated seven hundred and sixty thousand dollars for an expedition of three thousand men under Hand's successor, General Lachlan McIntosh, who had fought his way up to command in the East. He, too, was to find Pittsburgh the grave of seaboard military reputations.

Of course, Congress knew nothing of Henry's secret instructions to Clark or they would have ceased to be secret; and Clark, beating up and down the Monongahela for recruits to defend the distant Kentucky posts, only had his difficulties increased by the crisis after the fiasco of the "squaw campaign."

"Meeting with some disappointments," as Clark puts it, Bowman and Helm had been able to gather only a handful of men, and were having trouble to hold them. There was no use of further recruiting effort. The only encouragement that Clark had was from Smith in Tennessee who said that he would be on hand at the rendezvous with two hundred men. Smith's optimism, which was to prove to be baseless, at least presently alleviated Clark's fear that he was to be a commander waylaid without an army.

So, meeting with "some disappointments," it was May before Clark could leave the Redstone settlements. In addition to Bowman's and Helm's little bands, which set out down the river, "there were a considerable number of families and private adventurers." At this statement the modern officer, who is habituated to the military ways of a different day, would cry out: "Where was his discipline?" The answer will develop.

For the restless of a large area the trail centered at the Redstone settlement, the Monongahela's way station on the downstream route to the greater way station of Pittsburgh at the rivers' junction. Clark was not disturbed when he found that he was leading a tourist party instead of a military expedition. The families wishing to try their fortunes away from the war's pressure, and the adventurers, too, welcomed the protection of riflemen under an officer who resolved their uncertainty into a definite departure.

It is unlikely that Clark could have held them back, if

he had chosen, without the use of force. They had a right on that river as well as he. No authority was given him, or any militia officer, to interfere with citizens on their lawful occasions under the new democratic system of all men "created free and equal."

Clark understood the families. They were the same kind whom he had organized into defense in Kentucky. Every man had a rifle which could be used against the Indians. Further observation might develop individuals who would be worth winning as soldier recruits. Even for the others and for the women he was to find a use in support of his expedition.

As for the adventurers, he also knew them well. Among them might be good fighting material; and probably among them tory sympathizers seeking the British lines. He could keep any whom he found worth while when he reached Pittsburgh and shunt the others.

At Pittsburgh he found Hand awaiting the arrival of his successor, McIntosh, who already had a Virginian regiment and a Pennsylvanian regiment from Valley Forge on the march to the frontier. Hand was in bitter mood against the machinations of the Tories. Captain McKee, a brilliant frontier tory leader who had been a prisoner at Pittsburgh, had escaped.

McKee, Matthew Eliot and Simon Girty and others of their type had joined Hamilton for gold and revenge and in the conviction that his was the winning side. McKee seems to have been the most resourceful specialist in organizing Indian outrages, but it was Girty who won the most infernal and notorious reputation as the archetype of white savagery because he had turned against his old settler comrades. His treachery was in keeping with his half-Indian nature. Sinewy, Indian swift, cunning, dauntless, a marvelous shot, he was as gifted in woodcraft as Boone or Kenton. For two or three generations his name was the synonym for horror on the frontier and "Girty will get you if you don't watch out!" a warning to children to be good.

Nothing in Indian ferocity was beyond the frontier renegades against the settlers who met ferocity with ferocity. More and more men had been witnesses of disembowled women and scalped children as the Indian warfare spread. At such sights even the Quaker ceased to be a gentle soul.

"There is no good Indian but a dead Indian," was a maxim born of murderous realism. War conditions gave the natural ruffian full license as a partisan of either the buckskins or the redcoats. The landscape could not be pleasant in this stage of chaos of a new forming world. Such men as Kenton, McKee and Eliot and such French loyalists as Quendre and La Mothe who were equally good shots, equally shifty and enduring and even better versed in Indian ways, organized an élite of white rangers as allies and runners up of the Indian bands for Hamilton's drive of frightfulness in the Summer of 1778.

At Detroit were hatched the rattlesnake's eggs. This was, indeed, the nest to be scotched.

"Since last May," Hamilton had written in January to Sir Guy Carleton, "the Indians of this district have taken 34 prisoners, 17 of which they delivered and 81 scalps." These were the early returns of the investment of the red-handled scalping knives, wampum and ornaments.

Experts in tonsures had to keep watch lest the braves cut a scalp in two and get double pay for a single casualty. What became of the prisoners whom they did not deliver up need not be left to the imagination. For the men it was running the gauntlet and then torture; for the women, ravage; for some children death and a few adoption.

Lieutenant Governor Edward Abbott, commanding Fort Sackville at Vincennes, understood this. He was closer to the front than Hamilton. His right hand could not conceal from the left what it was doing. He wrote to Carleton protesting that the Indian preference was not to attack armed men "but the poor inoffensive families who fly to the deserts to be out of trouble and who are inhumanly butchered, sparing neither women nor children."

However, Hamilton was covering his tracks. He reported that he was also giving the Indians gifts for not attacking the inoffensive. Either he had a sense of very grim humor or none at all.

In the House of Commons William Pitt had voiced the indignation of the Parliamentary opposition. "Who is the man who dared to authorize and associate to our arms the tomahawk and scalping knife of the savage? . . . What! To attribute the sanction of God and nature to the massacres of the Indian scalping knife!"

And it was Lord Suffolk, a member of the Cabinet, who said in the House of Lords that "there were no means which God and nature might have placed at the disposal of the governing powers to which they would not be justified in having recourse."

The Cabinet might say that it, and not the opposition, had the business of winning the war in hand against renegade Englishmen who had turned savages, themselves, in monstrous persecution of loyal colonists. Hamilton, with the Cabinet behind him and his methods not squeamish to the Royal Breast which hired Hessian mercenaries, might think of Pitt in terms of a radical orator who was stabbing redcoats at the front in the back.

"It is all very well," one can imagine him saying about Pitt, "for an orator, who goes home to port wine and plum pudding for dinner in a comfortable London house, to air his views, but I should like to have him put in a few weeks with soldiers of the king on this frontier."

And the Quaker settler, who took a scalp in revenge for his neighbor's or his wife's or child's, might make a response, interpolated in the language of our time, to horrified paci-

fists of his gentle sect in a peaceful village on the Susquehanna:

"Come out and meet a few braves on the warpath and
see how you like it!"

Vain the protests of Pitt and of Governor Abbott in face
of the military success of enlisting the savages. Early in
June, about the time that Clark's party arrived at Pittsburgh, Hamilton spoke to the Indian chiefs whom he had
summoned in grand council in order that he might blood
them for a decisive offensive to follow up the bands who
were already on the warpath. He had become adept in Indian imagery.

"With these strings of wampum I open your eyes that
you may see clear and your ears may listen to my words. I
speak by order of the Great King who is the Father of us
all, whether white or brown skins."

A British commander, who represented a king, had an
advantage over one representing the kingless Continental
Congress in an appeal to chiefs of royal mien who had no
superiors except the Great Spirit whose white counterpart,
as Hamilton made it appear, was His Majesty King George
III who by divine grace was the supreme father over land
and seas and peoples far and near. No Indian chief would
have subscribed to "free and equal " to stir up insubordination among the young bucks.

"For myself," Hamilton went on, "I shall never forget
the manner in which you have acted since I resided among
you, nor the good will with which you took up your Father's
axe, striking as one man his enemies and yours, the Rebels.
You know the consequences have been good, as you have
succeeded in almost all your enterprises, having taken a
number of prisoners and a far greater number of scalps.
You have forced them from the frontiers to the coast."

He told them that some Delawares who had just arrived
"have presented me with two pieces of dried meat (scalps),

one of which I have given to the Chippewas, another to the Miamis, that they may show in their villages the dispositions of the Delawares."

One of the Ottawa chiefs who replied to Hamilton was a practical warrior who wanted an end of words. Let him have his wampum and be away on his errand.

"You know my business here," he said, "is to bring you some prisoners and scalps. I had not thought of a council."

So with wampum and richly beaded belts and strings of beads, ornamented pipes and gay tokens and ammunition and new rifles as Hamilton's gift, and the McKees and Gertys as mentors to show them where the scalping was best, the braves took the trails toward the Ohio.

At Pittsburgh, Hand, a very conscientious man, was doing his mediocre best in disposing his troops for defense when appeared more trouble in the orders on him from Governor Henry brought by the young Lieutenant Colonel of Virginia militia who had a little band that was strictly on a mission of its own. Doubtless Clark was at his affable best. There is neither praise nor blame for Hand in the Memoir. Clark rarely indulges in either. The practical side of his nature took the measure of men and circumstances for their worth as facts with which he must deal. Hand gave him ammunition and such supplies as he could spare, very likely as the best way of removing one portion of the motley congestion on the river bank.

There was news at Pittsburgh which must have led Clark to a good deal of thinking on things in general. At the command of the Continental Congress Patrick Henry was raising twenty five hundred Virginia militia for McIntosh's advance against Hamilton's lair. So Henry's interest was turned from helping Clark with recruits.

Evidently he had not much faith that Clark would take Detroit. Doubtless he knew from expresses that Clark had not started from Redstone until the end of May instead of

February 1st as planned. "Select gentlemen" who had been won to youth's dream had the consolation that Virginia was out only twelve hundred pounds in paper money and that Clark had not enough recruits to be much of a loss to McIntosh. However, he had the better assurance that they would hold fast the secret of an enterprise that appeared to be still born.

Colonel George Morgan, Indian commissioner, was also at Pittsburgh. He was engrossed in a matter which was as confidential as Clark's. He was sending in estimates of the supplies for twenty days' marching for the fifteen hundred men of McIntosh's right wing which was to start from Pittsburgh through the enemy country to Detroit. It would not be less than one hundred and eighty thousand pounds, equivalent to four or five million dollars to-day.

For transportation there must be six hundred packhorses, and one hundred and twenty oxen; for the principal articles of food there must be two thousand four hundred forty cattle and six hundred thousand pounds of flour. In addition were the clothing, shoes, ammunition, tents, tools, artillery, hospital stores and officers' baggage.

When Congress faced this budget it resolved to defer the expedition to Detroit hoping that the very public threat of it had forced Hamilton to look to his defenses. Washington, in his distressing situation, was too wise to consider detaching any such amount of supplies from his own hungering and ragged army as he waited for the aid that would come as soon as the alliance with France was formally established.

After Hand's experience he may well have wondered if the Indians would not get many of the packhorses, cattle and oxen before they reached Detroit. McIntosh must operate with half the four thousand he had expected.

Meanwhile, Hamilton had, at this time, less than two hundred white troops, including regulars and militia, at

Detroit, which, however, if you will look at the map, was a long way in a wilderness, without supplies for an organized army with its baggage trains, if not for the men of the type whom Helm and Bowman had been enlisting.

Secure in his lair, with his small garrison, Hamilton was carrying on his aggressive campaign with Indians and the white rangers. It was a singular military situation very harassing to the human temper.

When McIntosh was wondering if he should attempt an advance on Detroit with only two thousand men, when reports of the increase of Indian activity down the river were coming in to Pittsburgh, Clark's flotilla with something over one hundred riflemen, pushed into midstream. The young patriarch of the great valley was still fathering all the families who had attached themselves to him at Redstone. Their company was protection against any suspicion of his plan.

Indeed, his secret would have been safe, I judge, if he had shouted it aloud at Pittsburgh in the midst of the alarms, the wild rumors, tales and visions of haggard, sick and famished men in from the trails. The sane would have considered merely that another man had gone out of his head in what might be called, using the phrase of a later era, the "lunatic fringe" of the frontier.

Clark remarks in his laconic way, where big issues are concerned, that he proceeded "with caution"; and also, I am sure, merrily, to keep up the morale of his followers and as a challenge to any further disappointments he might meet on his way to a performance so incredible that it has the lure of legend even when it is a matter of historical record.

XV

UNDER THE VELVET GLOVE

THE great river which had called him from boyhood! Its spell was to hold him to the end of his days which came in sight of its flow.

Now it was carrying him farther than he had gone before; beyond the forested hills that he already knew; beyond the tributary streams he already knew; on to other valleys; on to new vistas of rich bottom lands which asked for tillage by such families as those in his party. The families' migration was the fulfillment of his real vision, with the war only a means to an end.

He writes in his letter to Mason that it was a "pleasant voyage," this traveler who coined joy out of danger and treading the unknown.

There must have been much for him to tell those who were seeing the Ohio for the first time as they passed giant ash and sycamores overhanging the bank; of birds not common in Virginia; of the wild life of the forest; of how to start a plantation.

Probably he expanded his theory about the origin of Indian mounds. It was a century before scientists came around to his view.

Kind river! Kind in its great volume which made the James, the Shenandoah and even the Potomac seem small! A river that called for an expansion of spirit, an invitation to think much of things in general in a larger world!

Security for his passage was in the Ohio's breadth. If the Indians had had a few machine guns hidden in the thickets at the water's edge, or had been armed with modern Springfields, the flotilla would have gone through a murderous gamut. The round bullet from the flintlock of that day usually would not carry from the bank to midstream, or when it did, a few strokes of the oars would put it out of range.

The public purpose of the expedition in relation to its actual purpose still continued to hamper Clark. The commander of the post at the mouth of the Kanawha hailed him with the news that he had just been attacked by about two hundred and fifty Indians. An express had been sent to warn the settlers up the valley.

With the aid of Clark's force the commander was sure they could overtake and rout the Indians. Clark had to appear callous to a call for succor for the very people whom his expedition was nominally raised to defend. He could not afford delay or the loss of a single man. It was a relief to him to learn later that his view that the settlers would have word in time, and be able to hold out, was justified.

No further incident is recorded until he beached his boats at the mouth of the Kentucky river, familiar ground to him as the disembarking point for Harrodstown and the other settlements up the valley. This was to be a rendezvous where Smith's men from the Holston were to meet him. Not one was in sight.

He sent an express to Harrodstown for news while he looked over the ground on both banks of the Kentucky with the fresh eye of a new purpose. It had been his idea to build a fort at the mouth of the Kentucky which would be his base of communication in his future operations and a rallying point for the settlers. Now he saw that, in this location, two forts would be necessary. From what he knew he judged that a more strategic point for the larger outlook of the future, which required the control of both banks of the Ohio, would be at the Falls where the riffles in the river held up boats both coming and going.

The answer to his express was more than a disappointment. It was a blow. He had expected two hundred men from Smith who was recruiting in Tennessee. This would make the total which he thought necessary for success. Only fifty Tennesseeans under a Captain Dillard had arrived.

Clark had not only an excuse now but a reason for fulfilling only the nominal object of his expedition by marching his force inland to the defense of the settlements and his own land interests. In fact, it was military folly to have considered anything else.

This is one of the occasions in which he reveals what was going on in his mind. On one side, he was thinking how the officers and men of his pitifully small band for his objective would receive the news that they were to advance nearly "a thousand miles from the body of their country to attack a people five times their number, merciless tribes of Indians, their Allies and determined enemies to us."

It looked as if the rainbow's end which he had seen at Williamsburg was melting into quicksand.

On the other side, he was thinking of the effect of failure upon Governor Henry and friend Mason and neighbor Jefferson. He was not concerned, if so apprised, that they had doubtless already dismissed his as still another of the many military dreams of the Revolution that had been broken. As he saw it they had pledged their faith in him. His loyalty was stirred; his pride stung.

As usual when he had an obsession it took only tighter grip of him in face of adverse circumstances. On Jove's errand maintain the front of Jove. The next turn of the cards might be in his favor. Why be downhearted? Not before his followers. They should not know that there was bad news from Harrodstown.

"I knew our cause was desperate," he wrote, "but the more I reflected on my weakness, the more I was pleased with the enterprise"—yes, the more stimulating its challenge.

There was increased reason for guarding his secret carefully lest his own men desert to the settlements. He did not even mention the secret when he answered the express, I judge, but only told Colonel Bowman, in command of the Kentucky militia, that he was going to garrison the Falls of the Ohio. Bowman was asked to bring every Tennesseean who had arrived and all the militia he could spare from the settlements to the Falls.

Bowman's militiamen were accustomed to know where they were going and why. It was the season of the busy cultivation of their farms. Were they to absent themselves from the protection of their families and land when the Indians were becoming active again?

Boone, that tower of strength, was no longer with them. No worse blow to their morale could have happened than his loss and the manner of it. Boone, of all men, had been ambushed. He and twenty other settlers had been captured by Indians while boiling water for salt at a lick. (Knowing how to play on the Indian nature he mitigated harsh treatment and by the use of his wits eventually managed his escape.)

His own people were asking if Clark had deserted them after all. He had been a restless man, anyhow, full of schemes. Whatever was his latest one it did not concern them. His place was there in the valley defending his cabin as they were defending their cabins.

But this was not the only view in the tempest of discussion that followed his summons. Another sprang from the memory of Clark's service; of the flash of his eyes in action. Hadn't he beaten Henderson, brought the powder, made Kentucky a county, and stood by through last summer's siege? Whatever plan he had up his sleeve it had always turned out right. This one would, too. A few of the bold single men fell in behind Bowman on the march. They included the veteran Simon Kenton.

Meanwhile, having arrived at the Falls, Clark's soldiers

and his families and his captains were again wondering what next. They waited on the bank while he did more prospecting. He was looking over the site of the present Louisville, which later in a modern city-planning enthusiasm he would have laid out on spacious lines before L'Enfant laid out Washington. But although this was the place to build a city, it did not suit his military purpose.

The low land that formed an island (Corn Island) in the river promised better. He walked all around it as if judging the depth of the water and the distance ashore. Then he walked back and forth across it.

There was nothing for the soldiers and the twenty families to do but to wait on him. They were at his disposition. They had learned that all the answer they got when they asked him questions about his plans was his inscrutable smile.

The inspection over he put a prompt end to curiosity. The families were told that this was their destination; to bring their belongings ashore and make shelters. Each was assigned a section of the soft alluvial soil in which to sow their corn and vegetable seeds. Thus they would have food for themselves for the winter, and perhaps some to sell to the army. Their able-bodied men would consider themselves as militia henceforth and go through the prescribed paces in instruction as the home guard of defense of their gardens.

So much for the families in their part. They had been made useful after all. There was no farming or gardening for the soldiers. Theirs was quite another part. Soon they were realizing that it meant harder work than breaking ground for crops. As frontiersmen and good shots they thought that they knew all about fighting. All they asked was to be shown the enemy and let the war begin. Men who were recruits in the training camps in the World War will understand their feelings; and so will cowboys who served in "The Rough Riders."

"I first began to discipline my little army," Clark wrote, "knowing that to be the first essential to success."

It would have warmed Washington's heart and brought a smile to the stiff lips of Baron von Steuben to have seen that autocrat on his island who saw discipline as the first essential of the success, which, paradoxically, was to become another argument in favor of the thesis that you have only to put arms in the hands of freemen to win battles.

The recruits were feeling the steel hand under the velvet glove of a commander who up to this time had seemed a genial, easy-going leader. There was no rising and going to bed as they pleased. The full routine of an armed camp was established. There was no escape from it or from the drills for men he had securely under hand in order to mold them to the sword grip of the blade he was sharpening. If any disgruntled soldier was of the mind that he had served his country long enough and he preferred home and mother he had not only to swim to make his escape. Sentries were placed along the shore. He was warned of a deserter's fate as further stay to temptation.

Clark's men might wonder as soldiers always do what was the object of all these rules and regulations until, they learned the futility of speculation. And after that they might put their heads together, when officers were not looking, in grumbling mutual commiseration as the best of veterans will.

What had being on this island to do with the defense of the settlements up the Kentucky river which they had left behind them upstream? Was Clark to keep them at those antics all summer?

Clark could tell them that he would look after that. There would be action enough if they waited. They would be glad of all this schooling. In affable moments as he rallied them he must have made it appear that if they did as they were

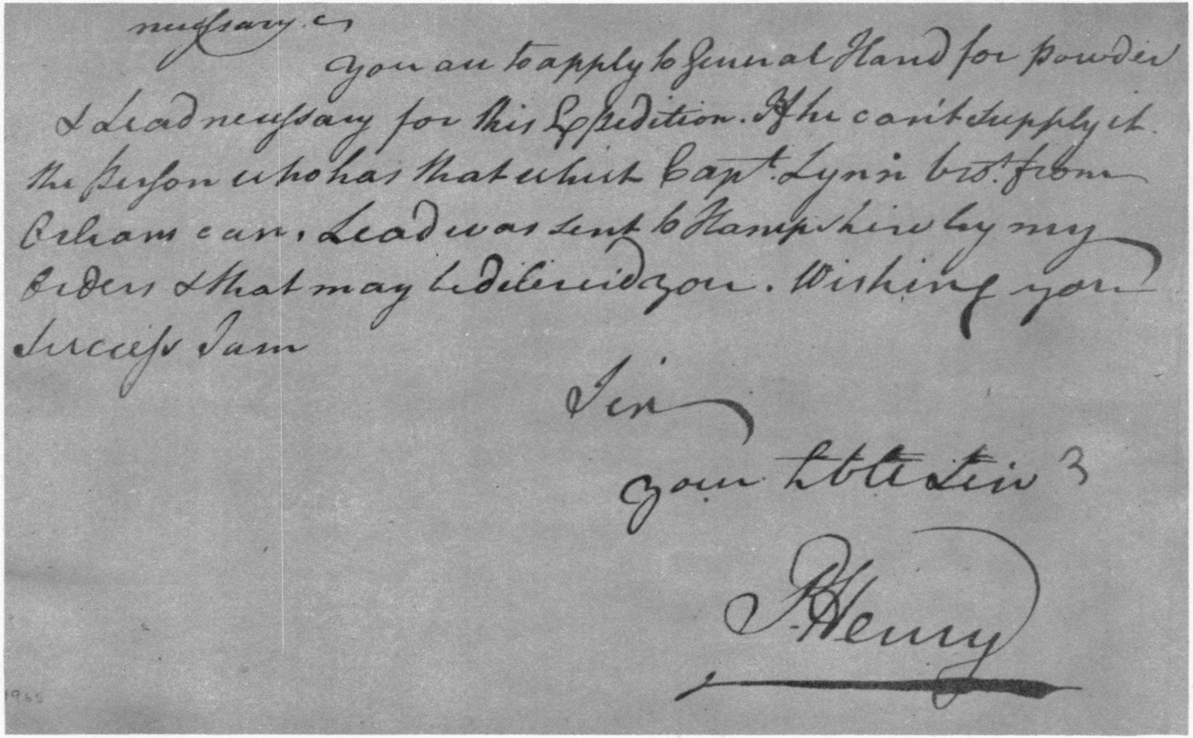
necessary.

You are to apply to General Hand for powder & Lead necessary for this Expedition. If he can't supply it the person who has that which Capt. Lynn brot. from Orleans can. Lead was sent to Hampshire by my orders & that may be deliver'd you. Wishing you success I am

Sir

Your hble Serv.

P. Henry

GOVERNOR PATRICK HENRY'S CLOSING PARAGRAPH ABOUT THE NECESSARY POWDER AND LEAD FOR THE EXPEDITION INTO THE ILLINOIS COUNTRY

told they would all inherit fortunes from rich uncles. While he awaited the arrival of Colonel Bowman and the Tennesseeans he was noting the capacity of his captains; noting among the men which ones could stand the gaff and which might be by nature marplots and malingerers.

Still he was hoping that with the reinforcements from the settlements he would be able to set out with three hundred and fifty men. Then he would move first on Vincennes and, Fort Sackville captured, he would force his marches over the portage to grapple with Hamilton. The dramatic stroke would cow the Indians, battle-tired after their summer campaigns. Once entrenched at Detroit he could hold out against treble his numbers. Winter would be closing in. The long stretches of snow and ice would be between him and any troops the British could spare from Quebec after Burgoyne had lost his army.

Detroit captured! What news for the post riders to bear back to Jefferson, Henry and Mason! What news along the whole Atlantic seaboard! What news for the Royal Breast! The States would hasten reinforcements to head off the reinforcements which the British might send.

Conviction became as bright as his dreams as he paced his island, gossiping with his families and organizing discipline. Less through any late information he had than through military intuition he was warranted in thinking that with three hundred and fifty men he could have taken Detroit while McIntosh at Pittsburgh was to give up the attempt for want of ten times the number.

But when he saw the less than a company of the Tennesseeans in addition to the county militia which Colonel Bowman brought, Clark realized that the first blow must be at Kaskaskia. He would not have enough men for the direct route by the Wabash.

Now Colonel Bowman should know why he had been summoned; now all officers and all men and all followers should know the object of the mobilization on Corn Island. Clark was too good a master of human nature to let the secret filter out. He would make the most of the dramatic surprise on all minds; direct emotion in the full flood of wonder.

So he did not make it an order that the men who had come down the Ohio with him should follow him on the hazardous march he proposed when the faint-hearted must understand that they would not be wanted to join in a lion hearted task only to falter by the wayside. So all might be free agents of decision.

Yet the psychology of leadership gave them no time to form groups to mull over the matter in camp corners. Wordy pessimists, with leisure to form their arguments, might not wait for the fallow field of cooling emotions in which to sow dissension, when Clark's plan, in its dazzling and definitely conceived whole, was tossed as a bright colored ball of discussion into public council out of a fireworks burst.

Some thought the plan wild, that it must fail. The ayes had the majority in the contagion of the prospect with its alluring gamble. They bore down the minority in the sweep of their enthusiasm which left the doubtful, if they hesitated, subject to reflections on their timidity by the lion-hearted. And the three hundred acres of land which Clark's secret instructions promised to each soldier in case of success gave a material appeal to the venture in a virgin country.

Colonel Bowman and other leaders from the settlements who were with him considered the situation. They told Clark how all, including the Tennesseeans, had been warned by the settlers that they must return. Possibly Bowman, the older man, may not have been very eager to lessen his own forces to contribute to a triumph by the younger man if his rash undertaking succeeded. He thought that he could not spare at the most more than a company and a half of militia for the expedition. A company and a half! About seventy five men! And of course they agreed that the Tennesseeans must remain. Their fifty were vital.

However, among the Tennesseeans themselves, the ayes did not have it. They had not been under the spell of Clark's personality and dominant will through serving with him. Outwardly they appeared amenable when sullen at heart.

Lack of courage was not the dissuading factor in the attitude of these typical frontiersmen; but they had marched far and past the blue-grass region where they had seen land which was so rich that they were not interested in the bird in the bush.

As they saw it, this lordly Virginian, this sprig of aristocracy, his head touched with vain glory, had tricked them. They had enlisted for the defense of Kentucky, where they would be defending the land they were improving, and now they were expected to scald their tired feet on a wild goose chase into the unknown where there might be only deserts and marshes.

When he understood the disatisfaction of the Tennesseeans Clark says "the boats were well secured and sentries placed where it was thought there was a possibility of wading from the island." Clark mentions a certain Tennesseean lieutenant "of whom I had previously a tolerably good opinion," his name not being given, probably out of consideration for his relatives. Speaking Clark fair was a part of the lieutenant's cunning.

The Tennesseeans went in swimming and found where the water to the Kentucky shore was not over their heads. Then, having dressed, they escaped the observation of the sentinels, and they were across before the alarm was sounded.

For a few minutes, Clark says, he was in doubt what to do. A few minutes was a long time for him to hesitate in an emergency. Possibly realizing that his temper was up he was waiting for it to cool. To him these fifty Tennesseeans were just as important as a division of twenty thousand men who were counted on for an offensive action by an army of a hundred thousand against an army of a hundred thousand.

If such were their spirit he was well rid of them. Time would be lost in pursuit. However, there was more than this at stake. The disciplinarian in him prevailed. The steel under the velvet glove had to be shown now lest he should have to show too much of it in the future to those who presumed upon soft-handedness. These men had presented no petition in a manly fashion. They had broken faith. They were deserters.

He must not blink the fact when every man under him must yield absolute obedience or his expedition would fail. He gave a ruthless order. The Kentuckians who had horses were to lead the pursuit and men on foot act as relays. If the fugitives resisted when overtaken they were to be "put to death."

"Follow me if you are lion-hearted," was the meaning of that to the others on the island, "and if you do come, I offer you an example of the fate of deserters who endanger the lives of their comrades."

Eighty years later, when Colonel William T. Sherman was the first commander to have his regiment in order after the Federal rout at Bull Run, a lawyer stepped forward from the ranks saying that their three months' enlistment was up and they were going home. "I know one who is not," said Sherman, pointing his revolver at the lawyer, which ended the argument.

When the Tennesseeans had gone about twenty miles they saw the pursuers approaching. They scattered, every man for himself in the woods.

"Only seven or eight were taken," Clark wrote. The rest made their way to the different settlements. "Many that were not woodsmen almost perished. The poor lieutenant and the few that remained with him, after suffering almost all that could be felt of hunger and fatigue, arrived at Harrodstown."

Their reception was hardly in keeping with the anticipation that was warranted when, as they marched away to the Falls, they had been told they must return to the defense of the settlements. Some of the pursuers had arrived at Harrodstown before the fugitives. They had brought news of Clark's plan. This fired vehement reaction among the settlers which broke on the heads of the Tennesseeans who were seen as slinking curs who had deserted their beloved leader in the hour of his need when he was about to strike the boldest blow yet in their behalf.

The settlers refused at first to give the lieutenant food and shelter. Some of the returning militia hung his effigy and burned it as an example to all white-livered traitors. In some cases individual deserters were hounded back into the wilderness. Had Clark himself reappeared at Harrodstown, so completely had his prestige been restored, probably the whole population, women and children included, would have been ready to follow him. Surely, enough militia would have been spared to permit of the Vincennes rather than the Kaskaskia objective.

However, the Tennesseean flight was ancient history to Clark as he counted heads in his final muster. He was weeding out others who were unfit although they implored him to take them along in their conviction that they could keep up with the best he had on the march.

There is no mention of any doctor who might assist him in the task. Probably Clark himself knew simple remedies and how to set a broken leg; that salt is good for wounds as the ancients knew and which practice is realizing again. In view of the nature of his enterprise his frontier experience told him that one laggard would be equal to the loss of four or five men; a dozen laggards might mean delay that would spell failure.

A factor more conclusive than medical examinations was proved fitness, a test of endurance, which chest thumping or the stethoscope could not diagnose, in the survival of the wilderness trails' gamut of danger, exposure and hard fare. It was not just that a man had not flat arches to the anatomist's eye. The roughest going had shown that his arches would not fall under the pack's weight as so often happened to those who passed the recruiting standard in the World War.

Teeth? They had shown their quality on jerked buffalo meat. Eyesight? It had been proved on the rifle sight covering live targets. Heart? The human pump had stood the strain of rowing and poling and hill climbing.

Morons? Although a man could not read or write, he passed the intelligence test if he knew how to make camp, to make wet wood burn, and could detect signs of hostile Indians in the wilderness. He had tactical intelligence which shone where scholars would be babes in the wood.

The intestinal tract? Proof against parched corn when it was getting musty and buffalo meat when it was tainted or that of a tough old father bear. Tuberculous tendencies? Survival in rugged health after sleeping in wet clothes on the wet ground was evidence of immunity.

There was no man who had not been measured by Clark's own eye as commander, major surgeon, recruiting sergeant, drill sergeant, chief of operations and chief of welfare. He had a line on each man's temperament and he was to know each better as all were to know him better—all those who were finally selected in councils with his captains.

No man who was in any way ailing could be permitted to go; no chance taken that he would recover on the way. There would be no ambulances to transport the sick; no dressing stations, no hospitals, the shelter of no villages on the line of march.

The joy of it! The glad gamble of it to youth his foot in

the stirrup! At last, after all his journeys back and forth, his harassing of governors and Councils and Assemblies, while he nursed his dream, he was ready for the take-off.

There they were formed up for the final review, his four companies, The Captains were Leonard Helm, John Montgomery, Joseph Bowman (not the same as Colonel Bowman) and William Harrod (a brother of the founder of Harrodstown).

If you are thinking of picked force consider this one. Never in our military history was one that was more expert for its task; not Grant's or Lee's veterans; not the veterans of shock divisions in the World War.

In all Clark had a hundred and seventy-five men. Every one was of the old American stock, the founding pioneering breed, canny, often proud to truculency, sharp tempered, self-reliant to a you-be-damned independence and willing to take a chance for a stake.

Few were very young. Hardening does not come until a man is twenty-five. And they were hardened, raw-hide tough. Some were close to middle age, their gimlet eyes set in the weather-beaten wrinkles. To a top sergeant of the barrack parade ground their drill would have seemed a painful one but they would have put him through paces that would have made him appear and feel painful.

The object of that drill was what soldiers know as fire discipline requisite to the kind of action they must face, as is that of all drill. A modern chief of staff striving for harmonious organization of the complex forces of artillery, infantry, tanks, gas, all the powers of land and air, if he could have looked on at that little band in buckskin, which had not a single cannon, would have understood that the drill had been right for the kind of fire discipline expected of them. Otherwise he would be a poor chief of staff in time of war.

Yet it was not the fire discipline which George Rogers

had most in mind, thinking of things in general and human beings in the terms of geography and history. He knew these men would fight. His fear was that they would fight in the wrong way at the wrong time. They must fight only at the right time; and, at the right time, too, individualistic as they were, be ambassadors of a well planned diplomacy. Else, after they lost their scalplocks, they would be food for wolves.

A hundred and seventy-five men! Hardly enough for a minor trench raid on the western front. Cæsar had small numbers in Gaul, although they did a lot of map making. Washington had only sixteen thousand, including the French, at Yorktown; Wellington seventy-five thousand at Waterloo. But they made a decision not of trifling importance compared to the four million under Marshal Foch on the western front; and Nelson with his wooden ships at Trafalgar had not less influence on the history of this time than all the allied fleets in the North Sea. The one hundred and seventy-five were to decide the future of more territory than all the armies that raged back and forth in Europe's Thirty Years' War.

XVI

DOUBLE MAN THE OARS

THIS young man of Virginia had many strings to his bow. He could switch quickly from grim to merry tunes. All tunes had spirit of corps in mind. He delighted in surprises which kept interest alive in his soldiers who would think less about their troubles if they were wondering what he would do next.

His ruthless pursuit of the deserters, his censorious inspection of the loyal and stern elimination of the unfit who were so sure that they were fit, might be taken as a sign that he had thrown away the velvet glove for good. Those who were going with him on the expedition must have been gloomy at the prospect of being set in a harness of steel with a martinet for a driver.

Their thoughts were suddenly diverted when he gave the word for a day of entertainment before their departure. Again he was the merry commander who would make the start a merry one. The men should have a break in training to accumulate spring for the take-off and strength for the championship test. We may be sure that the island autocrat, with his sentries posted, had kept "likker" out lest some of his soldiers might have to be carried on board the transports the next morning.

Entertainment in those days meant physical games or dancing to the fiddle. There must have been running and jumping; and there was certainly wrestling which was one of the prime pastimes of the frontier, wrestling "square holt" and "side holt." Roars of laughter rose when some "shorty" got a trick "holt" on a giant and threw him.

It was a meaning farewell for Clark and his old friends,

191

the Kentuckians, who had not gone after the deserters. When would he and Bowman meet again? Where would Washington's army be then? And what then would be the state of feeling in the Royal Breast of King George III?

When the little army embarked on the morning of June 24th, 1778, it was as simple a business as tourists going for a row. There were no packhorses, no wagons, not even mounts for the officers, or for Clark himself. The only baggage beyond what each man carried was a little for the down-river trip.

No rolling kitchens were to come up with the infantry after iron rations were exhausted, no relieving supply trains prepared for or expected. The only base of supplies in the rear was the little gardens and corn patches of the families on Corn Island.

It was a telling farewell, too, for the families and for those envious of those who had been chosen to go. All must have joined in shouts which were a throaty stirrup cup toast of good luck as they put their shoulders to the gunwales to push the flatboats free of the beach.

The boats bristled with the long black barrels of the rifles held upright between the soldiers' knees. They had to row a mile upstream before they could swing into the main current. And just as the boats came to the falls it became almost as dark as night. The flotilla ran the falls during an eclipse of the sun.

Frontiersmen had a larger superstitious strain than people back in civilization who, in turn, were more influenced by omens and less likely to walk under a ladder than people of to-day, many of whom, however, do not relish sitting thirteen at table. Men who live close to nature know how her rough and variable moods may make sport of their plans. Soldiers, being subject to the gamble of war, know that death may be in every bullet.

Realists, as they must be, they have even more reason to propitiate all the gods of fate than one who likes to be on the safe side in case there should be anything in the thirteen superstition. Everything that may mean a favorable or unfavorable sign at the outset of a great hazard is noted. So that eclipse was bound to be taken as a good or bad omen.

Soldiers of other more superstitious lands, whose traditions were different from those of the practical seaboard colonization, might have found in the eclipse such sure evidence of predestined failure that they would have lost heart. This was not the way of Clark's men. They came of the school which taught, "Trust in Providence, but keep your powder dry!"

To those who saw it as a bad omen it meant only a heavier handicap to overcome. You may be sure that Clark and his officers hailed it as a good omen; and veteran Simon Kenton could cite favoring precedents out of his frontier lore. And all would know at the journey's end whether it was a good or bad omen. Meanwhile it gave the expedition a new sense of importance. It was something no one was to forget. And even those who saw it as a bad omen would be saying one day, "I knew things would go all right when we had that eclipse of the sun."

Before the boats were past the falls it was apparent why only the strong might be chosen for the enterprise. This was no party of settlers drifting with the current. The command that bent backs in hard labor required no explanation when they must travel faster than their secret.

The plan of the expedition was already the gossip of the trails on the Kentucky side. Should anyone warn the garrison at Kaskaskia that it was on the way this disposed of the surprise upon which success depended. The incentive for speed was brought home to the frontiersmen, who were used

to Indian ambushes and stratagems and lightning strokes
out of the forest, better than to a modern force on a similar
errand.

With oars double manned they rowed in alternate shifts
night and day. There is no record of this, but surely Clark's
own boat must have been in the lead, his big shoulders rising out of the morning mist with the rising sun at his back
and outlined in gold by the setting sun.

Every man saw the future as under the leader's black
hat. His river, the expedition of his conception! Williamsburg, the seat of civil authority, was more than a month
away. There was no calling him back, now.

He had no way of paying his soldiers except the promise
of land. His little stock of paper money was exhausted.
Everything had to be done on a shoestring woven of the
strands of hope, will and audacity. It was young madness
and a glorious madness. The joy of it, the free rein of it!

As he passed the mouth of the Wabash he must have looked
up its valley with longing eyes. That was the way to Vincennes, the direct route to Detroit. But Fort Sackville at
Vincennes had a garrison more than double his force supported by artillery. Moreover, as he says, "there was an
Indian town adjoining, and large numbers of Indians
always in the neighborhood. There were more inhabitants,
more able-bodied white men who had arms in the Kaskaskia
than in the Vincennes region, but they were scattered in different villages. There was less danger of being overpowered
by the Indians." He would be better able, with small numbers by surprise to get the rallying point of the fort, and
thus be established behind defenses with local supplies at
his command.

More tributaries for his river! The waters of the Wabash
were added to its flow; then the waters of the Cumberland,
and in a short distance the waters of the Tennessee. It was
not much farther until the Ohio, which had absorbed so many

rivers, would in turn lose its identity in the Mississippi.

By boat he might make his way up the Mississippi and then up the little tributary Kaskaskia to his destination. But he had no thought of going by this route. It was in the French region where there was much more going and coming than on the lower Ohio. Unfriendly eyes, if not those of posted spies, would see the flotilla, and then, a horseman, faster over the French roads which were hard in summer than the boats could go upstream, would carry the alarm to Kaskaskia. The final advance must be overland in a region where, hopefully, the pace of the expedition could keep up with any tale bearer.

A brief landing, the first since Corn Island, was made at the little island of Barateria at the mouth of the Tennessee. Here the leader would inspect his men again to see how they were shaking down, give his captains further instructions, stiffen the spirits of any that had grown down-hearted, make final preparations for the march.

They were in the region where seventy years later the paddle wheels of steamboats, loaded with soldiers in blue, were to lash the waters of the Ohio, the Cumberland and the Tennessee. On their banks many camps were to rise as soldiers beat the earth into mud. Here Grant was to win sudden fame at Fort Donelson and to move on to the bloody field of Shiloh, leading Federal against Confederate armies in both of which were descendants of Clark's men.

It was significant of how little peopled was this section of the wilderness world, a neutral ground between Indian tribes, that Clark had not seen a single human being since leaving Corn Island. However, he must have been teased by the uncertainty that some stealthy Indian brave from the cover of thickets on the bank had observed those swiftly rowed little forests of rifles and was already on an Indian lope toward Kaskaskia with his tale.

Now John Duff and a party of hunters "were brought in

by one of our boats." The expedition is mentioned as a "surprise" to Duff, but whether or not his first inclination was to retreat is not stated. It was certain that there was no officer on the expedition who would not have tried to cut off his retreat.

Hunter was a broad term. It might mean settlers out hunting. Usually, and in this case clearly so, it characterized all the free lance wanderers beyond the rim of the settlements who formed a class by themselves in frontier life. They had no part in the war on the American or British side. In a sense they were men without a country, connecting links between French and American settlements and Indian camps, suspected but allowed freedom of travel, retailing news, knowing portages and trails, familiar with the Indian sign language. Their password was "furs." The pelts they brought in were usually from the Indian traps in exchange for the ornaments which they had to barter.

Sudden historical importance had descended on Duff. He had good reason to be polite when he faced a leader who was surrounded by nine score of armed men with their gimlet eyes; and Clark had good reason to be polite to him. There was no concealing the fact that the nine score were not seeking buffalo meat or looking for land for a settlement. They were plainly on the warpath against the British garrisons.

All the men of the Duff party had come originally from the States. They belonged to an American class of frontier soldiers of fortune which had sprung up in competition with the French *coureurs de bois* since the seaboard migration over the watershed. Clark told Duff frankly what his objective was. He invited Duff and his men to come with him on his march. They said they would be delighted to accept. They responded readily to Clark's request to take the oath of allegiance as Governor Henry had prescribed it in his

letter of instructions, and which would give Clark the same
authority over them that he had exercised over the Tennesseeans.

It happened that Duff had recently been in Kaskaskia,
which was ground for holding him under suspicion at first.
This meant most valuable information, if correct, for Clark,
who had had no reports since the return of Linn and Moore
twelve months ago.

Duff had been bidden when he left Kaskaskia, as all
hunters were, to keep a close watch for rebels and lose no
time in bringing back word of their approach. Rochblave
was still in command there. To give him his full name, he
was Phillippe François Rostel sieur de Rochblave, who had
served as a French officer in the French and Indian War.

He seems to have been a survival in spirit of the medieval
days—and even in the seventeen seventies the Royal Breast
was not considered out of form in Europe in hiring Hessians
to teach the rebel colonists loyalty to Britain—when the
professional men of arms, the swashbucklers, went from one
war to another offering their service for sale to the king
which would pay them best or held out the best prospect for
loot in victory. All causes were alike to them. They were
honest fighters as worthy of their hire as honest brokers.
They fought well. Their contempt of death and the soft
bourgeoisie who worked for a living fortified their courage
against all amateurs who took up arms in what were to
them the naïve illusions of local patriotism.

Rochblave's allegiance was readily transferable with that
of the territory of the great valley when the British flag
was raised in place of the French on the northern Mississippi.
He settled in Kaskaskia, married there, lived on the Spanish
side for a time, profited in his ventures and had such influence over the French inhabitants and had so well proved
himself to British authority that he was given command of

the militia at Kaskaskia when the garrison of British regulars was withdrawn. And command meant many perquisites, slaves, an autocratic position.

In common with the New York loyalist, Major De Peyster, who succeeded Hamilton at Detroit, he had the proselyte's extremism as the best voucher for his loyalty. He despised the American rebel *bourgeoisie* and longed to meet them in action. He improved on British propaganda and on the French tradition about the ruthlessness of the ruffian, godless, seaboard people who had come over the watershed, by picturing the Big Knives as more savage than the Indians. If they took Kaskaskia they would give no quarter to the men, ravage the women and drive any survivors into the wilderness, taking their homes, fields and gardens as the spoils of their thieving victory.

Rochblave had ample munitions. He had organized the males capable of bearing arms into a well-drilled force. At the first warning they would hasten to the places assigned to them in defense, these minute men of the Illinois country, and resist the despoiling Big Knives in the desperation of citizens fighting for their lives.

There had been alarms that the Big Knives were coming; but Duff said that the apprehension had passed before he left Kaskaskia. If Clark could arrive by surprise and get possession of the fort and its cannon, before the militia could man it and the men of the outlying settlements could concentrate, he could make an easy success out of the confusion.

Clark might still wonder if Duff were not telling him what Duff thought he would like to hear. In any event, Clark knew that here was good propaganda to arouse the confidence of his troops. He bade Duff circulate among them, repeating what Clark wanted him to say, about how readily victory would be won if all played their part—"which," says Clark, "put the whole in the greatest spirits, sure, by what they heard, of success."

The eclipse now seemed a good omen to many who probably had seen it as a bad one, while doing a galley slave part at the oars had made the advance thus far anything but a pleasant junket in summer weather.

Clark was not discouraged by the report of the terrible reputation of the Americans among the French inhabitants. The "frightfulness" would serve his purpose.

"I was determined to improve this," he writes, "if I was fortunate enough to get them in my possession, as I conceived that the greater the shock that I gave them at first, the more sensibly they would feel my leniency, and become more valuable friends. This I conceived to be agreeable to human nature as I observed it in many instances."

For he must have the French inhabitants on his side; their remarkable power over the Indians, which so far had been in Hamilton's service, at his own service. This was the keystone of his plan of making his venture with so few men.

A few miles from the mouth of the Tennessee was the ruin of Fort Massac which the French had built long ago to control the Ohio at its entrance to the Mississippi. North from this ran trails which the *coureurs de bois* and the Indians still used. These Clark would follow under a guide, John Saunders, who knew the country.

When the march was over, although news of it had not reached Rochblave, he would be facing Kaskaskia across the Kaskaskia river which was unfordable. How was he to make the crossing which might be under fire from the fort and riflemen in the houses? Clark had to leave some things to improvisation, which would be the easier with Duff as his walking map of the town at his elbow. This was a detail which was doubtless included in the censorship ban in telling Duff what to say to the troops. Clark would do all the worrying for them.

There was no further use for the boats which had borne the expedition down the Ohio. They were hidden in a bayou. As the hundred and seventy-five stepped ashore to begin their march, they were light infantry, relieved of every ounce of extra weight; every unessential thing which a man might want to take was left behind.

XVII

THE LEAN MARCH

A WITTY member, "Sunset" Cox, when the first Chinese Exclusion Act was before Congress, won laughter in the lower house by saying that the best reason for excluding the Chinese was that they wore their shirts outside their trousers. This does seem an exotic foreign custom which we associate with the subjects of autocracies as quite alien to life under our Constitution.

One of the curiosities of the change of fashions which salutes us from old prints is that shirts were worn outside the trousers by the most virile of freemen of the old American stock long before they appeared at our ports on Chinese and Russian immigrants. The frontiersman's buckskin shirt, which reached down to his knees, itself probably a descendant of the smock of the British yeomanry, was too long to be tucked in even if it had been cleft at the bottom to facilitate the process.

It fitted rather closely around the hips and its length was a protection against the cold and winds. At night it took the place of a blanket, keeping in body heat, and was much lighter to carry. It was moderately waterproof. It took the place of coat and waistcoat. On hot days, when it became a parboiling encasement, it might be carried over the shoulder.

The old adage in favor of eating the food and wearing the clothes of the country was practiced by Clark when he left his jackote behind at his father's house and put on buckskin. Army boards which discuss soldiers' clothing in relation to climate and duties, and expert outfitters for camping tours and polar trips, would probably find that, considering conditions and requirements, the frontiersman's

201

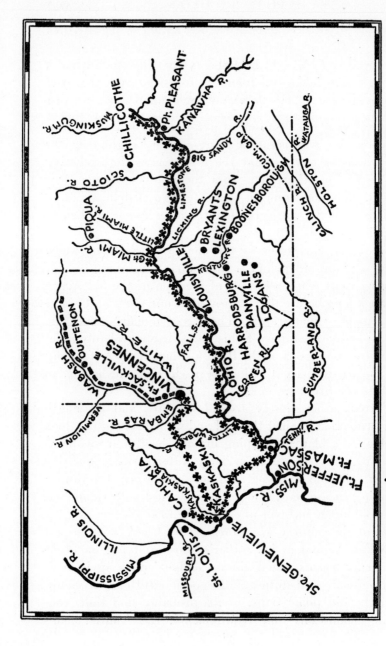

CLARK'S·ROUTE✠✠✠HAMILTON·FROM·DETROIT ▬▬

THE REGION OF CLARK'S ACTIVITIES, SHOWING THE ROUTE OF HIS MARCHES TO
KASKASKIA AND VINCENNES AND OF HAMILTON'S COUNTER STROKE.

garb was a product of experience best suited to the life that he led.

On the broad belt which bound in the shirt to the waist the owner expended the fondness for ornament that the cowboy expends on his spurs and hat band. It was set with bright beads and studs, his pride no less than his ruffled shirt to the young man about town in Boston, New York or Richmond.

The frontiersman, too, had a fancy in hats. But it did not run to the ten-gallon variety. This would have been no less impracticable in forest thickets than the cowboy's chaps which mean warmth for the rider's legs and protection against sage brush and cactus, although this does not always occur to the summer visitors on "dude" ranches. They, by the way, would have had as much of a taste of the real thing following Clark as they would have had following the Forty Niners.

We think of the frontiersman as always in a coonskin cap with a coon tail dangling behind. This he favored in cold weather in northern climates, and he had to wear it when no other head covering was available in warm weather. But luxury, and the vogue, when procurable, in summer, was the soft black felt of the type, although of a narrower brim, which is still worn by Southerners, and for which a much higher price is still paid by the affluent of an older generation than for the silk topper of ceremony. The great majority of Clark's men must have been in black hats.

The hunting knife was thrust in the belt. So also was what was called a tomahawk, which was really a hatchet which was used to cut firewood, clear away underbrush, whittle a peg and drive it in and in case of extremity to meet the Indian tomahawk in kind.

In dry weather and extreme dry cold moccasins were worn. They were cheap and readily made when shoes of good leather were expensive and new ones not often available on the frontier. Feet used to moccasins suffered in shoes. Moccasins did not bring blisters. An extra pair was light to carry. They gave the foot natural elasticity, a good toe hold as everyone who has used them in the frozen North well knows. In padding softness and swiftness of movement they put the wearer on a par with the stealthy Indian. Probably some of Clark's men were in moccasins and some in boots.

Long leggings of buckskin or wool, usually buckskin, were laced close to the calf. The buckskin was less likely to be torn by brambles.

Over one shoulder was hung the powder horn, a cow's horn which was sometimes carved. A buckskin bag held the round lead bullets. Over the other shoulder hung the game bag which contained the rations of parched corn, jerked buffalo meat, and also any extras, which included some salt, pepper as a rare luxury, and lint for wounds and any medicines and small tools which the bearer favored.

Thinking in terms of the extras which soldiers, at the outset of a march when they are fresh, always want to add to their packs, it is easy to imagine one man starting for the "hike" to Kaskaskia putting up an argument for bringing a saw, and another for bringing an auger. Else how were they to build cabins when they had that three hundred acres of land which were promised to them by the "select gentlemen" of Virginia?

There was no pack then, as soldiers now know it. The weight which each man bore for the march of a hundred and thirty miles was lighter than that borne by a fully equipped infantryman of to-day when the regimental wagon train is close behind him. Only the rifle was heavier and much more awkward to carry. If you doubt it take down the long-barreled flintlock from the museum wall and balance it in your hand in comparison with the modern Springfield or sporting rifle.

Quartermaster and commissariat details have been too often neglected from the narratives of Xenophon to the present. They leave us in the dark about the factors that make for fatigue and exhaustion as against endurance in a physical business. Although we all know that an army lives on its belly the rations of Napoleon's men, whether plodding across the snowy stretches to Moscow or the sands of Egypt, are rarely mentioned.

It is a matter of conjecture just what Cæsar fed his men when crossing the Alps or what was the travel ration of a legion which he hastened to relieve a distant garrison. We may be sure that the practical Roman looked to this; and that his was no soft hand with an erring quartermaster.

Soldiers must have the fare to which they are accustomed or to which they have been habituated by training. The stomachs of the soldiers of the A.E.F. went sour on French rations which included the *pinard* wine in place of liberal portions of coffee which we must have to win victories as the British must have tea. Consider the care about diet at the training table of the pugilist or the football eleven! There is a legend that Napoleon lost Leipzig because of a plate of bad cabbage soup which weakened his strategic cunning and tactical finesse.

We know fairly well what were the rations of Clark's men. They had the iron rations to which they had been accustomed on the trail, and which would have put a modern expedition on the sick list, probably with a considerable percentage of cases of ptomaine poisoning. The frontiersmen took their calories and vitamins in meat; their salads in chewing birch bark or in wild berries and fruits in season. Long practice had made them practically carnivorous as the Indians were for emergencies. And the American pioneer had a mighty digestion. American indigestion seems to have moved westward with the pie and cake belt.

There was no worry because Clark's men had not enough

rations swung over their shoulders to carry them all the way to Kaskaskia. They relied upon the substitute of the day for the arrival of the regimental wagon trains and the rolling kitchens. They relied, as was the custom of all parties taking the trail, upon getting some game on the way. Otherwise, they confessed themselves poor shots, poor hunters and tenderfoot incompetents.

For the pioneers had great pride. When they looked eastward to civilization they had a feeling of a superior manhood. They were snobbish in their way as the tidewater aristocracy or as the old families of any of the early seaboard settlements which have now become great cities.

In what formation did the little army march—the one hundred and seventy-five who would screen their movement from observation, and would be instantly ready to resist an attack from ambush? This, too, was related to the "going under foot" no less than the advance of a modern military force to roads and bridges.

Single file was necessary for Clark's men in following the narrow trails through the woods. It left fewer tracks to be discovered even when they were crossing meadows where again any defined trail was sure to give the best footing. They were as an advancing limber, centipede-jointed arrow, an arrow of bobbing hats; but an arrow with a spread point of two or three old-timer scouts of the Kenton type who could set a fast pace; an arrow with a little feather spread of men who had the part of file closers, if you will, in the rear.

Every man's rifle was always ready. One detail which was never a cause for officers' reprimands was rifle inspection. Personal experience made a fouled rifle as out of the question as that a western sheriff in mining camp days should go into a barroom to make an arrest without his gun loaded.

No command had to be uttered if a word of alarm ran its swift course from point to rear. With a panther quickness every man would be down under cover, bullet bag and powder horn in reach to reload promptly, as eyes in the silence, with every man as still as a log, strained for a glimpse of a red face. The sight of an Indian did not warrant pulling the trigger, not unless the Indian were a fair target in good range. Otherwise, wait for him to come nearer, keeping a bead on him all the while. The thing was to make sure that your bullet hit the target.

There were not too many bullets in the bag; there was not too much powder in the horn. Far ahead were the days when, at sight of the enemy a thousand or even two or three thousand yards away, the machine guns and the magazine rifles send their hurricane even when there is no enemy in sight, but in the area where it is thought that he is under cover. Above all Clark would escape any action on the way to Kaskaskia. Aside from his advance being disclosed he might suffer casualties. The wounded would cripple his progress; or he would have to leave able-bodied men behind to guard them.

Being veterans of the march, although this was their first military expedition, his men marched in the manner of veterans, as Jackson's and Sherman's marched, although under a tauter discipline and homogeneity when numbers were small in the intimacy of a family. They had the free stride, which, after the drill ground stiffness of the essential fundamentals of mass army technique, usually comes to soldiers only with prolonged campaigning. No efficiency expert in the economy of pedestrianism need give them lessons. Travel to them was to reach the journey's end.

As the old workman shows the apprentice how to swing the hammer without waste effort, so they had been taught as novices by old timers of the trail to put the miles behind them in the easiest fashion.

Their muscles were not bunchy, but stringy, rawhide tough and trained not for bursts of strength but for marathonic endurance. They could extend themselves in the Indian lope, faster than a walk, for hours at a stretch.

If one could have a phonographic record of their badinage on the march and in camp it would tell us the pronunciation of the English language in that period and be a revelation of the slang words, not to mention the cuss words, then in vogue; or what Sieur de Rochblave of Kaskaskia would have referred to as the vulgar *patois* of the Big Knives and the Bostonnais.

It was summer weather, paradise for marching compared to the coming midwinter movement on Vincennes. At night the men had only to drop on the dry earth for their bed. For the first two days, in which they covered a distance of fifty miles, the column was passing through forests.

Thus far Clark found no incident worthy of note except the disappointment in getting no game. I wonder if that commander, who shaped all things to his end including what was "agreeable to human nature," was altogether surprised at this.

Nine score men in single file hardly made a good formation to stalk meat for the larder. Even the confiding deer and buffalo of a region little hunted would not wait for the march past of the column after its head had been sighted. Hunting parties had to be detached. This meant delay. Campfires at night for cooking would be seen by any Indians in the vicinity. Cooking by day, although every pioneer was an adept in making a fire so as to keep smoke from rising, took time out of marching hours.

Few hunting parties seem to have been sent out; these seem to have brought in little game. The counterpart of the modern growl when the rolling kitchens are not up must have risen from the ranks. There is no incentive like hunger when the only restaurant is a long way ahead. The sooner Clark's men reached Kaskaskia the sooner they would be fed.

They came out of the forest into an almost treeless plain where stalking game was out of the question. Then occurred an incident on which Clark dwells with a warrantable emphasis and which summons a vivid picture. Clark had little to say when things were going well. His memory dwelt on crises. Now one smote him in the face when the column had been swinging along in good spirits.

The guide's part in a military expedition is always a thankless one. If he is right about the route his services are soon forgotten. If he misses the route such is the dependence upon him that his excuses are all suspect.

On the third day out Clark saw that John Saunders, who had said that he knew thoroughly the country the expedition was to traverse, became hesitant in his directions. When Clark pressed the point he admitted that he had lost the way. As Clark surveyed the landscape, he could not understand how anyone who had been over the ground once could possibly go wrong.

Saunders might be leading him into a trap, might be in Rochblave's pay. All Clark's plans might be fruitless, his dream broken by misplaced confidence in this one man who was evidently either a fool, a knave, or a liar.

George Rogers' red-headed temper flamed. His language flamed, too. He must have been in many rages on his campaigns, but this one he was to remember through the years, and he regarded it as of such importance that he recorded it as faithfully as he did a successful horse swap.

His candor about his human self was delightful at times. It was not in his nature to try to suppress the fact that he possessed red hair. One sees that confused guide in face of his Jovian wrath.

"I never in my life felt such a flow of rage," Clark wrote. "To be wandering in a country where every nation of Indians could raise four or five times our number and a certain loss of the enterprise by the enemies getting timely notice. I could not bear the thought of returning; in short every idea of the sort put me in a passion that I could not master for sometime."

For the more Clark questioned Saunders the more he was in doubt whether or not Saunders were really lost. If he were not the inference was as sinister to the men as to the leader. Word was passed to them of the cause of the halt. Those in front formed a crowd around Clark and Saunders.

No game, the third day out, only one day's more rations and their little force struck blind by betrayal in a region to which all were strangers! Those gaunt pioneers knew too well what this meant. If Saunders looked away from Clark's angry eyes he saw the wrath in theirs and heard their mutterings.

Saunders begged that he might be allowed to do a little reconnoitering in the hope that he might orient himself. As there were no hills in sight breaking the level of the open plain the suggestion was not one to allay suspicion. There were raucous murmurs among the men lest he impose upon their leader and get a chance at "leg bail."

Clark reminded him again that he had said that he knew the country very well; sent a few men with him as escort to prevent his escape; and warned him that "if he did not discover and take us into the Hunter's Road that led from the east into Kaskaskia that he had frequently described— I would have him immediately put to death which I determined to have done."

An order for execution would have been unnecessary. Saunders must have seen his fate written in the stark grimness of the men's faces. He had endangered their lives, his should be the forfeit. Yet, when it came to the test, I have an idea that Clark might have tried to stay the extreme penalty of retribution.

So, in their suspense, we see the men lying about on the ground watching Saunders and his escort, suggestively close to his elbows, becoming smaller and smaller figures on the plain. The what next of the spectators' conjecture this time held them in a mortal spell.

To have to go back after they had gone this far! They might leave their bones bleaching with those of buffalo and deer in the wilderness. But they would not have gone back, not while there was fire left in Clark's eyes to stir the last spark of their strength to make this a fight to the finish.

After an hour the figures were seen growing larger. They were returning. Their attitude told the result before it was heard in words. Saunders said that he had found the way; he had seen "a place that he knew perfectly."

He might be saying it only to gain reprieve as he hoped that luck would yet be with him in stumbling on the hunter's road, as a blind man leading the blind. At all events he knew the joy of stepping from the grave's edge back to life and popularity when they did come to the road. "We now perceived," said Clark "that the poor fellow had been genuinely bewildered." Clark mellowed at the thought that the only charge against him was human error, not treachery.

How much farther had they to go was the ravening question besetting him on the fifth day. Rations had been stretched to the last morsel of meat. They were too near the goal to delay in any hazard for game.

There were no springs, streams had dried up. Men who had been used to traveling in well-watered country found themselves in a parched land. For a day they suffered from thirst.

In their empty provision bags they treasured some bits of colored cloth whose sentiment added to the urge of hunger's gnawing in speeding their steps. These were American flags which they would fly in Kaskaskia.

There is no mention that any man fell out from illness or fatigue or had to be carried. Self-preservation was the stern file closer. But, apparently, their feet were dragging, they were not advancing quite so rapidly.

No breakfast on the next morning after a day without food began to tell by lunch time even on those who boasted of Indian endurance. The stronger had to wait on the weak, carry their heavy rifles, giving them a helping hand over rough places. Up and down the line we can see Clark, head up, playing on all the strings of human nature's bow, now berating, now putting the spur to pride, now calling for a song of the time such as "Hot Time in the Old Town To-night" and "Hail, Hail, the Gang's All Here!" in future campaigns.

Merry comrade forced merriment to bolster faltering comrade; the optimists cried down the pessimists; and pessimists, turning optimists, rallied optimists who had turned pessimists. No use of lying down to die. Better die on your feet. It cannot be much farther. Keep on putting one foot in front of another. Oh, what wouldn't they do to a good buffalo steak when they got one! Come on for another lap! There may be fried chicken in Kaskaskia. Thus they kept on plugging to make the red-haired man's dream come true.

By the afternoon of the sixth day, in and out of the winding forest trails that followed the "traces" that the buffalo had made and through the wild grass knee high in places on the virgin plains, they had covered, I estimate, nearly a hundred and fifty miles.

Twenty-five miles is a good march for one day. But twenty-five for six days in succession even over good roads! Look up the records and see how often it has been surpassed when the rolling kitchens were up or there were plenty of beans to flash from the can and bacon to fry.

The fifth day was much harder than the fourth, but not nearly so much so as the sixth than the fifth. And on the night of the sixth, with aching legs and that very hollow feeling in their middles, this truly picked force was to go into action which should have seen them fresh with stomachs full.

The head of the column halted; orders were passed that lighted fatigue-glazed eyes with anticipation that the gamble's cast was soon to be made. The single-file procession broke into groups. The majority were to hide in the woods until further notice as the next move was with the scouts creeping sinuously in advance, Clark in the lead.

Then, just when they had the cover of dusk, those in the main body started on the final lap. This brought them to the river bank as darkness fell. Again they went into hiding; but across the water they could see the twinkle of their goal in the lights of the little town. There they were to get hell or breakfast, and it would have to be a very hot hell to keep them out of breakfast. And how were they to cross the river? The answer must have been the subject of whispered conjectures, with the sententious, as ever, remarking that this was for the colonel to arrange.

Meanwhile Clark was being polite again. He was drafting another man to his service as he had drafted hunter John Duff. He had taken possession of a commodious house, three quarters of a mile up the river from the town, which was occupied by a large family. The first thing was to glean all possible information from the owner which Clark would interpret with the aid of Saunders and Duff.

He was told that an alarm that the "rebels" were coming had put all the militia under arms recently, but it had been thought groundless, and at present all was quiet. There were many militiamen from the neighboring settlements still in the town but few Indians. The sound of voices and movements that was heard was made by negroes at a dance.

"I did not entirely credit the information given us at the house," Clark wrote. He thought that the man was contradicting himself under catechism, especially about the reason for the noise. However, it was quite in order that a peaceful citizen of the suburbs should be a little confused at the sudden appearance at his door on a tranquil summer evening, of a giant Virginian in the company of other Big Knives when the nearest rebel was supposed to be three hundred miles away.

The noise might mean the American's presence on the river bank had been discovered; the militiamen hurrying to their places; preparations to turn the tables on Clark's would-be surprise by a surprise sweep of bullets on the targets of men crowded close together as they were ferried across the river.

That four companies of armed men should approach the town by the artery of the hunter's road in the period of summer travel when the farmers were out in their fields, without being detected, must have seemed to Clark, now that he knew the topography of the environs of the town, a heavy tax on credibility, however alluring the prospect had been back in the camp on Corn Island.

But there was his goal, the goal of his years of planning, of his ordeal in beating up recruits and all his journeys back and forth through the wilderness. "It was do or die," as Captain Bowman said in a letter. And the sustaining practical thought was that every man under Clark knew that it was so.

The problem about the boats had been solved. Happily, the house owner seems to have been in the ferry and river transport business. He had enough boats for the crossing of the little army.

Clark now made his plan of attack. He not only told off his captains to their parts but took his men into his confidence in an action which required such thorough teamplay.

They were divided into three divisions. He was to lead

one to storm the fort. The other two were to rush the town when his party raised a cry as a signal of success.

Clark speaks of "various orders" which were given in case of opposition. Well they might be given and very carefully thought out. Had Rochblave been forewarned not only the advantage of position was with him behind the river moat; but darkness was also. Night actions are usually planned to break with the flush of dawn so that the attackers will see where they are going. This one relied upon completion in the darkness.

Every figure of the assailants would be a shadow in the open to posted defenders. Strong opposition meant loss of cohesion in a blind man's buff business in the streets. Morning might find the guns of the fort still commanding the town and Clark's men foodless on the outskirts with the militia and Indians from the rear closing in on them. For Rochblave knew his muttons as a frontier soldier.

Softly the moccasined feet stepped into the boats; softly the boats were pushed off from shore; the oars took the water with feathered strokes. Not a voice had been raised lest it carry in the still night, while every mind was at the peak of suspense and under the spell of the supreme "What next?" after all the what nexts since Redstone, on that evening of July 4th, 1778, the second anniversary of the Declaration of Independence.

XVIII

INTO THE TOWN

It did not take many strokes of the oars to cross that narrow river; but with every stroke rifle flashes and bigger flashes from cannon might break out of the kindly twinkle of lights. The boats grounded, and still there was no opposition. This was no assurance that there would be none. Rochblave might be biding his time when it took so long to prepare the second blast that the first blast from muzzle loaders was most important.

The men sprang from their boats with that thrill of relief which everyone who has ever been in a landing party against a concealed defending force so well knows. Something snaps in them. They are freed of close packed helplessness as solid targets of flesh which cannot strike back.

Stalled energy, panting for a full breath, is released; inaction, in which there is nothing to do but think, changes to action, in which there is no thought but a goal to be attained, as feet feel the touch of earth and rifles that had been dead in hand become alive.

Still, the little army, every man in the front line, no reserve, all the eggs in one basket, met no fire after it was on the river bank. Rochblave might be waiting for Clark to appear before the gate of the fort so that every bullet in a crash of musketry might count in abrupt concentration upon close ranks. The storming party disappeared in the darkness.

The rest of the force, faint skulking shadows in the night, spread out around the town. It was a small town with less than a thousand souls, yet it was the great, strong point of the Mississippi region. A few miles away, on the plans drawn by Vauban, the great French military engineer of the period, the French had built a stone fortress, Fort Chartres, as the supreme central stronghold of the great valley, whose foundations still exist. It had been abandoned for the wooden fort on the banks of the Kaskaskia as the more practicable according to a later conception.

The men on the outskirts of the town saw no signs of life in the streets, which might be taken as a sinister sign in the critical seconds after Clark began his dash. It had not been long, hardly as long as it takes to run around the block, when they heard the cry—the fort was taken!—which was the signal for them to carry out their planned part.

They let up a cry in answer as they were bidden. They were to keep shouting as they ran back and forth through the streets to give the impression of being in much larger numbers than they were. Those who knew some French, or could fit their tongues to a set phrase, had been told off to pound on the doors, calling on the people to remain in their houses on the pain of death as the terrible Big Knives, the Bostonnais, were upon them.

What Clark's "various orders" were in case of opposition he did not consider important enough to relate when they had not to be put into effect. In less than a quarter of an hour the town was won. All the resident militiamen were prisoners in their houses with sentries pacing on the outside.

A bloodless victory! This was the merit of it, and its drawback in the popular conception not only of that day but of the present day. It seems "agreeable to human nature" to judge the importance of victory by the number of casualties rather than by the prevision, the care, planning and discipline to gain the maximum of result with the minimum of cost which is the prime economic principle of military technique. In time, gossip, "back East," was to see this "wonder man" Clark as having overwhelmed some peaceful villagers without having a single one of his men wounded. The most ardent pacifist who reads this account may remark in disappointment, "Nobody hurt! Why, that was no battle at all."

When Clark was to gather rifles from more than his own numbers in trained militia and the defense had a three to one advantage over the offense, what kind of opposition would he have met, what would have happened, if Rochblave had been forewarned of his coming and all "set" to receive him? Had Clark's storming party been riddled by rifle blasts at close quarters and Indians sprung upon the survivors out of hiding, and then, in the scrimmage which followed, the town had been burned and women and children hit by stray bullets, the affair would have been immortalized in history.

Or, if a dozen or so, all that were left alive of "the heroic band," had been chased into the forests to starve, Illinois would have its Alamo tradition. With reasonable prevision there need have been no Alamo; and if the Minute Men had taken the pains to have up accessible stores of powder they would have repulsed the British charges, and Bunker Hill would have lost some of its glamour of a bloody stand to the death. In fact, probably not one quarter as many patriots would have been killed or wounded.

There is the story of a professionally canny old general who said to his chief of staff, "Young man, you are making this operation appear so easy that we shall not get any credit for it." Commanders who would be assured of the laurel permanently crowning their brows should manage to achieve victory by very bloody action, and then the blunders that caused the losses will be painted over with gold through which their faint lettering will be seen only by experts who never forget the cardinal principle in war.

The absence of any satisfactory supporting evidence makes one piece of theatrics in the taking of Kaskaskia, which was long accepted, only a legend which appeals to novelists. According to this the sentries of the fort had deserted their posts to look on at a ball which Rochblave was giving in the great hall. The men in their ruffled shirts were enjoying their punch, the ladies were displaying their new Parisian gowns which had come up the river with the Spring convoy.

Their gayety was suddenly interrupted by the warwhoop of an Indian, who was lying athwart the door, at the sight of a stranger standing above him in the flickering light of the torches. And the merry-makers saw Clark an interested spectator in the doorway. With unchanged and grim face he was said to have told them to go on with their dance, but now they were dancing under Virginia and not Great Britain.

Even if there were truth in the story this does not sound like Clark, but more like Andrew Jackson, by the Eternal God Almighty. The polite Clark would have been in the ascendant in such an event, enjoying its humor and considerate of the feelings of the women. More probably he would have said something like this:

"I am Lieutenant Colonel Clark of the Virginia militia. You will pardon my abruptness, but we have overpowered the guards and have you surrounded. I must ask the men present to give up their arms and then the ladies will be escorted to their homes, as all the population must remain indoors until they receive further instructions."

Reason precludes any likelihood that so good a soldier as Clark would have wasted time standing in a doorway when he had such a pressure of business in hand. He makes no mention of the incident in his Memoir or in any of his letters. It is hardly probable that he would leave it out when the manner of the taking of Rochblave would not have been a detail to escape his memory or unimportant enough not to be mentioned.

Clark found the postern gate of the fort open and his surprise of the guards, if there were any, prevented resistance. He tells us that Rochblave was in bed when the town was occupied.

Rochblave made use of a petticoat shield, not from lack of courage, but for a sound reason in war in which all is fair. He could not be induced to come out of the conjugal chamber; and throughout the night the son of Ann refused to enter by force to make a search while Madame Rochblave was there.

Such consideration would not have characterized officers on either side in the World War under similar conditions when war had become much more scientific and the intelligence departments more impolite. Probably Madame would have been allowed five minutes in which to dress—and again she might not have been!—while her husband himself would have been bidden to appear instantly on pain of breaking in the door.

As it was, the price of Big Knife chivalry—let army staffs take a note for class room lectures—was that Rochblave was able to destroy official papers and correspondence which would have revealed information of great value to Clark; or else Madame Rochblave carried them away in her trunks later on. She made the most of her feminine indignation when Clark had no callous customs inspector with his expedition. How could a young gentleman of Virginia search the trunks of so outraged a lady who was so sure no rebel colonial ever was a gentleman?

"From the idea she entertained of us," wrote Clark, "she must have expected even the loss of her clothes."

It was a very busy night for George Rogers. The fort taken and Rochblave taken, the militia in town must be disarmed; his position made secure against treachery.

His conduct after his bloodless victory wins admiration for those qualities which are rarely included in the equipment of a military genius. When they are the soldier becomes a ruler, and when they exist alone in a commander his military discomfiture usually precludes his having an opportunity to display them.

In this small field, which was so valuable as a precedent and which was to have such a wide influence, he was to be both the leader of the legions and a civil administrator. He had learned lessons in law and the wisdom of the law from his able mentor, George Mason, proving again that to be the favored disciple of a great tutor, who is at once scholar and man of the world, may be a useful substitute for a college education and post graduate courses.

The real test of his discipline, of the dominance of his will over his men, was yet to come. Soldiers may obey orders implicitly in taking a town; but obeying them is another matter after the town is taken. The harder the march, the heavier the suspense before the decision, the more difficult is this problem. There is no break in training like that of victory; no such warrantable excuse for commander's lenience to the license of men whose effort and loyalty have gained the guerdon for him.

Soldiers feel that what they have won is theirs. They have endured restraint in order to succeed. They see nothing as so unfair as that it should still be imposed after the game is over. Years of barrack training, grinding routine into the very bones, and regular spirit of corps and veteran precision all fail to keep men from going on the loose after the goal is reached. There are examples in the World War itself if you wish ones later than the march of the allied forces to Peking in the Boxer Rebellion.

Here were no regulars, automatons of routine, but militiamen, individualistic frontiersmen with a "you-be-damned" independence, unaccustomed to restraints. They had no rations in their packs, remember; no regimental wagon train was on their heels to park in the public square. Two days' hunger was gnawing them. They lived in an age when to the victor belong the spoils. It was not until well into the next century that the British ceased giving captured cities in India over to plunder.

Any license would have been fatal to Clark's plan, as it has been to many leaders who could not restrain their men, or their officers, or even themselves, when weary harness-galled human nature would spring free of the harness in emotional compensation and diversion. Clark returned to the street to find that his men had all the population penned indoors. The long effort which began at Corn Island was at an end, the job finished.

There was wine in the houses; there was food in the kitchens; wine, when a celebration was in order, stimulation in groggy fatigue and hunger.

Had Clark loosened the reins his soldiers would have soon been out of hand. Morning would have found many figures dead to the world in the streets, brawls with the inhabitants who would have seen all their fears about the Big Knives fulfilled. The first man seen with a bottle of wine or brandy in hand—and brandy would have been the hard stuff of American preference—must be relieved of it as an example; the man raiding a kitchen warned off.

For all the men must be kept out of the houses as well as the people off the streets during the night. Every soldier was forbidden to hold any conversation with any inhabitant. Sternness or "bawling out" alone would not keep control. This would sow the seeds of sulkiness and future insubordination, when Clark needed the loyalty of all for the future.

Adequate personality, that of the natural leader, was the prime factor in control; and the son of the majestic Ann had it. The proof of its adequacy was that no report has come down to us showing that his men did go on the loose in that hour of temptation; there are no stories handed down

GEORGE MASON, WHO WAS CLARK'S PRECEPTOR
AN ENGRAVING FROM A PAINTING

of outrages on women, as there were of the Hessians for generations in New Jersey.

However, the credit for this good repute must not be assigned altogether to Clark's discipline. It was in keeping with the attitude toward women of the men of the little valleys carried on by the settlers in the mutual protection of lone wives and daughters in frontier cabins; an attitude which persisted through the westward movement to mining camp days, and which still lives.

Clark had a list of the leading citizens. He sent for them at once. Through them he would learn the situation. But his first thought, as is that of every good leader, was commissariat when men are hungry. If they were not allowed to raid the kitchens in private requisition, there must be prompt official requisition of food.

On the list were two American traders at Kaskaskia, Richard Winston and Daniel Murray. They knew where to lay their hands on provisions which they promptly gathered. And the men had that breakfast for which their mouths had been watering for two days.

Their hunger satisfied, and more meals in sight, they were posted in the edge of the town soon after daybreak. Then those who were not on sentry duty might sleep until further order or they were hungry again, leaving the sleepless son of Ann with a free hand for an essay in the kind of statesmanship as a proconsul which he found "agreeable to human nature" in the present situation.

XIX

THE NEW GOSPEL

WHAT a scene when dawn broke on the Kaskaskians' white-washed houses and the dew-sprinkled flowers of their gardens and touched their ripening fields of wheat with gold after that dreadful night with its promise of the end of the world in the morning!

The well-to-do, who had solid silver plate on their sideboards, and the humble, who had pewter, had shared the common fear of losing all their possessions. There must have been stealthy digging of holes in cellars in which to bury both silver and pewter; and stockings and bureau drawers, the safe deposit boxes of the time, must have been emptied of treasured gold coins to be sewn in under-garments.

After more than a century the moving outpost of one of the two mothering civilizations, which were so widely separated in character although by only a channel's breadth in the old world, had come up with the sleepy stationary outpost of the other in the freedom of virgin continental expanses of the new world which was so meagerly tenanted by savages.

Generations of Frenchmen had been born and died in the great valley since the day of La Salle. Kaskaskia was no new settlement. It was the old home town to its people. After the French and Indian war they had shared the fate of their kinsmen of the more populous Quebec.

They saw their Mother France, the France of the great Louis, whom they had served so loyally, as having deserted her distant children. In the temperament of French patriotism and in the inheritance of racial traits, theirs was the mood which, a century and a quarter later, made French Canadians lukewarm in the cause of Mother France in the World War because, in their view, she had fallen under the wicked spell of atheism and false gods while they remained true to the faith of their fathers.

Just as the peasant's plot of land in the France of to-day is France to him so was each plot of land in the great valley to its owner. He held fast to the ways and the tongue of the land from which his ancestors had migrated; and these in Louis XVI's time in Kaskaskia were those of Louis XIV's time as they still remain in French Canada.

And before his door in the night had appeared the advance guard of a new civilization, as one of the strokes in freeing itself from the rule of the old, in the course of keeping abreast of changing environments and the spread of opportunity.

The French settlements had accepted British sovereignty with the more philosophy in their devotion to customs which kept them French if not under the French flag. All they asked was to be left to themselves; to render unto Cæsar the things that were Cæsar's.

So the British governors found that the *laissez-faire* policy, which was to be the universal British colonial policy after the lesson of the American Revolution, was easy through the French settlers' inclination. It was also wise and fruitful in that it economized in the personnel of British garrisons and encouraged the shipment of peltry over the long-established trails and portages to Detroit.

In fear of the Big Knives and the Bostonnais, with their harsh reputations of ruthlessly molding all in their communities to their heretic ways, the support by the French settlers of the British side in the Revolution had been in the instinct of self-preservation as long as it required only the armed defense of their homes. Kaskaskians, with the exception of a few *coureurs de bois* for pay or adventure, would

not have put on red coats to march away to offensive action
to gratify the Royal Breast of King George. Would they
now be, as the Acadians were, exiled from their gardens and
farms and their church? If allowed to remain, at what
price?

After that night of grilling suspense, with every footstep
out of doors an alarm, the people peered out at dawn for
a glimpse of the masters of their fate. No approach of Cos-
sacks in Eastern Prussia or the tramp of German infantry
on Belgian roads in 1914, held so horrible a prospect as the
arrival of the Big Knives. There had been no opportunity
for flight. The complete surprise had precluded the old
war picture of driven refugees who, in this case, would have
taken trails into the wilderness rather than to relief stations.

Clark's men had not yet moved out of town at daybreak.
They were pacing up and down as sentries or standing about
in groups. Ravenously eating the food that had been brought
to them, they looked the fierce wolfish part of their reputation.

Pictures which show them in Continental uniform carry
romance and idealism to preposterous absurdity. This is a
likeness as out of keeping as the full dress uniforms of the
Ancient and Honorable Artillery company in the trenches
in France. Their appearance had no more of the glamour of
war than a battalion after four days' action when it had
mopped up the last bit of the third objective in the mud of
Flanders or the Meuse-Argonne.

These victors were lean to emaciation, tanned Indian
bronze, their ragged beards matted with dust; and the wrinkles of cheek and brow were caked by summer sweat with
accumulated layers of dust. Their rough exteriors displayed
no sign of a finer inherent chivalry to women than flourished
where silver buckles glinted on the dancing floor and a mas-
culine hand in lace ruffles gracefully met a lady's in the
halls of Versailles.

Everything which they could not carry on their backs having been left in the rear, they had had no change of clothing since they left Corn Island. Bare toes showed out of worn moccasins. The shirt and breeches were torn by brambles, and so was their flesh which was also blistered by exposure to the sun. Ragged buckskin and wool was grimy from cooking and preparing game for the pot and sleeping on the ground.

The only thing about them that could have seemed clean were the whites of their eyes in which were set those relentlessly watchful pupils. Those among them who had been used to good beds and spotless linen at home were inseparable from the rest. All had been daubed by the same smutty brush.

Clean also were their rifles and the tomahawk and knife in their belts ready for instant use by sinewy arms. The very way that their grimy hands gripped their rifles was truculent; the brigand-like felt hats, drawn over the eyes and gray with dust, added to the aspect of ferocity, suggesting that they who had come so swiftly without warning from afar and were in rags expected to be clothed afresh with a victor's bounty. If Clark's object were to frighten the people of Kaskaskia, theatric art in make-up and costume could never have succeeded in simulating so wanton a piratical effect as this reality.

And these invaders had disavowed the true faith. They were so godless that they had brought no priest with them. No leniency could be expected from such human wolves. All the legends that had come up from New England to the St. Lawrence and across the lakes and portages about the terrible Bostonnais and all Rochblave had said about the Big Knives must be true.

And Clark continued to send for leading citizens to come to him. He was not going to them in that juncture, you may be sure. He was asking them questions, checking off answer against answer. How many Indians were there in the neighborhood? How well armed were they? What was their mood? How strong was the garrison at Cahokia? For he had to take more than Kaskaskia; there was more than Kaskaskia to be held to assure the security of his little army.

He had to require some of his legionaries to force strength out of their exhaustion for still another dash. Horses must be found to mount thirty chosen men. They were to ride swiftly at once to storm the fort at Cahokia, hope, will and audacity having to tranquillize more than their numbers of armed men in villages on the stretch of sixty miles to their destination. Cahokia was on the Mississippi, opposite Spanish St. Louis, the outpost of Kaskaskia in the defense system. Thirty men, to be lead by Captain Bowman, responded in spite of their fatigue.

He told the people that they might now walk in the streets on their private business; but they were not to form groups and enter into conversation. He would take no risk of cabals against him. The officers of the local militia were included in the permission. Even Rochblave, himself, seems to have been.

However, the late commander was in no mood to appreciate such generosity. His professional martial pride had been gored raw and peppered by being trapped by this low ruffian of an amateur. He had no inclination to change his allegiance again, not to the new flag of the filthy rebels, not he who had served two kings as an officer and gentleman of the old school.

Such were his splenetic upbraidings of his own officers as poltroons and his abusive open expression of his contempt for Clark's ragged soldiers that he was confined to his house. Otherwise he might have felt the impact of an angry Big Knife's fist on his jaw when he had no sword with which to run an assailant through. This would have been final humiliation when a Frenchman of that day considered the use of fists to settle an argument as the lowest form of barbarism.

Clark, seeing that the people were disobeying his order by forming groups and talking together, put the military officers, whom he had given freedom, under arrest. He could afford to tolerate no suggestion that he had not all under close scrutiny; to allow them to presume upon no sign of weakness to plot any counter action.

Meanwhile the people were placing their hope upon their shepherd. If anyone, the priest could soften the pirates' wrath. Father Gibault and a few elders appeared at the door of Clark's headquarters asking to be heard.

"However great the shock they had already sustained by reason of their situation," Clark wrote, "the addition when they entered the room where I was sitting with my officers was obvious and great. . . . We presented a dirty and savage aspect. So shocked were they that some time elapsed before they ventured to seat themselves, and still more before they could speak."

Finally they were asked what it was that they wanted. Then Father Gibault inquired which was the commander. No epaulettes, no recognizable insignia of authority identified him! Unshaven for days, his ragged red beard, his great stature, eyes sunk deeper than ever under his promontory brow, nose a beak rising out of gaunt cheeks, his appearance held out anything but a promise of merciful treatment to that fearsome delegation. The red haired king wolf was as savage as his lean pack.

"Salute no red haired man nearer than thirty feet," said an old French proverb, "with three stones in thy fist to defend thee."

"I knew that they supposed their very religion was obnoxious to us," said Clark, and also how obnoxious his religion was to them. Both were something to capitalize for his purpose.

Father Gibault took the worst for granted. He said that he knew that the members of his flock would be parted from one another. Clark, his face a mask, his eyes deep wells hiding his thoughts, did not disabuse him of the idea. As many of his people might never have a chance to meet again, when they had been so long neighbors, Father Gibault asked if the commander would permit them to gather in the church for a final farewell reunion.

Clark replied indifferently. He had nothing to do with the church. Father Gibault might go there if he pleased; but he must tell all the people that they must not leave town. When Father Gibault and the elders essayed further talk, Clark dismissed them, in keeping with his present part, with a word as hard as his looks.

They saw their darkest fears confirmed. There was no use of trying to leave town when it was encircled by the line of Big Knives every one of which could shoot as well as a *coureur de bois.* At such time as it pleased the king wolf they would be driven forth into the wilderness, their homes, farms and crops confiscated and all the results of their labor in cultivating the rich bottom lands in that sequestered valley lost to them forever.

When the word was passed for assembly at the church all responded. The aged came hitching along on their canes, mothers came bearing their babes in arms with frightened children clinging to their skirts. Clark mentions his own realization of how they felt.

They spent some time in that wooden church where all had worshiped. Probably they were bent in prayer. No soldier was allowed to enter to disturb them.

When they came out it was to find that nothing had been molested in their empty houses. No soldier had broken orders by crossing a threshold looking for souvenirs or better clothing in place of his rags or a piece of home bread with honey spread on it and a bottle of wine to wash it down.

This was very surprising in the Big Knives; but, too, it was sinister as part of the working of the harsh and calculating destiny which they had seen in the deep-set eyes of the leader of the wolf pack.

Again the cassock was before the conqueror's door. This time Father Gibault had a much larger delegation. All the members' hair was not white like his own. There were leading citizens who were not yet in the elders' class.

They thanked Clark for allowing them to meet at the church. Evidently counsel as well as prayer had taken place there. Would the commandant listen to an appeal on a subject that was dearer to them than their lives, their women and children?

C'est la guerre, Monsieur le commandant! They told him that they realized that theirs was the fate of war. There was no quarreling with it; to the victor belonged the spoils.

But would not *Monsieur le commandant* be appeased by taking all their property? Must they be parted from their families? Might not their women and children keep their clothing? Might they not retain a small quantity of provisions to enable them to make another start to support themselves by their industry? The venerable priest must have been eloquent out of the long tradition of the mother church in mercy's plea of the cross upraised to protect the weak from the rage of the strong.

Still Clark's face was a mask; still there was no softening of the measuring glint of his eyes.

The truth was, the good father told him, while the others agreed, that many of them had been in sympathy with the Americans; but all had had to obey the orders of their commanders.

And then some of the deputation spoke of Gabriel Cerré in a strain which Clark had already heard from others. Cerré was the leading merchant of the region, always going and coming; in high favor with the British at Detroit, profiting by British favor. He was now in St. Louis; but his family was in town and he had storehouses full of valuable goods which would yield a large sum of money to the Americans.

Evidently the petitioners were ready to save themselves— and that too was "agreeable" to one side of human nature— by throwing their wealthy neighbor to the hungry wolf pack. Clark judged that a number of the accusers were in debt to Cerré. He would put a guard over Cerré's house and goods. When Cerré heard of this he would return promptly to town, reasoned Clark who thought that here was a man he would much rather have inside his glass house than on the outside throwing stones.

For none could realize so well as Clark that he was in a glass house whose walls he must make appear of rock. He did not forget that his real base was far away at Pittsburgh. What was McIntosh doing there? Had he started an expedition to Detroit? If so Clark knew the value of his part to its success. If it were a failure then his own position was highly precarious.

His men's time would soon expire. He had no rewards for them in sight except by the confiscation of property; no pay except as his drafts were honored. Their enthusiasm would pass. They would demand to return home. Where would he get recruits to take their place? This was the question behind the measuring glint in his eyes. Its right answer the object of his hard looks.

The weaker the legions behind it, be the measure by platoons or army corps, the stiffer must be the front of Jove in its pretense of vast reserves of men and munitions at its command. A faltering line must always be told that the reinforcements will soon be up although a commander fears that they have missed the road.

So the people of the Illinois country must have a sense of Clark's power and their own weakness drilled into their

very bones. Despite the ease with which he had taken the
town, he was none the less acutely aware that if they realized
their potentialities and his weakness, and Cahokia and the
other adjoining settlements found a leader who roused the
Indians, he would be in siege.

As soon as he had arrived he had spread the word that
the force the people saw was only an advance detachment
of the main army forming at his new base at the Falls of the
Ohio from recruits fast coming down the river from Pittsburgh. All his orders were dated from "Headquarters, Falls
of the Ohio" to justify the idea. He had imparted it to to his
soldiers. His dream a father to conviction, he must have
almost believed it himself, when he had no authority for
thinking that a single armed man would come to his assistance.

Yes, Father Gibault, with head bare, and all the other
leading citizens with heads bare before the conqueror, must
understand that a big wave was following the little wave
which had swept through the town.

Clark knew that Father Gibault was more than a local
priest. For twenty years he had been vicar-general of the
Illinois and Wabash country. He was deeply beloved by all
the French settlers. His was a powerful influence both with
whites and Indians for Clark to have on his side. So was
that of the other much-traveled man, Cerré, captain of industry, notable British partisan.

Looking into the faces of the deputation, while the rest
of the population hung in the background awaiting the
word of their fate, Clark saw that he had gained the primary
effect which he had sought. He was convinced that they had
"really expressed their sentiments and the height of their
expectations," without guile.

"This was the point to which I wished to bring them,"
Clark wrote.

It was time in the swift drama which he was stage-manag-

ing for him to play another part; time for the invading
army, having established order in the town, to yield place
to civil authority. Soldier Clark became civil governor Clark;
the leader of the wolf pack became shepherd. There must
have been a shining first moment, when the old vicar-
general, who bore the lamp of culture for his people, detected in Clark's voice that there might be kindly men
brought up in good homes even among the lawless heretics
of the seaboard valleys.

Clark followed sternness by upbraiding. The face that
had been a mask was livened by indignation that flashed
from eyes which had been all cold scrutiny. He was rounding
on the petitioners in the appeal of his own injured feelings,
of the wrong they had done him.

"I asked them very abruptly, whether or not they thought
they were speaking to savages, and said that it was certain
that they did, from the tenor of their conversation. Did
they suppose that we meant to strip the women and children, and take the bread out of their mouths? Or that we
would consent to make war on the women and children or
the church? It was to prevent the effusion of innocent blood
by the Indians, through the instigation of their comman-
dants and emissaries, that caused us to visit them, and not
the prospect of plunder."

One can hear across the span of years their voluble protests of "*Non, non, Monsieur le commandant,*" in their polite eighteenth century ingratiation.

Now Clark mellowed. He played another tune on the
human strings. He was the George Rogers of the winning
ways, of fellowship with all manner of men on the trail; the
George Rogers who had won the heart of George Mason as
a boy, who, the petitioners might understand, would be at
home in a ruffled shirt, dance with the best of them, meet
Father Gibault's wilderness tale with one of his own around
the crackling wood fire.

Again the pity of it is that we have not a report of what he said! But his meager account gives us the sense of it. And it was a talk which embodied the principles of the Declaration of Independence on the morning after its second aniversary when no great nation except Britain yet had a parliament other than in name; embodied them better than records of later Fourth of July orations; embodied the practical application of the Constitution of the United States which was yet to come.

The man, his career, the audience, the occasion, which could never be repeated, gave his words their weight.

He brought the message of the little valleys to the great valley. He expressed his vision of the coming settlement of the west; the characteristics of the enveloping American movement in its absorption of the French and Spanish settlers and all manner of future recruits from foreign lands.

His eloquence was in the eloquence of the deed, of the precedent he set in the wilderness six hundred miles from the main seaboard frontier. What a different precedent he might have set in disorderly looting soldiery, in confiscation, in military tyranny, in outrages on women, when the temptation was so strong and succumbing to it so justifiable, even considered the only sound way according to the canons of the age!

What tales of the savagery of ruffian frontiersmen and loathsome rebels there might have been to soothe the conscience of the Royal Breast and to bolster it in employing Indian fiends to fight white fiends and to be quoted for generations to come in terms of "The Kaskaskia massacre!" In this instance Clark would have wide fame as the subject of controversy between defenders and accusers with the future historian trying to throw the light of truth on the event. Clark was a man of many parts; but, as we proceed, we shall understand more and more that he did not know

how to become famous. This is one of the defects which make
him so interesting.

He was a crusader in the distances for the new dispensation for which the Americans were fighting. There was to be
no state church as there was in European lands. Every
man's worship was between God and himself. All religions
that did not teach disloyalty to the state would be tolerated
and respected. The right to free public worship would be
protected. So far from meddling with the local church, this
conqueror from the lawless and godless seaboard valleys said
that any one who "who insulted it would be punished by me."

What a man earned was his own; the land he improved
was his. For that Clark had labored before the Virginia
Assembly. In this cause, the practical economic cause, the
new flag which was now raised in Kaskaskia had come into
being. Destroy their homes and gardens? Not the man whose
vision was homes and gardens out on the trackless prairies
and villages rising at new crossroads and cities rising on
the river banks. Nothing was so good in his sight as a crop
of grain. He knew the effort it took to raise it.

The Kaskaskians' homes, gardens, farms, all their property were theirs; and to-day and to-morrow they would be
as free to go about their affairs as they had been yesterday.
No soldier should molest them.

This from a conquering army, and from such a ruffian
looking army! Instead of the crushing steel hand, a velvet
glove, fleece lined. Clark was making the most of the value
of the dramatic surprise which gives the glow of relief after
fear and despair. Now, as he revealed to the Kaskaskians
the sweet nut in the rough burr, his part must have become
very enjoyable to him.

And it was the right moment to spring a piece of news on
them. Had it been sent ahead through an agent, then Rochblave, if he had failed to suppress it, would have derided it
as a lie and a ruse. If Clark had advanced it at the outset

of his occupation of the town when all were prisoners indoors the same view might have been taken. At least its truth would have been questioned. Now it could be sown in warm moist soil under a gracious sun.

Before he had left Corn Island he had received an express, cheery company for the little American flags which his men carried in their bags on the march, announcing the publication of the pact by which France gave her support to the Revolutionists.

"This information affected them very visibly," Clark remarked in his restrained fashion. Well it might!

Then he told them that whether they chose to take the American side or the British side in the war their property and their daily lives would no less be disturbed under the American occupation. He bade them, all in keeping with the new principle of freedom of opinion, to retire and talk it over and let him know their decision. Anyhow, they might be certain—here the dominant light must have again appeared in his eyes with a suggestive glint that there was still steel under the velvet—that the Americans had come to Kaskaskia to stay and that American victory, which had already been in sight, was guaranteed by French support.

So, under the spell of their awe and wonder at the turn of affairs, they retired to confer. Their homes and gardens safe! No Indian warfare to be started! Everything as it was yesterday, and even better! The King of France on the American side! His Catholic Majesty had not finally deserted this distant flock, after all.

Doubtless the imperious George Rogers was already assured of the result before he gave the permission for the council which would make the decision by their own will rather than his command. The council was very brief. Acclamation did not have to wait on the motion being seconded. And Patrick Henry's oath of allegiance was awaiting them.

The petitioners became messengers running about the

town with the glad news. It was a scene of bright color, with the women in the gay peasant costumes of old France, as the flock fluttered around the black cassock of the white haired Father Gibault. Laughter was back in the throats of the children who had been affrighted by the Big Knife goblin. All the bells in the town were ringing.

The cracked voices of the old joined with the voices of the young in seventeenth and eighteenth century songs. They decked themselves with flowers; they brought out all their flags and marched behind them as they sang. It was gay France in the valley of Kaskaskia, making rainbow holiday after the black thunderhead which had promised a destroying cloudburst but dropped only a shower that made the sight of the glad sun so much more welcome.

Doubtless wine was opened. The Big Knives with flowers stuck in their rifles, were offered the best the pantries afforded without having to take it by *force majeure*. Fires were set roaring in the ovens to make big bakings of bread for the hungry guests who had brought the amazing news.

But the faithful must not forget *Le Bon Dieu* to whom they owed thanks for all blessings. He had looked after them in their hour of trial; He had tested them and then been kind in His mercy. All moved to the church for a *Te Deum* in answer to Father Gibault's summons.

And then the leading citizens were back before Clark with an offer more gratifying than any petition. They had heard that he was gathering horses to mount men to go to Cahokia. He should have the horses. But why limit the size of the party? There were many more than thirty good horses in the town.

There would be no work in the fields to-day. Spirits were quite too *exalté* for that. Thirty men might not be enough. Indians might be troublesome; there might be armed resistance by some whites who had been forewarned by the news of the Americans' arrival and still believed them to be as terrible as their reputations.

Kaskaskians knew the roads, they had friends in the outlying settlements to whom they could explain the truth. A few hours after the able-bodied men of Kaskaskia had feared Clark as a murderer they were volunteering to serve under him. Among them were several of Rochblave's former militia officers.

The local force kept growing until it not only outnumbered Bowman's force but was equal to Clark's total. He seems to have had no suspicion of Greeks bearing gifts, no apprehension that Bowman might be the object of treachery. He saw their new loyalty as real, at least temporarily, as their faith in Father Gibault. To have suspected them openly would have been an error. His own eggs had to be placed in the same basket with theirs.

So they rode west, with sixty miles to go, bearing the new flag and doubtless the pennons of the local militia. It would have been all out of keeping with French character if some one of the elders had not brought forth from hiding an old *fleur de lis* flag of the Bourbons which gladdened the eyes of the disciples of La Salle as it floated over them again.

They rode fast, stopping only to rest their horses, their number increased doubtless by acquisitions, as those Kaskaskias in miniature, the villages of Prairie du Rocher and St. Phillippe, in turn blinked at the sight of that cavalcade in which French settlers were making boon companions of Big Knives.

The Bostonnais had come. Yes, yes. And learn, *Camarades*, how they had been wronged! Bowman had to do no talking at all. He had only to watch the gestures and listen to the flow of eloquence explaining that the age of miracles was not past. The flaming red-headed youth of Clark had made the miracle only the more wonderful and appealing.

Supported by such enthusiastic numbers from the capital the sweep of the procession was quite convincing to the people of the suburbs. Every man met on the road, as he looked up into the faces of the eager horsemen and heard the tidings, was warned either to get his horse and join the party or not to pass the news ahead.

They would make it a surprise for Cahokia as Clark had for Kaskaskia. After his bolt out of the blue the Frenchmen must have appreciated surprise as a very vital element both in war and propaganda.

The first the commander at Cahokia knew of what had transpired at Kaskaskia was when the expedition appeared in the streets of the town and surrounded the fort. Surrender was the only alternative when his own garrison was being infected by the siege of eloquence.

But, take the oath of allegiance at once! This did seem to the commander and some of the loyalists to be rushing matters a little too fast. So, Bowman, Clark-wise, let the siege of eloquence continue in the open discussion of a public council. As a result, more than a hundred men took the oath, and this was a good percentage of the able-bodied citizens.

After their six days' march, Bowman and his thirty had been three nights without sleep. That flag, then so new in the world, and whose future then seemed so uncertain, was raised beside the Father of Waters. Without shedding a drop of blood Clark had taken the key posts, which controlled the junctions of the Ohio and Missouri from the east bank of the Mississippi, in the destiny of the rivers of the great valley.

After the taking of Cahokia it would seem that the red-headed son of Ann, himself, was entitled to a break in training; but to have rested on his oars would have been to drift to certain disaster. More surprising than his easy military success were the problems which it entailed as the legacy of the temerity of his enterprise.

The more territory that he took the thinner he had to spread his little army, the more funds he required when his stock of paper money was exhausted. Responsibility kept pace with his expanding ambitions. He was a youth of many troubles which were to make him old before his time.

XX

MANY AFFAIRS

WHAT of Vincennes? Clark did not forget that this fort and garrison were between him and the American frontier. No sooner was he in secure possession of Kaskaskia than their fatigue did not stay the steps of the veteran Simon Kenton and a companion in answer to the summons for immediate departure upon a scouting trip to Vincennes.

What of Hamilton, the British commander in the West, when news reached him at Detroit of the loss of Kaskaskia? He was too bold a soldier not to try for its recovery if he knew how small was Clark's force which he had in a pocket.

If Kenton were captured, or opportunity presented itself, he would spread the word, as all Clark's soldiers were spreading it, that they were only a flying column of the American army forming at the Falls of the Ohio. Should McIntosh be advancing from Pittsburgh as Clark hoped, the prospect of two converging forces approaching Detroit might incline Hamilton against risking a retaliatory expedition which would leave Vincennes and Detroit inadequately defended.

Considering the information about Hamilton's numbers and plans which she had destroyed or secreted, Clark might well have regretted his politeness to Madame Rochblave. Happily, without waiting on the return of Kenton, he was to find a good substitute in a new friendship that he had won.

The venerable vicar general, Father Gibault, was the favored ear for all the information which was brought over the trails by those of high and low degree, by merchants, hunters and braves; for all the whispers and rumors about the doings at British headquarters which he knew so well how to evaluate out of his long frontier experience.

242

He personified the tradition of Father Marquette; of the pristine bearers of the Cross in the romantic days of the *voyageurs* in the great valley. He could tame the savage breast where others made it swell with greater rage. His cassock was a passport where another traveler's life would be forfeit.

Fear was not in such pioneer priests. They went unarmed except in their faith. Father Gibault's white hairs appearing in the midst of the orgies of a war dance represented all that was good and wise and sacred in the palefaces. He was the evangel of the Great Spirit of the whites. It was bad luck to harm him; to lay angry hands on the Cross he wore.

But, the church, riding with the storm and keeping its bark on the crest in subtle pilotage, ever knows when to yield to Cæsar the things which Cæsar can make his by force. This was as true on the frontier as in complex modern politics or wars on a world scale.

And Cæsar had seen fit to blood the Indians into fierce war on the whites in war between the whites. The labors of the Cross were being sacrificed in horrors; the mass was yielding to the frantic rites around the peeled post. And this was the policy of the Royal Breast under the flag that had raised its sovereignty over French missions and settlers. But time, time! The church which can reckon in days, hours and minutes can also reckon in years and centuries.

Well met and strange allies in a heart to heart talk were the restless young Virginian, with Detroit humming in his mind, and the old priest of the frontier, in the simple faith which held for such as he when mighty Cardinals were more worldly. Clark was aiming to mold all his influence to service of the new flag and his vision; Father Gibault, regardless of new flags or old, or earthly plots, was aiming to use the dynamic force of this conqueror for the good of souls, whether under red or white skins, of which, in his serene con-

viction, a divine mission from infallible Rome had made him
shepherd.

Mother Ann might have squirmed a little at the thought
of her restless son in close counsel with a Papist. Very far
away, indeed, were the little Clarks in the family pew in
Caroline County from this conference in Kaskaskia when
George Rogers, the learner from men rather than books,
was broadening his education by listening to a new in-
structor.

Clark heard fresh and illuminating information about
British methods on the frontier; of how widespread had been
the propaganda among the Indians. The tribes of the northern Illinois country and of the recesses of the forests bor-
dering the rivers and lakes of Wisconsin had been encouraged
by gifts to join the eastern tribes on the warpath.

Clark wanted the Indians to bury their hatchets which
were raised against his countrymen. To keep the Indians at
peace was the mission of the church, in which it had so skill-
fully succeeded before the Revolution. Souls were not saved
around the peeled post. Looking into the minds of each other
young soldier and old priest saw eye to eye.

Father Gibault had just learned that Lieutenant Governor Abbott of Vincennes was on a visit to Hamilton at Detroit. With the commander absent Clark was thinking of another surprise by a handful of chosen determined men, say
only forty or fifty, against the leaderless militia of Vincennes.
Doubtless he told Father Gibault that the taking of Vincennes was the next step as a matter of course, once the main
force from the Falls of the Ohio had arrived. If Clark had
Vincennes, Hamilton would be inclined to retake it before he
tried for Kaskaskia.

The priest, looking into the glad faces in the peaceful
streets and seeing the fields of ripening grain in the distance,
was thinking of the happy harvest time transformed into
horror. He pictured his beloved Kaskaskia as a cockpit for

THE EARLIEST VIEW OF PITTSBURGH. A PRINT WHICH WAS MADE
EARLY IN THE EIGHTEENTH CENTURY

the Big Knives in their grim defense against an attack by Hamilton and his Indian allies.

Why should Clark send an army to Vincennes? Father Gibault suggested another kind of expedition. The Vincennes people were under martial law. They knew no such freedom as Clark had brought to Kaskaskia. They were not bearing arms gladly for the British king, but if their homes were attacked they would fight as the only alternative.

Vincennes was in Father Gibault's vicar generalcy. He knew the people and their priest. Many Kaskaskians had friends in Vincennes who might be won over to Clark's side if the good news of how happy the Kaskaskians were under the new régime should be brought to them in a convincing way. The Indians of the region might also be won if they, too, learned of the mighty stroke of the Big Knives at Kaskaskia and how the great white Father of the French, His Catholic Majesty, was now fighting on the side of the Big Knives.

Thus much bloodshed might be prevented, many a hatchet buried. Clark praying for a battalion to take Vincennes had found one in the vicar general. His plan accepted, the circumspect ambassador said that, although out of his experience he would direct all policy, it would be better that as a spokesman of the spirit he should be accompanied by a temporal representative.

He suggested for the part Dr. Jean Baptiste Laffont who always had been secretly sympathetic with the American cause. Little is known of Laffont. It would seem that he was the local physician of Kaskaskia whose cure of bodies may have been a more substantial example of paleface magic, as is that of the modern medical missionary, than the cure of souls.

Clark sent no soldier—this would have been an obvious mistake of policy—with that little mission whose part was that of the cavalcade which had made the dash to Cahokia.

Priest and physician, company for each other on the trail, were riding three times the distance to Cahokia on a neighborly visit. They might call also on some Indian chiefs, who would welcome spiritual and medical attention, not to mention political advice. Their surprise was in the good news they carried; their arms were the letters from friends in Kaskaskia to friends in Vincennes telling them that the good news was true.

They also bore instructions from Clark, instructions which would make the most of the overnight prestige that he had won. His letter in French to the temporal legate, Dr. Laffont, began, "having the good fortune to find two men like M. Gibault and yourself to carry and to present my address to the inhabitants of Vincennes, I do not doubt that they will become good citizens."

So he assumed at the outset that there was no alternative but for them to yield; and he was good enough to counsel a gracious yielding for their own interests. This, he further assured them, was the only way to avoid the miseries of war, for by reason preferably, but in any event by force, the Americans had come to stay. The citizens were to "elect a commander among themselves, take possession of the fort and defend the inhabitants until a greater force arrived."

Where was Clark to get the greater force? He did not allow that to appear to concern him when he had the big imaginary army forming at the Falls of the Ohio.

Much that Clark did not put on paper the priest and doctor might say for him. They could tell of the good nature, frankness and kindness of the Big Knives if you rubbed their fur the right way and how the wolf pack instantly showed their fangs if you rubbed the fur the wrong way; of how the people were to be delivered of all the exactions of martial law and elect their own magistrates just as the settlers did in the new county of Kentucky in becoming a part of the new American family.

Clark kept faith with his promise by holding elections immediately in both Cahokia and Kaskaskia. In Cahokia, where there was some grumbling over having yielded the fort so readily, the inhabitants, having been summoned to cast their ballots, without time to groom local candidates and not yet having gained political confidence in themselves, cannily chose Bowman as magistrate which further strengthened his position as master of the town. Clark remarks, however, that on occasion the magistrates had to come to him for advice and support, probably taking care not to wear through the velvet to the steel.

The young ruler had won the church and the people to his side. There remained the leader of what we now call "big business." In this undertaking he did not eschew finesse. One criticism of him, among idealists, is that he was too much of a politician; another is that he had no gift for politics as illustrated in his later career in dealing with his Virginian superiors. He was frank about the tricks of the trade which rulers fail to mention in their memoirs and we learn second hand through the memoirs of others.

A special department is supposed to take charge of all chicane for some modern rulers who are thus saved responsibility for everything but the noble postures of a transparent simplicity in their statesmanship. Clark's Memoir in this sense was at least a hundred and fifty years ahead of his time—this is written in 1929—and perhaps two or three hundred years.

Sometimes Clark seems to rejoice in his diplomatic stratagems in a boyish desire to show that although he was so young he could be as shrewd as the elders of the Virginia Council. He had learned politics from Jefferson and Henry as well as equity from Mason.

As a youngster under the tutorship of a thrifty father, who had sold his own tobacco crop in the market of Fredericksburg and later planned to make himself a rich landholder, he had some training in business. He knew that what was "agreeable to human nature" in other people would be to a captain of industry. So the response of the great merchant of the valley, Gabriel Cerré, to a guard over his house and goods was as anticipated. Cerré rose at once to the bait.

Having tried in vain to secure passport to protect him under the flag of the States from the Spanish authorities in St. Louis, where he was when Clark took Kaskaskia, he wrote a very capable and well expressed letter to Clark, showing that he was both a man of intelligence and of education. In this he asked for a safe conduct "to return home so that I may clear myself of the accusations that have been made against me and attend to my affairs there."

A safe conduct meant that Clark assured him that he might depart in safety. Clark refused that bait. Cerré had been too friendly to the British cause for Clark to allow him out of hand at will if he did not sincerely accept the American cause.

His answer was through the friends who were interceding for Cerré and who seemed in the majority in town as he reminded them. "I intimated," says Clark, "that I wished to hear no more of the subject, nor would I hear any person who had anything to say in vindication of him. I told them that I understood M. Cerré to be a sensible man. If he were innocent of the allegations against him he would not be afraid to surrender himself."

The friends hurried off with their report to Cerré. They could assure him that his goods were unmolested and his wife going about her personal affairs as usual, but there was only one way for him to join her and that was to put himself at Clark's disposal.

He crossed the river, and without delaying even to call on his family, appeared at headquarters. It was his turn now to be measured by the smoldering deep-set eyes of the *diable au corps* of whom he had heard. Would they emit volcanic sparks or be appeased? A dignified captain of industry was M. Cerré. He was respectful, but not cowed.

Clark warned him that his delay in surrendering himself was convincing of guilt. Cerré knew what was being held against him, that he had incited Indians to murder, "a crime" as Clark warned him, "that ought to be punished by all people who were fortunate to get such culprits into their power."

Cerré defied any man to prove the charge. He was a merchant; he had no concern in politics except to conserve his interest as a merchant; he had not been in position to form a fair opinion of the issues in the present contest.

No interest in politics? Clark read to him a part of a letter from Hamilton to Rochblave in which "he was alluded to in affectionate terms." Cerré answered that in Detroit he had behaved himself as became a subject under the sovereignty of Great Britain. This did not imply he had favored Indian warfare. He disapproved entirely of such cruelty. On this score he welcomed thorough investigation.

There were people who owed him money and were trying to ruin him. He was beginning to explain why he had been so slow in reporting when Clark asked him to wait in an adjoining room. The prospect must have seemed gloomy to Cerré as he withdrew; for there had been no friendly sign in the smoldering eyes.

Meanwhile the people had heard of his presence. They were gathering in groups to learn the fate of the town's wealthy malefactor. Clark sent for his leading accusers. Others who wanted to appear as witness or be spectators of the *cause celébre* came with them. Then Clark gave certain citizens another surprise. He called in Cerré.

With both prosecution and defense present Judge Clark was ready to start the trial. He said for the benefit of all present and all people of the Illinois country that it was not the way of the Big Knife to condemn a man unheard.

It was time that Cerré were either proved innocent or guilty of the charge of inciting Indians to murder; if guilty, he should be properly punished. Cerré began to make a speech; but Judge Clark silenced him with the warning that it was for the prosecution to present its evidence first.

But the prosecution had many more lawyers than witnesses. They began whispered consultations. Gradually, they were slipping out of the room. When only one was left, and the Judge called on him to speak his mind, he, too, had nothing to say.

It was a smiling Judge Clark who congratulated the defendant upon having been acquitted of "so black a charge" and borne himself so well. One imagines Clark of the vision in his best winning manner picturing the future prosperity from the spread of settlements and the growth of markets in which the foremost capitalist of the Illinois country would share.

Again there was cozening by the velvet glove which is grateful after the feel of the steel. Clark hoped that Cerré would come into the family as a citizen of the United States. Whether or not he did, he could go where he pleased and do as he pleased with his property which would be protected.

Cerré had found that he now fully understood the issues at stake. He decided to take the oath of allegiance at once. Capital as well as the church was now on Clark's side. The people had learned that whispering judgments did not prevail under Big Knife justice. Accusations must be backed by evidence, all sides would be heard. There was to be no looting from the storehouses of the rich man or the poor man's home. Clark was Cadi as well as conqueror. He might be certain of one thing. Cerré, after this experience, would not use his influence to send Indians on the warpath.

Clark now had a problem as alien property custodian. His men had found all the good land in the neighborhood taken. There had been few plots that appealed to them in the region which they had traversed on their lean march. They had been covetous of a division of the spoils of Cerré's warehouses. Since Cerré had taken the oath Clark could answer that what might have been permissible requisition of enemy property had become robbery.

But Rochblave had not taken the oath. He met the suggestion with a blasphemy that indicated he would not turn his coat again. It was evident that he must be treated as a prisoner of war taken in British uniform as the commander of a British post. Madame Rochblave had left town to go to the Spanish side of the river, but such a permit might not be given to Rochblave who might slip across country to Detroit.

He had a number of slaves. It was quite normal in the custom of the times that Clark's soldiers should think that they should be sold in their own town and the proceeds divided among the victors. It was the only recompense they saw.

The people seem to have favored the plan. They saw Rochblave now as an avaricious commander who had exploited them. Clark's officers opposed the plan, until, when they did the gracious thing by inviting the vanquished commander to dinner with the French militia officers, Rochblave's feelings got the better of him in an outburst of abuse of his hosts. It cost him his slaves. The sum for which they were sold was divided among Clark's soldiers, his officers refusing any part.

Clark, who could ill afford to weaken his meager forces by messengers to a chief who was a thousand miles away across the wilderness, now spared Captain Montgomery and one private to carry the report of his operations to Governor Henry, and to escort Rochblave as prisoner to Williamsburg where, later, he broke his parole by rejoining the British forces.

The Governor was asked to send reinforcements in addition to men to fill the places of his time-expired veterans. Thinking of himself as holding an officer's commission and not a civil appointment Clark also asked that a civil administrator be sent to govern the immense region which he had won to American sovereignty, and which would require garrisons to uphold the hands of the administrator.

For Clark now had news from his embassy to Vincennes. Governor Abbott and the British officers had been withdrawn. Probably Abbott's protest against Indian outrages was too acute a reminder to Hamilton's left hand of what his right hand was doing. Hamilton, who had not yet heard of Clark's expedition, concluded that the best way in which to give the Indians a free hand, when he was financing and blooding them from Detroit and was depending upon them for his offensive against the frontier settlements, was to leave Vincennes to the French militia.

Under Father Gibault's leadership, the people had assembled at the church in "solemn conclave" and taken the oath of allegiance, to the disapproval of British residents. They had elected a commander of their militia and the new flag was floating over their fort, with no American present.

Clark thought that he should have at least one representative on the spot. He sent Captain Leonard Helm who was of middle age, a veteran of the frontier and who had proved to be of resource and sound judgment, as American commander of the post and "agent for Indian affairs for the department of the Wabash." Helm, who had one American soldier in his garrison, could be certain of a busy time when Hamilton heard that he had lost Vincennes. It ceased to be a negligible quantity to British strategy when the enemy possessed it.

Hope, will, audacity! So far they had succeeded. They must continue to succeed. Clark assured Helm that he should have adequate support as soon as Governor Henry sent the reinforcements.

XXI

TAMING THE SAVAGE BREAST

IT was not enough to have the support of the church, which included the school system, and the people, judiciary, industry and local militia and health department. Our young autocrat must be a cormorant of cabinet offices until a civil administrator arrived. It was vital that he should succeed as Chief of the Department of Indian Affairs.

Thought on things in general became very specific in determining what was "agreeable" to Indian human nature. Here again he was to defy precedent; break away from the policy which was the inheritance of royal governors, peace commissions and the suitors for land grants. In preparation for his expedition he had studied the latest British treaties which had made the Indians allies on the warpath and also the treaties and policies of the French and Spanish who had managed signally to keep the Indians at peace.

With this background of information he was a learner on the spot from Father Gibault, merchant Cerré, leading citizens and *coureurs de bois*. The mill of his searching mind was open to all grist which had a possible grain of wheat in the straw. He concluded that the States' method of dealing with the Indians had been wrong. At least it was for him in his present situation when he must capitalize the prestige of his victory in the alternative which became a routine, even a habit with him, in making virtue out of a necessity with his slender resources.

The old method had been that of bargaining. The Indians had been approached with bribes in return for land grants or raising or burying the tomahawk. The British could afford bribes and Clark could not. He would not ap-

pear to yield, thus disclosing his weakness, but to give out
of the generosity of his power. Any small largess at his
command would be the reward for proven good behavior.
The Indians should have presents for being good, not to
make them good.

They were great gossips as are all primitive peoples who
receive news only by word of mouth. Their occupation and
livelihood being on the trail they were ever traveling. One
tribe, even in moods of mutual suspicion and enmity, was
in touch with its neighbors. Any happening of importance,
particularly with reference to the palefaces, was carried by
the birds, as they said, with incredible swiftness.

Speedily the birds bore to the nearby lodges, to be passed
on speedily to the more remote, the story of the mighty
event at Kaskaskia. Could the account be true as they had
heard it? Many thought that an evil spirit had put a lie
in the birds' beaks.

To the Indian mind, which dwelt on stratagems and ambush, here was a supernatural achievement by a paleface
in the kind of warfare in which the redskin was certain that
he excelled. He saw the palefaces' advantage in plentiful
ammunition, superior rifles, greater numbers and the cannon
which shook the earth.

Now some of the Big Knives had broken free of their
settlements in the great Kentucky hunting ground where
they had been in siege. After marching for many days, without a single bird having seen them, they had struck by surprise in the night; and in the morning they had all the
people of the biggest paleface town in the land prisoners
in their houses.

Without risking one of their own scalps this Big Knife
war party could have had their belts festooned with hair,
taken as many women as they chose, drunk all the wine in
the houses and stuffed themselves with French pastry and

sweet preserves. They had done none of those things. It was all very strange.

Thus the Great Father of the Big Knives had prevailed over the Great Father of the British and taken the great chief Rochblave in his bed; and thus the Big Knife braves had acted after their victory. What said the Great Spirit of the Indians through the medicine men? Probably the medicine men looked wise, talked of portents that had warned them that a miracle was coming, and otherwise reserved decision until they had further information.

Chiefs and bands of bucks would see for themselves if the birds had been lying. They took the trails toward the great river. Processions of canoes were being paddled down the Mississippi, which brought them to Cahokia, easier to reach by water than Kaskaskia by land. There they found that the palefaces' fort, which the French and then the British chieftains had said would forever command the Father of Waters, was, indeed, flying a new flag, the Big Knife flag.

Impromptu parliaments of tribes were forming at Cahokia. When an Indian appeared in town he was always a good Indian, or had to be accepted as such, although as soon as he was out of town he might be a bad Indian looking for scalplocks. Indians were always coming and going in the French settlements. To put bodily restraint upon them, when all carried rifles, or had rifles concealed near town, might bring reprisal. The French inhabitants were becoming worried at the number of self-invited week-end guests.

The braves learned that all that the birds said was true. Gravely they sat about, gravely they grunted, as they considered the amazing situation. The Big Knives had all the settlements; and the French Father had come to life again and had bidden his children to be friends with the Big Knives.

Clark, himself, arrived at Cahokia. All the warriors, their

faces expressionless as tanned leather, would have a long look at the warrior who had performed a wonder worthy of a devil brother of the Great Spirit. He was tall as the tallest buck. His eyes were dark like an Indian's, but his hair was red like fire. He bore himself as became a mighty chief, mightier than any paleface they had ever seen. He passed by the Indian chiefs in the streets with an indifference which implied that, in the "haughty and violent disposition" of the Virginians, he could snatch lightnings from the sky and destroy them all.

His men bore themselves in kind; for this chief had put his stamp on all his braves. Each, indeed, was a haughty chief in himself, very unlike the British redcoats, or the French militia, or the old French regulars which the elder bucks remembered. Doubtless the haughty rank and file laconically communicated the idea that they were only an advance guard; an army as numerous as the blades of grass in the fields was coming. All who were interested might tell this news to the birds to carry back into the forests.

For the present, in their awe, the visitors appeared to be extremely good Indians. Clark's problem was how to keep them good when treachery was the father of their method of warfare. They begged that they might have talk with the mighty paleface chief, hear the winged words of wisdom from his lips. If those words had issued in cannon spouts of flame and the red hair had blazed as fiercely as pitch pine they would not have been surprised; not when they had been told that, in the eclipse of the sun, darkness had fallen upon the land when his expedition started.

He received them as petitioners to whom he would condescend to listen. They were humble in all the tricks of Indian ingratiation. Bad Indians, and bad birds sent by the British from Mackinac, had deceived them, they said. Now they knew the truth from the good birds. They desired peace. After their speeches some of them stamped on flags and belts of wampum which they had received from the British.

But the mighty warrior of the red hair, who could blot out the light of the sun, was unmoved by such theatrics. He was determinedly playing his part as the creator of a new Indian policy. The chiefs were bidden to come the next day when they should hear the truth upon which the fate of their people depended. He refused, and bade his officers to refuse, their offers to shake hands.

"I told them," says Clark, "it was time enough to give the hand when the heart could be given also."

They were not to be surpassed in high-flown phrase and replied that "such sentiments were those of men who did not speak with a double tongue."

Much Indian argument must have passed among them in the next twenty-four hours, whetting eagerness to hear the miracle warrior's address. He had gained time for its prep- aration which was as important in his statecraft as an in- augural address to a President of the United States, or a pronouncement of policy in an international crisis by the Premier in the House of Commons.

Although Clark was so laconic in his Memoir about the taking of Kaskaskia and the mid-winter march to Vincennes, he was quite expansive about his dealings with the Indians. In no other part of the narrative is he so manifestly pleased with himself. Capturing forts and towns with inferior num- bers were military incidents, but Indian relations was a most engrossing business. Indian lore and character deeply in- terested him. He seems to have had a liking for the children of the forest; to have felt a sympathy with them in the foreseen fate of their race in yielding to the advance of the whites in working out his vision for the great valley—which was to include the first proposal to educate them.

Many writers have been inclined to pass over his Indian relations as belonging in the category of ethnological his- tory; but it is a part of his achievement which should be emphasized. It spelled the difference between military success and failure. When Washington, in his alarm, spared troops for Pittsburgh from his meager forces at Valley Forge, Clark was trying to prevent not only the rout of his own little army but to lighten the burden of the defense of the whole western frontier.

There is a touch of boyish pride in the way that he prints in full in his Memoir his speech to the first lot of chiefs, as if to say, "You have heard about palefaces' speeches in the Indian style. What do you think of mine? Not so bad, eh?"

I, too, am inclined to print it in full. It makes a sharp contrast with the speeches of Hamilton who was blooding the Indians for the warpath, while Clark sought to keep them off the warpath, not only as a military measure but as an aid to the peaceful settlement of the land.

We may picture the audience that listened to Clark, the orator: braves squatting in front, braves with arms crossed standing in a circle behind them, silent as the forest in winter, while their eyes, as dark as still water in winter's dusk, wandered from his lips to those of the interpreter. It was mighty medicine from the mighty warrior, his idioms so clear to them that it further suggested that he was in close harmony with the Great Spirit.

There was no "comic relief" in the speech. The Indians took their oratory very seriously. Clark's every word, even in the repetitions of thought, must be attuned to the somber dignity of Indian eloquence; the dignity of the rivers and the forests through which they flowed, of the great plains and the black clouds of buffalo which coursed them, and of the blue dome overhead where the Great Spirit dwelt. An interesting bit this speech, aboriginally American—with the accompanying ceremonial as requisite to the occasion as that of the King opening Parliament—which appealed to the red children of the great valley, when the new flag

ORIGINAL OF CLARK'S MEMOIR. THE PASSAGE DESCRIBES CLARK'S TRIP BACK
TO VIRGINIA WITH GABRIEL JONES. *Draper manuscript*

had just been raised over the Mississippi which had not yet a settlement of a thousand whites on either bank north of New Orleans.

"Men and warriors, pay attention. You informed me yesterday that the Great Spirit had brought us together, which you hoped was good, as He is good. I also have the same hope, and whatever may be agreed upon by us at the present time, whether for peace or war, I expect each party will strictly adhere to and henceforward prove ourselves worthy of the attention of the Great Spirit. I am a man and a warrior, not a councilor. I carry War in my right hand and in my left Peace. I was sent by the great council fire of the Big Knives and their friends to take control of all the towns th   _nglish possess in this country, and to remain here watching the conduct of the red men.

"I was sent to bloody the paths of those who continue the effort to stop the course of the rivers, but to clear the roads that lead from us to those who wish to be in friendship with us, in order that the women and children may walk in them without anything being in the way to strike their feet against; and to continue to call on the Great Fire for warriors enough to darken the land of those who are hostile to us, so that the inhabitants shall hear no sound in it but that of birds that live on blood.

"I know that a mist is yet before your eyes. I will dispel the clouds in order that you may see clearly the cause of the war between the Big Knives and the English, that you may judge for yourselves which is in the right. Then if you are men and warriors, as you profess to be, prove it by adhering strictly to what you may now declare, without deceiving either party and thus proving yourselves to be only old women.

"The Big Knives are very much like the red men; they do not know well how to make blankets, powder and cloth; they buy these things from the English (from whom they formerly descended) and live chiefly by raising corn, hunting and trading, as you and your neighbors, the French, do. But the Big Knives were daily becoming more numerous, like the trees in the woods, so that the land became poor and the hunting scarce; and having but little to trade with, the women began to cry to see their children naked, and tried to make clothes for themselves, and soon gave their husbands blankets of their own making; and the men learned to make guns and powder, so that they did not want so much from the English.

"Then the English became angry and stationed strong garrisons through all our country (as you see they have done among you on the lakes and among the French) and would not let our women spin nor the men make powder, nor let us trade with anybody else. They said we must buy everything from them, and since we had become saucy they would make us give them two bucks for a blanket that we used to get for one. They said we must do as they pleased, and they killed some of us to make the rest afraid.

"This is the truth and the cause of the war between us, which did not begin until some time after they had treated us in this fashion. Our women and children were cold and hungry, and continued to cry. Our young men were lost, and there were no counselors to set them in the right path. The whole land was dark, and the old men hung down their heads for shame, for they could not see the sun.

"Thus there was mourning for many years. At last the Great Spirit took pity on us and kindled a great council fire that never goes out, at a place called Philadelphia. He stuck down a post there and left a war tomahawk by it, and went away. The sun at once broke out, and the sky became blue. The old men held up their heads, and assembled at the fire. They sharpened the hatchet and put it into the hands of the young men, and told them to strike the English as long as they could find one on this side of the Great

Water. The young men immediately struck the war post and blood ensued. Thus the war began, and the English were driven from one place to another, until they became weak and hired you red men to fight for them, and help them.

"The Great Spirit became angry at this, and caused your Old Father, the French king, and other great nations to join the Big Knives and fight with them against all their enemies, so that the English have become like deer in the woods. From this you may see that it is the Great Spirit that caused your waters to be troubled, because you fought for the people he was angry with, and if your women and children should cry you must blame yourselves for it and not the Big Knives.

"You can now judge who is in the right. I have already told you who I am. Here is a bloody belt and a white one. Take whichever you please. Behave like men, and don't let your present situation, being surrounded by the Big Knives, cause you to take up the one belt with your hands when your hearts drink up the other.

"If you take the bloody path you shall go from this town in safety and join your friends, the English, and we will try like warriors to see who can put the most stumbling blocks in the road and keep our clothes perfumed with blood the longest. If you should take the path of peace and now be received as brothers to the Big Knives and the French, and should hereafter listen to bad birds that will be flying through your land, you will no longer be counted as men but as persons with two tongues, who ought to be destroyed without listening to what you say, as nobody could understand you.

"Since I am convinced that you have never heard the truth before, I do not wish you to give me an answer before you have had time to counsel if you wish to do this. We will part this evening and when you are ready, if the Great

Spirit will bring us together again, let us prove ourselves worthy by speaking and thinking with but one heart and one tongue."

After Clark had finished speaking we see him turning away from them in his sedulously preserved grand manner as they in their own grand manner went to council. Their response to the mighty warrior must be no less ceremonious than the presentation of his ultimatum. It was a splendid opportunity for histrionics in which it was gratifying for the braves to find the miracle man of the Big Knives proficient.

Indian etiquette was as formal as old world diplomacy and must have been as boring after a first experience to a creative and impatiently active mind; but it was the oil for the machinery of Indian international relations.

A chief spokesman was chosen; the elders arranged the agenda and the formalities. All the people of the town were invited to be present for the ceremony.

The orator advanced bearing the belt of peace to Clark who was seated. Another bore the pipe of peace; another the fire to light it. When the pipe had been presented to the earth, the heavens and the Great Spirit it was offered to the great white warrior for the first puff and in turn to all the other important personages in the order of their rank.

Then the orator spoke. What Clark had said to them had been put into his heart by the Great Spirit; and the Great Spirit had taken pity on his red children and opened their hearts and cleared their eyes so they could receive the truth. They would call in their warriors and cast the tomahawk into the river where it would never be found again.

No bad birds should again be allowed to disquiet their women and children who would smooth the roads for their Big Knife brothers as guests in their villages to see how the faith had been kept. The word of peace should be borne back by good birds to the other tribes who would want to hear it and in turn smoke the pipe of peace.

Gravely the braves departed, after a surpassing emotional experience in treaty making, when treaty making shared first place in public spectacles with the war dance after they denounced treaties. If treaties were never broken they could not have the thrill of war and the happy business of making more treaties. How long would this one last?

Other parties from greater distances continued to arrive just as later parties of the curious in the motor cars of to-day replace others in viewing the scene of a sensational murder or fire. The best tribute to Clark's speech and method was their success. He had to continue repeating the speech which, however, was fresh to each audience which could not have read it in the newspapers or have heard it over the radio. Again and again he went through the same rigamarole in befitting solemnity as he maintained his lordly mien in keeping with his prestige, taking care not to allow his youthful sense of humor to betray him.

However, there were some bucks of the Meadow Indians who concluded that he might not be as mighty as others thought. They would prick the bubble of the miracle warrior's reputation; demonstrate, in ancestral faith, the absurdity of this new idea that any paleface was as good at Indian tricks as such bright Indians as themselves.

Great would be their honor, far into the forests would the birds bear their fame, if they should take Clark in his bed and bear him away as a prisoner to be paraded before the chiefs who had bent in fear of him. What an offering to the Great Spirit the scalp of this Big Knife chieftain! What triumph to make him run the gauntlet and see if he would moan under torture! Then all the other Big Knives would be in flight and rich the rewards from Detroit for the heroes. All the braves would smash their peace pipes and raise the tomahawk. And it is not too much to say that, at this juncture, the Clark patriarchy would have soon collapsed for want of a patriarch.

The Meadow Indians had a place in Indian life which reminds us that the first tramps in America were not white. They were a characteristic band of vagrant cosmopolitans, composed of members of different tribes who traveled over wide areas, depending upon opportunism and social tolerance and making themselves useful go-betweens as masters of a gypsy chicane and barter.

The house that Clark occupied as his headquarters faced the little Cahokia river. Accomplices in the Meadows' plan would fire shots on the opposite bank in the middle of the night. This would be a signal for the ambushing party to approach the sentry before Clark's door, saying that they were good Indians peacefully asleep on the near bank when they had been fired on by bad Indians who were crossing the river to pursue them. Then they would kill the unsuspicious sentry and any other soldiers inside the house.

But, under the Clark discipline, the sentry was very much on the alert. A burst of shots at one in the morning! The sentry instantly aroused the guard indoors; for Clark knew better, despite all the peace pipe smoking, than not to have more than one soldier between him and the street when he was in bed. It was the Indians who had the surprise in the size of the guard which met them with ready rifles.

Clark, who remarks that he was sleeping lightly as he had many things to think about, had also heard the shots, and himself sprang to arms. It was a light summer night, and when the Indians saw his towering figure in the doorway behind the guard they became good Indians in fact as well as pretense. They told their tale about the bad Indians who had attacked them from the other side of the river when they were on the Cahokia side. They might have succeeded in having it believed if it had not been observed that when the earth was summer dry their moccasins and leggings were wet from fording. Clark ordered that they should be put under arrest; and then he would leave the local authorities, whose peace they had disturbed, to decide their fate.

Here was further proof of the miracle warrior's magic. The plan had been just as good as his own against Rochblave, probably patterned after it. But the king Big Knife had as many eyes as he had soldiers; he slept with his own eyes open; he divined all stratagems against him.

When he had the offending Meadow bucks brought before him in the next day's peace council, he ordered that their irons be removed. He said that everybody concerned had agreed that they ought to die. But a bird had told him of their plan, and so silly were they to think that they could catch a bear asleep that he found "they were only old women and too mean to be killed by a Big Knife."

"But," Clark went on, "as they ought to be punished for putting on breech-clouts like men these should be taken away from them, and plenty of provisions given them to go home, as women don't know how to hunt; and as long as they stayed here they should be treated as all squaws ought to be."

To Indian warriors this was an insult emphasized by the most indifferent contempt, an insult worse than death. To add to their humiliation Clark went on talking to others present without even noticing them except that they were much agitated. Savage egoism could not bear the strain.

They begged that they might be heard again; but Clark refused to have their words interpreted. He was busy holding council with brave warriors with no time to spare for the breech-cloutless. Finally they offered him a peace belt and peace pipe. Now he appeared to be insulted. He broke the pipe in two and laid his naked sword on the table impressively.

Let them sit down and enjoy themselves in the part of spectators as became women. But he did listen when it was clear that they wanted to confess their guilt. The bad bird from Mackinac (Detroit) had put the wicked idea in their heads. Wouldn't Clark take pity on their women and children? When their lives had been spared might not the Meadows also have peace?

Clark kept to his adamantine part. Other chiefs joined in the appeal. They said that they knew that the Big Knife was above little things. Wouldn't he take pity on these erring warriors?

"I told them," Clark wrote, "that I had never made war upon them. If the Big Knives came across such people in the woods, they commonly shot them down as they did wolves to prevent their eating the deer, but they never talked about it."

And so Clark closed the discussion, or appeared to have closed it, as he turned to other business. The Meadow bucks withdrew into a corner for further discussion in a desperate crisis.

"At length," Clark wrote, "two young men advanced to the middle of the floor, sat down and flung their blankets over their heads. At first I did not know what to make of this action."

Two of the chiefs with peace pipes in hand took their place beside the young men, and explained that the two were offering their lives in atonement for their guilt, and it was hoped that their sacrifice would be accepted. When Clark was again offered the pipe he again refused it.

The two pulled their blankets aside for a peep wondering why the sword on the table had not descended, impatient to know their fate. All the dark Indian eyes were on Clark. There was very rapt Indian silence. It was deepening the impression of the alarm all felt over Clark's power and that there must be peace at any cost. Clark concluded that the expiatory offer was sincere. The two expected to die.

"I had intended all along to grant peace to these people," Clark wrote, . . . "You may easily guess my feelings on this occasion and the pleasure with which I regarded these young men. I had read of some such action as this, but had never known whether or not to credit it. I ordered the young men to rise and uncover themselves. Upon this there was a very visible alteration in their countenances, which, however, they appeared to try to conceal" —in stoical Indian fashion.

The miracle warrior hailed them as warriors of his own kind who had been ready to face death calmly. It was such brave men that the Big Knives wanted in friendship. He and all his officers shook hands with the two; he promoted them to be chiefs. Then he had the garrison salute them.

"Our new nabobs were now treated with great respect on all occasions," Clark remarks.

Finding that the old chiefs were a little too much cowed and possibly a little jealous, Clark gave them some presents to give to their friends on their return home.

The incident was most fortunate for the peace parleys; its effect enormous. The birds bore it far and near, adding to the saga of Clark's prestige.

It brought in still more remote chiefs who would see and talk with him. "Mr. Blackbird," as Clark refers to him, was coy. He was a powerful personage whose home country was in the environs of the present city of Chicago. His young warriors were on the warpath for Hamilton.

Word came to Clark that he was standing on his dignity as he had received no personal invitation for a diplomatic *pour parler;* and Blackbird, who had learned white man's ways from the British at Detroit, was self-consciously particular that he should receive the proper respect of being treated according to the etiquette of paleface diplomacy. Clark sent the invitation saying that he would meet him at Kaskaskia.

Blackbird arrived in style with eight attendants. Clark made the customary preparations for the ceremony of an Indian council in receiving him. Blackbird replied through a buck, who acted as his diplomatic secretary, that he did not care to spend his time on ceremonials when he had come to confer with Clark on matters of "consequence to both our nations."

Blackbird might be from up country, but he wanted it understood that he was as much of a man about town as any white. Before the Virginia Council he would have been out of feathers and beads and in jackote and ruffled shirt. He sent word through his diplomatic secretary that he would like to talk across a table with Clark, as potentate to potentate, both being seated on equal terms. Clark was agreeable, and doubtless secretly amused at first, although he must have soon been stifling yawns after all the treaty making he had been through. He never forgot that all Indian chiefs must be taken very seriously.

Far from stalking into Clark's presence in the grave Indian manner, Blackbird simulated the affable and polite circumspection of a meeting of European rulers. And more than this, there was a Frenchman with him in order that he might be formally introduced, as further assurance that he was no hat-in-hand petitioner. In European fashion, as he understood it, he began the exchange of compliments.

"He said that he had long desired to have some conversation with the chief of our nation," Clark wrote, "but never before had the opportunity of doing so. He had conversed with prisoners, but he placed little confidence in what they said as they generally were afraid to talk. He said that he had been engaged in the war for some time, but had always doubted the propriety of it, as the English and Americans appeared to be the same people. He was sensible that there was some mystery with which he was unacquainted. He had heard only one side of the story, and now wished me to explain it fully to him in order that, having heard both sides, he might be in a position to judge for himself."

Not all European rulers, ambassadors or premiers could have made a better approach when so many of his braves were fighting the braves of the ruler with whom he was conferring. The more questions Clark answered the more Blackbird asked. Clark had not only to explain the causes of the Revolution, through an interpreter to an Indian mind and not in Indian similes, but to gratify "this inquisitive Indian I was obliged to begin almost at the first settlement of America and go through its entire history to the present time . . . I was the better able to satisfy him as I was now pretty well acquainted with all that the British officers had told the Indians."

Blackbird said that the British must be afraid or they would not give the Indians so many presents to fight for them. He was content. He would call in his young men from the warpath. If any of them took any Big Knives' scalps before they got the word they must be excused. Clark granted his request to send one American with him to give support to his message to his people. Relations having now been so happily established, Blackbird, in his farewell in the best foreign manner, said he would be gratified that they should keep up a correspondence as became two good friends.

So one more treaty was promoted and signed by Secretary of State George Rogers Clark. More dramatic and more in the Indian manner were the negotiations with the Big Gate who took his name from having shot a white soldier at a gate. He, too, had been much at Detroit and his warriors had been winning Hamilton's bonuses for rebel scalps; but, pleasing as his action had been to the Royal Breast, he had been as unaffected by associations as the Rhodes scholar who is untouched by the broad "a" in his career at Oxford.

Without an invitation or saying a word, Big Gate had strutted into one of Clark's peace councils, to reappear the next day and the next. He always sat well forward in "great state" as unmoved and silent as a statue of Buddha, while, in truculent impertinence, he was wearing around his neck the bloody belt he had received from the British.

Clark went on with his business. Although having Big Gate in mind in some of his remarks, he appeared to pay no attention to him until at what seemed a propitious moment. Then he approached Big Gate and greeted him with the remark that of course he knew who the distinguished guest was; that none other than the renowned Big Gate had honored the council with his presence.

"As he knew public business must be attended to before private business," Clark remarks, "I hoped he would excuse me for not having spoken to him sooner. I said it was customary among white people when officers met in this manner, even though they were enemies, that they treated each other with greater respect than they did common people, and esteemed each other the more in proportion to the exploits they had performed against each other's nation."

Indian chiefs of that day liked attention no less than some white chiefs of this. Great warrior had paid tribute to great warrior in the freemasonry of the guild, but what was caviare to Blackbird was not caviare to Big Gate. Clark not only studied the Indian mind in general but the peculiarities of the different leaders. And Big Gate was as much of a snob in his way as Blackbird in his.

"As he had come designedly to see us," Clark told him, "and our business was now over, I hoped he would spend a few days with us and that he would dine with us that evening."

This was a reminder that, although the manner in which Big Gate had appeared in the council seemed rude and in violation of etiquette as understood between chiefs who must recognize amenities not understood by the masses, Clark would overlook the dereliction and act the part of great host to great guest. The loss of face was a factor as influential in Indian as in oriental life.

"He appeared to be on nettles," Clark says, "and, rising, began to excuse himself. I would not listen but ran on upon the same theme. I would stop, he would commence, and I would begin again until I had him worked up to as high a pitch as I desired."

Then Big Gate had the floor to himself. The leash was off his gathered emotions which had brought him to sudden decision in cataract force.

The British had told him lies. The Big Knives were right. He tore a small British flag from his breast and threw that and his war belt on the floor. Having stamped on them with a savage fervor to his own raucous accompaniment he continued his divestment until he retained nothing except his breechclout. His red skin rippled with the play of his lithe muscles in the emotion of further passionate declamation. He had been a warrior from youth; war was meat and drink to him; he delighted in it; three times he had fought the Big Knives.

Then he kicked the pile of clothing and trinkets across the room in token that he was forever through with these loathsome rags. He struck his breast a mighty thump. He was now a Big Knife, the naked warrior of him. This demonstration concluded, it was the time for pleasanter amenities. He shook hands with everybody present.

"A great deal of merriment ensued," Clark remarks. There must have been more of it at the dinner which took on the character of an armistice celebration.

"As our new brother was naked, it was necessary that he should be clothed," says Clark. A suit "covered with lace," worthy of a dandy in town, was found for him.

"Captain Big Gate was quite the finest man at table,"

says Clark. "In order to appear in as much state as the rest of us he had ordered one of his men to wait on him."

What a scene! What a display of buttling! Life was not without its variety for the son of Ann.

After dinner, Big Gate indicated that he desired a private conversation of Chief to Chief. Clark remarks that he was on guard lest so dramatic a person might be seized with homicidal mania; but the loyal ardor of the proselyte had only been accentuated by wearing lace ruffles.

He wanted to take the warpath for the Big Knife brothers at once. He knew Detroit. Give him the word and he would soon bring back a British prisoner or scalp.

Clark would make no exception to his policy even to gratify a champion who so delighted in war. Big Gate might bring him information, but no scalps. Every true Indian brother of the Big Knives must remain neutral in their quarrel with the British. Big Gate promised that he would and resist all temptations of wampum from Detroit. Had not the chief of the Big Knives told him as he told all the Indian chiefs, that a noble Indian warrior who took pay for fighting for the whites would be playing a hireling's part, thus shaming him before the Great Spirit? War was outlawed for the Indians for the present.

Farther and farther, the legend growing with travel, the birds carried the story of the wonder doings of the miracle warrior who dropped out of the sky in the midst of the wilderness, and of the bright blaze of his hair and the words of wisdom that fell as golden leaves of Autumn from his lips; carried the story not only to the north but to the west. Deputations from the Spanish domain on the other side of the Mississippi appeared. Treaty making for them was a Spanish matter; but they said that they could not resist satisfying their curiosity.

Clark gave these also ceremonious attention. Among them

were some who had come very far, indeed, from the land of great thirst for all who did know their way.

"They were somewhat different in their manners and complexion," says Clark, "being much fairer than any other Indians I had ever seen. I suppose it was this that gave rise to the idea of there being Welsh Indians in that quarter."

The Welsh Indians! Memory of a forgotten epic poem, "Madoc," by Robert Southey on the basis of a legend, is revived. In the twelfth century, Madoc, a Welsh prince, weary of home strife, set sail on the western ocean, and finding in America the promised land of peace that he sought, his blood and his followers' were mixed with that of the natives. Probably the Indians of fairer skin were the Mandans who lived in the upper reaches of the then mysterious Missouri. It was a long journey to make for a sight of the celebrity of the Illinois country.

In the meantime, Captain Helm, Clark's proconsul at Vincennes, reported that his garrison of one, or of two including himself, was in good health and peace reigned in his domain. While Clark was winning the Big Gate the doughty Helm had won the Grand Door of the Wabash who had been an equally sturdy harvester of Revolutionist scalps. He was called the Grand Door because "nothing of importance could be undertaken by the league of the Wabash without his consent." He, too, when Helm had read Clark's letter to him, after he had heard of the miracle warrior's doings through Father Gibault, had thrown down his bloody belt and taken an oath of loyalty to the Big Knives which he never broke in the stern days to come.

This and other treaties with chiefs of the Vincennes region were sent for Senator Clark to confirm and President Clark to sign. Not only Father Gibault and Gabriel Cerré, but other French priests and merchants as well as hunters and small traders were missionaries of Clark's propaganda.

Practically all the tribes from the forests of Wisconsin and the shores of lake Michigan through the present states of Illinois and Indiana to the Ohio had agreed to bury the hatchet. It was fortunately so when Clark was having to send his time-expired men home and no reinforcements were to come. There were braves in Detroit, white braves in red coats, who would not be won to neutrality. Hamilton, finding his Indian allies deserting and his recruiting grounds becoming sterile, was preparing to meet the challenge of the new flag which was flying from Vincennes on the Wabash to Cahokia on the Mississippi.

XXII

HE MUST HAVE MONEY

A younger generation, which is so used to having government notes redeemable in gold at par, may learn from old Southerners who remember the "shin-plasters" of the Confederacy something of the financial problems of the founding fathers of the nation. Benjamin Franklin's presses were running off paper money, which was depreciating in ratio to its increase, when to stay the output was to leave the treasury empty of the only kind of funds available. The confidence of all effort at the front and the rear suffered from the bankruptcy of credit.

Among the other offices that Clark held was that of Director of the Budget. His little stock of paper money had been exhausted when he arrived at Kaskaskia.

Where was he getting the funds to pay for his army's food, clothing and shelter, and for those little presents which he gave the Indians? Whence came his ammunition when he was so far away from his base?

He was paying in metal, or in as good as metal; in British guineas and Spanish *piastres* which were the gold basis among the Kaskaskians. Continental script was unfamiliar to their eyes for months after they had seen the new flag floating over their fort.

Again the destiny of the rivers was serving Clark. His banker was far away on the delta of the Father of Waters. He was drawing bills in gold to be honored by a young man who had the heart of a lion as a financier no less than Clark as a soldier and the Clark gift in cutting sharp corners; who shared the vision of Clark and had Clark's fertility of resource in action worthy of the conception.

The letters of this pioneer American business man might well be a textbook in the Harvard school of business. His career is an encouragement never to be downhearted, to loyalty, to think in a big way, to risk much for great stakes, to establish a credit in personality which may be better than collateral.

I am glad that those which are extant are to be published by Professor James Alton James. They should be read by all biographers of the great railroad builders of the West who did not foresee whence the capital would be forthcoming to complete the enterprises they had begun. Their methods were not those of to-day; nor were Pollock's in the emergency of a still more distant time no further from the period of the buccaneers of the Spanish Main than from the present.

Fortunate it was for Clark and the United States that the Pollock family emigrated in 1760 from Ireland to Carlisle, Pennsylvania; fortunate that son Oliver ventured forth in what was then called "mercantile pursuits" which brought him to Havana; and that when he went to the government palace Irishman met Irishman. For the Governor General of Cuba was Don Alexander O'Reilly, descendant of one of the Irish warriors who joined the Spanish Army and who were to show again that, despite the then accepted inability of the Irish to govern themselves at home, they were welcome recruits in assisting other rulers to govern their realms.

Why the Irish in recording the part of the Celts in the Revolution neglect Pollock's part is a puzzle unless they have mistaken his race because of his English name. The Governor General of Cuba did not forget that before he was a count and a don his ancestors were O's among the kings of Ireland.

Under the favor at the command of a Spanish governor general of the time, which enabled him to make friends with Spanish merchants and other Spanish governors, the sagacious Pollock was soon prospering. He settled in New Orleans. He had argosies going and coming on the southern seas.

Fortunately for Clark, years before Patrick Henry had cried "Liberty or Death!" or the tea was thrown into Boston Harbor, one of them was a cargo of flour; and, fortunately, it arrived before New Orleans just after the arrival of the Spanish army of occupation, which was taking over the city from the French, added three thousand soldier mouths to be fed to those of the local population.

Flour had risen to two hundred dollars a barrel. Pollock had the local market at his mercy, profit of two thousand per cent on his cargo in sight. He was not penny wise and pound foolish, not the type who killed the goose that laid the golden egg. His policy was live and let live. He was looking to the future; his Irish sentiment would not take advantage of famine. He told Governor Unzaga to name his price, which was the normal price of fifteen dollars a barrel. By way of a token of friendship, when Spanish governors were autocrats bothered by no Parliament, he gave Pollock permanent freedom of trade at the Port of New Orleans.

Out of this Pollock had soon made more than the profit he might have made out of the flour. His perquisite was confirmed in a close friendship with Unzaga's successor, Galvez, who was only twenty-nine, the son of a great viceroy of Mexico. Before the outbreak of the Revolution Pollock had made a fortune. He thought of himself as an American; all the power and influence he had were on the side of the colonies trying to free themselves from the ancient enemy of his race. The need of the United States of an able friend in New Orleans revealed the man.

When the new flag was raised at Kaskaskia and Cahokia, the vision of Clark and the vision of Pollock became one.

This spanned more than the breadth of the great valley from the Alleghenies to the Rockies. It spanned the depth from the headwaters to the Gulf of Mexico in a whole of which the Illinois country was only a small territorial part, clearing the way for the advance from frontier cabins from the Mohawk valley to far past those in Kentucky and on the Holston.

Soon after the close of the French and Indian war, when France in defeat left the country east of the Mississippi a legacy to Spain to keep it out of British hands, the British were brought to a halt in gleaning the spoils of victory. They were thinking covetously in terms of the "ideal island of New Orleans." The gateway of the great valley was under the flag which, from the days of the buccaneers of the Spanish Main, had disputed with broadside and cutlass the attacks on ships bearing gold from the mines of Peru and Mexico and all British trade rivalry in the southern seas.

In return for Cuba, as a part of the diplomatic bargain at the end of the French and Indian War, the British had received Florida which included the hinterland of what is now the states of Alabama and Mississippi, thus completing British sovereignty over all the present United States east of the river. Florida was entirely loyalist, its recent white settlers fresh from the motherland, their emigration officially promoted. Britain had spent much money on roads and improvements and in fortifying Pensacola as an outpost which should prevent the Gulf of Mexico becoming a Spanish lake.

Keeping in mind that law of gravity which had so much to do with our continental history, we must remember the simple fact that it was downstream from Pittsburgh and the Illinois country as well as from the Spanish side of the great valley; downstream to New Orleans on the way to the Paris market and upstream and over portages and across lakes before it was downstream to Quebec on the way to the London market. The British might hold all the eastern part of the valley, but still water would seek its own level in defiance of all commands of the Royal Breast.

Still the convoys came up the Mississippi with goods from Paris. St. Louis had been French as well as Kaskaskia and Vincennes. French traders were on the spot; they knew the sources of furs and how best to procure them at a bargain. Their commercial relations from Indian villages to Parisian buyers were established. They formed new ones with the Spanish, new links completing the old chain where it had been broken.

They might accept British sovereignty but they were not giving legs to British trade to follow the flag at the expense of their own livelihood. Traffic charges were less by the Mississippi than the St. Lawrence route. New Orleans was paying higher prices for furs than Quebec. So Britain found the furs of the valley still going to Paris, which was not at all pleasing to London financiers.

On the outbreak of the Revolution New Orleans was annually exporting five hundred thousand dollars' worth of furs. The total trade of the port was three millions, which we may multiply by five for a modern equivalent, having in mind how much greater a factor fifteen millions were then in international trade than to-day. The British were making a big investment in Florida and still not getting much business, which was not in keeping with their practical habit in empire building.

That "ideal island of New Orleans"! They must possess it. The forward party in England, the "jingoes" of the time, advocated war with Spain to make both banks of the Mississippi British and perhaps retake Cuba, incidentally gathering in some other useful bits of the Spanish empire. British troops were even mobilized in New York for an attack on New Orleans when the battle cry might have been "All the furs or none!"

However, weakening old Spain with memories of the ruthless Drake, in face of the doughty young aggressor, which is now called old England, made concessions in some other quarter which the Royal Breast, short of funds after so much recent warring, found acceptable for the present. There would never be lack of incidents enough for a *casus belli* in all the privateering, smuggling and lawlessness, when the British had half the navigable rights on the broad expanse of the lower Mississippi, with Natchez their fortified stronghold on the east bank as a base of operations against New Orleans commanding the west bank.

Such were the muddied and often bloodied waters, although there was nominally peace between Spain and Britain, in which the busy brain of the solemn-faced Patrick Henry found good fishing. The suggestion that he might be impinging on the preserves of the Continental Congress did not disturb this eager volunteer diplomat. His justification was the wisdom of prompt action in making that his own business which a conflict of views in responsible quarters reduces to nobody's or enlarges to the equally ineffectual result of being everybody's.

Enterprise of this sort had a considerable part in winning the Revolution when we lacked the cohesion which today would make a communication on foreign policy by a governor of a state such an absurdity. Virginia thought she must win the war or it would not be won; and so thought Massachusetts, Pennsylvania and the other states. Shades in the archives of State libraries must still be disputing as to which did win it.

Everything which makes an enemy expend strength in men or money, or diverts concentration through alarms or threats, is a military asset. Spain in Cuba, New Orleans and

St. Louis was a thorn in the side of Britain. Press in the thorn!

Henry was writing most engaging letters to the Governor General of Cuba and the Governor of New Orleans expressing the value of friendship with America, while he hoped that friendship could be encouraged into armed alliance. Although he had been lukewarm about the early proclamation of the Declaration of Independence, once it was a fact he made the most of the States being, as he said, "now free and independent, capable of making Alliances and Treaties."

He explained how American success was the best guarantee of the security of all Spanish possessions in the western hemisphere which Britain, in case of victory, would attack while she fattened on the trade that had been Spain's. His messages were well buttered.

"We are well acquainted, Sir," he wrote to the Governor General of Cuba, "with the Honor, Spirit and Generosity of the Spanish nation and should therefore glory in an intimate connection with it." This recalls some of the pleas to bring new allies into the World War when so many nations learned that all their men were noble and all the women fair.

He said that the States could supply "Beef, Pork, live stock, Stores, Shingles and several other articles" to the Spanish and "we have vast quantities of Skins, Furs, Hemp, and Flax which we could, by easy inland navigation, bring down the Mississippi to New Orleans from our back country."

He invited friendliness by expressing the interest of the United States in having Florida restored to Spain. "You must be too well acquainted with the nature of our States to entertain any jealousy of their becoming your rivals in Trade, or overstocked as they are with vast tracts of land, that they should ever think of extending their territory."

It is one of the ironies of history that Henry should be thinking in this fashion. He was probably thinking too much in terms of the opportunism of the moment to include the vision of the future which would have made his plotting in his study at Williamsburg so Machiavellian. His "Give me liberty or give me death!" had started the flame which spread in revolution in France and then in the wars for independence in Spain's American colonies which ended her American empire; and the success of the American Revolution unleashed the migration of settlers which swept the Spanish flag off the Mississippi.

But Spain took his view of the moment to gore the ancient enemy Britain; acted on it at once in conniving assistance, skirting the edge of actual war. The fact that a governor of one of the States was conducting a correspondence on foreign affairs was an assurance to Spanish councils, in their old world conception of nationhood, that the States were heterogeneous entities which would make them the less dangerous as neighbors. They were only small populations scattered in a wilderness, too individualistic and lawless for cohesion in peace when they so signally lacked it in war.

We went to the markets of Spain as buyers as well as sellers. In face of the British blockade our need was dire for arms, munitions and medicines; and the medicines included quinine in which Spain had a monopoly as it came from the bark of the cinchona tree in her colony of Peru. Its therapeutic value, first discovered when the wife of a Spanish governor took it for a fever, was recognized two centuries before we learned that the mosquito carried the malaria which was the curse of the frontier.

At first we paid for consignments in cash through a Portuguese banking firm. When even neutral ships were subject to the blockade and British search on the high seas was ruthless the Mississippi appealed as another route.

Early as the Summer of 1776, Captain Gibson and some armed men, disguised as hunters, made their way by the river route to New Orleans. The British Consul learned of the presence of an officer of the Virginia militia and his object. He demanded Gibson's arrest.

Governor Galvez complied, as friend Pollock advised. With Gibson in jail the nominally neutral Spain, which had harbored him, had kept faith with a rule of international law; but there had been no request for the arrest of William Linn, Gibson's second in command, a brother of the Linn whom Clark had sent on the scouting trip to Kaskaskia during the siege of the Kentucky settlements.

Pollock procured nine thousand pounds of powder and a supply of quinine. With these Linn started upstream. It was heavy labor for his party of armed oarsmen and wearily slow in taking all precautions against attack; but in seven months, at the rate of about six miles a day, Linn arrived safely the following May at Pittsburgh when ammunition was short against the Indian attacks and frontier defenders, suffering from "fever and ague," welcomed ample doses of the favorite remedy. Later, the trip was made in from three to five months. The ammunition, which Clark received from General Hand for his expedition, presumably was being taken back down the Ohio by which it had come.

The mind of Oliver Pollock was no less busy than Patrick Henry's and often with more material results. He was gathering supplies to be forwarded by sailing vessels; but the blockade stiffened. The eyes of the ranging British skippers, and the guards at the straits leading out of the Caribbean, grew more alert at the prospect of the bounty of contraband which meant prize money as they searched every ship they could overhaul.

Pollock could know the fate of the cargoes only when word came back by sailing vessel, which might be captured, or by express across country or down the river, or when a cargo was so long missing that it must be accepted that the British had garnered another consignment of munitions for Washington's ragged army. The diminishing means of the States' treasuries had to pay for those that were lost as well as those received.

Pollock was sending forth bread upon the waters, casting hazards into the horizon of the gulf. The high hope placed on the departure of each cargo was tortured by the long suspense awaiting news of its fate. Not for months was it known that every cargo sent in the early part of 1778 had been taken. And the British promptly strengthened their patrol of the river when they learned that those damned, thieving, pestiferous rebels were slipping supplies past the forts at Natchez and Manchac to Pittsburgh.

Downstream, in January, 1778, back to his old haunts, came Captain James Willing, a Pennsylvanian by birth. He had been living and prospering as a trader in Natchez when the news of Lexington and Concord sent him north as a passionate volunteer for the patriot cause.

Meanwhile, numbers of Scotch-Irish settlers, to escape the tory and "rebel" plots and frays, in which they had no side in their business of bettering themselves in the new land, had migrated across country to Natchez. There they found that they had jumped from the frying pan into the melting pot which already was boiling out a few old world prejudices in making a new amalgam.

Conditions made many of these settlers Revolutionary partisans. The battle of the Boyne was forgotten. Orangemen were secretly striking hands with that ingratiating Irish Catholic, Pollock, so quick to make the most of their dissatisfaction for an asset in his own fervid purpose. Willing brought the news of Burgoyne's defeat, which Pollock might capitalize in convincing Galvez that he was on the winning side, and which Willing capitalized by winning recruits from the settlers to his little army of forty-five men with which he took Natchez.

Pollock fitting out an armed boat in one of the bayous—how could Galvez know what was going on in all the unguarded bayous of that great delta between floods and low water!—took a British frigate and captured Manchac. He seemed to have manned the frigate, or at least have armed another vessel, with which he made captures of indigo and other valuable stores including some British slaves in a catch-as-catch-can business up and down the deltas, searching the bayous and waylaying British ships off the river's mouth.

Meanwhile Willing, who had not looked to his defenses, had been on the loose along the banks and inland and, profiting by the full license of the customs of the time and the region in which Spanish Main traditions held, seems to have been unworried by any of Clark's scruples about the requisition of either public or private property. He was finally taken prisoner at Mobile.

Galvez might not be concerned with the prizes that friend Pollock had taken. They were Pollock's property to do with as he pleased, which meant more funds for his cause. He considered his private purse to be only a subtreasury branch of the States.

The British asked that he be delivered to them as a prisoner of war; but neither friend Galvez nor Don O'Reilly, Governor General of Cuba, would surrender so engagingly Irish an Irishman although they ran out of plausible excuses for not complying with the request.

When word came to the British commander at Pensacola, that strong point athwart the sea lanes between New Orleans and Cuba, that the devil was to pay on the lower Mississippi, his part was clear. He had ships, guns and a large garrison on which to draw for an expedition. Natchez and Manchac were retaken and fortified in the course of reprisals that taught the Willing adherents among the settlers the better part of valor.

Under no circumstance would the British yield the control of the Gulf and the lower Mississippi. This concerned the future land expansion of Britain when the American rebels had been properly chastised and were back penitent in the fold for their misdeeds. Pollock would certainly have never been among the contrite, not while there were Irish in Spain.

With things going against him and with the British in Philadelphia, this intrepid trader, separated by such distances from the battle front, was as good at keeping up a front of Jove as Clark. Patrick Henry no longer had any cash to pay for goods, but he still had ink and paper with which to write orders for Pollock to fill. If his cause had failed one imagines Henry, a recluse in his old age, still with quill in hand, the Don Quixote of volunteer foreign ministers. As the Revolution was won his shade may warrantably consider, in history's perspective, that his best title to fame was his part with reference to Clark, Pollock and Spain.

When bad news came from Washington's army he always had the solace that he could write another note to a Spanish governor. When Washington was holding on with his toenails Henry could propose that the States annex the Florida country—in reversal of his previous suggestion that it be returned to Spain—which, if the pen is mightier than the sword, after the pen has sung the sword out of its scabbard, would have removed the Pensacola thorn from the Spanish side and placed friends of Spain on the east bank of the lower Mississippi.

The Spanish did not object, but rather favored the idea; anything to encourage the rebels to keep on fighting ancient enemy Britain. In the same breath, perhaps as the reward

EARLIEST PICTURE OF NEW ORLEANS. A PRINT MADE IN 1803

of his suggestion, Henry asked Governor Galvez for the loan of one hundred thousand pistoles, or four hundred thousand dollars, in gold, to Virginia.

The useful Irishman might arrange that, too. Nothing could be gained without asking; and the Revolutionists became adept at asking in every possible quarter.

As much as he would like to be agreeable to his great and good friend, the Governor of Virginia, Galvez had to regret the refusal of the loan for the lack of funds.

Out of the sales of his contraband prizes and loans on his private property Pollock kept on buying supplies and shipping them. Henry was well warranted in thinking that when the need was so crying in the present fortunes of the cause, he had developed a real financier in New Orleans of the useful kind which could find money when the public treasury was empty. There must have been times when Pollock wanted to put ice on his head; but it was in the days before the making of artificial ice in hot countries and before the days when rich Louisiana sugar planters brought it in ships from Maine to put a crust of frost on their mint juleps.

When Clark received his paper money for the expedition another question arose. Inwardly, it must have been quite remote to Henry. This mad youngster might never be able to raise an army. If he were, the army might never get down the Ohio or it might be dissipated in defeat on the march. But in case of success—the question was one of future credits after the paper money was exhausted. Henry made this seem a detail. Nothing simpler. Clark would not pay in paper money. He would draw bills on Pollock to be paid in Spanish gold.

And Clark may have been glad that it would take so long for an answer from New Orleans as he drew on Pollock with the assurance that this was as much a matter of routine in national solvency as for Hamilton at Detroit to draw on Quebec. He probably made the most of the further impression of how wide had become the dominion of that new flag when it had a treasury agent in New Orleans.

If the bills had not been honored, he might have lost more than the support of merchant Gabriel Cerré. He would have been in the position of drawing worthless drafts at the expense of all the communities of the Illinois country.

With a few soldiers at your back in face of superior numbers it is easier to keep the front of Jove than with an empty purse in face of the clamor of creditors who feel that they have been bilked of their money under false pretenses. All that stood between Clark and the collapse of the empire built on his personality was the personality of that Irish trader to whom the States were already in debt.

When Manchac and Natchez had been lost and every express brought the news of a loss of a cargo at sea or another order, with no cash, for goods to be filled, Pollock received, in August, the news of Clark's success. His Irish imagination was as stirred as the Indian chiefs' wonder by that brilliant march and victory which raised the flag at Cahokia.

"I have succeeded agreeable to my wishes," Clark wrote to Pollock, "and am necessitated to draw bills on the state and have reason to believe that they will be accepted by you, the answering of which will be acknowledged by his Excellency, the Governor of Virginia."

More bills to be paid, more money wanted for the cause; but here were obligations not for a hazard yet to be made but for a hazard already won. Clark was asking for ammunition and clothing and quinine for victorious soldiers. Here was action that appealed to the active Pollock as a shining deed gleaming in the sunlight through a rift in a cloud of broken promises and collapsed schemes.

There was the ring of achievement in Clark's letter in character with Pollock's own pointed and business-like letters to Clark. These are preserved in the Draper collection with the ornate address on the thick rag paper envelopes which are still fresh although the ink is faded, showing how carefully the messengers guarded them.

What Natchez and Manchac were to New Orleans, Cahokia was to St. Louis. Pollock saw the Ohio junction to Pittsburgh as now secure. He hailed the prospect of this soldier after his own heart leading an expedition which would clear the Mississippi of the British all the way to the Gulf.

Just then creditors were pressing Pollock very hard owing to the loss of many of his cargoes. With his personality as collateral he got a further loan from a friend against funds expected from Henry. Clark should have the supplies he wanted. Pollock was finding a way to get them past the British river guard.

Word came back to the merchants of the Illinois country that the drafts were honored; and with it Pollock's vision appealing to Clark's to gather a force and push down the river "so as not to lose a valuable conquest which might now be easily obtained."

XXIII

TERESE DE LEYBA

CLARK never had to call a Cabinet meeting. His Cabinet rose when he rose and marched when he marched. As his own Secretary of State he had to look after other foreign relations than making treaties with Indian chiefs.

The new flag over Cahokia was a welcome sight to Spanish St. Louis. Any flag would have been in place of the British. No dispute about the boundary line arose when the old neighbor had been dispossessed. For the time being this was marked as distinctly by the Mississippi, although the crossing took only a few minutes by paddle or oar, as the British Channel marks that between England and France.

On the remote frontier Spanish etiquette was likely to be more punctilious about an exchange of official calls than nearer Madrid. There was the routine that concerned passports and traffic to be looked after. The treatment of merchant Cerré was an example in point which might allay the apprehensions of Spanish merchants about interference with trade by the new régime.

Clark and Don Fernando De Leyba, Governor of Upper Louisiana with headquarters at St. Louis, had a personal surprise for each other. De Leyba must have been prepared for a boastful swaggering conqueror of the uncouth and crude mannered Big Knife type of which he had heard. Although Clark was offensive De Leyba must be ingratiating in keeping with the hint that came up the river from New Orleans by way of Galvez from O'Reilly, and to O'Reilly from Madrid, that Spain might soon be at open war with Britain, with the American colonists as allies. On his part, Clark fully appreciated friendship with Spain.

To be trite yet expressive, De Leyba's first thought upon meeting Clark must have been, "Why, he is a gentleman!" The son of Ann's careful breeding could also be a gracious grandee.

"An intimacy had commenced," Clark wrote in his letter to Mason, "between Don Leyba and myself. As I never before was in the company of any Spanish gentleman, I was much surprised in my expectations; for, instead of finding that reserve, thought peculiar to that nation, I here saw not the least symptoms of it. Freedom almost to excess gave the greatest pleasure."

Such progress had Clark made that he wrote to Governor Henry, "This gentleman interests himself much in favor of the States—more so than I could have expected. He has offered me all the force he could raise in case of an attack of the Indians from Detroit."

It was not the prospect of armed aid, should Spain be at war with Britain, nor the Governor's own affability which, probably, gave his hospitality its chief appeal.

In the Governor's household, aside from his wife, the Lady Maria de la Conception y Zerar, was his young sister, Terese De Leyba. Some historians find no documentary evidence of a love affair between George Rogers and Terese. This is true in that nothing in Clark's hand and nothing in hers or her brother's in the way of proof has come down to us. The family tradition of the letters exchanged between them tells us that his letters were long since ashes mixed with the soil of Spain for reasons which will later appear.

The historian, who is so captious in discounting every item which is not on paper or sworn to, might be reminded that even in the modern days of publicity a phonograph is not set up in an arbor on a moonlight night to record the words of betrothal. Nor do the blissful pair, lacking a dictaphone, rush to a public stenographer for a prompt re-script while memory is fresh, and then have it attested before a notary public in order to make future research easy for what is called "human interest stuff about celebrities," should the groom become President of the United States or one day pay the largest income tax of our millionaires.

In this instance to remain wholly sceptical, after reading John Todd's letters to Clark at Vincennes, requires a literal archivist whose part is not to concern himself with probing for the causes of surprising actions and inconsistencies which the available documents reveal when the vitally important explanatory ones have evidently been destroyed.

"If I could get an opportunity of sending you something good to Toast your Sweetheart in I would," Todd wrote. "Perhaps I may by Colonel Bowman." And again: "Madame De Leyba is dead. Mlle. Terese still a maid."

There is no record or suggestion in the many volumes of the Draper manuscripts of interest in any other woman by this spirited passionate youth whose soldier sternness melted into gayety at dances and parties. Did he never fall in love? If he did fall in love, with whom if not Terese? Else why the toast to his sweetheart? Else why, when he was fiercely campaigning and out of touch with St. Louis, did Todd mention Terese in otherwise strictly business letters?

Clark, who was so given to keeping his own counsels, would have hardly carried his heart on his sleeve when its beat was speeded by the love of a woman. Here was a precious secret to be guarded by one to whom guarding secrets had become a habit. For her sake he might well conceal their love in his realization that the hazards of his situation might make it fruitless except as the happy dream of a future possibility when all his battles were won. In lovers' meetings, as well as in councils of war and of state, the words on which action and decision are pivoted are often never set down in writing.

When Clark was striving to compass so much by sheer

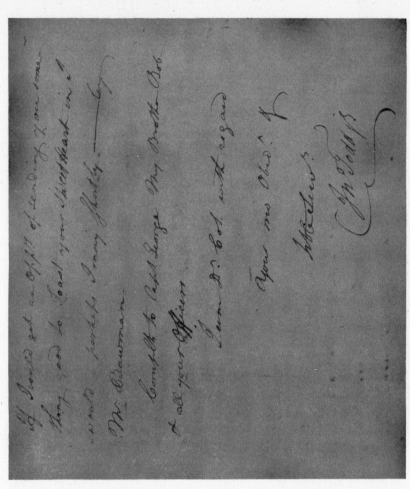

THE LETTER TO CLARK FROM JOHN TODD, JR., REFERRING TO TERESE DE LEYBA. *Draper manuscript*

force of personality he was under a bright light no less, even more so in the little gossiping settlements, than if he ruled a thickly populated region. His every movement was watched for a sign of his thought and intentions or the first suggestion that he might have a heel of Achilles. He could not afford the repute of philandering trips to St. Louis which was sixty miles from Kaskaskia.

In one passage of his Memoir there is a hint of the lover's self-consciousness, either reflective of the desire for concealment or a self-reminder of his obligations to duty in the face of temptation. He mentions how the friendly exchange of visits "between the Spanish officers and ourselves added much to the general tranquillity and happiness." And he adds:

"It was not my fortune to enjoy pleasures of this kind. I found myself embarked upon an enterprise that would require close attention and all the skill of which I was master to execute for the service of my country which now appeared in prospect, with honor to it and credit to myself."

After going through the Draper manuscripts it does not seem to me to be embellishing fact with imagination to accept the family traditions about Clark and Terese. I would not compromise verity by yielding to the old saw that where there is much smoke there must be some fire. Here was fuel tinder-dry for a great flame which can be managed, Indian fashion, to send up little smoke just as well as a tiny blaze of wet wood may be smudged to broadcast a signal column of smoke that rises above the tree tops.

I was of a mind, too, to resist the old entreating quest of *cherchez la femme* which, however, is based on the sound premise of the mighty factor of love of man for woman in affecting careers both great and small. But conviction as to the actuality of a high romance, unsurpassed in our history, led me to surrender delightfully to the thought of this young Virginian, spearhead of the advance of the absorptive seaboard civilization, losing his heart to the daughter of old Spain on the banks of the great river.

Love of Terese helps to explain Clark after Vincennes; the Clark who became a recluse; the Clark who, after winning an empire, acted as if he had lost an empire.

What a meeting place in 1778 for contrasting human backgrounds, creeds and social conventions and governmental systems, the Governor's house in St. Louis! On one side of the river was the flag of eager youth; on the other that of husbanding old age wrapped in formulas of the past which was to be its death shroud. The world saw the young flag on a slender trembling reed of a staff set in the quicksand of vain teachings of democratic rule. After hungry marches, sheer audacity had brought it to what seemed the goal of ambition gone mad, when it was not yet half way across the continent.

So, too, in Cortez' and Pizzaro's time the old flag, when it was young, had been borne by little bands of men sweating in steel armor through the blistering heat of deserts and the parboiling heat of jungles and up high mountain passes. But that was in a far yesterday, farther than our first settlements over the western watershed from to-day. Age, which developed quickly on bonanza riches, rested on what youth had won and drew checks on its capital which it mistook for income.

In the Philippines and Cuba, on the opposite sides of the earth, and from Patagonia through all the climates spanned from the extremes of the temperate zones, the Spanish flag still floated. The marvel of the island of Britain as hub of the present British empire is not more wonderful now than the possession then by the Spanish peninsula, with its small population, of such vast areas.

Standardization has not been carried farther in our mechanistic civilization of to-day than in the forming and the ruling of the Spanish empire. While the seaboard communities were extending streets along irregular cowpaths in individualistic bent, the Spanish laid out towns according to a single blue print bearing the royal stamp. They were all governed by the same covering set of laws, having the sanction of the divine authority of church and state which was far more arbitrary with the Spanish than with the French under the Bourbons. There was one way to do a thing and in this way all must do it. This foresight, in which autocracy prides itself, sowed for a bad harvest while individualism, which is supposed to have no foresight for the whole, sowed for a good harvest.

In every town was a plaza. Facing the plaza were the government buildings, the Governor's palace, the barracks, the church, the seminary, the priest's house or the Bishop's palace. With the exception of the wives of the officials and rich merchants, few women immigrants came. So were bred the future generations of half breeds who were one day to become the ruling caste of the ins and outs of succeeding revolutions, when Spanish emperors had gone mad or effete from the strain of autocracy, and the house of cards, which was set up by ancestral standardization, began falling about their heads until the last was down and there was only the glory of the past for consolation.

The Spanish plan was sound enough, granted the soundness of its premise, and Spanish laws sound in theory, as we learned when we took over the Philippines, the last outpost of decadence. Failure came in practice as in all autocracies, in the weakening of the standards down through the grades when all authority came from the top.

Spain's pioneers, the *conquistadores*, as we know went for gold. They enriched themselves in the loot of gold that was already mined or in opening new mines. And so, in turn, those who succeeded them, on through the generations, went to the colonies to enrich themselves.

A Spanish governor was not of the mind to live on his
pay. His credit was in making virtue of that moderation
which Warren Hastings pleaded as palliation in face of his
temptations. The other links made common intrigue against
the very highly courageous official who in his honesty defied
custom and thereby broke the chain of connivance in corruption. In England, at least, there was a public opinion
which was vented in the voices of protesting members on the
floor of Parliament against royal governors guilty of excess.

Appointments, preferments and promotion were gained in
the Spanish colonial service through family influence, friends
at court, the favor of superiors and presents in the right
quarters. But for her trained civil service, under so rigidly
a selective process which drew such a high class of personnel
with its superb traditions of incorruptibility, Britain might
long ago have lost India.

The amazing thing was the endurance of those thin
threads of authority which were spun into the distances from
the throne in Madrid as a web in holding the parts of the
Spanish empire together. It was a tribute to the high ruling
qualities of one of the great imperial systems of history
which had more *laissez-faire* and wisdom than it is credited
with in the control of peoples who labored for its profit.

All dons, all with inherited grandee pride, these Spanish
governors were as certain as all aristocracies that the plum
tree would never cease bearing. The fall of the Spanish
empire was as inconceivable to the average Spaniard in the
seventeen seventies as the fall of the Roman or the Russian
empire to the average Roman of the Augustan period or
the average Russian when the late Nicholas succeeded his
father on the throne.

The young dons of Spain were brought up in the at-
mosphere of far flung dependencies. When family fortunes
ran low they sought colonial berths. It was their call to

travel much the same as the Ohio had been to Clark. In Madrid the thought was not of dying empire but of expanding empire which supplied still more berths for officials and army officers in the recent addition of all that domain which is known now as the "Louisiana Purchase" on maps which block off the successive territorial acquisitions of the United States.

We may see Don Fernando De Leyba and his wife and young sister leaving New Orleans on the way up the Mississippi to the North American wilderness. There were official courtesies for him at New Orleans, stirrup cups and farewell dinners. The British flag was dipped for him at Natchez.

The new Governor of Upper Louisiana was on his way to his post at St. Louis! Parties of hunters, or of wandering Indians, had this explanation of why a gentleman was traveling in such state. His were all the available honors in the great valley which are given to a touring monarch in the present time.

We may see the De Leybas on cushions in the stern of the big boat under an awning to protect them from the sun and rain. Whole days passed without a sign of human life. It would be cooler when they reached their journey's end, as cool in Winter as the Pyrenees they were told. They might even see snow. Midstream was best. There were not so many mosquitoes. It was well to take quinine even if you had not a touch of fever. Mississippi! What a word! So many "esses" in that English language which resembled the hissing of geese to ears used to sonorous Spanish!

There was little to talk about, not much impressive scenery. There was no sound except of the dipping of the oars in the stream, the heavy breathing of the twenty black oarsmen, or their soft voiced jokes and plaints. Again the strumming of a guitar, perhaps by Terese herself, broke the monotony with old Spanish airs.

It was a tedious journey, but all in the life of Spanish governors no less than six or seven days in a steamer across the Atlantic for the tourist of to-day. Servants looked after every practicable want of him who was the great man of Spain in all the wide region of forests and plains in the remote north. St. Louis was not so bad a prospect. Don Fernando would send the delicacy of a smoked buffalo tongue to his friends at court. There were good profits in furs. Don Fernando might yet have a comfortable old age in a castle in Spain.

What was the life of the convent bred Terese in St. Louis? What companionship had she? The wives of Spanish officials and merchants and French on the other side of the river, and young officers of the garrison. There were trips across to Cahokia, occasional balls. Traders brought pelts to sell. Terese might have her pick of furs. Grave Indian chiefs appeared with their arguments and petitions. When one mail arrived from Spain you might look forward to the next. It might arrive in a week or a month or three months. Long letters were to be written for the outgoing post.

There was the majestic companionship of the river which was to weave its spell over Mark Twain who passed it on to his readers in prose that had the power of the Mississippi's flow. Sometimes the river was placid as a lake. Again it was swollen in flood as islands detached from forests rushed past. Its daily temper was set by rains and snows of regions which the Governor knew only through the tales of traders and Indians.

And Terese had embroidery and a flower garden, prayers and masses and the many *devoirs* of a Spanish girl of the period. She heard such gossip as her sister-in-law thought fit for her to hear. Perhaps she heard some forbidden bits from servants when her sister-in-law was out of the room. She might not go riding and walking alone. This was dangerous when Indian moods were as uncertain as the river's in the Spring.

No young man might accompany her. This was not proper, not even if she were engaged, only if she were married. She must have had a dull time, or perhaps she did not know that it was. At all events it was not proper for her to say so, or to be natural. Convention forbade this no less than laying out a town without a plaza and placing the Bishop's palace at one end of the main street and the Governor's palace at the other end.

Then monotony was broken by news as startling to St. Louis as to Buffalo, in our day, that an aërial force had landed at Toronto and raised the flag of another European power. The Big Knives had taken Kaskaskia. They were at Cahokia. With glasses you could see their colors over the fort.

Terese had heard about the awful customs of the American colonists, although certainly the Lady Maria could never have imparted to virgin ears the indecency of the "bundling" method of courtship of the Bostonnais. However, as an example of the social license of the heretics from the Mother Church, she might be told how both Big Knife and Bostonnais mothers permitted their daughters to sit alone before the fire, or to go riding along little frequented lanes with a young man, unaccompanied by a married woman. How could any girl remain virtuous when such practices were in vogue? It was against sex nature.

A frank discussion on the correct upbringing of daughters between Maria De Leyba and Ann Clark would have been diverting. We may see the majestic scorn of Ann, in her faith in womanhood's right thinking after maternal tutoring, of the carnal hypothesis of Spanish mothers—while Maria concluded that it was useless to argue with heretics who never went to confession.

The girl who may not think aloud may think in secret. When Terese had letters from friends in Spain about the gay times they were having she might imagine the glad day of her return. She had many idle hours for dreams, which her sister-in-law could not censor, there at the lonely outpost on the Mississippi.

When she heard of Clark's feat and how young he was she might wonder if this Big Knife barbarian, this Cid of the wilderness, was as terrible as his reputation. Would he put his feet on the governor's table and swear monstrous oaths between Indian grunts and eat his meat raw with his fingers?

When she met him he had the advantage of surprise no less than he had for the people of Kaskaskia. Again the fact was a complete reversal of anticipation. If her dear sister Maria's pictures of Big Knife uncouthness had been so much in error her dear Maria possibly might be wrong about other things.

He was tall and fair, and she, we are told, was small and dark. His manners were not those of the dons, but they were charming and refreshing, the more interesting because they were different. When he spoke to her he had to bow his great head and she had to lift hers and his eyes had laughing gleams in their mysterious depths. The miracle warrior to the Indians who had made her brother and all soldiers marvel! He was as a giant red headed Visigoth who had such power over palefaces and savages when he was so young. Yet one who was small and dark might have power over him.

Virginian girls riding with their beaux along deserted lanes homecoming from the hunt! Virginian girls sitting out dances with their beaux under honeysuckle vines on a summer night! Demure Bostonnais girls loitering with their beaux on the way home from prayer meeting! Spanish girls in lace mantillas! Spanish girls listening to serenades

behind barred windows and tossing out a note or a flower
in daring coquetry!

And Virginian voices were soft in those days. Probably
Clark had a pleasant accent. In what language could he and
Terese make each other understood? She must have known
convent French. He may have learned a little French from
the people in Kaskaskia.

Love that laughs at locksmiths does not need an extensive
vocabulary of mere words. It has a language of its own in
which Spanish girls are still highly proficient and in which
Clark was far from deficient when he had such brilliant
eyes.

Spanish girls could use their eyes over the shoulders of
their elders from the edge of a flirtatious fan. Perhaps their
eyes were the brighter in compensating reprisal on the
rigid conventions. And Spanish mothers, or aunts who
took their places, were not opposed to skillful fan play.
They, no less, even more, than those of other lands, were
thinking of the marriage market; and they would display
the goods, but inside a locked glass case to enhance their
value to a prospective groom who was warned that any
intimacy was procurable only by the key of marriage.

So inside the case, the jewel might sparkle its best, and
eye sign language was well developed in Spain in want of
other means of communication between lovers. Spanish custom may have been the product of the universality of lus-
trous dark feminine eyes.

Terese's eyes caught the message, a message which other
than Spanish women can quickly detect, from the eyes of
the warrior who had set her heart to tripping in the realization that the chief of the Big Knives had winning qualities
in other things than war. He might have told her of Virginian ways and she might have found it pleasing that one
did not have to stay all the time in a glass case, as she saw
in his eyes that respect for womanhood by man which, in

the seaboard custom, was its truest protection. She might have increased his French vocabulary by teaching him new words or introducing him to Spanish words.

This is an old form of play which gives eyes an excellent opportunity. It might be enjoyed in one of the so strictly conversational conversations which were one of the most characteristic bits of mechanization of the standardized Spanish etiquette.

Such conversations went on from the Pyrenees to Gibraltar; from Patagonia to St. Louis. The men were ranged in one straight row of chairs facing the women who were ranged in the other. There was no "switching" to the right and left; rarely had one a choice of the person who was his *vis-à-vis*. The object was to converse. George Rogers' fate may have been that, owing to his rank, he had to sit opposite the aunt instead of Terese when time was so precious to him. In love as in war he had to be swift, and he had also to keep his objective from the prying eyes of the enemy scouts.

Did Governor De Leyba know of the infatuation? If his wife had a suspicion of it she was more than ever the guardian of convention to prevent Terese ever being alone with this strange adventurer of the conquering manner. Terese may even have been brought from Spain because she had fancies, after leaving the convent, which would not warrant her being left at home with relatives.

The De Leybas' conjugal concern about the domestic situation was complicated by the necessity of keeping friends with Colonel Clark. In his heart the Governor may have been a Spanish tory who held with the old régime of the Phillips. Those strange, stubborn, narrow, devotional Spanish kings who wrought so much through such errors even as other rulers have! Squandering their treasure won from the colonies in wars for family reasons! Expelling the Jews who took with them their hoards of gold with which extravagant grandees parted so readily! Trying to subdue the heretics of Flanders instead of conserving the profits of their over sea empire!

Charles III was now on the Spanish throne. The "philosophical monarch" was bent on building roads and internal reforms, but getting into wars which were hard on his neglected army and navy. Even his comparatively liberal mind could have hardly had any sympathy with the American cause except in purely political policy. His rejoicing over the anarchistic Declaration of Independence was that it was such a bitter pill for Protestant enemy King George who, after all, had only his heretic self to blame when he allowed a Parliament to indulge in as much loose talk as it chose and to make all the silly laws it pleased.

Deep in his royal heart, touching the freemasonry of kings, Charles must have felt that this colonial rabble, happily Britain's and not Spain's brood, should suffer the punishment for defying divine right which Spain would inflict upon transgressors of the same kind. If the kings of France and Spain had then struck hands in class interest the first revolution in the new world might have failed. When, later, they joined in the Holy Alliance the mischief had been done. So we owe much to official diplomat Benjamin Franklin serving at the court of France, and something to volunteer diplomat Patrick Henry who was so liberal in drawing bills on Oliver Pollock's credit.

And, moreover, De Leyba had to consider his personal fortunes in not offending Clark who was acting generously toward Colonel Vigo, a former officer of the Spanish army, who was the Governor's partner in his business ventures. Vigo became such a ready proselyte of the absorptive Clark vision, so sturdy a partisan of the American cause, that a county of the future state of Indiana was named after him. He may have also been a partisan of the romance and understood, as one who had been long away from Spain in strange lands, how the very limitations of convention and the contrast of backgrounds added to the glamour which the giant had for the lady who was small and dark, and which she had for him.

Her slightness and daintiness must have appealed to the male protective sense of the powerful frontiersman. No explicit vow may then have passed between the two. A glance was enough to bridge the Mississippi for them. The girl whom he left behind him knew that she had his heart.

Castles in Spain! But he would not build his castle for her there! The pioneer would raise his cabin in the wilderness to which he would bring his bride, according to the custom of the Bostonnais and the Big Knives. He would be rich in lands when the war was over and his vision of new towns and settlements came true. He would sweep her away to a new mansion in the blue grass region, one as grand as those of the great planters of Virginia, where there would be many servants to do her bidding and they would look out upon their prospering domain from their white-pillared porch.

Family traditions, when taken in connection with remarks of his own, suggest that this was the dream that he carried as his supreme secret. A sentimental Clark! He imbibed sentiment in childhood in the little valleys. It flourished on the frontier, expanded in the great valley. Leave it so. The lady must wait, and she did wait.

He might not see her often when autumn rains made going heavy to Cahokia and he must be always in touch with Kaskaskia and Vincennes. The absence of familiarity may have heightened the enchantment. If he were ever to have that white-pillared mansion for his Terese he must not lose the country he had won, America must not lose the war. It was as simple as this, the love of the young Colonel of the ragged rebel militia and the daughter of old Spain.

XXIV

TRACKS IN THE SNOW

No replacements for Clark's time-expired men had arrived; no word of any being on the way, no word from Governor Henry acknowledging his reports, no word from home, no word of the fortunes of Washington's army in the summer campaign. Winter was closing in. On his twenty-sixth birthday Clark had reason for concluding that he was a forgotten son of Virginia lost in the wilderness.

"It was now that I saw that my work had only begun," he wrote.

This called for a different brand of eloquence than that which had won Indian chiefs. If it failed Vincennes might not be the only town in his empire which had a garrison of two. He must win service-weary, homesick soldiers, who had so faithfully earned their over due honorable discharges, to further service in a region where they had found no free land to their liking.

He rallied the time-expired men as brothers in arms on the lean march, rekindled their imaginations to the great cause that had set them on the trail. Would they desert what they had won, refuse to finish their task, quit before the trail's end? When they had followed his red head as a flaming banner they could not resist the dominant call of his flashing eyes—not those who had no families at home, no excuse except their own pleasure.

"Remember me to Kaintuck! Tell Governor Henry we are still here. My regards to all my friends in Fauquier County. If you meet a girl in the inn at—"

Such must have been the messages to the outgoing, bearing

many letters, as they pushed off the boats from the Kaskaskia bank.

About one hundred men remained. And the sight of them was good to George Rogers Clark. He was again the stern commander who explained why he must be stern to veterans to whom he refers as "still raw and undisciplined troops." It was a comment that would have been surprising to drillmaster von Steuben who was used to colonels of American militia thinking that they already knew it all, and had taught it all to their volunteers, after three months' service.

"Strict subordination was my first object," Clark writes, "it being the matter of the greatest consequence to persons in our situation."

Had he, who studied French and Spanish treaties and methods with the Indians, taken a note out of the great book of colonial experience which enabled little garrisons of long-service British regulars, and before them little detachments of Roman legions, to hold in order large populations through conduct, prestige and appearance no less than by skill at arms?

He knew that every one of his soldiers was an example in conduct to impress the sense of American power and standards upon French and Indians. They had come as the missionaries of a new dispensation in government. They must live up to this idea and act up to it in honor and for their own self-preservation. He did not bandy words in telling them of his resolution to carry out thorough regulations and drill which were so much more necessary now that their numbers were reduced.

They were no automatons who took discipline blindly in fear of royal displeasure or because their ancestors had accepted it. Theirs was the then new American "Why?" of which our officers still complain. Although it may be an excuse for lawlessness it never leads to stagnation, and when convinced it means the teamplay which is the flower of discipline.

Clark's men understood his purpose in the instinct of the pioneers, of the cult of the seaboard civilization whose character won the Revolution and strove to set in its own mold all the immigrants which were in the future to be dumped into the melting pot. Occasionally these veterans might slip, occasionally they might drink too much, but they knew the why of their presence in remote Kaskaskia, as something other than an adventure or a land prospecting trip.

"You must be sensible of the pleasure I felt," Clark wrote in his letter to George Mason, "for them to return me for answer that it was their zeal for their country that induced them to engage in that service; that they were sensible of their situation and danger; that nothing could more conduce to their happiness than good order which they would try to adhere to; and hoped that no favor would be shown those that would neglect it."

This was not so bad for these rebels whom the Royal Breast had proscribed as a rabble of ruffians while some of our historians have come to accept the same view after reading tory pamphlets of the time. It was to be a sustaining factor in the crisis that Clark was soon to face.

And the son of the majestic Ann says that, having striven for discipline, he "effected it."

December drew to a close with no word from Patrick Henry, which Clark found mystifying and irritating if not ominous. Pollock, who was selling his property and winning new loans from friends, was dispatching more supplies and also some cannon up the Mississippi. Everything in Clark's empire seemed secure until campaigning weather began in the Spring.

All the Messrs. Clark of the different departments seemed to be giving a satisfactory administration. The Indians were still friendly. The fur trade was flourishing. Young men in both Kaskaskia and Cahokia had formed companies of militia who were drilling under the new flag. Clark was looking forward to a merry Christmas for all hands.

What of Hamilton? What of Detroit? Clark's apprehension on that score had been lulled by an express from the Falls that McIntosh's army had started from Pittsburgh. Clark momentarily expected to learn that Detroit had been taken.

Then bad news piled on bad news, the first item revealed by an incident at Cahokia. A man named Denny was arrested there by Major Bowman. He was found to have recent correspondence with Hamilton in his possession. The penalty for a spy in time of war then as now was death. But Denny received a punishment in which the people had a part.

"He was tied to the tail of a cart," Clark wrote, "and driven through the town, receiving a lash at every door. He was also branded in the hand for other misdemeanors. This was the first and the severest punishment inflicted by us on any of the inhabitants. It was necessary at this time to convince the people that we were capable of extremes either way, and that the good treatment we had heretofore shown was due to our principles of government."

There might be other spies. This was a warning to them. It was a light penalty for the time for a man who had on his person a letter containing "dangerous information" which he was about to send to Hamilton. Any citizen who might have pitied Denny if he had been hanged as a spy might now remember that he had added his lash stroke to the victim's back.

Other papers taken from Denny told how Hamilton had roused all his Indians to resist McIntosh; then how Hamilton, having learned that McIntosh had returned to Pittsburgh, was preparing an expedition to clean Clark out of the Illinois country. Further confirmation of one particular soon came from the Falls of the Ohio. McIntosh had spent the Summer in parades and abortive forays and in building a few forts. He had not had Clark's success in "effecting discipline" of his militia which he had disbanded upon the approach of Winter.

Trails to the north were snowbound, ice had formed in the lakes and rivers. It would seem that Hamilton would wait until Spring for campaigning weather before attacking Kaskaskia. Yet what of Vincennes where Captain Helm held the fort with one American soldier? The bi-monthly post had not arrived. Although bad conditions for traveling might readily account for the delay, Clark sent scouts toward Vincennes.

With a portion of his troops at Cahokia he did not parade his Kaskaskia garrison as a whole lest the weakness of his numbers be realized. His pretension that his force was only an advance guard of the main army coming from the Falls was having a hollow sound in the gossip of the streets. The Indian chiefs might be listening again to bad birds. He knew that Detroit's emissaries, well supplied with wampum, were circulating among the tribes with whom he had signed treaties.

The nearest armed Americans were two hundred miles away in the Kentucky settlements. There was no hope of aid from them. The families who had been the garrison of Clark's new base at Corn Island had, by Clark's orders, reaped their harvests and moved to the mainland where he thought that they would be more secure. That hard-bitten mercenary, McKee, was concentrating braves to attack Boonesboro; but Boone, who had been a prisoner of the Indians, escaped in time to warn the settlers.

McIntosh on the defensive at Pittsburgh! The latest word from Pollock, as he cadged funds at New Orleans, that the British were heavily reinforcing their Pensacola garrison and strengthening their river guard! Hamilton with three hundred British regulars at Detroit aside from his Canadian militia and Indians!

Clark's work, indeed, had only begun. He was occupied by much thought about "things in general" as he seemed to surrender in apparent freedom from all worry to French merry making in the Christmas holiday season. If no reinforcements came from Henry he might have to abandon Cahokia and concentrate upon the defense of Kaskaskia. Anyhow, Hamilton would probably take Vincennes before he attacked Kaskaskia.

Was it only to judge the situation in the other settlements that led Clark to set out for Cahokia in a snowstorm? Or was it that he wanted to see Terese?

The storm abated soon after he was out of town. All the land was white. Those fresh tracks in the snow, along the road for some distance before they broke away from the main road! Probably they were made by Kaskaskians, but usually the townsmen did not set out on a journey in a storm, and rarely on foot.

Clark, as usual, had a small guard. Some of the civil members of his party were in *charrettes*. One of the *charrettes* sank in a swamp. His fellow travelers enjoyed a laugh over the predicament of its occupant before they went to his assistance.

There were other spectators of the incident, the men who had made the tracks, hidden behind some logs nearby. Before them sharing the raillery was the prize whom they sought. Clark had too many rifles with him for them to dare an attack which might defeat their object should he be killed in the exchange of shots. They had learned that he planned to go to Cahokia, but had not expected him to start in a storm. They were scouts from the hidden camp of an expedition of white rangers and Indians whom Hamilton had sent to capture Clark himself.

Orders were positive to bring him in alive. Under no circumstances was he to be harmed, but treated with all respect and courtesy and zealously guarded. When word should be passed that he was the prisoner of Hamilton's ambush, there would be an end to his prestige as a devil brother of the Great Spirit, and all good birds would be British again and all bad birds Big Knife.

Clark did not know that the men were behind the logs or of their purpose. This time his trailsman's eye and instinct failed him. But this was not to be the end of the tale of the tracks in the snow in that wilderness world.

After Clark had dinner at Prairie du Rocher the people would celebrate in honor of the visit from the commandant. The presence of any guests in a settlement was always an excuse for a dance. One was in full swing when a messenger brought word to Clark that a party of white men and Indians, all strangers to the region, had appeared on the outskirts of Kaskaskia. They said that Hamilton with an army of eight hundred whites and Indians would attack Kaskaskia that night. It would seem that Hamilton's scouts had made the tracks in the snow. Clark was in the humiliating position of a commander who was absent from his command in desperate case.

Grim alarm silenced the fiddle and struck the smiles from the faces of the dancers who envisioned behind the messenger in the doorway an Indian with an upraised tomahawk. They knew the savage license that would have free rein in their little settlement if fighting began at Kaskaskia. They gathered around Clark warning him that he could not resist such numbers and begging him to retreat to the Spanish side of the river.

Of course, he laughed at their fears, although he was sorely worried. Let them go on with the dance. He would take care of the Indians. He made so light of the danger that after the horses for him and his guard had been brought some of the young men asked that they might join him; but they would be only a handicap in executing the ruse he had in mind.

If Hamilton's army had surrounded the town Clark must rejoin his garrison through its lines. Having borrowed frontiersmen's garb from the inhabitants he would join the attacking Indians, who he thought, in the confusion, would mistake him for English. Thus he would reach the gate of the fort and be admitted.

His horse was given the spur until he came near the town. Then, in his cautious approach, he became an intense student of tracks in the snow. There were not many—not enough for an army. The streets were silent. It was a "joyous welcome," he tells us, that he had from his men who were on the alert. Their commander was back. His face had never looked so "good" to them or theirs to him. They, too, had heard the report of Hamilton's approach. It was brought in by negroes who had been warned on pain of death by the scouting party not to tell of having seen them.

Sentries were out, scouts sent farther. Hamilton's horde at least was not near enough to attack that night; but there was no sleep for Clark. Morning showed that he had time for further preparation no matter how swift Hamilton's onslaught when it was sprung. Many other details than having his soldiers at their posts must be arranged. If the fort had been on a hill with a clean field of fire around it the problem of standing siege would have been simpler. It was in a town. The part of the inhabitants had to be considered. They must not hamper the free swing of the swordsman's arm in mortal fence.

Leading citizens were again before Clark in a very different situation than when he had taken the town. The people, certain that Hamilton's army was near, were in panic. They were burying their treasure again, locking their chests, and in a babble of confusion. King Louis of France might be on the side of the Americans, but that held no promise that if the Americans won, the settlements would be under French rule. They would be under the Big Knives. If King George won they would be under him. In either event they were lost to France.

And the Indians fought on the side of the British. They would loot, murder, scalp, take babes in arms away as prisoners in their camps. From their ancestors' stories the Kaskaskians knew the ordeal before them. They sought peace under any Cæsar. Where was that army which was coming to succor Clark? It was clear he was hopelessly outnumbered. They warned him that the British would fire the town. They begged him to retreat to the Mississippi.

Although they had seen him angry, this was the first experience of him in a supreme red headed rage. He had suddenly become as terrible, this kindly ruler, as the fiercest Big Knife of legend. President Clark, civil administrator, executive of all the cabinet offices in his government, was now in the part of the ruthless soldier reading the riot act.

He wrote in his letter to George Mason:

"I seldom found that I could govern my temper at pleasure"—a fact about his disciple that the serene lawyer must have known almost as well as mother Ann—"but this declaration of theirs and some other circumstances put me in a most violent rage, and as soon as I could curb my passion I gave them a lecture suitable for such a set of traitors, although I could not conceive the whole of them to be such."

They could expect no favor from him, no pity. Burn the town? He was going to set fire to it himself. So he did to the buildings, adjoining the fort, which interfered with a free field of fire for his men and would give the attackers cover. This was a military precaution no less in order than that of French gunners of a later generation shelling a French town in which the enemy was posted, or destruction of adjacent houses by a fire department to prevent the spread of flames.

"Never was a set of people in more distress," Clark writes, "their town set on fire by those they wished to be in friendship with, at the same time surrounded by savages"—and in midwinter.

The Kaskaskians were between the devil and the deep sea, their lot that of neutral communities, time out of mind, to have their town made a battlefield. They had asked for war no less than for a hurricane, an earthquake or a pestilence, but here war was in its cloudburst, a fact.

The snow on the roofs prevented the spread of the fire beyond the houses Clark would destroy; it would prevent Hamilton easily firing his wooden fort. Leave the rest to his riflemen at the loopholes.

The panic of the people changed to helpless lethargy at the sight of the flames, and then to action under commands that set them to work bringing in provisions for the siege. For they realized that they better do as they were told by this *diable au corps* of the red hair. He had made his fate theirs in a vivid application of the argument of the founding fathers about hanging together so as not to hang separately. The courage of self-preservation revived. The young French militiamen were ready for their part to supplement the part of Clark's veterans at the loopholes.

We are from the Holston, from the Monongahela and hills and valleys still farther away. Come on you Hairbuyer General! Colonel Clark is waiting to entertain you. Come on you ramrod-backed British redcoats and you massacring, wampum-bribed savages! When you are through with us you will know you have been in a fight.

XXV

HAMILTON'S COUNTER STROKE

LITTLE that a Bostonnais learned at Harvard or Yale, or a Big Knife at William and Mary, would be of service in the great valley in the seventeen seventies. If, in one sense, education were not high among the frontiersmen, in another it was postgraduate with honors in special courses to fit them for their careers.

They learned their lessons altogether in the laboratory rather than in theory. Their ruthless teachers might summon them to an examination at any moment. To fail of passing mark in the emergency might mean death or starvation.

They had instruction in a logic as unanswerable as that of mathematics in their battle with nature—a battle not only of the courage gleaming in the straight glance of their eyes but of trained wits. For two veteran trailsmen to look into each other's minds was about as complicated a process in projection as for two highly sophisticated lawyers before they present highly technical cases in court.

Old hands had learned tricks in subtlety from the Indian, that master of the "poker face," and from wild animals. The fox was cunning; there were squirrel answers; the weasel was quick. Men prevaricated with weasel words, they dissimulated by playing 'possum. To work hard was to be a beaver. The rattlesnake sounded a warning, but not the panther; the bumblebee buzzed, but not the hornet. A skunk fouled the premises of others.

Old hands knew how to march twenty men in single file so that their tracks looked as if only two or three had passed. They could decipher many messages from tracks which

were just tracks to the townsman. Clark's scouts brought
back word soon after he had Kaskaskia in a state of defense that the only sign of a number of men in movement
within several miles of the fort were tracks leading toward
Vincennes.

The present danger was over but not the apprehension.
As the soldiers and civilians settled back to routine, and
Clark, still sharply on the alert, waits for the return of
other messengers from the snow covered trails, the scene
shifts to Detroit, eight hundred miles away, and the actual
response of Hamilton to Clark's successes.

Hamilton directed British military policy over an enormous area. His sector stretched from the great lakes over
the St. Lawrence watershed and then downhill and then
uphill across many valleys in the great valley. It ended on
the natural east and west frontier of the Cumberland range
which was the bastion of fierce give and take between the
western armies of the North and South in the Civil War.
On the other side was the Florida country which was under
the British commander at Pensacola.

An expedition against Pittsburgh was Hamilton's great
ambition. He had instructions from his superiors reminding
him that his forays were not to be limited to that region
or to the Kentucky settlements. He was sending bands to
the mouth of the Ohio to cut off any Revolutionist supplies,
which might pass the forts on the lower Mississippi, from
reaching Pittsburgh.

So carefully had Clark guarded the trails that it was
not until August 6th, five weeks after the event, that Hamilton had an express telling him of the capture of Kaskaskia, and this came by way of Cahokia. Every day of this
delay was invaluable to Clark in establishing his authority
and winning over the Indian tribes and still more vital for
another reason as we shall see.

Even on August 6th, Hamilton did not know that Clark

was in command of the expedition, but as he wrote, "it seems that they are but a part of those marauders who left Fort Pitt last January under one Willan (Willing) a man of one of the best families of Philadelphia, but of infamous character and debauched morals, a proper head for the band of robbers he has conducted down the Mississippi."

When all the good families in the colonies, according to tory propaganda, were on the side of the king, who held that all men who did not agree with him were traitors, only a black sheep among the good families could be with the rebel rabble.

Hamilton, in his partisan fervor, may have written this quite honestly just after entering a note in his diary that the Delaware Indians, who belonged to one of the really old American families, had brought in fifteen settlers' scalps. Later, on September 16th of the same year, he was to write:

"Since last May the Indians in this district have taken 34 prisoners, 17 of which they delivered up, and 81 scalps, several prisoners (children) taken and adopted not reckoned in this number." This made a total in excess of the total of Americans Clark had after the departure of his time-expired men.

War is never nice whether in the great valley in the seventeen seventies or in Europe in 1914–18. It was then and still is the way of either belligerent to think that his side is conducting it in a nice way and his enemy in a barbarous way.

Willing's methods were hardly nice. He believed in giving the other fellow as good as he sent. Had he taken Kaskaskia he probably would have soon had the population in sullen if not open resistance and have blooded the Indians to fight on his side. Variations in the nicety with which war is waged are often more related to individuals than to sides.

In preparation for his campaign against Pittsburgh, Hamilton was already receiving reinforcements of regulars and gathering supplies. The loss of Kaskaskia changed his situation. He now had to look west instead of east. The loss of Vincennes was alarming and called for prompt reprisal.

Vincennes was on the Wabash. The short portage over the watershed from the headwaters of the Wabash, which flows into the Ohio, to those of the Maumee, which flows into Lake Erie, was the main bridge between the two great continental valleys. It made Vincennes the key position of all the region between the lakes and the Ohio river and the Mississippi river and the eastern boundary of the present State of Ohio. Vincennes must be retaken before Winter set in. Although it was off the main route of advance to Pittsburgh it would threaten the advance in flank. Moreover, its continued possession by the Americans would alienate the Indian warriors who were wanted in large numbers and in very war-like mood to concentrate on Pittsburgh.

Hamilton's information about the paucity of Continental numbers was too good, he was too sagacious a soldier to accept at their face value the reports, originated by Clark, that Clark had trebled his actual numbers and that an army was advancing from the Falls of the Ohio to reinforce the Americans in Kaskaskia. Hamilton had spies keeping touch with Vincennes. He knew that only the French militia held it.

However, the reports disturbed him. They must be taken into consideration. He credited the one of a considerable American force at Corn Island. This could move by boats up the Wabash to Vincennes. It might be the reinforcement which Captain Helm so confidently announced as coming to increase his garrison of two. Therefore, Hamilton would not rely on a flying column of small numbers to retake Vincennes.

He had word that Clark's pretensions as to numbers was believed by the French settlers and the Indians; word of Clark's peace treaties with the chiefs and the savages' awe

LIEUTENANT COLONEL HENRY HAMILTON, THE BRITISH
GOVERNOR OF DETROIT, FROM A MINIATURE IN
THE LIBRARY OF HARVARD UNIVERSITY

of the miracle warrior. He learned that even the tribes at the important center of Ouitenon, commanding the portage at the head of the Wabash, had accepted Clark's plan of neutrality when they had been previously very loyal scalpers.

Therefore, it was that emissaries of counter propaganda, well supplied with wampum and trinkets, were at once sent out from Detroit as far west as Wisconsin. Let no one be deceived by the bad birds who doubted the power of the British White Father. This miracle warrior who spoke such big words would soon be silenced.

"The Spaniards are feeble and hated by the French," Hamilton wrote. "The French are fickle and have no man of capacity to advise or lead them; the rebels are enterprising and brave, but want resources; and the Indians can have their resources but from the English, if we act without loss of time in the present favorable conjuncture."

Yet Hamilton would take no risk of a discomfiture which would be fatal to the morale of the Indian allies upon whom he must depend for his future operations. He would make thorough preparations; he would go in such commanding strength with such a show of force to impress all the tribes with British power that there would be no wavering between Clark's moneyless inactive neutrality and British wampum and victory on the warpath.

Other objects were bound up with the recapture of Vincennes. As the Gibraltar of the great valley Hamilton would build a fort at the mouth of the Ohio to prevent the passage of American boats. Having cleaned Clark out of the Illinois country he would secure control of the mouth of the Mississippi, undersell the Spaniards, win Indian coöperation and thus recover all the Mississippi trade to Britain. These gains would strengthen the Florida command for the mutual effort against the whole Revolutionist rear when Hamilton should strike his decisive blow at Pittsburgh which would open the way to the command of the Allegheny and Monongahela valleys.

Hamilton need not depend upon an Irish trader's depleted purse for his funds. He had sinews of war in plenty. There was a war chest of wampum and ornaments for the distribution of largess on the route of his advance. He was not in suspense for want of word from a governor in distant Williamsburg. He was in regular communication with Quebec by messengers that were never waylaid. His soldiers received real money on every pay day.

There are records which supply details of the astounding amounts, for that period, which the British spent on their western campaign. The expense was not incurred at Detroit alone; but at Michillimackinac where the northern lake Indians were blooded to cross Lake Michigan to "Chicagou" for the portage down the Illinois river, or to Green Bay for the portage to the Wisconsin river, and thence into the Mississippi.

In 1777 there was a single draft by Hamilton for cash for twenty thousand pounds on New York, then in the possession of the British, for presents, "not including rum and rations," and not to mention the fourteen thousand pounds for a single "great council" with the Indians. In all, eighteen such councils, or grand "powwows," were held at Detroit representing, at this rate, a total entertainment expense of two hundred fifty thousand pounds, or a million dollars in gold.

Hamilton is known to have received eighty thousand pounds in cash during 1778 from New York while the total of drafts on New York alone during the Revolution from both Detroit and Michillimackinac was over eight hundred thousand pounds. This was exclusive of all manner of supplies bought in Canada and brought direct from England. Making war, in the seventeen seventies, in the Ohio country and the great lake region was certainly very expensive in the values of the time unless you did it on hope, will and audacity.

The High Command in Quebec tried to cut costs by eliminating the traders as middlemen; but this created friction as the traders, being whites and thrifty, wanted no less than the Indians to share British gold. Major Hay wrote from Detroit, July, 1778, in appeal for more liberal allowances, that five thousand Indians "will be dependent upon this place" during the coming year.

Altogether Britain's western campaign, in ratio to the whole cost in trying to suppress the American rebellion, was about the same as that of the Gallipoli, Salonika and Mesopotamian campaigns in ratio to the whole of the British part in the World War. The two diversions from the main theater had much the same tactical object. The British, although never prepared for land war, open their purse strings wide to all useful supporters when war begins.

Hamilton's chief, General Sir Frederick Haldemand, Commander-in-Chief in Canada, when approving his plan to attack Pittsburgh, said that he was not to be limited "in anything which shall be requisite for the good and advantage of His Majesty's service, the exigencies of which, in the department entrusted to your management at that distance from me, can only be judged of by you, and, therefore, must be left to your discretion, in which I have full confidence."

So Hamilton had a free hand with ample support. Clark had a free hand with no support. Thus the gauge was set on that immense stage of wilderness with the Indian population the uncertain quantity which intensified the gamble. It was a contest of tens and hundreds of white men. Again I suggest that those who use numbers as their measure of events should multiply each squad into a regiment, platoon into a division, and company into an army corps.

With further regular reinforcements on the way, Hamilton had, exclusive of Indians, in garrison early in October, over three hundred British regulars and about six hundred Canadian militia and volunteers. From these he chose those most fit for his expedition.

The regulars were of the King's Own Eighth Regiment, seasoned men of the kind that repeatedly charged at Bunker Hill. They were far from home but that was their lot whether in Canadian snows or tropical heat. Among them were Gallaghers and O'Briens. Oliver Pollock might have liked a word with the sons of Ireland who were fighting England's battles.

For guides and transport experts Hamilton had the most experienced of *coureurs de bois* and trailsmen who knew the route. He picked the militiamen who were tested in loyalty and endurance. His *corps d'élite*, superior to the regulars for frontier fighting, were the volunteers, veteran French frontiersmen including border ruffians who gloried in an opportunity, when gilded with gold, to prove theirs was a harder skill and deeper woodcraft cunning than that of the Big Knives. Captain Guillaume La Mothe was their commander, a hunter, trader, frontier soldier of fortune, a genius of his kind, toughened in the same processes as his followers.

All the French power over the Indians, which the Church had helped to win, he knew how to use for anything but Christian ends. He was an exponent of the Indian ferocity which the French had loosed on the settlements when they had fought both British redcoats and Big Knives and Bostonnais, a ferocity worse than that under Hamilton who had some compunctions as a limitation. The French populations of the Illinois country, who had rejoiced less than a score of years ago in the savage reprisals on the advancing seaboard colonies, had the memory of past outrages on an enemy which they would not have turned on themselves.

So eager were the Indians to go on the expedition that

Hamilton found it difficult to get capable ones as messengers on his various errands over his wide area of command. With the ones chosen for proven valor and dependability to go on the war path with the great British chief himself, he sang a war dance in honor of their departure.

Here was the prospect of much excitement for the children of the forest, not of occasional scalps from scattered settlers' cabins, but of license in ransacking a town. Hamilton knew his Indians. Probably he was already wondering how he could keep them out of the town and prevent a general massacre of the inhabitants in case of victory after prolonged action.

Cozening them was Major Hay, British Indian agent at Detroit, who was the staff organizer of Indian raids and dispenser of gifts and who would make sure there were enough bloody belts to go around among volunteers on the line of march. As his aide, who had long experience in the field and much power over the Indians, was François Maisonville, trader, hunter, adept trailsman and scout, who had brought Hamilton word of Clark's capture of Kaskaskia.

Provisions and presents for Indians in fifteen vessels had preceded the expedition. On October 7th, completely equipped, the main body of the chosen, about two hundred whites in addition to the Indians, dropped down the river. They had cannon under a detachment of the Royal Artillery.

Here was no mean enterprise in transport and organization so far from British arsenals and factories. It was a bold undertaking with its destination six hundred miles away across a region which afforded no shelter and no succor except in game. Hamilton must have welcomed action after three years of such exacting and irritating garrison routine in which he had pandered to Indian ferocity to do his field service for him.

Across the thirty miles of open lake to the mouth of the

Maumee, where Toledo now stands, a storm scattered the flotilla and forced boats ashore to avoid shipwreck and to wait for better weather before proceeding. War was hard labor in the seventeen seventies as it always has been and always will be, each generation thinking that conditions are unprecedently bad in its time; ever much labor for the thrill of brief action.

The lighter boats must be poled and rowed up the Maumee, the Falls of the Maumee passed, until shallow water forbade further progress. Cannon must be dragged over the narrow trails of the portage in the mud; kegs of powder, cannon balls, every pound of supplies had to be packed and light boats and canoes borne on the shoulders. Additional boats were waiting at the headwaters of the Wabash.

It was not the habit of the British army to travel light; and the Continental Army imitatively, as in Hand's and McIntosh's case, fell into the same error but not our old regulars of the plains, after frontier lessons, or Jackson's or Sherman's men in the Civil War. Hamilton and his officers had tents. Doubtless they "did themselves well," and home luxuries and liquors were not missing from their messes.

The Indian auxiliaries would bring in game and lend a hand now and then when it suited their mood; but they were not much given to the drudgery which made the advance of paleface warriors so slow. They were privileged persons, who, as fellow aristocrats with Hamilton's officers and gentlemen, might watch the whites at ignoble toil which it was their own habit to leave to their squaws. They were slow to approach the cannon until assured that those big black muskets contained no charge. Their interest, to put it materially, was in pay day and when the scalping should begin.

Hamilton passed out war belts and wampum to new savage recruits from local tribes. He listened to more eloquent Indian speeches, made speeches in answer, smoked more pipes of peace and joined in more war dances. It was all in the life of a British Lieutenant Governor, in the expansion and defense of the realm, no less than the pomp and march past of brilliantly caparisoned elephants in honor of a subject Maharajah of to-day and reviews of battalions of Sikhs, Gurkas, Pathans and Punjabis in British service.

Did Hamilton's officers, who cursed the damned pestiferous rebels for getting them into such a mess which they hoped would mean promotion, relish the companionship of savage allies who were fighting their own race? "Blood is thicker than water" was not a battle cry of that campaign. There was no sentiment for an English speaking union in the Kentucky settlements.

It took more than a month to get all the supplies over the portage. Dry weather had so reduced the current of the Wabash that it would not float the boats. Cargo had to be unloaded and packed around shoals, dams built to float stranded boats; and this was not in the bargain. Those regulars of the King's Eighth knew little of politics, few of them knew how to read and write; but, as they slept in wet clothes, after wading in icy waters, with backs sore from packing, they must have favored letting the damned pestiferous rebels have this worthless wilderness and do as they pleased with it.

God save His Majesty, but all the British soldiers who were serving him in the Illinois country asked was a seat in an ale house in a British port. They grumbled as British soldiers always have; but stubbornly kept on with their task. There was a doctor and medical supplies if they were ill; rations of rum when they were chilled. In the political and military philosophy of the time there was no defending and expanding the realm without rations of rum.

In the midst of the growls blessings for the beaver with his flat tail and sharp teeth were more heartfelt than for the king. Twice the beaver's industry saved many days of labor, as it had for traders' cargoes before. The boats were floated in his little lakes and through breaches made in his dams which he immediately repaired in the stubborn industry of peasantry after an army has left destruction in its path.

At last the guides could say that free navigation was certain all the way to the destination. How long it would have taken that expedition with all its supplies to have compassed the distance overland when no trails ran south to Vincennes is not a matter for speculation. It would have been mired. On the bosom of one of the important rivers in the destiny of the great valley the boats and canoes had only to keep their bows downstream.

The Indians were in canoes, which adroit shepherding aimed to keep in the rear of the flotilla, while these aboriginal freemen would be in front lest they miss something of interest. When there were halts they did war dances on the bank. Their faces were painted, feathers fastened in their scalplocks as for a costume ball; and they were beating their breasts and uttering war whoops.

When the chiefs at the important tribal center, Ouitenon, at the headwaters of the Wabash, had felt the pleasant touch of wampum in their palms and saw Hamilton's numbers accompanied by the terrible cannon, they concluded that once more they had been listening to bad birds when they were won over by Captain Helm and Father Gibault to Clark's policy of native neutrality. Who would be a neutral with such a scalping prospect in Vincennes?

This meant more recruits for Hamilton's army. He had more Indians than whites now, a force of five or six hundred. There was no refusing a volunteer. He might vent his war spirit in a troublesome fashion in the rear. Hamilton was suffering from an embarrassment of redskin auxiliaries who took camp followers' liberties and considered the bonds of discipline as something applying only to the whites. Even as the cat the Indian warrior "walked alone." If he became peevish Hamilton gave him another present. Learning the method by which to obtain presents from the British Father he became peevish with increasing frequency.

As Hamilton approached the town he captured two of Helm's scouts which assured him that as welcome as the Indians might be in case there was to be any hard fighting, they would not be required for this emergency. The scouts must have been French as Helm could not dispatch his army of one on such errands and still have a morning parade of his garrison. One of the two, apparently, was the man who was bearing the bi-monthly express from Helm to Clark and who would have the latest news of the military situation for Clark before he started.

Thus Hamilton learned that he had only two Americans to overcome except in the improbable circumstance that the French militia should make a stand on its own. There was also just the chance that American reinforcements might be on the way from Clark's mythical garrison at the Falls of the Ohio. With so many Indians to spare Hamilton sent parties on to scout in that direction, to attack boats on the Ohio and to intercept any word reaching the supposed garrison of the Falls that the British were before the town.

As Hamilton looked at the Indians who remained, beating their breasts and uttering war whoops in accumulatory frenzy as they drew near to the town, the thought of their methods probably influenced his plan. He halted his army twenty-five miles from Vincennes and sent picked troops ahead. Aside from a detachment of the regulars and of the Royal Artillery which was to put the six pounder in position to command the fort, was La Mothe and his volunteers. With Major Hay, in command of the whole advance guard, went some Indian chiefs as a sop to their self-importance and a means of holding their braves in control.

"Had our whole force moved forward together," Hamilton wrote in his diary, "it would have probably been impossible to have restrained the savages from destroying the settlement. As it was, the young men took alarm, that they should have no share in the business, and threw themselves hastily into the canoes, to follow. They were, however, prevailed upon to return."

A "placart" was sent warning the inhabitants that if their militia resisted the Indians would be upon them. As soon as it was found that there was no resistance, Major Hay was to hoist the British flag over the fort, as a signal for the rest of the force to enter the town, when, hopefully, it would be well enough policed to control the Indians.

When Hamilton, himself, with his main body, moved down the river on December 17th in a blowing snowstorm, he saw, as the air cleared, that not the cross of St. George but the Continental flag was floating over the fort. Most assuredly interest now returns to Captain Leonard Helm and his one soldier.

We know what he was doing chiefly through a bulletin letter which he was writing as Hamilton's army approached. The messenger who bore it was captured, but happily this choice bit of historical data was preserved. We see the calm narrator, with his scratching goosequill, his garrison manning a cannon, as he watches the approach of the enemy. There is a trace of worry in the letter lest that red haired chief of his should expect that garrison of two to repulse five hundred.

"At this time," the letter begins, "there is an army within three miles of this place. I heard of their coming several days beforehand. I sent spies to find the certainty. The spies being taken prisoners I never got intelligence till they got within three miles of the town."

At first, he had had "assurance of the integrity of the militia." They were to take their posts on the signal of the

firing of a cannon, but none had come. "Before sight of an
army no braver men," Helm comments. This was not new
in the history of war's abyss between the march out from
home and the firing line.

But Helm had no time for sarcasm; he was not in humorous mood. He knew the cause of the timidity of fathers,
sons and husbands when the best hope of the protection
of the women and children was in their kinsman La Mothe's
influence with the chiefs whom his guile might not be able
to restrain if bloodletting began. The "fickle" French preferred British rule to massacre. Hamilton's Indian policy
was working out so far as efficiently as Clark's in military results.

"You know how I feel," Helm appealed to Clark. "But
I am determined to act brave. . . . Their flag is at a small
distance. I must conclude. Yr. Humble Servt, Leonard
Helm."

Determined to act brave! The thrifty Helm was not to
lose a point which he might conserve. He was a stickler for
etiquette, this white haired veteran frontiersman dealing
with a British commander. If he had to yield it would be
as if he were conceding a favor.

The reason that the British flag was not up appeared
when Major Hay reported to Hamilton that, although
Helm realized resistance was hopeless, he would not surrender until he knew the terms. That garrison of one officer and one private should have the honors of war and
be treated with respect.

With a six pounder in position and detachments of regulars and militia and volunteers with fixed bayonets behind
him, Hamilton, in person, approached the fort. He sent a
messenger to demand surrender. Helm, in all dignity, set
his goosequill scratching in reply. He would have everything
official and on the record. He asked for a written answer
as to whom this messenger represented.

The colossal conceit of this rebel! Possibly Helm's keen trailsman's eyes had a twinkle of appreciation of meeting stiff British punctiliousness in kind. Hamilton "advanced to the wicket" with the verbal answer: "The King's Lieutenant Governor from Detroit!" A picture, that British lieutenant governor with his motley army at the door of the fort and that veteran frontiersman behind it, while all the people of the town were so silent in their houses and the grave Indian chiefs awaited the war cry!

Helm was told that he should have humane treatment. Hamilton could not resist admiration in his irritation even when Helm refused, upon command, to lower the Continental flag. The British must do that, themselves. But they refused as they ran up their own cross of St. George which seems to have floated beside the stars for the first time in history. The sight of that was too much for Helm. He lowered his flag, and apparently kept it against the day when it should float again over the fort.

And Hamilton was busy, meanwhile, posting sentries to keep the Indians out of the fort; but "some of them got in at gun ports that had not been secured." Those supple, sinewy children of the forest who wanted their part in the paleface's show! And Hamilton had always to talk to them through a third person when they might only look blank and then do as they pleased.

"I called to the interpreters," Hamilton goes on, "and used my best entreaties with the chiefs, who really did all in their power, but the torrent was too strong for such feeble barriers. They bore down the sentries, and seeing that I had posted another at the commandant's quarters, they went to the windows which they broke and fell to plundering. The disorder lasted until the curiosity of the savages was gratified."

They had "generously restored to Captain Helm whatever was required of his private property. Some stout horses

—32 lately purchased on the account of the Congress—
they found in the fort, which I would not deprive them
of, as they had not committed a single act of cruelty and
treated the inhabitants with all the humanity which was
recommended to them. Had a single shot been fired, probably the settlement would have been destroyed in an hour's
time."

"Poor savages!" comments Hamilton. The "generously
restored" was probably after much palavering. As for the
horses, no Indian could be won to give up a horse, nor could
any frontiersman except in a swap or in face of a musket's muzzle. Whether the original owners ever received
their pay from Congress is left to the detailed history of the
claims which buffeted the members for generations after
the war was won.

"Poor savages!" Hamilton's mood toward them varied.
At times he was irritated and disgusted by having to be
their bear leader and baiter. Again he was minded that no
unfavorable reports reflecting on their methods of warfare
should reach the ears of those mischief-making members
of Parliament, Pitt and Burke, who were hampering the
Royal Breast.

"Poor savages!" Hamilton shared with Clark a sports-
man's feeling for them as the pawns of the white man's
chicane. How bereft they looked as they shrugged in
obedience to the orders of their chiefs to keep their tomahawks in their belts! They had come far in the promise
of being favored guests in a grand party where their own
social customs would prevail, and then had been kept outside with no "look in" except a raid on the butler's pantry.

"Poor savages!" They were more decent in Hamilton's
stiff soldier philosophy than the craven French settlers.
Perhaps he thought that the local inhabitants deserved to
lose a few of their scalps as retribution for their treason.
He summoned them to the church, his temper raw for sol-

dier emphasis after his seventy-one days' ordeal on the way from Detroit.

"In pretty strong terms," he writes, "I painted their ingratitude and poltroonery" for having turned on their royal master. They, too, could plead that they had been listening to bad birds when any bird that protected their homes and gardens was a good bird. For their signature he presented an oath in which they acknowledged that in taking an oath of allegiance to Congress, they had "forgotten their duty to God and failed in their duty to man" and they asked "pardon of God" and hoped "for the goodness of their legitimate sovereign" to take them again "under his protection as good and faithful subjects." Many signed it, and some evaded signing.

It was now mid-December. Hamilton had a force of five hundred and Clark had a force of one hundred; but Clark was more than two hundred miles away across winter snow and mud which would grow worse. Hamilton was warranted in his thought that in any event he had Clark at his mercy, although he waited until Spring.

By this time he was realizing Clark's forcefulness. If he could capture Clark, himself, his object would be gained without the misery of the winter march. The forty Indians and whites whom he sent for the purpose gave the alarm that he was before Kaskaskia with his whole army. As Hamilton would not go to him Clark was to go to Hamilton.

XXVI

WIN ALL OR LOSE ALL

HAMILTON dreaming of Pittsburgh! Clark dreaming of Detroit! Hamilton was the nearer of the two to his goal and between Clark and his goal. The coming summer promised Hamilton the triumphant climax of his three years' plotting and labor in exile. He could now cry "Check!" but not yet "Checkmate!"

Under a downpour of bad news Clark welcomed any ray of light in the gloom. When he was so heavily outnumbered every additional determined man with a rifle became a majestic figure. It was good to see the recruits which Major Bowman had brought in with his garrison when he arrived from Cahokia in response to the alarm of the unexpected attack on Kaskaskia.

Some of the young Frenchmen from the other settlements would serve with Clark, too. They were badly armed; they lacked uniforms. Clark outfitted them as best he could. They managed many flags if their clothing were not regulation. Flaunting their colors, as they marched and drilled, they boasted that they were much better men than the Kaskaskian youth. Clark stopped this rivalry, which was whetting *esprit de corps*, in time to prevent civil war.

Assured, now, that Hamilton was no nearer than the Wabash and they could be summoned in time for an emergency, Clark sent them and Bowman's little legion back to Cahokia to continue their guard of the Mississippi outpost.

He learned that Vincennes was taken. He could not imagine Hamilton, with all his impedimenta, undertaking the winter march. It was now almost a year since he had a

333

"scrape of the pen" from Governor Henry, not since he had left Williamsburg. Either Henry's expresses had been captured, revealing to the enemy the route by which he was sending reinforcements or that he was sending none, or he had dismissed that fractious youth, who had bedeviled him so much, from his mind.

Clark was hemmed in by the mystery of the wilderness which was harder for his high spirit to bear than if Hamilton's regulars and Indians had been besieging his fort. But gradually the mystery was being resolved, gradually reports padded in over the trails fitting the part of the picture puzzle together in a map of his situation.

Bands of Indians which had been sent by Hamilton from his new base were already seizing boats on the Ohio. He was calling a grand powwow of the northern and southern tribes for common action against the frontier in the coming Spring.

Just how many men had he in garrison at Vincennes? Were there eight hundred as reported? *Coureurs de bois,* or wandering Indians, who might be only simulating friendliness, could not be depended upon for exact information on this score. Clark must cut through the rumors to the truth.

Here his amicable foreign relations served him well. Colonel Vigo, Governor De Leyba's partner, offered to make a business trip which would include an expert's observation of the state of Vincennes' defenses. Clark's decision about his next move waited upon Vigo's return.

As a merchant and subject of a country which was still officially neutral, Vigo might be detained by Hamilton and again he might not be. Or, if Hamilton did not find an adequate excuse for detention, there was always the chance that a party of Indians could be utilized in waylaying the most innocent of travelers and holding him prisoner.

Hamilton suspected Vigo, and, it is said, made him promise that on the way to St. Louis he would not tell Clark what he had seen. Anyhow, Vigo construed this as unwarrantable compulsion on a neutral subject when the British plan to drive Spanish trade out of the valley would ruin his enterprises; when Clark had won his friendship and when perhaps his gallantry had been stirred by a more romantic friendship of a giant warrior and the small and dark Terese.

Vigo returned on the second of February. He told Clark, in technical precision, all that he had learned. Hamilton had been strengthening the fort, making its walls bullet proof with deep embrasures. He was settled for the winter with ninety British regulars as the nucleus of his garrison under the protection of his well mounted cannon. The majority of the Indians had scattered to their villages or on forays to the Ohio and some of the militia had returned to Detroit.

Clark had the last piece to fill in the picture. The whole was clear in its formidable challenge for a desperate stroke.

"It was at this moment," Clark said, "I would have bound myself as a slave for seven years for five hundred troops."

His account of the succeeding weeks may not be subject to complaints by the most captious of the prolixity of his narrative of Indian relations. He was laconic as usual when he was preparing for action. But he gives us diagrammatic outlines which leave no room for imagination of what was passing in his mind.

He was thinking of his families on Corn Island whom he had made hostages of his fortune; of the Kentucky settlements he had defended in that summer siege. He saw savage war parties going down the Wabash; the concerted action of bands crossing the upper Ohio to make common cause with those from the Tennessee mountains against the groups of cabins.

When he might have to fight his way he could not reach

them, if at all, with men enough to save them. They could hope for no succor from Williamsburg whose expresses had failed to reach Kaskaskia.

Further supplies from the lower Mississippi might be cut off. Pollock was reporting that he was at the end of his credit; he could not honor future bills unless his appeals to Governor Henry for funds were answered. Clark had not even Continental script for money when it was already making its appearance in the Illinois country where the settlers were beginning to realize, after the traders had passed it on them, its low value in gold.

The place to scotch the rattlesnake's eggs had been at Detroit. Now it was nearer, it was at Vincennes, when destiny had set Clark against Hamilton as the personification of an issue as distinct as the rivers with no highways or railroads sharing their dominance of the white expanse of the map.

It was win all or lose all in the gamble for the mighty stake between the substance of empire and a broken dream; the stake of all the valley from the Holston to the lakes; of his vision and Pollock's vision, all he had fought and labored for. It was better to lose before Fort Sackville in Vincennes, when success was only in its capture, than to accept certain defeat by stagnation in garrison or retreat to the Spanish side.

Many leaders have taken such mad chances against odds hoping for luck in their favor. But Clark was not given to depending upon luck. The commanders of great armies were no more calculating than he in the elementals of success which never change. There have been many conceptions which had the flash of genius without the steady flame of genius which made them victorious. Forlorn hope battalions or great armies are not formed in victory alone on the drill ground. Their spirit is founded far deeper in the habits, will, ardor and mettle of peoples.

FORT SACKVILLE. A DRAWING FROM DESCRIPTIONS

All the painstaking attention of Clark in his cabinet parts, every friendship he had won with Indian, priest or trader, was now an asset. He had to depend upon all those imponderables of human nature which are not purchasable, and more than ever chiefly upon George Rogers Clark himself.

He did not underestimate his enemy. He was fooled by no fostered tradition of innate racial superiority or the magic power of patriotic talismans and causes; of one American frontiersman being equal to two frontiersmen of any other race or three British regulars.

Much depends upon the conditions under which adversaries meet. Clark knew Hamilton was a very able soldier. He knew that with the support of cannon behind bullet proof walls one British regular with the ample reserve of food and munitions which Fort Sackville had, should hold off three men of any army.

The British regulars had bayonets. Clark's men had none. Bayonets, in the skillful hands of long-service veterans, were better at close quarters than big knives, no matter if the frontiersmen, used to the knife or tomahawk against the tomahawk, thought the contrary. But Clark would not disabuse his men of their idea. This would weaken their confidence.

He knew that he would have to traverse two hundred miles of "drowned" country, as he called it. The trails, easily passable in summer, would be spongy. This time the rivers were not to be the path of destiny but barriers. He must cross a series of them, their currents running with ice and overflowing the land in winter rains and February thaws.

Those who, from a Pullman window in swift flight, look out on this region of towns, cities and farms, which the vision of Clark foresaw, will please imagine themselves marching across the fields over inundated plowed ground in February. Or, if they spin along hard roads in an automobile over good bridges, they may look down on the streams and

think of fording them in February; and then, after having marched twenty-five or thirty miles in a day, no wood
dry enough to make a fire when night comes, half-raw buffalo meat for supper with no hot coffee to wash it down,
and not even a tent for shelter over a bed in the mud.

This is what Clark's men did, and their French comrades
did, under the spur of his temper and the cajolery of his
winning ways, in order that the towns might rise and the
automobiles spin and the cash registers click under our
present system of government when it was a young idea
in which Clark had such faith, whether or not we like the
manner of its present application. For the more I studied
the subject the more I was convinced that the decision as
to the future of the Northwest was made on that immortal
march when George Rogers carried the flaming young idea
under his flaming red hair.

Vincennes was on the opposite side of the unfordable
Wabash. But before Clark reached the Wabash there were
the Little Wabash, and the Embarrass and little streams
whose banks would be submerged under the surface of lakes.
Here was a task for an engineering train with pontoons,
but Clark could afford no such luxury as that.

If Hamilton learned that Clark's little army was on the
way to attack him and he chose not to wait on its destruction before the walls of his fort, or its drowning in the
Wabash under the fire of his cannon, he had a resource
better than garrison sorties in bands of Indians who were
aboriginally toughened against winter rigors. They would
not lack ammunition or good rifles from British stores.
They could shoot as well as the average frontiersman. Here
was business in keeping with their tactics in ambush for
flank attacks and sniping fire on that struggling, mired
and shivering column.

Such was the terrain for that march, and such the promised reception at its end from an outnumbering garrison

supported by cannon in a fort on the bank of an unfordable stream!

When temptation was so strong, in lack of either information or relief, Clark resisted the occasion which would have given gloomy opportunity to so many generals, who have foreseen failure for want of means against an enemy whose strength they overestimated, as their attitude engendered caution in place of confidence in their own troops.

Clark's letter announcing his decision to Governor Henry, which was written the day after Vigo's return, carries no word of caviling or complaint beyond the brief reference that he despairs of aid as he takes it for granted there is good reason for Henry's silence and inattention. He had to make the most of what forces he had. He was not sighing over what he lacked. In this letter he once refers to Hamilton as the "Hairbuyer General" but otherwise as Mr. Hamilton.

"I am resolved to take advantage of this present situation and risk the whole on a single battle. . . . You must be sensible of the feeling I have for those brave officers and soldiers that are determined to share my fate, let it be what it will. I know the case is desperate, but Sir, we must either quit the country or attack Mr. Hamilton. No time is to be lost. Was I sure of reinforcements I should not attempt it. . . . Great things have been effected by a few men well conducted. Perhaps we may be fortunate. We have this consolation, that our cause is just and that our country will be grateful and not condemn our conduct in case we fail."

"In case we fail!" was for Patrick Henry's private ear. It was also for that of cousin John Rogers who had been with Clark on the march to Kaskaskia. Young John had been given the command of Clark's new navy. Best of all the items of good news had been the arrival of four swivels, four four pound and one nine pound cannon which that genius in procurement, Pollock, had bought with money that he begged or borrowed. Clark mounted them on a big Mississippi boat which he named the Willing.

With thirty of his veterans for crew the galley gunboat was sent downstream to swing into the Ohio and then up the Wabash. Thirty miles below Vincennes she was to go into hiding until she had word that Clark's army was approaching. Then she would take the place of an engineer train acting as his ferry and would cover the attack of his infantry on the fort with her cannon fire.

Her presence was as important to Clark's plan as covering naval artillery and shore boats for debarking an army in a landing operation. On the way Rogers could be certain that one shot from his nine pounder would readily scatter any Indian band, but not prevent them from taking the news of his coming to Hamilton. He also carried ammunition and rescue supplies for the infantry.

Joint army and navy operations are always ticklish. What if Rogers should not arrive on time? What if Clark should never reach the Wabash?

"In case we fail" to cousin John was that he should join Colonel John Rogers, who, Clark had learned, was on the way up the Mississippi with a convoy which had succeeded in passing the British forts. Clark had sent the Colonel word not to enter the Ohio until he had learned the result of the march on Vincennes. The Colonel either did not receive, or, if he received it, did not heed the warning. He and some of his men were killed by Indians under one of Hamilton's white leaders, and another cargo of supplies failed to reach the Continentals at Pittsburgh.

There was no "in case we fail" to the veterans who remained with Clark after manning the Willing or to the native militia; no repetition of the thought to himself. The Kaskaskians had seen the galley being armed and had been duly impressed by the arrival of cannon from far away New

Orleans. There was no keeping Clark's coming advance secret from the people.

All knew that *Monsieur le Commandant* was planning one of his surprise strokes. By this time he must have known personally every man, woman and child in the little community. He was the patriarch of this family as he was of the settlers whom he had brought down the Ohio to Corn Island. He took the Kaskaskians into his confidence.

Yes, it would be another surprise just like that of Kaskaskia; and he was just as sure to win. Colonel Vigo who had just come from Vincennes said that he would. Hamilton would never dream that Clark had a galley with cannon. He would never dream any soldier would attempt to cross all those rivers and swamps in February, but Frenchmen and Big Knives were the hardy braves who could do it.

So Hamilton would have no scouts out; he would be all unaware of danger, battened in like the bear for his winter rest. One morning the galley's cannon would be pounding his fort and Clark's men at the gate when Hamilton was still in bed just as it was with Rochblave. Ah, but that was a good joke on Rochblave, but he could not join in the laugh over it.

Far was it from the interest of Clark to put any limit to the local imagination. The versatile son of Ann was occupying himself with the department of propaganda. No feature of war, from spies to intrigue, or depressing enemy and inspiriting your own morale to expend the last ounce of strength in the hazard of action, was missing in the councils of so small a force dealing with so large an area. Town gossip took the place of the influence of the press. Clark was his own censor.

Any smoldering public resentment over his burning of the houses adjoining the fort was swept away by the new excitement. Citizens who had seen how terrible Clark had been in a rage, how he had risen out of the night to become master of the town, had proof of how terrible he would be against his enemies who, they had become convinced, were their own.

Bowman with his thirty and the militia of the other settlements arrived. Clark made festival in their honor in a grand Virginian planter manner, in which the Kaskaskian militia joined to make holiday for all the people. As the fervor grew young men swelled their chests and stood erect to win the glance from the giant Big Knife which assured them that they would be among the chosen for the great adventure.

The streets of Kaskaskia were bright with the throb of colors as the women made more flags in a contagion of public industry and zeal. The men were picking the best horses, making pack saddles, hastening to execute all commands, gathering provisions. The old days under the Great Louis were recalled. It was a gay business when the French King sent his legions to war.

Clark's numbers being relatively so small for his undertaking, was he tempted to form a band of Indian auxiliaries? His desperate situation was a good excuse. He had only to sound the call that the time had arrived for the braves and the Big Knives to fight together, and to distribute bloody belts and amulets; and many chiefs and young bucks, who were restive under the neutrality policy, would have come loping in from their villages to follow the devil brother of the Great Spirit in the working of another military miracle. How well they would have fought under him!

But no such thought occurred to him. Assuredly he would rather have given up the expedition than compromise with his principle. He could be very stubborn on certain points, without losing his temper. For the future, after the war was over, he seems to have had in mind teaching the Indians husbandry and the arts of civilization as the outcome of his policy. Its eventual result was the government schools and the reservation system.

He might have been thinking that there was too much parade of his objective, of the danger of spies among the people preceding him on the trails to Vincennes. However, there was no use of worrying about that except in every prevision to guard exit from the town.

Doubtless his own way, if he had to lead only his own veterans, would have been to slip quietly away in the night, perhaps leaving word that he was going toward the Ohio to meet that army of reinforcements from his new base on Corn Island. But this was not according to the local manners and customs when he must depend upon French enthusiasm supplying volunteers and then upon keeping them up to their work once the hardships began.

There are many details we should like to know about that lean midwinter march to Vincennes which was to make the lean march to Kaskaskia comparatively a summer jaunt. Our data are Clark's own accounts and the brief journal that Major Bowman kept. We do know that, as well as fifers, there was a drummer, a merry little French drummer, who was to win laughter which wrought another effort out of despair in a crisis.

With him drumming busily at the head of the troops, with flags for every squad, we see the little army marched to the river bank, to the cheers of all the population in their gayest costumes. It must have seemed to the less emotional American frontiersmen at the river bank that the embraces would never end. Probably they, too, had to endure being kissed on the cheek by men although they did not find it any more disagreeable from the girls than a soldier of to-day.

It was a solemn occasion, too. The men, who might never return, must not depart without absolution. Father Gibault, Vicar General, whose faith in that heretic Clark had never faltered, gave it to his soldier children; and, Cross upraised, he blessed the whole expedition, bidding it godspeed to victory. Some of the people probably crossed the river with the troops and saw them start on their long tramp on February 5th. The drummer was drumming; the fifers tootling; marching songs of the seventeenth century were sung. To the English, Scotch, Irish, Germans and Swedes who were fighting in the Continental Army were now added the French settlers in the heart of the great valley.

Half of the force of a hundred and twenty odd men were French. And the French were not going for pay, when none was available to bribe them. It must have been the call of more than adventure, more than the spell of Clark's leadership, or even fighting on the side of the king of France which led them to face the ordeal which they knew so well was ahead of them. Going to war in Summer would have been quite a different thing. They must have found some merit in the idea which was expressed by the new flag under which they were marching.

Modern allowance, in terms of bronchial troubles in February in that climate for a force that had no tentage, would be about twenty-five to thirty per cent, which would have brought Clark to Vincennes with less than a hundred men fit for duty. As for the sick the injunction of the red-faced British Colonel about to go into action on the Somme in 1916, "There will be no shell shock cases in this regiment," applied.

On leaving Kaskaskia all the officers had mounts. Clark, with his planter's eye for horse flesh, had one which must have been suitable to the red-headed leader and the occasion in the eyes of his impressionable allies. His huge figure was on a Spanish stallion which had been passed along by Indian traders in a succession of swaps from New Mexico which then extended to Arkansas and Kansas.

We know that the horses started. We know the officers

did not ride for long; and in the end there were no horses left to ride or to eat. We know that there were heavy winter rains adding to the flood from heavy thaws in the head-waters country; that the march was almost immediately over land partly overflowed; that the route varied in rail fence fashion from the line of a crow's flight in breaking away from inundated trails to get better footing; and that, in the first stages, buffalo were available for meat.

Every night, in the first stages, each company formed in a square with baggage in the center and sentries out on guard against surprise. Evidently the packhorses were used for bringing in game. Evidently, one reason officers were not riding much was lest they appear to be favored over their soldiers.

Clark speaks of how the officers acted the part of woodsmen "shouting now and then and running back and forth through the water like the men themselves. I suffered them to shoot game on all occasions and feast on it like Indians at war dances, each by turns inviting the others to their feasts, which was the case every night"—that is, in the first stages.

And this he remarks was to keep the "men in good spirits." Good spirits when wet to the skin! Good spirits as they felled trees—"still raining," Bowman remarks—to make a crossing of the River of the Petit Ford.

It seems incredible, but there is the record, quite indisputable. With their feasting and their hunting game and tramping through the mud and finding fords they had been averaging twenty-eight miles a day.

"The men quite fatigued," remarks Bowman. One would say that this observation must also be indisputable.

They were on the banks of the swollen Little Wabash. Beyond that were the big rivers. Thus far the going had been comparatively easy.

XXVII

THE ICY MARCH

THE weather might have been worse as they were to realize later. A sudden seasonable freeze might lower the water, making their clothes encasements of ice; a heavy melting snowfall or heavier rain might raise the water. Anyhow, no Indians had harassed them and no human being, so far as they knew, had seen them on their march. "It might be worse!" is one of the consolations with which optimism rallies pessimism on a campaign.

The final fifteen miles had been across the mire of a "bad plain," an open overflowed meadow. This explains Bowman's remark that it was late before the troops and baggage were assembled in camp.

As it was dark the men could not see what was ahead of them. They had anticipated no trouble in crossing the two forks of the Little Wabash. The forks were usually fordable even in flood. But the next morning there was no sign of land as far as one could see toward the other fork which was three miles away. Along the bank the water was from two to four feet deep; the channel itself impassable except by swimming which, with heavy rifles to carry and powder to keep dry and baggage to ferry over, was not even in Clark's purview. And beyond this lake as they were shiveringly reminded were the Embarrass and the big Wabash itself.

It looked like a forlorn hope. An army might as well try to cross the Mississippi itself without transports. But Clark would have that forlorn hope—"precipitate it" as he said—on the other side of the second fork. Then the men would not think that what was ahead of them was any worse than what they had been through; and their only prospect of salvation would be to go on.

Dripping in the rain, which was raising the water every hour, they stood on the bank in the moist morning light watching to see what their chief would do next. Soon the axes were biting into a tree trunk and then adzes chipping the heart out of a log to make a dugout. Details of men took turns at the labor, but meanwhile the rest were idle. All must be occupied in some way. Otherwise they would soon be mulling gloomy talk; the active French imaginations would be picturing a dismal prospect.

If the fork of the Little Wabash was so bad, what of the Big Wabash? Did the Colonel think that he could take them and all their baggage in one dugout all the way to Vincennes? "Might as well give up now as ever." "I know the Big Wabash in flood!" "The weather is agin us!" "I've had enough of this!"

"Pains were taken to find diversion for the rest," Clark remarks. One wonders what the diversions were on an island of high ground in the rain. We should have details if Clark had been entertaining Indian chiefs; but this was soldier business. Probably the soloists sang the public favorites; probably they led choruses of songs; the Big Knives sang and then the French sang.

Probably Clark went from one group to another rallying spirits with jests and assurance. He may have poked a little fun at himself over his pronunciation of French. Jokesters were incited to display their wit. The drummer's wrists must have ached with effort; and it must have been a muffled rattle that came from his moist drumhead. The fifer's instrument, which he carried in his pocket, was good in drought or flood. Together drum and fife made an orchestra. Cheer up!

No one was to worry about the little delay necessary to locate dry ground for the next camp. As soon as the dugout was finished it was sent on its mission paddled by chosen men whom Clark could trust to heed his instructions. They were gone a long time before they found any ground above water. This was on the opposite bank of the second fork. They reported, as they were expected to do, that they had found a high and dry spot and the going was much better ahead.

"Still raining," Bowman says. "Orders given to fire no guns except in case of necessity." And necessity meant a shot at a deer or in defense from attack.

The scouts in the dugout, sounding depths with a pole, had blazed trees to mark the shallowest route for the morrow's march. Clark challenged the frontiersmen's pride in their fortitude. After a day's "rest and entertainment" when they were used to having their feet wet, anyway, what was the difference of a foot or two of water to them?

Floundering in the water they felled trees and built scaffoldings on the banks of either fork. Then the men and baggage were ferried across in the dugout, the horses swam and their packs were replaced.

The dugout was the hospital ship of that aquatic march. It carried the "sickly." No officer was riding now. Each must share the lot of the privates or he was not man enough to be an officer. The advance men, keeping their direction by the fresh scars of the axe on the trees, felt for better footing when they came to holes and gullies. Following in single file came the others in water never below their knees and again up to their hips.

They slipped and plunged often falling full length in the water. The answer to the curses of the subject of a mishap was laughter from the others; and in turn he had to laugh, if wryly. When men can laugh there are still shots in the locker of morale. In bad moments, when the water was deeper or the ground underneath very spongy, someone would start a song.

Blessed was that "little antic drummer" of the chronicle. He was not among the sickly; he might not be in the dugout. But when he struck a place over his head and the others saw him floating on his drum—*élan, messieurs, élan!*—and making merry over it in superior personal privilege over them, this brought the heartiest laugh of all. A giant lifted him on to his shoulders and bade him play. The fifer fifed. Everybody felt better, although the remaining flour and bread which had been brought from home were being water-soaked.

It took all day to make three miles. Night found all the marchers in camp on the opposite bank of the second fork, with two rivers and a lake behind them, that antic drummer the hero of the achievement as he gave banter for banter. Clark had his army well into the forlorn hope and in high favor with themselves, boasting of what they had endured.

"They really began to think themselves superior to other men," says Clark who had certainly encouraged the view, "and that neither the rivers nor the seasons could stop their progress. Their whole conversation now was what they would do when they got about the enemy, and they now began to view the main Wabash as a creek, and made no doubt that such men as they were could find a way to cross it. They wound themselves up to such a pitch that they soon took Vincennes, divided the spoil and before bedtime were on their way to Detroit.

"This no doubt was pleasing to us that had more serious thought. We were now as it were in the enemy's country; no possibility of escape if our enemy should discover and overpower us, except by means of our galley (Rogers' gunboat), if we should fall in with her. We were now convinced that the whole of the low country on the Wabash was drowned; that the enemy could easily get to us, if they discovered us, and risk an action."

How easily a little weight in the turn of the balance might have sunk the men in gloom! One imagines that in his description of their high spirits the wish was so much the father to the thought that it held its spell over Clark when he wrote this years afterward; that, inwardly, their elation was not as deep as he pictured it when the eye of the commander was on the watch for the first sign of discouragement that might seep under the bulwark of morale, which is will. Inwardly all must have realized that they faced more misery than they had behind them. It was the "whistling to keep up courage" gayety; it was the gayety that defies the worst which is yet to come.

No matter what of the morrow! See what we have done to-day! It shows that there is nothing that we cannot do. Our unbeatable chief says so. To-night eat, drink and be merry. Eat? "Our provisions grow short," Bowman records.

The march on the 17th, was like "finding a river in a lake," as Temple Bodley says. First, I shall quote Bowman's diary.

"Drizzly and dark weather," he says. "Marched early. Crossed many rivers (meaning evidently tributary creeks) very deep. About one hour before sunset we got near the river Embarrass; found the country all overflown. We strove to find the Wabash. Traveled till 8 o'clock—found it impossible to cross the Embarrass river. We found the Water falled from a spot of ground; staid there the remainder of the night."

There is an epic in that if we imagine all the emotions the men had been through since the previous evening with its gayety as pictured by the indomitable optimism of Clark.

We return to him and his part as leader. On the morning of the 17th he knew he was within ten miles of Vincennes as the crow flies. Between him and the goal were the rivers Embarrass and the Big Wabash. What if Rogers with the galley should not arrive in time? Could that be expected when Rogers had to row against the current in a heavy flood?

Clark sent four men in the dugout to cross the Embarrass for information and to bring back any boats if they could find them. They confirmed the impression that the Embarrass was impossible for horses or men and that all the country was a lake. They found no boats. But Hamilton had plenty of boats and ammunition. He might send a flotilla which would maneuver around Clark's waterlogged exhausted men who had little dry powder left and who so direly needed the gunboat as a ferry and its reserve of food and powder.

Obviously Rogers would stick to the main stream as directed in the assignment of rendezvous. Bowman's "We strove to find the Wabash" meant that Clark was marching, away from the town, down the bank of the Embarrass to locate in the lake its junction with the Wabash.

There was little to cheer Clark that night of the 17th although more than the next night. The men were too worn to be either cheered or depressed. They could have hardly cared whether their powder was wet or dry. For fourteen hours they had been sloshing through water that must have been under forty degrees Fahrenheit.

It was not so bad during daylight, not comparatively. The sickly were in the one dugout. Others were probably on any remaining horses; and more horses foundered and had to be left behind. There was halt after halt as officers and the strongest men leading shuffled along the banks of the hidden streams feeling for a ford.

If the water were up to the necks of the tall men it might be over the heads of the short ones, but they could hang on to the gunwales of the dugout acting as a ferry. The little antic drummer could always float on his drum over deep places when the giant was too tired to carry him. He could bring a laugh—a dry laugh in such a wet world—

when the last laugh seemed to be out of the throats of all. And when they had to halt they felt the cold more; and there could be no taking up the advance until every straggler was up.

The thin, sunless light of day went out with no camping place in sight, with nothing to do but to continue moving or to sink and be drowned. So they struggled on bumping against driftwood, caught in the roots of bushes, as they peered into the dark, to the accompanying sound of the swish of legs and the paddle of the canoe and warning calls back and forth, keeping close in single file, shadow following shadow.

Clark's deep-chested voice rang out at intervals a word of encouragement or he stood by, as the line passed, giving his shoulder to a faltering man. Still the rain fell to add to the weight of the water against progress as feet were lifted out of the sucking mud. The strong cheered on the weak whose steps were roweled by the fear of being isolated or stepping off a bank into a channel whose current would bear them away. The strong took the heavy rifles of the weak on their own shoulders. The weak must have clung to the gunwales of the boat; or to the pack of a horse, only to fall when the horse fell for the last time and the strong succored them. Remaining provisions were lost with the horse packs.

Famishing men and famishing horses and a famishing hope which had started so gayly from Kaskaskia when they had not yet one shot at the enemy! And that redheaded devil brother of the Great Spirit calling it a picnic! So they must continue to summon strength for still another step out of the great reserve force of will, self-preservation.

And "a small spot of ground!" The hand of the stricken swimmer in the night touched something that floated. No "Land Ho!" was ever more of a relief to a shipwrecked sailor than that space where the "water falled" to Clark's soldiers.

They dropped on the wet earth in their wet clothes in the fatigue that dulls keen appetites of a few hours ago and leaves body and mind in the coma of the spent runner who falls across the goal. In time to come they might wonder how they had ever managed to arrive. The thing was that they did arrive.

Hunters, campaigners, and those who "rough it" in summer camps, know what it means to sleep in wet clothes. It is the foremost "Don't" of their lexicon although they have eaten their fill.

And the cold that so saps the strength when there is no fuel for the human furnace which has to be so regularly stoked! The cold at three in the morning on the wet earth in February! One sees the Allies of that campaign of 1779, in Indiana, their backs against tree trunks and against one another's backs huddled together for warmth when they would have that great adventure which took them away from featherbeds and the odor of bacon in the frying pan in Kaskaskia.

And Clark had many "things in general" to think about during that dismal night and also of the things "agreeable to human nature" to make this aquatic enterprise a victory over Hamilton.

His men were three miles farther away from Vincennes than before they began their fourteen hours' wade. On the map this was not what is called progress. The next morning the irrepressible optimist reports everybody being much "amused" when through the mist they heard the report of the morning gun of Fort Sackville which they were to storm.

Anyhow, they knew that their guides had not deceived them. When landmarks were inundated they had not wandered away from their general direction. They knew that their hosts were at home, and hopefully, as another day

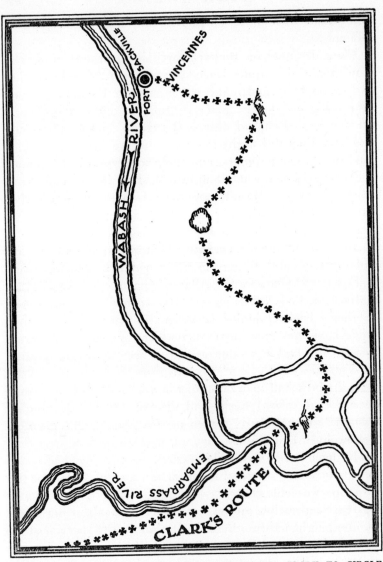

SHOWING HOW THE SWOLLEN RIVERS COMPELLED CLARK TO CIRCLE
SOUTHWARD IN ORDER TO CROSS THE WABASH AND ARRIVE
BEFORE VINCENNES.

had passed without seeing any human being, that the hosts did not know that guests were on the way.

Certainly, the pincers were now tight on the forlorn hope. For breakfast the men seem to have had the last of their horses, or, if not, they did the next day. The going looked better ahead.

"Set off and marched down the river," Bowman related.

If they kept in sight the streak where the water was in movement and bearing driftwood, this was the current of the Embarrass, and it would lead them to the Wabash. Once across the Wabash they were on the same side of the river as the fort and town. How were they to get across the Wabash? But why should soldiers ask questions?

Bowman was not so tired or hungry that his eyes did not light in the settler's quest for new eldorados of virgin soil as they looked over a strip of meadow which was above water.

"Saw some fine land," he notes.

This cheered the veterans of Corn Island who remembered the promise of reward from the "select gentlemen" of Virginia in place of the unsubstantial pay from Ben Franklin's printing press when even that was not being received. As they plunged along they might discuss the value of the overflow in fertilizing that "fine land" and what they would plant and the easy water transportation for their crops down the Wabash to the Ohio.

In the afternoon they stopped on more high ground for a camp where the currents joined. As far as they could see beyond the current it was all lake. The water measured by the height of the tree branches above the surface would be deeper than any they had yet waded through. In that case there would be no marching. There was not even any high ground on the other side of the current for a ferry station. Old timers had to admit that they had struck a record freshet.

Clark's army must wait a while in this new camp. It was again time for entertainment and also time to eat with very little to eat. Clark posted sentries in dry spots, probably some in the branches of trees, to apprise him of any naval expedition from Hamilton which might arrive before his own. He set his men to making new dugouts.

The lack of tools made this a slow business. It is only a guess that they had even an adze for which the useful big knife was a poor substitute. Probably tools had been lost with the pack horses. Ship building had not been contemplated as a part of the expedition's activities.

The original faithful dugout was sent downstream to locate Rogers and his galley and bid him to keep to the oars day and night until he arrived. Four men on a hastily made raft of drift logs were off to the other side of the Wabash to locate the next camp and to bring back any boats they might find.

Even if the galley did not arrive Clark was certain that by increasing his own flotilla he could ferry over unfordable reaches and thus attain his goal. He was hardly borrowing trouble about how he was to take the fort. He had enough present business to occupy him in navigation, commissariat and maintaining morale.

There was little prospect that any game except ducks could be found in this overflowed region. But an effort must be made. A hunting expedition in one of the new canoes might have some result. At least, it would put more hope in the forlorn hope.

Why be downhearted? Things might be worse. His army might have been drowned. There might have been no drift logs out of which to make rafts and canoes. And his men were great. He loved them. It was good to find how sturdy they were.

Indeed, Clark says that he was feeling quite cheerful. He must feel so. The master spirit in leading a forlorn hope develops an auto-intoxication in this respect. He is the actor who is true to a merry part when he knows that personal tragedy may summon him to a deathbed as soon as his make-up is off. Simulation leads to self illusion in imparting the illusion to others. All news must be received as good news. The worse the news, the closer it brings the disaster which only confidence will prevent, the more convincing must be the pretense.

But auto-intoxication could not have been quite complete. Recollection was not altogether unconscious of realities in this crisis of his career. Although he did not include the thought in the public memoir written at the request of school-mate James Madison, he wrote to George Mason:

"If I were sensible that you would let no person see this relation, I would give you a detail of our suffering for four days in crossing those waters and the manner in which it was done; as I am sure that you would credit it. But it is too incredible for any person to believe, except those that are well acquainted with me as you are, or had experience something similar to it. I hope you will excuse me until I have the pleasure of seeing you personally."

The next day, the twentieth, the son of Ann had enough bad news to make it, in his sense, the most cheerful day yet. Far from locating any dry land the crew of the raft, who had gone so far to find it, had to spend the night on their old logs as a bed. Captain McCarthy, who then went in a canoe on the same mission, had to return, in fear of being discovered, at sight of what he took to be a camp of a party of whites and Indians. La Mothe, the master guerilla, might be in command of them. He would have relished so fair a chance for his tactics as an attack on the marooned army.

Clark could be sure of holding his own veterans, men of his own blood. Not so much was to be expected of the French. A weaker bond controlled them. They were in their own land; the people of Vincennes were of their own race.

Hamilton might curse them, but would hardly punish them severely; they would probably be allowed to return to their homes if they made the most of their situation by giving themselves up and thus ending Clark's enterprise in certain fiasco.

Hollow eyed in their misery and hunger, appealing in their plight into which Clark had led them, some of the French came to him. They wanted to give up the hopeless effort. At least, they could float down the Wabash to the Ohio, and finding game to sustain them, work their way back to Kaskaskia.

Clark did not round on them in a martinet's upbraiding. He did not refuse them permission to go. He had sent out a hunting party which might bring in a deer. Why didn't they go for a deer themselves? Any moment the galley might heave in sight with its cannon and plenty of food making success certain. His dark eyes were wells of challenging confidence. With his personal power he must hold them; and without them his numbers would be insufficient for victory.

They walked away quietly. He was sure by their manner that without using force to restrain them, "they could be detained for a few days in the course of which our fate would be known."

Bowman says on the night of the twentieth that "the arrival of the galley is our last hope. Starving. Many of the men much cast down. Hard fortune!" Even his stout philosophy was weakening on an empty stomach.

Another day dawned in mist and drizzle on that saturated band waiting for starvation to finish them. "Camp very quiet, but hungry," says Bowman. "Some almost despair." Still they were waiting for the galley.

A sentry brought in five Frenchmen who were going south on a hunting trip. They said that there were many Indians in Vincennes; La Mothe was there with his irregulars. Otherwise the strength of the garrison was as Colonel Vigo had reported it. Hamilton was just completing alterations and additions in strengthening the fort. Some of the inhabitants were friendly, many lukewarm to the British. There was absolutely no way of reaching the town until the water fell except in boats.

The hunters reported that the advance of Clark was not yet known in Vincennes. The invitation for them to remain with him was made so very politely that it was as out of the question for them to refuse to accept it as for him to risk their rowing back to town with the report of his numbers and their condition and situation.

And the only kind of "kitchen wagon" the hungry might expect arrived. "One of the men killed a deer," says Bowman, "which was distributed in camp." Bowman was restrained even in his hunger, the last to make literary capital out of his emotions. "Very acceptable," was his comment.

One deer would not go far among one hundred and twenty men. This was the only food they had had since the previous day. Bowman says for "two days" which may have referred to his own command.

"I would have given a good deal for one of our horses," remarks Clark. The stallion from New Mexico must have been long since sacrificed. Clark had started with enough supplies for the maximum march; but they had been lost in the water.

The scouts who had been looking for Rogers' galley returned to say that it was not at the rendezvous. Clark must go without waiting longer for its aid. He must move his men before they were too weak and low spirited for effort.

Dawn of the twenty-first saw the canoes paddled back and forth until all were across the Wabash and on a small hill, called the Memel, which had been located. There was no baggage left to be ferried. Anyhow, optimism could dilate on the fact that transport had become much less complex.

And now Clark was on the same side of the river as the fort and town. What next? The French hunters said that there was no land nearer than a sugar camp three miles distant and this could be reached only in boats. Scouts, who were sent in a canoe to make soundings, confirmed this view.

Clark, who was probably the tallest man of his army, waded in to see for himself. Soon he was up to his neck in depths which would be over the heads of many of his men. In famishing intensity they watched their Colonel returning—slowly as he says "in order to give time for reflection." Was there no way to cross except by ferriage which would separate his force to be attacked in detail?

A field of bushes rose above the water. The canoes would have to work their way through them very slowly. Much time would be lost.

Not only hunger was in the men's eyes but something more alarming. At any moment they might reach the breaking point of morale from which a score of antic drummers and fifers and a thousand marching songs might not rally them. The harder and the longer the effort to hold it back the greater must be the collapse when it came.

As Clark came to the bank, the men, whose eyes had never been off him, could not overhear what he said to one of his officers. They saw that his face was very serious. So, even the leader's mask of cheer was off, even he was despairing. The rope of his will which had held them from falling into the abyss was frazzled and snapping. When he gave up all was lost.

It takes little to turn the strongest men in such a plight into panic. In the group psychology of veterans, who had been molded together by long effort against hopeless odds, the communication of alarm was electric. Some were staring; others were moving restlessly about and "bewailing their situation."

Their confusion would feed on itself. They would soon be

in the mood for anything but storming a fort; in a mood to run up a white flag to get a square meal no matter if it came to them as prisoners of war. The need was some kind of action to snap them out of their woeful thoughts.

Clark whispered to the men near him to follow his example. He cupped some water in his hand, mixed some powder in it and blackened his face Indian fashion. This would seem rather cheap theatrics to the average colonel of to-day, although he may find a situation where he will be wise to have the inspiration for its counterpart in his own age. He never had one hundred and twenty wet Frenchmen and American frontiersmen who were stalled on Memel Hill in February and who had had nothing but a sliver of vension to eat for two or three days.

Clark knew that all had the one common bond of Indian precept and surroundings. Always the challenge to the frontiersman was to prove that he had Indian hardihood; and "No Indian can outdo me on the trail!" was the boaster's catchphrase. Clark uttered a war whoop and sprang into the water. The war whoop Indian influence is not out of America yet. We have the college yells which have not yet been one of the influences in the Americanization of Europe.

A chorus of war whoops was the answering "Rah! Rah!" to the leader's signal. The emotions which might have broken into another form of hysteria sent all after him into the water. Now the game was for everybody to go in up to his neck.

Clark's plan was to get them as far as he could by wading and then ferry them over unfordable places. But one of those in the advance felt a ridge under his feet. He followed it a distance while he was getting no deeper, and his comrades were. The glad word was passed, so quickly changing the situation, that he had found a raised road. So, never in water above their waists, now in the regular

marching order of single file—and on a road, a road!—
the army made all the distance to their next stop, the sugar
camp, while the "sick and faintish" as Bowman says were in
the canoes.

The French hunters had been wrong; the scouts had been
wrong. Clark had been right. Again he had triumphed;
he had found a way, in keeping with his reputation and
prestige which were glowing bright again to his followers.

The sugar camp, apparently, was better and larger than
recent camps: the land although wet had been drained.
There must have been firewood: and Clark must have had
to restrain too large blazes for fear of revealing the presence of more than a band of Indians or hunters. Boots and
leggings could be dried, scald feet relieved.

The antic drummer must have dried his drum to be ready
to beat a march to victory. Both the morning and evening
guns from the fort were heard, Bowman tells us. If only
they had food! "No provisions yet. Lord help us!" Even
he was getting emotional. And he may have felt that Clark
had been wrong in not accepting the offer of the French
hunters.

The hunters said that they could easily return to town
and bring back food. Refusal must have been hard, when
Clark was hungry himself, in face of the gaunt specters
around him. His military instinct prevailed. It was not
"agreeable to human nature," when the hunters were asked
to explain for whom they wanted the food, that the intelligence with which they were bursting should not be revealed.

Every hour the secret was kept, if it were not already
known that he was coming, was a gain for success. He was
now only six or seven miles in a direct line from the town.
Its prompt possession meant rations.

The overflow extended all the way to the town; but three
miles ahead rose a stretch of high woods. Beyond he was
told it was easy fording except for a short distance; but

the French hunters were sure that the woods could be reached only by boats. Thus more time would be wasted by ferrying; a whole day might be lost.

So far the weather had been unseasonably warm if so rainy for midwinter. That night there was a sharp change. Ice three quarters of an inch thick formed. "Having frozen in the night and so long fasting" was the way that Bowman expressed the common feeling.

At dawn the men straightened out their stiff joints, rose and hoarsely answered the call of their names and formed to attention in groggy routine, when they were missing their breakfasts more than they had felt the lack of dinners. The sun sparkled on the frost. Sharp dry air whetted appetites. It also made life worth keeping; put a fresh edge to renewed nervous energy for warmth through movement and to reach food. There would be no rain that day to raise the water. Reefs were taken in belts for a tighter grip on the gnawings.

The Colonel was speaking to his soldiers. Their faces were ashy blue in the bright chill light. They were not tidy to look at compared to the morning parade of Hamilton's garrison. Their clothes were torn and streaked with river sediment, and starched by frost. Clark's were no better.

All they had been through he had been through, not to mention that he had had to think so much on things in general and had to deal with so much that was not at all agreeable to human nature. Certainly no member of that band had shaved on the march. There was eighteen days' growth of stubble on their chins, and Clark's was a red flame in the winter sunlight.

"What I said to them I do not remember," Clark said in his Memoir, "but it may be easily imagined by anyone who can understand my affection for them." To him, grubby as they were, both French and Americans, they were good to look at. They had been starving for the cause of his vision. This affection of man to man may be as gentle as the conditions which form it may be rough.

Clark's nose stood out more than ever a beak before his hollow cheeks; his eyes, sunk deeper than ever under the heavy brow, had the glitter which called for the answering glitter to make the final effort. Before them was the Horseshoe plain—good omen to men who were all horsemen—and once they crossed the lake that covered it and reached the woods "there would be an end of their suffering and in a few hours they would be in sight of their long-wished-for goal."

Clark put the climax to his speech by being the first to break the ice as he sprang into the lake. "A huzzah took place." In one sense there was every reason for a cheer; in another very little for men who had to fight a battle in order to be fed.

"Never were men so animated with thoughts of revenging the wrongs of their back settlements as this army was." Bowman wrote.

They were in line rather than single file. They moved rapidly as they broke the ice for half the distance, the water only up to their knees. Then the whole line seemed to slip off into a ravine. They pressed on, but into greater depth. This time there was no raised road to confound the French hunters' statement.

The canoes hurried to put the "weak and faintish" ashore and came back for more in hectic ferriage. Clark, who had kept the strongest men near him, in order that he should have a dependable band to dispatch to meet emergencies, sent some of them wading ahead. They were to cry "land!" as they approached the woods as encouragement; for he saw how the icy water was taking it out of everybody.

Others of the strong were sent to assist the faltering which the canoes could not pick up. Every man's thought was to keep his powder and rifle dry as he might soon be going into action. There were no bushes to cling to for support in passing. When the cry of "land" was passed back by those in front, shivering muscles answered will's call for a final spurt. There were appeals for help from those whose eyes were seeing only mist as they felt that they were about to fall.

Sometimes one man and again two men, who still had some strength to spare, held up one whose strength was ebbing. And yet the water remained deep despite the cheery calls of "land!" It was up to Clark's shoulders, he says, at the edge of the camel's hump of woods.

With canoes leaving the exhausted on the shore, and men foundering and holding on to drift logs and all energy being spent in the sheer business of escape from drowning, here was an army that was *hors de combat*.

What a prospect for La Mothe's volunteers and Indians, tomahawks in hand, should they shoot in surprise around the cover of the woods! Yet there would have been wicked fighting, hand-to-hand battles in the water, after canoes were overturned; and it would not have been only the blood of Clark's men that would have been spilled when the one bullet in the musket had a sure target.

He was warranted in saying that "This was the most trying of all the difficulties we experienced." Men who had arrived were lying still, their bodies half out of the water on the shore. Others were clinging to overhanging branches or to the logs that had been their salvation. Men who dragged comrades ashore sank in collapse beside them. As Clark surveyed the forlorn hope it hardly looked like a capable storming party to take a fort.

But the island was high ground and really dry after the morning's frost and sun. "A delightful spot of about ten acres," optimist Clark described it. The strong were set to building fires. "We soon found that fires answered no purpose, but that two strong men taking a weaker one by the arms was the only way to recover him; and it being a delightful day, it soon did."

That is, it was known that the prostrate were going to live. With food and rest, if pneumonia did not set in, a doctor would have said that they would soon be all right again, as he called for ambulances.

It was good to have a delightful day, but they could not eat sunlight. Could they rise and go on without food? There was no further nourishment in tightening a belt. Clark had reason to regret his "piece of obstinacy," as he called it, in not having allowed the Frenchmen to go for provisions.

Luck had been against him in the unseasonable freshets; against him in the failure of the galley to appear. Now he had a stroke in his favor.

"But fortunately as if designed by Providence," he says, some Indian women were seen coming in a canoe from town by "a nigh way," as Clark expresses it in the language of the time. They might have information of value to him. When his canoes brought them in it was found that they had something better, which they were taking to their men in camp,—corn, tallow and a half quarter of buffalo. Even the tallow was a delectable morsel.

But a quarter of buffalo would go no further than a deer among one hundred and twenty men. They did not break the bonds of discipline by becoming ravening beasts. This was not the way of frontiersmen used to sharing short rations.

"Broth was immediately made," Clark wrote, "and served out to the most weak, with great care. Most of the whole got little, but a great many would not taste it but gave their part to the weakly, jocosely saying something cheerful to their comrades. This little refreshment and fine weather gave new life to the whole."

Unlettered these men, yet they had the very soul of spirit of corps. Their immortal march took high courage;

but here was a finer courage of self-restraint which held hands from snatching for the first food they had seen for three days. Boy Scout masters, if they run short of examples in the ethics of fellowship and grit or tire of modern instances, are referred to an older one.

So the weak were on their feet again and ready with the others to go on. The glitter of their eyes was answering the challenge of Clark's again. "Thus," as Clark puts it, "they passed from one extreme to another as is common under such circumstances."

The canoes ferried them across a narrow place that was over their heads. Then, after marching in shallow water another two miles, they came to a grove on a hill. Hidden themselves by the trees, they could see their goal. The worst was over. All they had to do now was to storm the fort in order to break their fast.

XXVIII

AGAINST THE FORT

Visions of richer land than their ancestors had farmed; of settlements on the wastes they had traversed; of white pillared mansions beside pleasant streams; of a Spanish girl in St. Louis; of revenge for the wrongs on the back country!

The symbol of each man's vision was in the whitewashed houses and palings above which rose the towers surmounting the walls of the wooden fort. Through his glasses Clark could see the dark holes of the embrasures in which the cannon were mounted. He was glad that the houses extended up to the walls of the fort. This would give his riflemen cover for the approach unless Hamilton, forewarned, should burn them.

Shallow water covered the plain, which was broken by ridges, between the grove, where Clark's army was hidden, and the town. There were no bushes to interfere with a rapid advance. The only human beings in sight were some mounted men nearby hunting ducks.

One of the hunters was won into camp by an "active man," presumably a French volunteer, who slipped between him and the town. The other hunters, perhaps because they heard their own tongue spoken, did not flee, but awaited events.

There were still many Indians in town. So far as known Hamilton had not been appraised of the coming attack. Again Clark was told that some of the inhabitants were at heart friendly to the Americans, others indifferent.

A happy item of fresh information, gleaned from the hunter, was that the Grand Door of the Wabash, Tobacco's son, whom Clark's policy and Father Gibault's appeal had won to smoke the pipe of peace six months ago, was also in town. He was a great power, called the Grand Door of the Wabash because of his influence as the most powerful chief of the region.

In the veteran Captain Helm, as the miracle warrior's legate, he had found a brave after his own heart whose fate he would share. When Helm had to surrender to Hamilton the Grand Door insisted that he, too, be regarded as a prisoner. He had remained near Helm, visiting him often to make sure he was well treated.

As the Grand Door refused all wampum and all flattering appeals to accept the bloody belt, or even enter into Hamilton's Indian councils, Hamilton made an occasion of presenting him with an "elegant sword." Gravely the Grand Door inspected the ornamented scabbard, then drew the blade, and bending it on the floor to test its steel, gravely remarked that it would be useful in sticking frogs when the grass grew in the Spring and their brother Big Knives came to release him and Captain Helm.

There was great awe of him even among the young bucks of the other tribes who had slipped away upon the warpath without his approval. He had warned them that a day of reckoning with the Big Knives would come.

"We were now in the situation I had been laboring to attain," Clark says, "with no possibility of retreat in case of defeat. We knew that nothing but the boldest conduct would insure success."

As soon as his army broke out of the copse of woods his advance must be disclosed. Hamilton might put some men in barricades in the streets to rake Clark's line exposed in the open. Or, if Clark entered the town without opposition, his men might fall to raiding pantries in their hunger and get out of hand, prejudicing his plan of attack in which every man must be supremely effective and cool. Confusion

might be increased by sniping from the houses or by a tomahawk rush by a party of hostile Indians. All this was "agreeable to human nature" and of soldiers in action "passing
quickly from one mood to another." Clark's only hope was
in "getting the jump" and keeping it.

The French were nearly half of Clark's force. They had
received the vicar general's blessing and godspeed. They
had not been drafted; they were volunteers who had had
time to learn the true nature of the terrible Bostonnais
and Big Knives. For three weeks they had been on that
midwinter march, whose rigors everyone on the frontier
understood, and the fellowship of the allies had held through
the test.

If the French kindred in Vincennes knew this it might
stiffen the friendly, win the indifferent and cow the British party and some of the militant Indians. Then Hamilton would have to make his whole resistance from the fort;
the houses and palings of the town would be held by Clark's
own riflemen, their famine relieved quickly and in an or-
derly manner to give them strength for the siege.

The captured hunter who had come out for an afternoon's
duck shooting was having unexpectedly interesting sport.
He was to be the bearer of another "placart" to the much
placarded Vincennes. The wonder is that the message written by a commander who had been four days without food
was not wholly incoherent.

"To the Inhabitants of Vincennes—
"Gentlemen: Being now within two miles of your village,
with my army determined to take your fort this night, and
not being willing to surprise you, I am taking this means
of requesting such of you as are true citizens and desirous
of enjoying the liberty I bring you to remain quietly in
your houses. If there are any that are friends of the King
of England I desire them instantly to repair to the fort
and there join his troops and fight like men; and if any

that do not repair to the garrison shall hereafter be discovered they may depend upon being severely punished. Those, on the other hand, who are true friends to Liberty may expect to be well treated. I once more request that they keep out of the streets, for every person found under arms upon my arrival will be treated as an enemy."

War's weapon of the threat! If you are for the British King fight openly for him. Otherwise you will be safe in your houses. But all were warned against clandestine opposition. Hamilton had not allowed any choice in the matter for the citizens when he retook Vincennes. He had in mind that all were in British territory and British subjects. Opposition was treason.

"I entertained conflicting ideas as to what would be the result of the letter." Clark says. "I knew however that it could do no damage."

The duck hunter, who was its bearer, departed with the words of the men of his own race in his ears begging him to make it appear to his fellow townsmen that there was an army of one thousand in the grove. Compliments were sent to Vincennes friends in the names of the men who were supposed to be in Kentucky.

Clark would still utilize his much heralded main body of which the force that had taken Kaskaskia was supposed to be only a detachment. He would chance the impression that the Big Knives before Vincennes, in the company of French allies, were the army that his imagination had mobilized at Corn Island. Much depended upon what the duck hunter had to say when he reached the town.

Through his glasses Clark watched his arrival. There was soon a stir in the streets. The people rushed to the common and heard the message read. Then all were looking toward the grove where Clark was waiting.

But there was no sign of life in the fort. No drum or signal gun was heard. Clark's conclusion was that Hamilton had been forewarned; his preparations made to receive an attack, he was only waiting for the game to be flushed.

Once Clark's line broke from the copse it would be in full view of the town. If his men failed they knew that they might fall into the hands of Indians and be tortured. At least they would be prisoners of war who would be sent on to Detroit.

Clark warned them again of the value of implicit obedience when so much depended upon each man in so small a force. They answered that they hoped he would put to death any man who disobeyed. No commander could ask more when he knew that in a prolonged action they might run out of ammunition, and then their only weapons would be their knives.

They had lost their baggage, but they had kept their flags. Each little group of volunteers, which had been enlisted by the officer who led it, had a flag; and Clark's veterans had shared in the bounty of the enthusiastic needlewomen of Kaskaskia. There was a brave flutter of pennons out of the grove just at sunset as the little army began its final advance. The famished march had become gay display.

At the foot of the copse was a shallow ravine. Several officers were mounted, having borrowed the horses of the duck hunters. They rode in and out among the pennons which were being marched back and forth, so they appeared above the crest of the ravine. It was a schoolboy trick that served its purpose. There being a company pennon for every ten men instead of every fifty the townspeople might see with their own eyes what a formidable force was coming.

The people concluded that this could be none other than the big army from the Falls of the Ohio. Clark himself could not be present. His signature to the proclamation had been used to overawe them with his prestige. Not until the tall man with the red hair—the famous red hair in all the Illinois country—had been pointed out to them would they believe that he was actually in command. A citizenry which had had so extensive an experience as the "subjects" of varying sovereignties was bound to be suspicious that anyone spoke the truth in war.

Twilight had come. From the distance of the town the advancing line became dim shadows that melted into the night. Clark swung around out of the direct line to the heights in the rear of the town. Yet no cannon had flashed from the fort; no rifle had flashed. Clark was mystified. What was the trap Hamilton had set for him?

He sent a small number of men forward to open fire on the fort. And still there was no answer. Their bullets had sunk noiselessly into the thick wooden walls.

The garrison had ascribed the sound of the firing to a salute of the fort at nightfall by drunken Indians and had paid no attention to it. Much of the ammunition which the British supplied to the Indians was used in the joy of sheer noise making. This waste of powder which came all the way from England was another item in the heavy costs of keeping the mercurial children of the forest in good humor as allies.

The battle began when one bullet was not buried in the wooden wall. A British soldier standing at a porthole struck a light which displayed him as a target. When he fell Hamilton knew that an enemy was in range. He had heard that some strange party had spent a night at the sugar camp, and La Mothe had been sent to investigate and intercept them, but by that time Clark, approaching by a route which hid his force from La Mothe's view, was in the copse of woods before the town.

Not one of the inhabitants had gone to tell Hamilton about the arrival of Clark's message. The town had hidden the debouch from the grove and the display of the pennons from the British sentries. There was some wonder at the crowds gathering on the common but not enough to make an investigation. It took little to bring people out of their houses in midwinter when idleness hung heavy on their hands. A dispute between frontiersmen, or the arrival of a hunter from a distance, was enough. The crowd had not remained long on the common. It had soon dissipated indoors in compliance with Clark's warning.

And then, when Vincennes was in the middle of a lake and all the country impassable and Clark was known to have only seventy men in Kaskaskia, the thought that he should be marching across country was inconceivable. For Hamilton to have kept outposts in the outskirts of Vincennes in February weather would have characterized him as a heartless martinet who enjoyed making his soldiers miserable. The hoped-for surprise in attempting the impossible had been effected.

There was to be noise enough that night to satisfy any Indian; more noise than had ever been heard before between the Alleghenies and the Pacific; as much noise as in the Fourth of July celebration in an Indiana town, in the height of the fireworks period one hundred years later, when the boys were well supplied with giant crackers.

The cannon, which held the Indians in such awe, were booming with mighty bursts of flame. Hamilton's rifles were flashing in answer to the fire of the thin line of riflemen with which Clark had surrounded the fort while he kept a majority of his troops in reserve. He was riding back and forth on his "borrowed" horse directing his dispositions with many things to do as well as to think about.

And he had the town. Soldiers behind the palings, Indians, faces at the windows were revealed by the cannon flashes between intervals or darkness. It was not the Big Knives but Hamilton's cannon balls which were shattering the houses as a further encouragement to the people that fortune if not conviction was making them Clark partisans. The lot of being a cockpit which Kaskaskia feared was that of Vincennes.

The apprehension which had been haunting Clark for days on the march concerned another famine than that for food, empty powder horns as well as empty stomachs in the midst of action. Again the seeds which his policy had sown came to harvest. Colonel Le Gras and Major Busseron, of the local militia, who had not heeded Helm's signal to repair to their post against the hopeless odds of Hamilton's advance, had nursed, under their external compliance, a growing irritation against Hamilton's rule.

They came to Clark with word of secreted treasure more valuable in this crisis than hoarded pirate gold. A quantity of powder and ball, which they had buried upon Hamilton's approach, was at Clark's service. Now there would be no lack of ammunition. Young men of the town carried it through the fire to their kindred and the Big Knives on the firing line where a number of them joined in the attack.

Perhaps there were enough to take the place of Clark's "sick and faintish" who were unfit for duty. But mention of the "sick and faintish" has passed from the chronicle. Perhaps the prospect of action started convalescence; and the moment of action brought complete recovery.

Meanwhile a famous brave was watching a famous brave in action. So this was the miracle warrior himself. He was as tall and quick as the man of the tales which the birds bore. This paleface chief understood the paleface's wonder weapons. It was not for big Indian chief to be abashed by the cannon's thunders when big paleface chief was bearing himself so carelessly before the iron balls the thunders spat. Big Indian chief, his own sculptured bronze face as impassive in the flashes as if it had been in council, saluted big paleface chief.

The Grand Door of the Wabash thought that the time

had come for red brother to fight side by side with Big Knife brother. Back of him were thirty tried warriors who had been long restrained from the warpath, their throats open for the war whoop.

Stirred by the example of Clark's fiery energy he would make sure by their prowess that the day of reckoning which he had promised foolish young bucks had come. Tribesmen who had defied his authority should know that the Grand Door had raised his tomahawk and have another lesson to nudge their memories in the force with which it could strike.

Here was the offer of a reinforcement of enormous, perhaps of decisive value, when Clark knew that La Mothe and his irregulars and many hostile Indians were near the town and might spring upon his line from the rear. Clark would not deviate from his principle; he would not make an exception which would be heralded far over the trails to convict him, when he had declared that he spoke with only one tongue, of being a liar to all the chiefs with whom he had made treaties of peace. But the Grand Door, who had so faithfully kept his promise, must not be offended. He was told that all was going well according to plan; and to wait until morning.

So white chief saluted Indian chief and then was away to the rim of flashes from the rifles of his own braves, who were against wooden walls which bullets could not penetrate, and who had no cannon with which to answer the fort's cannon. Such was the handicap in theory; but Clark, naturally, had studied the fort well. Even if he had not, the tactical thrust and feint of the soldier in action, which, in the early period of the World War often developed under fire a better position for a trench than an engineer had plotted, was serving Clark's men in the same way in confounding theory by practice with the weapons of their day.

They found that if they crawled to within thirty yards of the fort wall the cannon could not be sufficiently depressed to bear upon them. They could laugh at the balls passing over their heads, when those same balls would have made a hot duel of it against Rogers' galley firing from the river.

Hamilton's cannon were mounted in the towers of the fort eleven feet above the ground, and yet the embrasures were so open that the cannoneers exposed themselves to Clark's riflemen on the ground. There was a light inside the fort shadowily silhouetting them; and the flash of the gun illumined the face of the man who put the match to the touch-hole. Here was sharpshooting to the taste of frontiersmen. A dozen of them might be watching for a target as they would for game to flush from a thicket. There was a burst of bullets into the gunport when the target appeared.

The cannon had become useless except in destroying the town or hitting men in reserve. It was riflemen from the loopholes of the fort against riflemen behind palings or any breastwork they could hastily raise. And the only target the defenders had were the well-separated flashes.

After a flash it was dark again. But the man whose rifle had made the flash was no longer where the flash had been seen. He had moved a few yards to the right or left as he reloaded and waited for another shot. It was like shooting at the flashes of fireflies on the wing.

Captain Leonard Helm, who was a prisoner in the fort which he formerly commanded, was hearing sweet music. Hour after hour through the night the sniping kept up. The fort was a stationary target for that elusive dodging enemy with darkness for his shield. One by one the cannoneers were being picked off.

As Clark's men gained confidence cries rose in the intervals of silence; cries of raucous and profane defiance; warnings that only a part of "us" are in yet. Wait until the rest of the army begins shooting! Wait until "our" navy with its cannon arrives!

When the British closed some of their gunports they

heard taunts of a white-livered timidity which were hard for royal artillerists to bear. Where is your boasted British courage? Is your "Hair Buyer" Colonel "scairt"? Didn't he want some more scalps to send to King George?

You're not against women and children now, Come on! Bring on your redskin murderers, too! Are you afraid to use your cannon against muskets? Show yourselves! Fight, you snotty, redcoated sons of muck, or we'll come and get you! Answers in kind to swinish rebels and bloody traitors came from the fort.

When the artillerists opened the ports there was another burst of bullets and a war whoop of triumph followed by the demoniac baiting laughter of famished men in the exaltation of action.

But what of the morning when the men from whom the cries came, and whose hands held the sniping rifles, would be visible in that intimate action, and the fact of their small numbers revealed?

Clark had scouts on the lookout for La Mothe with orders that unless he and his whole band could be captured they were to be allowed to pass in case they wanted to enter the fort. It was better to have them in front in siege than free lancing in the rear.

Before dawn shadowy figures sprang out of the night and scuttled through the open spaces between the American line where it was thinnest. La Mothe, himself, passed within a few feet of one of the American officers. Ladders were lowered from the parapet for the reinforcement which was welcomed with joyous shouts from the garrison. Even then, apparently, so literally and subordinately did Clark's men interpret his orders, no one fired on them.

But Clark had not prohibited the use of language. In this there was no muzzle loading limit to the volume of the fusillade. The discharge was as automatic in its rapidity as the latest type of machine gun. With some of La Mothe's men slipping from the ladder rungs, a guffaw went with the gibing.

Get into your holes, you skunks! You have taken your last scalp, outraged your last woman. We have you where we want you when we begin our own job of scalping. Retribution is near.

How rigorous it would be if left to individual license appeared when François Maisonville, one of the most notorious of Hamilton's white leaders of Indians, was taken by two Americans. When Clark saw him bound and being used as a breastwork by his captors he was put under guard as a prisoner. But frontiersmen thought in terms of scalp for scalp as well as eye for eye and tooth for tooth. Some vengeful Big Knife took a nick out of Maisonville's crown as a reminder of what he had been doing to white settlers.

Just before dawn Clark drew off his firing line except for a few outposts of observation. He would be ready for any fresh emergency while he studied the situation. Another and more powerful reason for withdrawal was rations. Some of his men had had snacks passed to them; others seem to have had none.

Having been in action all night, after four days without food, they had a square meal from the town's supplies. The number of loitering Indians on the outskirts had not increased and the Grand Door of the Wabash was keeping watch of them. Any hostile parties approaching might now be seen at a distance. Eyes trained hopefully down the river were not rewarded by a sight of Rogers' galley. The fort was undamaged. It had provisions to last for months, Clark knew, and ammunition to hold out for a long siege.

Sniping into embrasures under the cannon balls had been excellent for morale; but the number of casualties inflicted on the garrison might easily be overestimated. In daylight Hamilton's cannoneers and riflemen could see their targets.

XXIX

HASTENING THE CLIMAX

THERE was quiet again. In this respect only was the morning of the twenty fourth like any other winter morning in Vincennes. The emaciated fighters were seen clearly in the daylight. Although they had gone so close to the fort, which had fired all night, they were not lying dead and wounded, as the inhabitants expected, but eating ravenously as wolves, these wolfish men.

Cannon balls were lying out in the fields which they had plowed. Chimneys had been smashed. There were gaping holes in wooden house walls. The people, who had been spectators out of range, were surveying the damage that had been done to their town. They and the Indians drew nearer as they saw a man bearing a white flag moving toward the fort gate.

The red headed Colonel, who looked far from a mood to give up the battle, had been writing a message for the Colonel in the fort. There would be no more firing until the white flag returned. Meanwhile the hungry wolf men continued eating.

Clark had reason to believe that Hamilton had captured an express from Williamsburg. This might have the letter from Governor Henry for which he had so long waited. He was thinking in terms of the bold course as usual. If Hamilton would keep up resistance he must know what to expect.

"Sir: In order to save yourself from the impending storm that now threatens you I order you to immediately surrender yourself up with all your Garrison, Stores, &c, &c., for if I am obliged to storm, you may depend upon such treatment justly due to a Murderer. Beware of destroying Stores of any kind, or papers or letters that are in your possession, or hurting one house in the town, for, by heavens, if you do there shall be no mercy shewn you."

It was a very red headed message, and anything but polite. Treatment justly due to a murderer! Yes, by Heavens! All the "haughty and violent dispositions" of the Virginians which Hamilton had proclaimed and all the ruthless Big Knife reputation were expressed by a commander in keeping with the cries and taunts of his men during the night.

The letter breathed the thought, "We are unbeatable." The sum of its threat was surrender or a massacre. Mother Ann, who knew that her second son would never cease to be a boy, if she read the words, would probably have said that he was indulging in "tall talk" and "showing off." She would have known that he would do no massacring; but he was bound to have his own way as usual.

Hamilton semed to be inclined to the same view. He may have thought that he would give a ruffian a lesson in manners in his brief answer. He had had only one sleepless night so far.

"Governor Hamilton begs to acquaint Colonel Clark that he and his garrison are not disposed to be awed into any action unworthy of British subjects." If Hamilton had won or fought to the death, Clark's ultimatum would have been futile bombast and Hamilton's an example of proud restraint.

Anyhow, this ended the repartee in words. The next move was with Clark. When he turned to his men, who now had a square meal under their belts, he found them eager to storm the fort. But ladders would be necessary in order to scale the walls. A rush to break through the gate would have met bayonets after point blank fire and in close quarters inside the walls where Hamilton's men could choose their positions. In that kind of fighting British regular stubbornness would be very much at home. Hamilton would have welcomed such impetuosity which he may have anticipated as in keeping with "the haughty and violent dispositions."

"This would have been a piece of rashness," Clark said.

He had no lives to spare for experiments. Considering how soldiers "passed from one extreme to another" a repulse might be decisive against him. He would keep the rein on refreshed strength which might easily expend itself, continue administering the medicine which had been proven efficacious by renewing the fusillade.

His riflemen had breastworks on the town side of the fort; they had already found the safe angles on the other side. Although they were now visible, they were such accurate shots, and so short was the range, that their heads were hardly more exposed targets than the eyes and foreheads behind the sights through the loopholes. They found that the cannoneers could be almost as easily picked off in daylight as in the dark. All day they were to keep up their sniping and their taunts, still casting glances down the river for sight of the galley which did not arrive.

Clark mentions having men wounded. Whether or not there were any killed is not clear. Doubtless there were. If not, then in face of so much musket fire, although the cannon balls were still going over their heads, this was amazing luck as well as a tribute to the fox and weasel tactics of the frontiersmen. Probably the eye behind the breastwork was a little quicker in getting the bead and firing than the eye through the loophole.

Anyhow, Hamilton's force was being whittled down faster than Clark's in the course of the day's attrition. As the afternoon drew on, what of the night? What of the next day? Clark hoped that when Rogers' galley arrived he could explode the fort's powder magazine with a hot shot.

Hamilton saw that Clark was evidently making preparations which suggested he was planning to undermine the

Colonel Clark's Compliments to Mr.
Hamilton and begs leave to inform
him that Col. Clark will not agree
to Any Other Terms than that of Mr.
Hamilton's Surendering himself and
Garrison Prisoners at Discretion —

If Mr. Hamilton is Desirous of
a Conferance with Col. Clark he will
meet him at the Church with Capt.
Helms —

Feby 24th 1779   G R Clark

CLARK'S SUMMONS TO HAMILTON TO THE UNCONDITIONAL
SURRENDER OF FORT SACKVILLE. *Draper manuscript*

fort during the night, when there also would be the danger
—which Clark does not mention—of piling inflammable material against one of its walls and igniting it which would
be another means of exploding the magazine. Surely Hamilton realized that so bold a leader as Clark would not be content with a leisurely and conventional siege.

Another white flag brought silence. This time it came
from the fort. Hamilton was in a changed mood. He asked
for a three days' truce in which he would undertake no defensive works and Clark no offensive works. He would like
to confer with Clark "as soon as can be." Either side was
to have two persons present at the parley. "Whatever may
pass" was to be kept secret until "matters be finally concluded to the honor and credit of both parties. If Colonel
Clark makes a difficulty of coming into the fort, Lt. Governor Hamilton will meet him by the gate."

His officers apprehending a trick to kidnap him, begged
Clark not to enter the fort. But Clark was not worried that
Hamilton, although he did hire Indians to murder settlers,
would be guilty of the foulest of all breaches of military
ethics. Clark's concern was Hamilton's object in the truce.

Was Hamilton expecting the arrival of bands of Indian
allies? Was reinforcement from Detroit on the way? Although Rogers' galley might arrive in the meantime, again
it might not. Clark seems to have dismissed aid from the galley from his mind.

It was Clark's turn to be brief. He replied:

"Colonel Clark's compliments to Mr. Hamilton and begs
leave to inform him that Colonel Clark will not agree to any
other terms than that of Mr. Hamilton's surrendering himself and Garrison Prisoners at discretion. If Mr. Hamilton
is desirous of a conference with Colonel Clark he will meet
him at the Church with Captain Helm."

Clark's grimly keen frontiersmen, and Indians and townspeople in gaping silence, were watching the gate after the messenger passed through. When it opened again Hamilton and Major Hay appeared with Captain Helm.

So unkempt himself, with the deep red stubble on his chin, Clark had his first view of the antagonist in his garrison valeted uniform. One may make much of the contrast. The essential thing is that manners never so much make the man as when he is in mud-stained clothes. They doubtless reflected a youth—he was only twenty-six—who would be at home in ruffled shirt or the best fitting buff and blue uniform a tailor could turn out. He seems to have known how to use his commanding height for effect. Probably in all punctiliousness, as he relished the situation, Clark was a little arrogant in emphasizing his confidence that he had only to keep on acting a bold part to conclude the business.

There was drama enough in the personal meeting itself; but here seems a good place to mention an incident, which occurred during the conference, and which expressed in stark realism all the passions, ambitions of kings and peoples and land hunger which had placed Clark and Hamilton facing each other on the banks of the Wabash.

A party of forty or fifty Indians were seen coming in from the warpath beating their breasts and shouting in triumph. They had news to please Hamilton, in two settlers as prisoners and in fresh scalps which they had taken on their raid, to cash in for wampum. As the British flag was still flying over the fort, and there had been silence during the truce, they did not know that the Americans were in Vincennes until Captain Williams and his company hurried out to intercept them.

Then the joy died in their throats; many escaped by flight; about fifteen were taken. To these the Grand Door of the Wabash might well have spoken his "I told you so." Their day of reckoning had come.

There was no restraining Williams' men who had been

seeing red in action as they feared that hostile Indians might strike the rear of their siege line. Their relatives and friends had been scalped and tortured by such fiends as these, who had been caught bearing the bloody trophies of the kind of an outrage whose avengement was the object of that icy march. Punishment should fit the crime and promptly, without waiting on orders from Clark for an execution which was so quickly over. When one of the French volunteers found that one of the two French guerilla leaders of the Indians was his own son, his life was spared for his father's sake as passion cooled.

There was the vivid fact of Hamilton, negotiating for terms, powerless as their employer to save the lives of his scalpers. The miracle warrior had warned all braves who went on the warpath against Big Knives that they would be hunted down. Word would go out over the trails to the Indian villages as far as "Chicagou" and even into the Wisconsin forests that the Big Knives had the power to punish and did punish.

Hamilton had prepared terms of capitulation which included all the honors of war and that he and his troops should join the British garrison at Pensacola. Clark complimented him on his skillful defense; warned him that his men were embittered against his Indian policy; that there would be no holding them when they broke into the fort. There would be murder done.

"It would be beyond the power of a single officer to save a single man." This was putting it strong for effect. Yet Clark had good reasons for providing against such an eventuality of bitter close quarters fighting inside the fort, when the victims would be British soldiers acting in their line of duty. The massacre of a British garrison would be a black blot on the Revolutionist record, a justification of employing "savages against worse than savages" to confound Pitt and Burke in Parliament.

Clark held out resolutely for unconditional surrender. Helm supported Hamilton's argument for more liberal terms. Helm knew how strong the garrison was and how well provisioned; and he was impatient to raise the flag again over the fort.

"Without viewing us as savages," Clark wrote, "they could not suppose that they would be treated worse in consequence . . . Governor Hamilton then said that Captain Helm was liberated from that moment and might act according to his pleasure. I told the Captain that I would not receive him on such terms; that he must return to the fort and await his fate. I told the Governor that I would not begin hostilities until one minute after the drums had given the alarm."

Clark turned to go, and Hamilton, too. They were back to back, apparently the last word spoken before they began a fight to the death in that contest for empire which permitted of no compromises. But Hamilton was thinking fast. His plight was now what Clark's would have been if Clark had failed.

Detroit, the nearest British post, was six hundred miles away. The winter conditions, which had been so against Clark on the march, were now in his favor as one looked over the flooded land that he had crossed. The survivors of a desperate British sortie, which made an opening in Clark's lines, would be moving northward, in the worst period of Winter through country in which the Indians would now be unfriendly, to starvation in the snow if not overtaken by the wolfish pursuit of these lean devils of Big Knives.

It was a hard position for the proud Hamilton, who had grown somewhat saturnine in three years of irritating dealings with French and Indian allies, while he dreamed of promotion and comfort in England. In the Spring he had hoped to close his career brilliantly by taking Pittsburgh.

All the money he had spent, all his preparations had been in vain. The indigent rebel had him surrounded.

In his final official report, Hamilton says that it was Major Hay and Captain Bowman who loitered and suggested further parley. Clark says that Hamilton faced about and called to him, and "politely asked if I would be good enough to give him my reasons for refusing any other terms than I had offered to the garrison."

The answer was that "in the name of the widowed and fatherless on the frontier," he would have the Indian partisans in the garrison in his power to do with as he saw fit. If Hamilton "chose to risk the massacre of the garrison it was his affair." Clark avers that he was talking less for the benefit of Hamilton himself, than for Major Hay, "who was paying close attention, and this in a great measure influenced my conversation."

Jehu Hay was a native Pennsylvanian who enlisted in a British regiment in the French and Indian War. A major of British militia, he had been in actual command of the Detroit garrison, under Lieutenant Colonel Hamilton as Governor, as well as the local Indian agent and responsible organizer of the raids of the Indian allies. All this Clark's men knew well.

The British regular officers at Detroit did not like Hay. Not all shared Hamilton's views as to Indian policy. As Britons born, they were doing their duty in the regular establishment for king and country. In their professional soldier code was the same instinct which led some British regular officers in South Africa to say, "If I were a Boer I hope I should be fighting with the Boers for my country." In the Revolution some were thinking, "If I were an American I hope that I should be fighting with the rebels," which was no compliment from the King's "officers and gentlemen" to the American Tories.

Hay had gone against his own people, and in the rene-gade's eagerness to prove himself, had become the instigator of the savagery that disemboweled women with child. Nominally he must be received as a fellow-officer in British uniform, but the sight of him, as the glad recipient of white scalps for which he paid, did not lead other redcoats to care for his personal company.

"Pray, sir," Hamilton inquired, "who is it that you call Indian partisans?"

Clark relished the opportunity to be specific.

"Sir, I take Major Hay to be one of the principal ones."

One judges Hamilton to have been too good a soldier to have quavered if Clark had named him; but the reply took the starch out of Hay. He was not equal to stoicism when the kismet of his career was so close at hand. Clark says that he was so stricken and "pale and trembling, that he was scarcely able to stand. Governor Hamilton blushed, and was, I ob-served, much affected at this behavior in my presence. Captain Bowman's countenance sufficiently disclosed his disdain for one and sorrow for the other."

Clark enjoyed that moment; it was one of supreme ret-ribution. It paid for sleepless nights and famishing days. He had relieved his mind. He had posted Hay for what he was; had seen him craven and suffering mental torture be-fore his commander. Clark told Hamilton that he would take a little time for counsel. If he did not send a white flag for further parley then the drums would give notice that he had not changed his mind.

His officers, who also understood how hard it would be to hold the men in hot blood, when their comrades were being shot and bayoneted in storming the fort, were for modify-ing the terms. Clark yielded to their view, quite readily, it seems, after he had made his point to Hay.

It was agreed with Hamilton that the fort, with all its ammunition and supplies was to be "delivered up"; officers were to be allowed "necessary" baggage; and the garrison to march out the next morning, the twenty-fifth, as prisoners of war.

Clark had to face further suspicion from his officers and men because the British were to remain over night in the fort. He knew, for one thing, that the British would have large rations of whiskey in the fort. It would be far more difficult to keep his men in hand in the dark than in the light. Hay might suffer something more mortally retributive than repartee.

Clark also wanted time to arrange for taking over the fort and its supplies in good order and for the secure care of prisoners almost equal in numbers to his own force. While the blood of his own men cooled, all except the parties posted in observation would have a night of real rest.

"I passed the night," Hamilton wrote in his final official report to his superiors, "in sorting papers and in preparing for the disagreeable ceremony of the next day. Mortification, disappointment and indignation had their turns." There was much blame for the poltroonery of his French allies in excusing his failure and he was depressed that "our wounded must be left at the mercy of a mercyless set of Banditti."

In order "that we might be spared the mortification of hauling them down" he did not hoist the colors the next morning. It was with "fix'd bayonets and the Soldiers with their knapsacks," he reminds us, that the garrison marched out, led by the veterans of the King's Eighth who may have been glad of an end of fighting white men in brotherhood with savages.

Major Hay and Captain La Mothe must have been the most uncomfortable of the prisoners in face of the ferret glitter from the eyes of that line of mud-stained frontiersmen as they stood to attention while the arms of their enemies were stacked.

It was a memorable spectacle too, this yielding of his

strong fort by the mighty British Father, for both the townspeople and the Indians. Of all, perhaps it was most gratifying to good friend, the Grand Door of the Wabash, a high honor to him in having recovered his own as a prophet in his own land. This is, of course, reserving an exception in white haired Captain Helm, late commander of the garrison of one, as he raised the flag he had kept secreted, while the little antic drummer must have been fully equal to the occasion.

Three days after the surrender Rogers' galley arrived. Having rowed their hearts out against the flood his men were bitterly disappointed at being late for the "party." What wouldn't they have done to that fort with their man-of-war if they had had the chance!

At the end of his report Hamilton does say, "The difficulties and dangers of Colonel Clark's march from the Illinois, were such as required great courage to encounter, and great perseverance to overcome." Elsewhere he says: "I must tender this testimony to the officers and men under Colonel Clark's command that they have treated our officers and soldiers as men of honor should."

Even in his report of exculpation to his superiors Hamilton made no charge that the "mercyless" banditti harmed one of the prisoners, not even Hay or La Mothe. But he had many complaints. In the night, when he feared that two "drunken soldiers" would murder him, he had to repair to Clark's quarters for security. He said Clark "robbed" his surgeon of the medical stores. But Clark had none for his own men; he had to care for the British wounded who must remain in Vincennes.

Hamilton said there was no time for making bread before the prisoners were sent away. But Clark was sore put to get transport and escort, and would be relieved of the burden of the prisoners as soon as possible when his own garrison was so small. His own men were used to going without bread. It

ROSTER OF THE BRITISH GARRISON OF FORT SACKVILLE WHICH SURRENDERED TO CLARK. *Draper manuscript*

is certainly not "agreeable to human nature" that the victors do better by the vanquished than by themselves.

Hamilton thought that Clark took a very meager view of what was "necessary" as officers' baggage. It might have been to British officers used to much impedimenta even on the frontier and to the young Clark who was accompanied by a servant when he first descended the Ohio. All Big Knives had learned the value of traveling "light" on such a journey as was ahead of the convoy of prisoners down the Wabash, up the Ohio and the Monongahela and then overland to Williamsburg.

In the gamble of war Hamilton had had the misfortune to meet a genius in frontier warfare, and I rather think in any kind of warfare if opportunity had come to him. Between the lines one reads that Hamilton suffered not only a military surprise but one in the quality and breeding of the son of Ann which was the more trying to Hamilton in view of a conscience pricked by the company he had been keeping.

On that long and arduous trip of the prisoners the small escort, which had to prevent their escape, also guarded them against public indignation when they reached the main frontier. It was then, as it has ever been, that the farther from the front the greater is the bitterness.

To Virginians, with husbands and sons in Washington's army and enduring war stresses, Hamilton was the arch fiend of Indian atrocities. They had him in their power. Although Thomas Jefferson was now governor, Hamilton was for a time put in irons. Maisonville committed suicide. Finally, the harsh treatment of the prisoners, relieved by individual kindnesses, was officially ameliorated by the intercession of General Washington.

La Mothe had been sent to Williamsburg. But Clark had a surprise for the French volunteers who had served under him. They were given provisions and boats and bidden to return to their homes and families in Detroit.

XXX

"FOR WANT OF A FEW MEN"

GEORGE WASHINGTON was sipping wine after dinner when an express arrived. All talk halted as the members of his personal staff, who were in the room with him, watched him open the envelope.

In their knowledge of their chief they could read signs of what was passing in his mind which were masked to others. They knew from previous experience that there might be revelations in this dispatch to draw an explosion of anger in that intimate circle at a further stupidity which would increase his heavy burden; and how the anger would pass as he girded himself afresh to his problem.

This time, apparently, the news, at least, was not very bad. They saw the muscles of his face relaxing. It must be good news. The muscles kept on relaxing. The lines which had been set through four years' determination against odds were melting into softness which was more glowing than a smile at one of Alexander Hamilton's after-dinner witicisms, or a pungent bit of military irony by Baron von Steuben, or a quip by the Marquis de Lafayette. It must be very good news, perhaps great news, when even a little good news would be welcome.

At length General Washington broke the silence over that message which had come a thousand miles by boat and trail by remarking that Colonel George Rogers Clark by a mid-winter march had captured Hamilton and his garrison.

Glasses must have been emptied then, and refilled. This was the Clark who had discovered to staff minds a place called Kaskaskia, which was opposite a place called St.

Louis, and now discovered to them another place called Vincennes—all so far away in the wilderness.

If, on the heels of the messenger, Clark, himself, had appeared at Washington's headquarters! If he had brought his winning ways to bear in his towering height and his frontiersman's Indian tan on members in the lobby, and appeared on the rostrum beside the speaker, to give the Continental Congress a reason for applause when they had so few reasons! If, in the fashion of the knights of old, he had been accompanied by one of his veterans as his herald, playing the part of the modern press agent, to describe the icy march and this marvelous achievement by so modest a hero who could not speak for himself!

At least, when victors can not return at once to make the most of their victory they are wise to have emissaries who will make sure that it is properly appreciated in high places and by the public. Clark's publicity department was entirely occupied with local affairs when no war correspondents were following him.

As Washington contemplated the news from the West he must have been thinking of it in relation to depreciated currency, the French alliance, the hoped for alliance with Spain; he must have been fitting it into its place in the scheme of his whole from the Mississippi's mouth to Maine and Lake Champlain in the continental area of the activities of the Continental Army which he commanded.

There was no wireless at his command; no telegraph, as even Lincoln had to tick into his office what was happening along the front from the Potomac to the Mississippi. By the slow means of the communication of the time, Washington waited for information of British movements and plans; and in the same way sent his orders, or more often his advice and recommendations in patient understanding, broken by bursts of temper to his staff, of the jealousies of the states and militia commanders.

Hamilton, master mind of the Indian campaigns in the West, a prisoner! Indian tribes from the Wabash to the Mississippi in control! Here was a breathing time on the Western front. This much the young Clark had accomplished in the scheme of the whole which was plotted in the live map of Washington's mind.

Pittsburgh would be secure for the coming summer. Colonel Brodhead had enough men in garrison there without expecting heavy reinforcements to meet a crisis. Provisions were assured from the back country if not enough money to pay for them. No harrowing outcry for relief from the settlements would be a further drain on the main army's meager reserves. Immediate troubles from one section might be eliminated. The Commander-in-Chief was sipping an excellent vintage that evening.

Two years later he was to write in a letter appreciating Clark's services, "I have not the pleasure of knowing the gentleman—" when he had to know so many who were bores, so many incompetents who wasted his time making explanations and ever calling for money and men he could not give. This young man, with the little army which he had raised himself, and no help except that little stock of paper money, had sent the word which every commander-in-chief wants to hear, that of victory.

Clark, himself, whose active years had been spent west of the Alleghenies, could have understood little of Washington's problems except that it was the duty of an American officer to fight any British in front of him. He was a youth with an obsession. With sufficient youths who have the right kind of obsessions any war can be won.

Clark had a further measure of his victory in the official spoils in captured Fort Sackville at Vincennes. His frontiersmen had never seen so much wealth before. It included British specie for future Indian bribes and soldier pay days; the value of the total was one hundred thousand dollars in gold. Out of it Clark's soldiers received back pay, and more than pay in the custom of the time. "They were almost rich." Clark and his officers took nothing except some needed clothes and boots from the stores.

Captain Helm and forty men, mostly French militia of Vincennes who were sent up the Wabash, learned for whom Hamilton was waiting when he asked for the three days' truce which Clark refused. Creeping up on their camp at night they captured forty British and the stores and gold which they were escorting. Here was more largess, one thousand dollars each for the French militiamen who must have concluded that going to war under Clark was more profitable than gathering furs. Six more captured cannon, including a brass six-pounder, in addition to those captured in Vincennes, gave Clark quite an artillery establishment according to the standards of the time.

What next? The hum of Detroit in Clark's ears had a nearer sound, but the goal was still very far away. The French volunteers from Detroit, whom he had sent back to their homes after their surrender, would bear fair news of the Big Knives to their neighbors. He sent word by them to Captain Lernault in command at Detroit that he would arrive almost as soon as they, and he was glad that the works were being strengthened as that would be less expense for him.

What was the strength of the garrison? Clark seems to have known that it was about one hundred regulars aside from militia. It had been cleaned of supplies until the lakes opened in the Spring. So busy had the people been in convoying and aiding Hamilton's expedition that they had not yet threshed the previous year's crop of corn at last accounts.

Clark decided to move immediately on Detroit. He was firing his weary men for another effort. They had captured British gold to fill their pockets, British provisions to feed them. His Kaskaskian French rose to the challenge. The Vincennes French would join them.

It was six hundred miles to Detroit which, except through trailless forests along the shore, was approachable only by crossing the lake. If Clark arrived at the mouth of the Maumee before the ice broke he could cross it in two days' march; if not, he must make his way by boat. Hamilton, with provisions and trailsmen sent ahead to prepare the way, had taken more than three months to reach Vincennes.

Twice Clark had challenged the impossible. Again he might be in the clinch of a forlorn hope with death by starvation in retreat and succor in storming a fort. Twice he had found the way, twice he had won. He would win the third time.

Once he had Detroit, as he said, all the country between the lakes and the Ohio would be in control. All the gambling spirit of him called for the cast. His instinct told him this was the time, as it had when he dared the march to Vincennes.

He was making his plans to that end, in the glow of the most daring venture yet, when the sight of Rogers' galley arriving assured him that he could count on the eager reinforcement of its crew. With them he had two hundred men. It was now fourteen months since he had heard from Governor Henry; but, no matter, he would keep on sending news to the Governor. No matter about Continental script! No matter about drawing bills on Pollock! Again he would make King George pay his expenses out of the British treasury. Youth was in a merry mood for another plunge into icy waters for the supreme prize.

If only the members of the original crew had been on board Rogers' galley, Vincennes would have been only a brief stop-over for that little man-of-war on the way to the portage to Detroit. But she had picked up an extra man.

He restored a bond that seemed to be broken, a band of responsibility.

This messenger brought Clark the first word he had had from Governor Henry for fourteen months. He was far from forgotten, as he had feared. His capture of Kaskaskia had created a stir up and down the James. Mother Ann had further reason to be proud of her wild son.

The Governor made no mention of credits. This little detail was still being left to Oliver Pollock. But only plain paper, not even Continental script, was required for printing the resolution of thanks to Clark for his victory by the Virginia Assembly.

Something more materially important was that the Governor was starting five hundred Virginia militia as a reinforcement for Clark. They were under Montgomery who had been one of his officers on the march to Kaskaskia and whom he had sent bearing an express and to escort Rochblave to Williamsburg.

Making allowance for garrisons, and adding his veterans and French volunteers to the five hundred, Clark would have six or seven hundred men in the Spring, when weather favored his advance. Still his instinct was to go with the force he had; to live hard and travel light in swift mobility. But reason was countering instinct. So were his officers, the more he talked with them.

Twice fortune had favored the desperate stroke that necessity commanded. Why take a risk which necessity did not command? All that he had won would be endangered by failure. He was realizing, through the reëstablished connection with the outside world, how much he had already won.

Everywhere else the Continentals were on the defensive on their own ground; but Clark's operations had carried an American offensive across the Alleghenies, across the Ohio, far into British territory. The flag at Cahokia was floating farther from Pittsburgh than Pittsburgh was from Washington's headquarters.

If Clark were absent when they arrived who would take charge of the reinforcements? If his expedition broke in starvation on the trail or before the walls of the Detroit fort, or if he were killed, who could take his place? Then all his prestige would be lost with the Indians he had won to peace. Not only would Vincennes and Kaskaskia be lost, but the Kentucky settlements might be overwhelmed.

His right hand man, Major Joseph Bowman, had been injured by the accidental explosion of some powder in the fort. Many of the veterans of the march to Vincennes were now ill. So much prosperity was not good for them after such long abstinence and hardship. Some had been too well entertained by the local inhabitants, eaten too much, and probably drunk too much of the stores of ration whisky among the captured British stores.

Even those who had been temperate were feeling the cumulative lassitude, in which nature insists upon a protracted rest to make up for the loss of periods of regular rest during extended strain. All frontiersmen were used to "laying up" for many days after a long trip over the trails. As they ate their fill in camp, after thirty miles a day on foot on iron rations, it became an effort to move a hundred yards to a neighbor's cabin. Rest areas in France in 1914–18 told the same story.

Either those veterans must be "jumped" on to the trail at once, or they could not be moved. Clark must make an immediate decision. It was to wait. The great question of his career will ever be if it were not wrong.

Had he gone on then, again trusting to hope, will and audacity, and had he succeeded, his name would be forever associated with the fall of Detroit, the one town well known to all the East as the strong point of the vague region of the wilderness. Reflected light would have thrown his preceding exploits into bold relief. So it would, too, even if he had fallen face forward in failure, with his surviving men still face forward under his spell. Death and success in the flood tide of youth would have glorified him as the American Wolfe, he who had the double part of a Wolfe and a Clive.

In his decision he had in mind loyalty to Henry, and to those "select gentlemen," Mason, Wythe and Jefferson, who had given him their faith. It was the wise decision for the Continental cause. In his Memoir and his letter to Mason, in all his actions, he was thinking only of Virginia as mother soil. He was the man of the rivers, of the vision of virgin meadows which were to become farms, of the forests that gave timber to build homes on the meadows and towns on the rivers' banks. This was the Continental cause to him.

He saw Detroit as certainly his before snow flew again, while he busied himself with all the details for supplies, training and transport for mobilization at Vincennes in June. Colonel John Bowman, commander of the Kentucky militia, was asked to send three hundred men. The Indian chiefs and their retinues were again coming for councils with the warrior who had repeated his miracle. They were worried lest the Big Knives take their land; for they lived nearer the Kentucky settlements than the tribes around Cahokia.

The Grand Door of the Wabash stood at Clark's elbow saying that his Big Knife brother did not speak with a double tongue when he told them that "the first white man that offered to take their lands by violence must strike the tomahawk in my head." It was destiny that the whites should come; but they should not come as robbers. In this Clark was forging a two-edged sword.

With all the Indians of the Wabash valley won over, Clark was down the Wabash in flatboats returning with the Kaskaskian militia to their homes. It was called a

"Joyful Occasion" when the townspeople rushed to greet them on the river bank from which they had departed on the march to Vincennes when the elders must have thought they would soon be very much in need of Father Gibault's blessing and absolution. Thirty citizens of Kaskaskia gave Clark fifty-four thousand pounds of flour for his army in its next venture and the Cahokians one-fifth of all their livestock.

In this period, while he was occupied in this portion of his realm, the autocrat must have, in the course of foreign relations, slipped across the river to St. Louis. Had the prospect of seeing Terese anything to do with his delaying his advance on Detroit? After his victory at Vincennes he must have been a still more marvelous Cid of the wilderness to her.

The civil administrator whom he had requested had arrived in the person of lawyer John Todd as the new County Lieutenant. The Virginia Assembly had hesitated about making a county of Kentucky, when Clark had threatened that a "country not worth protecting was not worth having"; but now that he had shown what a successful protector he was with twelve hundred pounds in paper money it was quite ready to make all Illinois into a Virginian county.

In its enthusiasm over the exploit of Virginia's son it had passed an act which assumed that all the land beyond the Ohio to the lakes and the Mississippi was Virginia's. This was sowing seeds for a heavy crop of future troubles. It was not pleasing to other states, the large as well as the small, that Virginia should have become so vast, bending her border around Pennsylvania and New York, while Massachusetts and Connecticut held that their own territory extended clear across the vague distances to the "western ocean"; not to mention the flutter of irritation in all who were interested in the land companies which had won overlapping concessions from Indians who impartially gave grants in return for wampum, to first and second and third comers.

Todd's new government was established with glad acclaim and the first printed ballots ever used east of the Alleghenies bore the names of the candidates for office. Clark had to discipline a few refractory Indians and refresh the friendship of others while he was in Kaskaskia and Cahokia. But there were signs that all might not remain serene. Pollock sent word that Virginia's bills were going to protest as his private credit was exhausted. The traders were pouring more Continental script into the length of the Mississippi valley. By loyally accepting it, at first, for its face value in silver, Pollock had dug a pit for himself.

Almost as productive as Benjamin Franklin's presses in printing the real script were British presses in British-occupied New York in printing counterfeits of the Continental note issues of April 20th, 1777, and April 11th, 1778, which, through loyalist agents, were widely distributed in the back settlements where their true nature would be less easily recognized. As if Robert Morris, financier of the Revolution, had not already enough problems to drive him mad, here was another.

The counterfeits must be removed from circulation. When it was announced that all which were not turned into the treasury in exchange for the genuine by June 1st, 1779, would be voided, the holders in the remote areas could only plead in the voice of outrage for postponement of the date of validation in their favor.

Was it money? Was money to stand in the way of the taking of Detroit? Clark emptied his own pockets; he emptied those of his officers and friends. He had lands which should be valuable. They were back of his personal signature to pay bills if he might no longer draw on Pollock. Colonel

Vigo put his own private fortune in the hopper in his devotion to Clark. All would be right when the flag floated over Detroit.

Colonel John Bowman had raised his three hundred Kentuckians; but he decided for a little military glory on his own by leading them in an expedition against the Shawnee whose braves still harassed the Kentucky settlements. He burned Chillicothe. Then he lost control over his men who fell to plundering. When they met the Indians, mobilized behind logs and tree trunks for the final test, they turned tail in disorganized retreat which took the war spirit out of most of them for the coming Summer.

This was good news for the New York loyalist, Major Arent De Peyster, who was promoted from the command at Michillimackinac to that of Detroit after the surrender of Hamilton. The region of the present state of Ohio with its portages from Sandusky and Cayahoga on Lake Erie, the present site of Cleveland, down the Miami, the Scioto and Muskingum to the Ohio river was the route for the British Indian raids on Kentucky. Clark had not operated in this region; but every warrior who coursed its trails knew his prowess. Detroit was the base for all the raids from Lake Erie and all would be stopped by taking Detroit.

This was realized by De Peyster as well as by Clark. De Peyster came to his task with fresh energy and fewer compunctions than Hamilton. Upon the opening of Summer, he was receiving the money, supplies and reinforcements which were gathered for Hamilton's anticipated advance on Pittsburgh.

His chief, Haldemand, was prompt to hasten more to him. Otherwise, as Haldemand said, if the Indians "quit us," the fur trade would be lost as a part of the penalty of a military disaster. Moreover, the attack on Pittsburgh had been part of the revived plan to close in on the Continental frontiers north and south, as Cornwallis' army was trans-

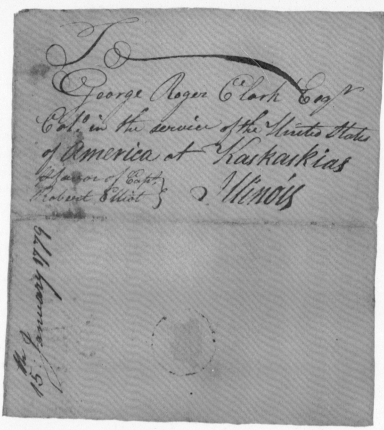

ENVELOPE OF A LETTER WHICH WAS SENT UP THE MISSISSIPPI
FROM NEW ORLEANS BY OLIVER POLLOCK TO CLARK IN KASKASKIA.
Draper manuscript

ported southward for the Carolina campaign after the British main army had failed of decision against the masterly tactics of Washington west of the Hudson.

De Peyster would keep the Shawnees and tribes of the eastern Ohio section hostile. He would call in more *coureurs de bois* and raise large numbers of fresh recruits from the northern lake region in its breadth and depth from the present Minnesota and Manitoba section to that of Ontario and Ottawa. But, in preparing against Clark's attack, after Hamilton's surrender the only offensives De Peyster undertook in the Summer of 1779 were two expeditions which had been already planned across Lake Michigan and the portages to the Wisconsin and Illinois rivers toward Cahokia and Kaskaskia.

Although one expedition was commanded by the master guerilla McKee, both were dissipated as soon as they met Clark's friendly Wisconsin and Illinois Indians in resistance. Clark's very name seemed to awe them as they came near to his stamping ground. De Peyster had been placed on the defensive for 1779, which accounts for Washington having found the vintage so good on the evening that he learned of the capture of Vincennes.

With Clark fuming with impatience at Vincennes to be started, when every day was putting more good campaigning weather behind him, thirty Kentuckians arrived instead of the three hundred he had expected. These were not of the type of his own veterans. Instead of the promised five hundred Virginia militia there limped in one hundred and thirty of a poor class, barefooted, ragged, unpaid, without ammunition or food, unused to frontier life and already wearied of it, in no mood for the rigors of a bold enterprise.

Promised supplies had not arrived. Clark lacked even clothing and boots to refit the ragged; he was without money and no one in sight to honor his drafts; he was worse off for his advance when Detroit had been much strengthened than he had been when instinct had bidden him to the third desperate hazard and reason forbade it. There was disturbing news from Kentucky. Right-hand man, Major Joseph Bowman, was dead.

He had to submit to the inevitable; to postpone again that long nursed project in which "my soul was wrapt up." His brief comment as he made the bitter decision was "all for the want of a few men," and yet without any fling of resentment at Colonel John Bowman or at Governor Henry who had not kept his promise about the five hundred. Why be downhearted? He would take Detroit yet.

XXXI

THE INCREASING STAKE

As the harvest of his own victories other things "agreeable to human nature" awaited Clark upon his return to Kentucky, which was now under civil government although his command of all the forces of the northwest included the Kentucky militia.

The news of the taking of Kaskaskia, which had reached Williamsburg in the fall of 1778, had inflamed the restless with an enticing prospect to escape the miseries of war. Security seemed to be assured in all the fair Kentucky region. Early arrivals would have a choice of claims. Beyond the Ohio Clark's conquest had opened another virgin field.

Families were packed close with their cattle on flatboats down the Ohio. They were tramping through the gaps and over the Wilderness Road and down the valleys. It was said that there were twenty thousand in this migration which overwhelmed the old timers of the pioneer Kentucky settlements.

Clark occupied himself, in keeping with his original plan as Henry had directed him, building a fort at the Falls of the Ohio. He was a patriarch looking to the defense of a suddenly increased family which was not of his choosing, but nevertheless the children of his vision which his successes had set in motion. He was feeling the touch of the other edge of the two-bladed sword which he had forged.

Cabins were raised fast in the new settlement of Louisville at the Falls where it would be under the protection of his fort. He submitted a plan to the surveyors to make it "the most beautiful city on the continent." Land would be reserved for a great esplanade along the river front; back of that would be a court house plot of two squares with a park half a square in breadth extending the length of the town.

He may have dreamed that one day he and Terese might walk under the shade of the avenues of trees of the city which he had founded. But his park system was not to be carried out by the newly elected trustees who were under the pressure of fractious individualism in rivalry for the possession of the most valuable locations.

While he was building his fort he built a cabin for himself which was to be his future home in sight of "*la belle rivière.*" It had a big room of hewn logs with a plank floor. His fondness for dancing and that of all the settlers would make a gala occasion of his house warming.

Trabue tells us of the journey of the guests from the other settlements to the ball. The ladies seem to have been in the ratio of one to five to the "Jentlemen" who had to halt on the trail in one instance to make sure that any lurking Indians might not be on the warpath.

"When the Ladys came to be dressed up they did not look like the same thing. Everything looked new. Colonel Harrod and his lady danced the first gig."

However, there was not much merriment when December came. A long remembered hard winter was that of 1779–80 in the West. It was merciless on the inexperienced and improvident. Emaciated deer and buffalo were driven by their hunger to the cabin doors to share the cattle's forage. Immigrants who were late in their start over the divide were caught in the cruelly inhospitable mountain trails and with them the disillusioned in retreat. Their relicts became the ancestors of the background and isolated mountaineers of to-day in their eternal family feuds.

The reward of the bold, hardy and provident in that

merciless test of the survival of the fittest was to be in
keeping with their character and favoring chance. Their
children and children's children were to found new towns.
Their family names are on the boards of directors of institutions and corporations, on bronze plaques, on public monu-
ments and tax lists and voters' directories all the way to the
Pacific coast, and in the cities of the seaboard to which descendants have returned.

Spain had now come into the war on France's side against
Britain, but not to recognize the United States as a nation
no matter how perseveringly and ingratiatingly John Jay
knocked at the doors of Florida Blanca in Madrid. Louis
XVI, of the then unlimited monarchy of France, who was
using the American rebels as a club to pound Britain and to
revenge the loss of Canada and the great valley, might
stomach this, but that parlor liberal, Charles III, of the
unlimited monarchy of Spain, would not hold hands in so
intimate a fashion with the godless and lawless who fulmi-
nated the anarchy of "All men created free and equal."

Spain had no Voltaires or Rousseaus, no fickle Parisian
rage over "quaint Ben Franklin" as a new thrill in which
the nobility might indulge as a relief from *ennui* in their
perfect confidence that their class was secure in all the tra-
ditional *droits de seigneur*.

In the eternal European feud the French wits made
quips about vulgar rough-mannered British officers and
the hairy half-savage Scots, bare of leg and groin under
their aboriginal kilts. The Spanish dons, to whom drunk-
enness was the negation of gentility, had visions of British
officers' messes in debauches when the weakest man was the
first, and the strongest the last, to be prostrated under the
table. They saw the British parvenus, who, themselves, had
taken no gold out of the earth, as the sea robbers of Spain's
hard-won treasure when the British knew little of ocean

navigation and Drake and his kind had lashed captured
Spanish pilots to the wheel with certain death as the pain
of an error.

And venerable Benjamin Franklin, no matter how much
Paris toasted him, and John Jay, with so old a head on
his young shoulders, never had any secret illusions in pursuing the main chance.

Oliver Pollock was finding relief from the hounding of his
creditors as a volunteer under friend Governor Galvez in
an army for the capture of the British posts of Manchac
and Natchez. Although these points were los', the indefatigable British, at war with two European powers while trying
to reduce His Majesty's American colonies to loyalty, would
keep the Father of Waters closed to American traffic between Pittsburgh and New Orleans. They had roused the
Cherokee and other tribes below the Ohio's mouth to the
prospect of better scalping and more loot on river boats
than on the trails.

In April, 1780, Clark set to building another fort at the
"Iron Bank" on the east bank of the Mississippi south of
the Ohio's entrance to safeguard the water route as Williamsburg desired. Vincennes, Cahokia, Kaskaskia, the
Falls, the more posts he had, the more garrisons must be
drawn from a total force of less than three hundred Americans when he would not use the Indians as allies; and this
while he was also responsible, in the broadening area of his
command, for the defense of all the new Kentucky settlers
scattering at will and refusing to build stockades for protection against vagrant Shawnee bands.

It was a hard task to hold the southern Indians to neutrality when they had not heard of his prestige and he had
no gifts for them and his own soldiers at Iron Bank were
complaining for want of pay. Detroit had seemed never
more distant while De Peyster was preparing a bold offensive campaign for 1780 in full knowledge, now, that

Clark was too weak to attack Detroit. Earlier in the year one of his Indian scouting parties had captured and killed the bearer of an important express from Clark to Williamsburg.

The intelligence service of both sides was amazing when one considers the distances and absence of roads. De Peyster depended upon single Indians, posing as friendlies, for his runners and spies, and upon parties, usually led by a white, for small guerilla operations. It was just the sort of service in which the Indians excelled.

Swift white trailsmen kept Clark in touch with his temperamental empire. Very serious news came to him at the Iron Bank in an appeal from the commander of his garrison at Cahokia and from Governor De Leyba. St. Louis was in danger from a large force of British whites and Indians who were mobilizing for an advance down the west bank of the Mississippi from the Michigan portages. A small dark Spanish girl at St. Louis might be at the mercy of savages.

Thus one part of the British plan of campaign of 1780 in the west had developed. Two wings were to close in on the region of Clark's control. On the right, now that Spain was in the war, was an easier prospect than meeting the resourceful Clark; a more direct method of strangling New Orleans' hold on the fur trade by capturing De Leyba and his garrison.

The red headed son of Ann with the few men he could muster kept the oars flashing day and night up the river. We know that he was at Cahokia the day before the attack on the garrison when the British force was busy in scalping and plundering in the outskirts. But his part is somewhat confused in want of explicit detail.

For Clark's letter to Mason was written after he had taken Vincennes; and the Memoir which was written for President Madison, ends in 1779 after his expedition to Detroit was balked. It was as though in that final account, which he

never completed, his pen faltered and faltered until broken
ambition laid it aside.

"For want of a few men!" What more was there to say?
A good soldier does not weep over spilt milk or make explanations.

It seems that he crossed to St. Louis in person and looked
to its defenses, and made his own plan for crossing the river
to strike the rear of the enemy. He must have seen Terese
for a few minutes in that crisis. The British attempt to
storm the fort failed and the attacking force immediately
disintegrated.

The accounts support the conclusion that once the Indians
knew that Clark had arrived and was "making medicine"
they bolted. There was no fighting him, they thought. He
had tricks in ambush which only the Great Spirit, who was
on his side, could fathom.

The presumption is that he rallied the Spanish garrison,
put his own in order and his prompt mastery of the situation, or at least the prestige of his presence, was a decisive
factor in saving St. Louis.

Madame De Leyba had died recently. Governor De Leyba
was wounded. Terese was having an experience of the terrible side of frontier life and in the course of it, another
glimpse of her Cid of the wilderness in the fullness of dynamic action as a deliverer.

It was not enough for Clark that the enemy should be in
flight. He who did not speak with a double tongue must
keep faith with his word that he would hunt down the Indians who entered the white man's quarrel. He called for
horses to mount the Spanish volunteers from one side of
the river and French from the other, which he rallied, and
they and the regulars he had brought with him, and others
from the Cahokia garrison, were sent in hot pursuit.

Some detachments seem to have gone as far as "Chicagou"
and "Milwakee", without catching up with the flying rem-

nants of the retreat of an expedition which had begun with seven hundred men and had for its trophies forty-three scalps, according to the British official report. But Clark's gospel had again been impressed upon the natives clear to the Wisconsin forests. So much for De Peyster's right wing while Haldeman was complaining that eighty-four thousand pounds in one draft seemed a great deal for the indulgence of the Indians, although the largess must continue in order to see the business through!

The call of duty prevented Clark from crossing the river again. His *au revoir* to Terese, as he must have thought of it then, had been in the midst of action.

Now he was apprised of the other part of De Peyster's plan. He had word across the trails from Detroit of the mobilization of De Peyster's left wing three hundred miles away down the valleys beyond the Wabash. Their prey would be all the scattered Kentucky settlers whose number had been further increased by the migration of the present summer, and who were wandering about and staking claims in their fools' paradise of security.

If the patriarch would save that fractious family, which had exploded his dream of "the most beautiful city on the continent," he must lose no time. He might expect no Red Sea dispensation in his Moses part when he came to the Ohio river as he hastened down the Kaskaskia. On the contrary only his ability to "see an Indian first" prevented his being taken by one of the scouting parties which were watching for him on the Ohio.

De Peyster had learned of his going to build Fort Jefferson at the Iron Bank. He hoped to capture Clark on the way back to the Falls, or, if not, to capture the fort at the Falls and complete his raid in destruction of the Kentucky settlements before Clark could return.

Clark was Indian wise in taking no foolish risks. Finding the ascent of the Ohio unsafe, when he had only one companion, they struck into the forests on the south side in a direct line regardless of trails. They dressed themselves as Indians, stained their faces, lived on what game they could kill, crossed the Tennessee river on logs bound together with wild grape vines; and there Clark was, a stark bramble-torn specter out of the wild, eyes flashing at the door of the land office at Harrodsburg which had been doing very much of "a land office business."

He ordered the land office closed. The amazed prospectors waiting to register their claims might grumble, but martial law was established. The young patriarch who had defended the fledgling settlements in the Summer of 1775 was again the dominant soldier. He called on the land hunters to enlist to save their lives and those of their families. He knew what they did not know.

Those who remained sullen against his warnings soon had confirmation in the reports of survivors who had escaped from the new Martin's and Ruddle's stations. They told of the attack by British and Indians with cannon which had forced surrender; and how the women and the weak among the prisoners had been tomahawked because they could not keep up with the march of their captors.

This was only a raid by a detachment, sent by Captain Bird who had come down the Miami with three hundred whites and seven hundred northern Indians, as the left of the enveloping movement to pinch out Clark and his garrisons north of the Ohio. When the raiders returned, after demoralizing the Kentucky settlements and forcing them on the defensive in stockades, Bird would be ready for his main stroke which was the capture of Fort Nelson at the Falls which he hoped to accomplish in Clark's absence.

Clark did not know of the plan against the Falls; but his tactic were bound to be the offensive for defense. He would go to Bird as he went to Hamilton. The settlers soon forgot horrors; but here was a fresh one for recruiting propaganda.

Boone, Logan and other leaders were ranging the trails. As they passed cabin doors men took up their rifles and flung their game bags and powder horns over their shoulders to join the growing bands forth for reprisal.

Speed was the word. Never mind how wet you may get yourself in the summer rains, but keep your powder dry. Clark had ridden back to the Falls, stripping the garrison there of all the sturdiest men for rapid ascent of the river in light canoes. By August 1st all the companies were ready at the rendezvous at the mouth of the Licking.

It soon became clear that the thing was to obey an order from this red-headed youth as his eyes from a mountainous height sent their boring command past the big nose, or perhaps broke into a taunting gibe that set everybody laughing; and clear that he led men to victory, which is what they fight for. Anyone who complained about rations was again held up to public scorn. He better return to the feather beds of the seaboard cities. Each man had a pound and a half of corn meal, nine quarts of parched corn and a little jerked buffalo meat.

This hastily raised army of all sorts, with Logan second in command, was immediately across the Ohio and on the march to Chillicothe. Stragglers had not only the apprehension of Indian ambushes to keep them up with the column, but file closers who put the fear of God into them in language they could understand. There was no vagrant prospecting for land; no side trips for hunting without authority.

Yet, the leader of the hand-picked, hand-seasoned and trained men of the Kaskaskia and Vincennes expeditions could get only from fifteen to twenty miles a day out of these tortoises when the going was good except for heavy rain, mud and morasses. That poor mileage record must have been very disturbing to Clark. Boone must have concluded that men were not what they were in his youth.

Bird did not wait at Chillicothe to join battle. When his

Indians heard that Clark was coming they bolted, and then he started a retreat with his whites which did not end until they were back on the Lake Erie shore.

But Simon Girty, the notorious guerilla, who was out with a freelancing band, did wait with recruits he had gathered from Bird's army. He, too, had legendary prestige. He longed to meet Clark and prove that he who was born to frontier life was a better man than this young Virginian who had adopted it. He waited at Piqua, his marksmen posted behind boulders and logs.

As usual Clark made an evolution with his forces divided into divisions. Logan did not get across the river in time; but he seems to have served the purpose of confusing Girty as to the direction of the blow, which Clark gave himself. Girty was routed.

During the action a man came running toward the Americans from the enemy with his hands up crying, "I am a white man!" He was young Joseph Rogers, a cousin of Clark's, who had been a prisoner of the Indians. Hit by a bullet, which was fired either by one of Girty's men or by an American who misunderstood his purpose, he died in Clark's arms.

Kentucky was safe again. The settler soldiers might return to their cabins; and the land office was opened again. Clark had extended the empire of his operations, strengthened his prestige. Both wings of the enemy's enveloping plan had been crushed.

If we indulge in the supposition that all the money that the British had poured into Detroit had materialized in the success of De Peyster's advances we may see how they fitted in with the grand strategy of the British campaign of 1780 as a whole over the broad area between the St. Lawrence valley and Savannah river.

In May Cornwallis had taken Charleston, the great southern port; his army, swinging into Carolina, decisively defeated General Horatio Gates at Camden. His main body was sweeping north toward Virginia. In the Tennessee mountains his man, Major Patrick Ferguson, was mobilizing an army of loyalists in combination with British regulars.

This was to clear the frontier of rebels and join Cornwallis' main body as a flank, in an advance through Virginia and Maryland and so on to Pennsylvania and the Hudson, to achieve the end which had not been accomplished by striking from the base of New York, the destruction of Washington's army. The war had reached its final stage when attrition had worn both sides to exhaustion. This was to be the last cast of the British in suppressing the rebellion.

De Peyster's purpose was to join hands with Ferguson in forming one large loyalist frontier force to win the decision which would clear all the country west of the Alleghenies of rebels. In answer to the alarm of Ferguson's threat that he would hang them if they did not yield, the Tennessee settlers hastened against him as a vital part of an enveloping movement.

If De Peyster's left wing had swept through the Kentucky settlements, the Tennesseeans, who had left their settlements undefended, would have had the British Indians in the full tumult of savagery, their lust fed by success, burning their cabins and closing in on their rear as they faced Ferguson in front. It is likely that the Revolutionists might not have won the important victory in the desperately fought battle of King's Mountain which hobbled Cornwallis' advance and allowed more time to Washington in cozening his opportunity.

Clark returned to the Falls in the autumn to find more paper money flooding all the area under his command while his soldiers had been unpaid for eighteen months. A band of Chickasaws under the half-breed Colbert had besieged Fort Jefferson at the Iron Bank at the mouth of the Ohio as their part in co-operation with De Peyster's right wing in clearing the Mississippi,

Captain George and his little garrison held out protecting the women and children of the settlement. When a cow strayed outside the stockade Nancy Hunter ran out to bring it in. Her clothing was cut by bullets but she saved the only source of a milk supply for the children. One of the six-pounders, presumably captured at Vincennes, was a saving factor when it put an iron ball into the midst of a group of the savages.

Instead of the aid which the besiegers expected from De Peyster's right wing came a handful of veterans from Kaskaskia, apparently under Captain Leonard Helm of previous distinction as commander of the garrison of one at Vincennes. Anyhow, he was there during the succeeding hard winter of starvation and illness.

And he was still determined to act brave; and still the philosopher. He wrote to Clark that he was "sitting by Captain George's fire with a piece of lightwood and two ribs of old buffalo which is all the meat we have seen for three days. Excuse haste, as the lightwood's just out and mouth watering for part of the two ribs. Captain George gives his compliments but has neither light nor paper."

Meanwhile a new actor, unasked for by Clark, had been striding that wilderness stage for a brief and instructive part as very distinctly a babe in the woods. His preparation was in the salons of Paris; his dream based on the traditions of La Salle and Duluth.

Augustin Mottin de la Balme was another friend of the Marquis de Lafayette, that pioneer of the *voyageurs* of the Revolutionary period who became so numerous about Washington's headquarters after France became our ally. They must have been a sore racial trial to brusque Prussian von Steuben who was happily freed from many playboys from his own land. Washington must have had moments when his secret thoughts were the same as those of a commander in France who said, "I hope in the next war we shall be able to fight without allies." All the *voyageurs'* susceptibilities must be considered no less than the jealousies of the generals of the militia of the different states.

La Balme was most unhappy. His position as a fifth wheel inspector general under von Steuben did not please him. He would have action and adventure, not in the part of America which was almost conventionally European but in the wilderness. He would put an old dream of Revolutionist policy into effect. It was to rouse the French Canadians to fight for their independence, too. Our abortive attempt to take Quebec early in the war had dashed this hope; but Mother France was not in as an ally then, reasoned La Balme.

He would first rally the French settlers of the Illinois country to follow him. Those in Detroit would rise in his favor; and, gathering recruits like a rolling snowball, he would sweep across Canada in a romantic crusade. Powerful French court influences were back of him, secretly nursing the hope of the recovery of the great valley to France. With the name of La Salle, the discoverer, would be linked that of La Balme, the restorer.

There might be something in the scheme. Anything that will in the least distress the enemy, when the men and resources for the enterprise are no drain on his own, is worth trying to any hard pressed commander. Washington gave his consent which he might have found a way of refusing, or deft young Alexander Hamilton for him, if a modern facility of communication had enabled Clark to have a few words in his ear over the long distance. But Clark was striving to find the means to pay for expresses to Williamsburg when the cost of each one was considerably more than the price of long distance calls, two hundred dollars in gold.

La Balme had what every European nation had in those days, and we had not, funds, for his venture. A messenger from the King of France, a gallant of the old régime, he was welcomed warmly in Kaskaskia and Vincennes. A few impressionable young Frenchmen joined his standard; he increased his force by recruits of young bucks impatient for the warpath, thus compromising Clark's Indian policy.

His plan was two converging columns. For either he was able to muster fifty or sixty men, as a nucleus to start the snowball rolling. But when Detroit learned they were coming, Indian bands were offered a prospect of good scalping. One of the La Balme parties got as far as St. Joseph which, in its fifty residents, then had a larger population than "Chicagou" across the lake. Its fate was ambush and massacre which was that of the other party under La Balme himself, who was killed fighting gallantly to the death when surprised on the Miami.

French scalps, including that of the man sent by the White Father of France, were hanging to Indian belts. Now De Peyster could spread the inciting word that the enemy was also employing Indians; Clark did speak with a double tongue. It meant a loss of French influence, on which Clark had depended, over the tribes.

But another summer was coming. He would yet have Detroit. He would be his own express to Williamsburg. His appeal would be to neighbor Jefferson who was now Governor, a man of larger caliber and straighter bore than Patrick Henry who did not always distinguish between service to the cause and to Patrick Henry, especially in the matter of horseflesh. Jefferson was as clean in such things as Mason or Wythe.

Posterity may be entertained and enlightened by it, although the solemn-faced Patrick saw nothing humorous in a letter to Clark in which he was as deliberately serious in detail in three foolscap pages as he was passionately serious in telling the Virginia Assembly that if this were treason to make the most of it. The letter was written December 12th,

THOMAS JEFFERSON IN 1786. AN ENGRAVING FROM
THE EARLIEST PAINTING OF HIM

1778, less than a month before Clark started on his march to Vincennes. Presumably, Clark received it with Henry's promise of the five hundred men in the Spring for the advance on Detroit; if not then, perhaps when the ragged quarter of them arrived and he had to give up the advance.

He refers Clark to "my public letters for everything I have to say on public business." He has heard that the horses in the Illinois country are fine . . . "I am very desirous to get two of the best stallions that the Spanish settlements can furnish." Clark is to enlist the aid of De Leyba to send any distance to get "the best," although Spain was then not yet in the war. A personal letter to the Spanish governor was enclosed.

"I would not have you value the cost of the Horses or the expense of sending them in . . . Get good men to bring them to New Castle Town in Hanover & give them handsome wages to secure their taking pains to bring them safe & have particular care of the Horses."

This convoy, when Clark was so pressed for men, was to go six or seven hundred miles by river and be strong enough to protect the precious stallions from thieving Indians. Henry, who dispatched no funds to pay troops and buy army supplies, sent no cash for this private venture. It would be brought by Montgomery. Perhaps Clark might have wondered if he were to draw bills on Pollock to improve the breed of horses on Henry's plantation.

And Henry also wanted mares. There was to be no delay about them. They were to be sent by a special escort if the best stallions were not immediately procurable.

"I want true Spanish Blood & the Mares to be large as you can get, & not old. Don't lose a moment in agreeing for the Mares, for vast Numbers of People are about to go out after them from here, & will soon pick them all up & raise the price very high. . . . Again pray purchase the Mares immediately upon receipt of this; & don't wait a moment for them, as you do for the Horses, but buy the Mares immediately & send them by careful People. I shall depend upon this."

It is unknown whether or not either the stallions or mares were ever sent. Clark had little time to get the stallions in his brief trip to St. Louis when he was busy saving the town from capture; and ferrying the mares on logs bound together by grapevines across the turbulent Tennessee would hardly have been giving them safe convoy, according to instructions, when he was rushing to the relief of the settlements.

Henry's cupidity for horseflesh may have been in Clark's mind, when at the Falls of the Ohio, in a crisis, he received a sword which Henry sent to him with the compliments of Virginia in honor of his victories. There was no inscription on the sword. Clark already had a sword, and what was of more value, a good rifle. He wanted men, money, understanding, answers to business letters, instead of requests to scout for stallions in the Spanish country. It drew criticism upon him for his ingratitude, when in a red-headed heathen rage, he threw that useless ornament into his beloved river.

XXXII

JOHN JAY INSISTS

CLARK had no spare time for days of rest with his family after the comparative holiday of his rough trip over the divide. Baron von Steuben was looking for just such a young man as Clark, in vital haste; but not to fight Indians.

Inquiries for news from horsemen riding west from town over Virginian roads had more intimate concern than when Washington was retreating from Long Island or across New Jersey, or Burgoyne was advancing down the Hudson valley. Redcoats might soon be at the door of the Clark homestead. Little brother William must wait for big brother's tale of adventures in the far-away Ohio country.

The northern states had had their turn as cockpits. Now it was Virginia's. Cornwallis' main army was threatening her borders while Benedict Arnold was preparing the way for its spring campaign. Von Steuben assigned Clark to a command in the operations against Arnold's plundering raids which burned Richmond and forced the state government to flight.

Refugee Governor Thomas Jefferson's popularity was in the eclipse. People were saying that his political dissertations were poor protection against bullets and cannon balls and blaming him for not having looked to the state's defense. If this were not enough to condemn the philosophical statesman he would give up territory—give up land, land!—which belonged to Virginia.

In his large outlook for the whole, and in political acumen that was not penny wise and pound foolish, he proposed to turn the jurisdiction of the immense new Illinois county of

Clark's conquest over to Congress. This was in keeping with Clark's vision which was unconcerned under what state sovereignty the future cities and towns were to rise. Jefferson's generous gesture soothed state jealousies in the lobbies in Philadelphia; but Congress was not in the mood to accept a new responsibility when it had more than enough inescapable afflictions. The only thing it was ready to annex at the time was something that would bring in funds.

Arnold's retreat relieved the danger of further invasion until Cornwallis should commence active operations in the Spring; and Clark was relieved of this duty on the request of Jefferson who had become a partisan of Clark's plan at Continental headquarters, while Mason and Wythe of the "select gentlemen" were supporting it before the Virginia Assembly. In addition to the Kentucky militia Clark should have reinforcements to make a total of two thousand men, sufficient to capture Detroit and garrison the whole region between the lakes and the Ohio river.

Jefferson urged that a commission as Brigadier General in the Continental Army should be given to Clark in order that he should have undisputed superior rank over his subordinates; but such had been the pressure of ambitious militia officers for national commissions that a rule had been made against further transfers. Clark must remain in the gallery in which he had begun his military career. Jefferson promoted him to be a Brigadier General of the Virginia militia.

Crockett's regiment of Virginians was assigned to him. Washington favored Clark for the command on the strength of his high achievements although he had not "the pleasure of knowing the gentleman" personally. He issued orders to detach two hundred Continental regulars under Colonel Gibson from Brodhead's force at Pittsburgh for the expedition. Jefferson dared the draft in Virginia to raise further recruits. He promptly gave orders for ample supplies and equipment. Money? He was more generous with paper money than Henry for the Kaskaskia expedition. There was more of it in circulation of much less value.

Back in Kentucky, if Clark's instructions before he started for Virginia were being carried out, militia companies were being raised and trained, buffalo meat jerked, corn parched, boats built for mobilization on March 15th.

Again Clark was down the Monongahela to Pittsburgh in high hopes. At last he would have Detroit. He was thinking in terms of large numbers for him, and making elaborate preparations. Moreover, he knew that Detroit's defense had been much strengthened, and De Peyster was being heavily reinforced by more northern Indians and Canadian militia.

Jefferson found that the residue of Virginia's man power which had remained out of the war, or had a surfeit of service would not be drafted. There were not rifles enough for the few who did respond.

Clark was waiting at Pittsburgh past the time for the rendezvous in Kentucky for troops that did not come; waiting, past the time when he should have been on the march to Detroit to make the most of summer weather, to settle the issue with Brodhead who was against his project.

Both Clark and Brodhead, who refused to detach Colonel Gibson's two hundred men from his command, sent expresses, which meant more delay, in appeal to Washington who had reports confirming Brodhead's fear that a large body of Indians and rangers from the New York State area were to join the Detroit forces in an attack on Pittsburgh, which was never to materialize. Of course, Clark's answer to that would be to draw off any advance on Pittsburgh in defense of his advance on Detroit. By this time the general situation had more clearly developed to Washington. The slight but useful French aid to the Continental war chest might not continue. Rochambeau's army and the convoy of the French fleet were a present asset to be utilized against

Cornwallis who was to be drawn into the trap of the York-town neck.

When, one way or the other, the war must end soon and main army was to meet main army in the final test, it were better to alienate no troops in a frontier offensive. A disaster at Pittsburgh, however, would be serious. So Brodhead had his way. Later, when he was under charges of peculation, and a large part of his forces signed a round robin against him, he was dismissed. Pittsburgh had been the grave of an-other military reputation.

At last, on June 1st, when his expedition should have been as far as Vincennes, Clark set out down the Ohio with four hundred men. Again he was trying to drill his experience into raw recruits who knew little of discipline or the kind of campaigning before them. But they were the best equipped and munitioned as well as the largest force he had ever com-manded.

Colonel Archibald Lochry and about one hundred Penn-sylvania volunteers were expected to follow him soon. With these and the Kentucky militia, whom he would have mobil-ized when Lochry arrived, Clark would make his dash for Detroit.

It was not until August that Lochry left Pittsburgh. He made a mistake which Clark, or one of his veteran captains, would never have made after hard-learned lessons of the tactical value of seeing an Indian first. Those New York State Indians under Joseph Brant, who had come as a re-inforcement to De Peyster's operations, had in mind quite a different objective than besieging Fort Pitt.

Brant had learned that Lochry was coming down the river. His braves were padding softly behind the screen of thickets, sharp eyes on the watch for an opportunity. And ten miles below the Miami's mouth Lochry allowed his men to go ashore. While some were cooking a breakfast, others were scattered cutting grass for their horses.

Richmond Jan. 13. 1781.

Sir

I received last night from General Washington a letter on your subject in which he has complied with my request. as every movement will depend so much on yourself in the Western quarter I leave to yourself to determine whether you should not as soon as possible repair hither & take the ultimate measures which are necessary.

I am Sir

your most obed.t serv.t

Th: Jefferson

GOVERNOR THOMAS JEFFERSON'S LETTER TO CLARK, WHEN HE WAS SERVING AGAINST BENEDICT ARNOLD'S RAID, ANNOUNCING WASHINGTON'S SUPPORT OF THE ATTACK ON DETROIT

The first they knew that enemies were near was in the crack of the Indian rifles. After that came the warhoop and the tomahawk rush. Some escaped to their boats; but Brant had prepared for this by having some of his party in canoes. All but one of Lochry's men were killed or captured. He and the majority of the other prisoners were murdered.

Clark found the Kentucky settlements a raging frontier democracy, more concerned with working out his vision locally than in providing ground for its future expansion on the way to Detroit. Immigration was continuing; the discouraged outgoing passing the incoming on the trails. The original county had now been divided into three counties. There were three land offices and three sets of county officials instead of one, among them the father of the future Chief Justice John Marshall. Furs were the only dependable means of exchange in all the bartering and buying and selling.

Clark was facing in county jealousies the troubles Washington faced in state jealousies. The militia had returned to their homes. They had not gathered sufficient supplies. The old leaders, who had served under Clark, were ready to follow him anywhere, the new leaders lukewarm. Word of the disaster to Lochry's armed force spread alarm. The county lieutenants could muster two-thirds of the militia, but these would respond with no spirit for anything except a punitive foray and wanted to get in their crops for the winter and look after their traps which would give them a circulating medium. Home defense was their first thought. And the loyal Clark saw how exposed and helpless were the inexperienced among the settlers and the numerous new families. Good campaigning weather would soon be over.

There was no money with which to pay the militia for service. His veterans in garrison, his own "regulars," had been two years without pay. They had not a cent with which to make the simplest purchases. Fate was against Clark in all these odds and arguments and in all the expresses he received. Continental script was at the ratio of one thousand to one in gold.

In all good faith in the script, through their confidence in Clark, the French communities had been accepting it until now the traders had their furs and excess grain and they had nothing with which to pay their bills. Colonel Vigo, Richard Winston, Daniel Murray, Helm, McCarthy, Busseron, Le Gras and other loyal friends were bankrupt: Cerré so hard pressed that he had gone to St. Louis where he had died. De Leyba was dead.

The new Spanish Governor had made a raid to St. Joseph which angered the French. Clark could not be everywhere to apply his personality in straightening out situations. He was signing his name as surety for bills in gold when drafts on Virginia in script would not be accepted; subordinates in desperation were also signing his name. It was anything to carry on as he kept the front of Jove while he swallowed his disappointment over Detroit which lay heavy on his heart.

Fortune would yet take a turn in his favor. He tried to make it appear to De Peyster that he was about to advance. De Peyster, who worried on this score, kept strong reserves at Detroit. Brant's success was good news for him. Then came word of the failure of the ensuing counter stroke from which he hoped much.

Brant's Indians, in the flush of victory, had joined with forces of white rangers and Indians under McKee and Thompson. They started toward the Falls with a view to attacking Clark in his stronghold. Again when the Indians learned that they were to fight Clark they refused to go on. They returned to their villages and the whites to Detroit.

This ended the fear of Indian attacks on the settlements for the time being. As Winter closed in Clark had word that called for expresses far and near, no matter how many times he gave his personal credit to pay the expenses, news to give cheer to Father Gibault, to Vigo, to his famishing garrisons; and to the Grand Door of the Wabash and all the Indian chiefs who still held him to be their brother.

Washington, who had played such a long and deliberate game on such an immense board, had made the checkmate move at Yorktown.

Cornwallis had surrendered. Negotiations for peace had begun. The war was over in the East, although the treaty of peace was not to be signed until fourteen months later. But the war was not over in the West.

The new governor of Virginia, Benjamin Harrison, set out to surpass Patrick Henry as a letter writer. He would have Clark build and mount with cannon a chain of forts on the Ohio. This would show the Kentucky settlers that he was their good friend if generals would only carry out his orders. But he confessed to having only four shillings in the treasury to pay for these elaborate defenses. Meanwhile, Clark did build a gunboat on personal credit.

De Peyster had plenty of shillings. Rochblave, the old commander at Kaskaskia, who had broken his parole, and La Mothe, the able guerilla, who had been exchanged, were back at Detroit seeking revenge against the Big Knife who had taken them prisoner and broken their influence over the Indians. British persistence in liberally supporting savage warfare against the settlers in the Summer of 1782, after orders had already been given for the withdrawal of British reserves from New York to England, could be explained only by the desire to influence the peace negotiations or in the interest of the fur magnates.

The victory at Yorktown had given fresh impetus to further migration to Kentucky from Virginia, Carolina, Pennsylvania and Tennessee. Now that the war was over the early birds saw the prospect of many juicy worms.

In order to rally the Indians to action De Peyster asked them to look across the Ohio where the clusters of cabins were rising so rapidly on the old neutral hunting ground. He continued to hope that he might capture Clark in the course of his comings and goings with a small guard. But he had learned his lesson too well to undertake a big offensive.

His plan now was swift raids of Indians and rangers under his best white leaders who were to have a free hand. Information of a raid could reach Clark's garrison at the Falls no faster than the raiders could travel themselves. The spread of the settlements into the valleys opposite the hostile Shawnee region offered an opening for a master Indian fighter of the Simon Girty type.

Clark was at the Falls when Girty with a large band slipped across the Ohio and struck the groups of cabins in the valley of the Licking. Boone, Todd and Logan were again rallying the riflemen from the cabins in the neighboring settlements. Each county had its little army. There was lack of cohesion, impetuosity and speed linked with caution and delay, with no leader having power over the whole.

And their commands were settlers of all types. They made war in intervals of necessity; many were going into their first fight. Girty was at war all the time, a professional, and his Indians and rangers were professionals. Girty used the feint and recoil against a divided command. After inflicting the disaster of the Blue Licks, in which Todd met a gallant death and Boone was wounded, he withdrew without waiting to give battle to Clark.

Why was not Clark there when the blow came, the settlers were asking? Wasn't it his business, as Brigadier General commanding the defense of Kentucky, to be there? They were like wayward children who depended upon father always to be on hand when they were in trouble. Governor Benjamin Harrison, when the news of the Blue Licks reached him, was very wroth. After the victory of Yorktown, and the war was supposed to be over, Clark had failed to do his duty in this fashion. The whispers that he was drinking too much must be true.

An anti-Clark faction in Kentucky was getting the ear of the Governor who was somewhat Pecksniffian. He censured Clark for not sending in reports, for his extravagances, and demanded vouchers so that his accounts would be settled. By this time the Governor had only one shilling in the treasury; but he had paper for letter writing when paper was very scarce on the frontier.

Clark offered to resign, but Harrison would not accept his resignation. The Kentuckians did not want it accepted. Who of all the smaller men, ambitious for his place, could step into the giant's shoes? Friend Jefferson understood the situation. He wrote to Clark that "enemies were the penalty of being eminent. If you meant to escape malice, you should have confined yourself to the sleepy line of regular duty."

Meanwhile, Clark had given the answer to the Blue Licks; meanwhile, the militia had rallied behind his regulars for another advance to Chillicothe. But neither Indians nor rangers waited to meet him. This was his last stroke in the war and he returned from it to receive the blasts from Harrison. His dream of Detroit finally broken, he was to hold what he had won.

It is vain speculation to ask what would have been the influence on the peace negotiations if he had taken Detroit. He would have looked ahead to another goal; for he included Canada in his vision for which his ambition had recklessly dared so much. Meanwhile, the boundaries of a new nation were being settled around the conference table in Paris as he began his thirtieth year.

When peace treaties are being formulated the question of one side to the other is, what do you possess? On what line had the armies set the frontier when firing ceased? The red-headed son of Ann had drawn a line farther beyond the

Appalachian range than from Pittsburgh to New York. Except in the West our soldiers were nowhere on enemy soil at the time of the armistice.

And the next point relates to the character of the delegates themselves. Our three, Laurens having arrived only in time to sign, were "bonny" John Adams; venerable Benjamin Franklin, who was now so near the end of his vital and far-reaching career with this as its climax; and young John Jay, that steadfast revolutionist when so many of his New York friends had been loyalist.

Bismarck once referred to delegates who were of steel and of lath painted to look like steel. John Adams was not quite soft wood, but he was not steel. He was slightly susceptible to European court flattery and rather inclined to believe in the monarchic principle. His home town of Boston looked to its Appalachian range as the Berkshires; but there was Massachusetts' interest in that charter right to a slice of the continent all the way to the western ocean, which was a calculable influence in his attitude.

To John Jay's home town of New York, during its revolutionary siege, and still so to some of its inhabitants, in the present western view, its Appalachian range was the Palisades and its river of destiny the Hudson; but John Jay, with such an old head on his young shoulders, was a sword's blade of steel.

That amiable philosopher of "Poor Richard," as his friends and the statesmen of France and England had long since learned, possessed cartilages, which, despite his old gentleman's stoop, were knitted together in a very firm backbone under the pads of flesh which indicated his fondness for the good things of life. The rivers that joined to make the Ohio had their junction in his own state of Pennsylvania. As far back as the Albany convention in 1754 his foresight included the future of the country beyond Pittsburgh, although he said it could take centuries for its development.

JOHN JAY. A PORTRAIT IN 1783 WHEN HE WAS
NEGOTIATING THE TREATY OF PARIS

And the son of Ann, born of a world so different and yet so like, and playing so different a part from John Jay in the teamplay of common purpose, had really set two lines. The first to be considered was the "populated" zone, which was won by the migrating families in the custom of the seaboard advance and which was the inspiration of Clark's boyish vision.

If Clark had not besieged Patrick Henry for powder and courted the "select gentlemen" and then organized the settlers whose power of resistance increased with the increase of their numbers, the populated zone might not have extended beyond the Monongahela watershed. In that wedge of settlements Franklin and Jay had an argument which was not new even then, but as old as the racial quarrels of Europe. In a recent peace conference it was styled the "self-determination" of peoples; and before that it was the right to hold the ground which is already occupied by your own nationals.

So, in the terms of that period, the Ohio was the boundary of a region in the possession of our own nationals from which all the enemy attacks had failed to remove them. It was not even in the mood of Adams, when the Bostonnais had spread their frontiers in the same fashion, to weaken on this point.

And should these nationals remain in a wedge which, including the Tennessee settlements, had its base from Pittsburgh to Carolina and its point on the Mississippi? This would make a strange boundary insuring future trouble when, after what they had suffered in this war, the states were determined never to have another.

What of the region north of the Ohio? This was in the zone of action. The British could maintain no garrisons from the lakes to the Ohio and Mississippi, except at Michillimacinac and Detroit. That is, the only headquarters they had in being were at these points on the lake shores.

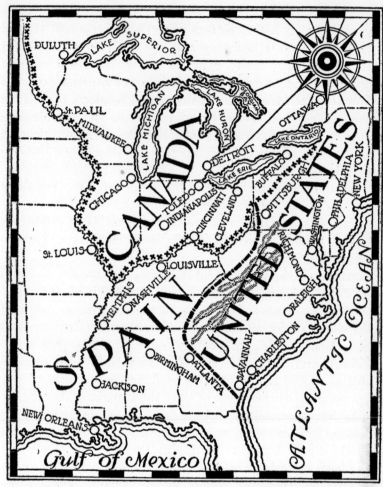

WHERE THE CANADIAN BOUNDARY LINE MIGHT HAVE BEEN DRAWN IN 1783 BUT FOR CLARK'S ADVANCE. THE LINE OF DASHES INDICATES THE AREA EAST OF THE MISSISSIPPI WHICH MIGHT HAVE GONE TO SPAIN AS PART OF THE FLORIDA COUNTRY, LEAVING THE APPALACHIANS AS THE WESTERN BOUNDARY OF THE NEW UNITED STATES.

They could make only sorties to the southward. Their guerilla bands had to retreat when Clark appeared. He had taken their posts and they had not occupied his. He held Indian chiefs by fealty while the British only held them by bribes for their forays. His influence was supreme from the Miami to the Mississippi. If this region became a part of the new nation, then the region of the Scioto and the Muskingum to the Pennsylvania border must be obviously included or it would become the counterpart of the modern Dantzig corridor.

Should the southern side of the wedge from the Tennessee settlements be left exposed? Should there not also be included all the land between the lakes and the Gulf of Mexico, except Florida, which old Spain must have for a while to satisfy her honor?

Although the Continental Treasury was empty, the steel of John Jay was unyielding that it should be. He would consider no compromise. If the Europeans were so sure that the states would soon split into several nations as the result of factional feeling, this only served his purpose. Clark and Pollock and Jay! Also Franklin with time-tested steel as stiff as Jay's! Canny old Ben said that he would not "give up one drop of those waters"—of those rivers of destiny.

In secret council the British delegates might look at Haldemand's, Hamilton's and De Peyster's account books and all the drafts drawn on the Royal Treasury for funds that had been spent in vain in blooding Indians for the warpath in that wilderness as remote as the African wilds before another European land rush began a century later. The British also had De Peyster's latest reports, in his alarm as he realized his personal position in the hour of British defeat, that the Indians would turn against the British as soon as the largess ceased.

It was a very long and expensive route up the St. Lawrence and, then, across the lakes and over the watershed, by which to send soldiers to hold a country against warring Indians and the advance of the American settlers who had shown such devilish initiative under this George Rogers Clark.

The cost was not worth the pelts. Those of the Mississippi valley were bound to go downstream to New Orleans, anyhow, and it was better to restrict the Hudson's Bay Company to developing the fur resources of Canada proper than to throw more good money after bad. The rapidly growing East Indian trade, in a region where the natives were less virile and every white man might be a nabob, was more profitable.

So all the land from the Gulf to the lakes and from the Appalachians to the Mississippi, and into the northwestern forests where it rose, became American, an area far exceeding that of the original states. Franklin might think that it would take centuries to develop it, but not only his own state but all the others of that pioneering civilization were brought up in the principle which was expressed by the Yankee farmers' view that it was always in order to annex a piece of land "jining" at a bargain.

XXXIII

MELIOREM LAPSA LOCAVIT

THERE was a family gathering in 1783 in Caroline County. It was the first real reunion since His Majesty's American colonies had taken up arms. Now a new nation was undertaking to run its affairs without the aid of a king.

Some of the conservatives among the late "rebels" were wondering if this were possible, while the home loyalists, shaking their heads in unison with Europeans, were certain that it was not. The experiment would not last. The States would have either to import a royal prince or put Washington on the throne.

For the majestic Ann, who must have been feeling quite majestic and likely a little more conscious than ever that she had done her part in the war, it was enough to have all her sons at home again. Only Richard was absent. He was still in the West where he had served four years under George.

Probably the devout mother inquired of her sons if they had attended the divine services held by the chaplains and had said their prayers faithfully in camp. Of course the regular going Jonathan had. George and Richard out in the back country might be excused owing to the lack of facilities. There were only the Catholic churches for them to attend in Kaskaskia and Vincennes. Doubtless Ann mustered all her brood in the family pew with George's red head towering over the rest.

George had seen many more stretches of rich land since he had returned in from his first trip down the Ohio. He was employing his winning ways to have the whole family settle in Kentucky.

Meanwhile, he had had his hearing with Governor Harrison who had ordered him home to explain the Blue Licks disaster, why he had not sent in his vouchers and why the Ohio river was not bristling with forts and it and all its tributaries patrolled by gunboats. When the auditor was asked about the vouchers, which covered all Clark's services since the Kaskaskia expedition, his answer was that he did not have them in his possession.

Either they had never arrived or they had been destroyed by Benedict Arnold's raids. One hundred and thirty years later, as we shall see, they were to be found. Harrison accepted Clark's resignation as Brigadier General, allowed in part, it seems, Clark's restatement of accounts from memory, and, reversing his previous attitude, wrote a letter to Clark in praise of his services.

When paper was so scarce in the wilderness and George was in the full tide of an obsession, and moving so fast and had so much on his mind, how many obligations for which he was personally responsible would turn up in the future? This was a question which father John might well ponder, gratified as he was by the Governor's praise. George had done great things. Father John was proud of him and mother Ann still prouder. But, now that he was out of the service, parental heads on the pillows, in privy council on family matters, were thinking of the future of all their brood.

Ann may have wondered how much there had been between George and that Spanish girl. George had always had a reserve about some things which there was no penetrating. The mother would observe signs that he was in love when the father would be quite blind to them.

As he listened to his brother's tales, young William, who was then thirteen, must have sighed because he was so small that he could not be in the war. His real hero was George. He hoped that when he grew up there might still be Indian chiefs for him to meet and he, too, might have adventures in the back country. Time was to yield prodigal response to the wish.

Whole hams must have been on the family dinner table to feed all those sons and daughters and in-laws. There was a christening, too, of one of Jonathan's children. Brigadier General George and Captain Edmond were the sponsors. Apparently brother John was not well enough to be present.

John's flushed lean cheeks and his cough had given the reunion a sad undertone. Having won his commission as a lieutenant, he had repeated his gallantry at Brandywine in a charge which left him surrounded in the defeat at Germantown, to become the victim of six years on a British prison ship. He was sent to the West Indies, which was the cure of pulmonary tuberculosis in those days; but it had not been for Lawrence Washington and was not to be for John Clark.

After John's death, his father and mother fell under the spell of George's vision. They were not too old to make a fresh start in life when a new era was beginning. Father John was still under sixty and Ann just turning fifty, although she was the mother of two brigadier generals. The farm was sold but not the negroes. These went with the parents and the younger children, William, Elizabeth, Lucy and Frances, in one big family party. Jonathan and the others were to follow.

Meanwhile, of close concern to George Rogers was a discussion raging in Virginia and reverberating back and forth between the legislative halls of Richmond and Philadelphia. Was all the western land which had been won by a Virginian not to be Virginian? Many Virginians were wroth over Jefferson's tender of the territory to Congress.

The question was put to George Rogers who was such a poor trimmer in political matters. He said that he was thinking in terms of the whole country. He did not forget that Carolinians and Pennsylvanians had served under him. He

saw himself only as the instrument for carrying through his
vision. This made him appear disloyal to those with strong
state views. It was no aid to his having the money he had
spent refunded to him when the Virginian treasury should
accumulate funds.

The Vandalia land company and other companies which
had pre-war grants were reviving their pretensions before
Congress. Pennsylvania and New York were acutely interested, also Massachusetts and Connecticut, about ancient
charter rights to the western ocean. All yielded in March,
1784, when the first of the territories, the North West Territory, including all the region north of the Ohio was established. Its official seal, which has so long slumbered in the
archives of the State Department, is on the cover of this
book.

Meliorem Lapsa Locavit was chosen for its motto by some
Latin scholar. "He has planted a better in place of the
fallen" might have been on the coat of arms of Clark whom
an imperial England would have created an earl with fifty
square miles of rich lands as his fief if he had done a like
service for the mother land.

The new nation for which he had won so much was not
giving titles. It was not even a nation yet, only a confederation. Imagination fired by victory in the zest of after war
recuperation, individualism took the bit when the new experiment in democracy loosed reins for a free for all race.

A tide of immigration from abroad set in to the new land
of "freedom and opportunity." In 1783, John Jacob Astor,
then twenty, who had worked in his father's butcher shop
and then as a piano maker, arrived in New York under the
influence of a successful fur trader he met on board ship.

Returning unpaid soldiers wanted some reward for their
services; their officers also, and in keeping with their rank.
In the lobbies of Philadelphia, where hotels and boarding
houses were crowded, new faces, and faces that were back in

old haunts, were appearing. Those who had been consistently near the throne, or who had friends at court, had an advantage over those who had been at the front.

The throne was the power of Congress which was overwhelmed, when the treasury was empty, by problems of demobilization, rehabilitation and reconstruction and of creating some sort of an integral system of government of the whole, which made the penalties of victory appear almost worse than those of defeat. Some loyalists were edging their way back into favor. The loyalists had better treatment than the South after the Civil War without reference to the custom of the times.

There might be no reward in money for the soldiers; but Congress did have plenty of land. The soldiers of the Continental Army should be the first served with quarter sections. To replenish its own treasury Congress planned the sale of the lands Clark had won when, to many of the members, he was a haughty wild Virginian frontiersman who had tried to annex all the Northwest to cormorant Virginia which certainly was not to be allowed more Senators in the upper house, under the new Constitution, than Rhode Island or Delaware which also had rights as states.

But Congress did hold Clark in enough esteem to make him one of eleven members of a commission to win land concessions from the Indians by peaceable negotiations. There must have been a flash of his temper when he was summoned to New York where the commission was to meet to receive the Indian chiefs. It could have hardly surprised him that the chiefs of the Mississippi region did not appear, when their traveling expenses had not been paid, and especially that the chief of the hostile Shawnees should refuse the invitation.

Although among its members were some of the men of mighty wisdom who made the Constitution, Congress had been too busy for eight years trying to keep all the States in harness and munitioning Washington's army to be well informed about aboriginal tribal customs and peccadilloes west of Pittsburgh.

As the chiefs would not come to Broadway from the Miami, the Wabash and the Cumberland, the commission must go to them, but with reduced membership which, in view of the exactions of frontier travel, must have been achieved without many heartburnings. Peace was made with the Shawnees as well as Clark's old friends; some of the concessions Congress wanted were won.

But Clark was not happy acting with a commission. He had not the articulate facility in counsel for that kind of service. He had created an autocracy which had accustomed him to an autocrat's rule. The Big Knife chief, who had been so successful in personal power over Indian chiefs, was incapable of explaining the instinctive sources of his personal policy. He foresaw that the tomahawk would soon appear out of the smoke screen of pipes of peace.

In one hand you must have force according to his experience in dealing with Indians. Congress was sending no troops. For peace service in the whole United States Washington was left with less than a hundred men. If soldiers were needed each state would look after its own situation by a call on the militia. Washington was to have a hard battle to win consent to a meager United States standing army while he was backing Hamilton's financial policy.

With force in the one hand you must have justice in the other. You must understand the Indian nature. You must not speak with the double tongue; and you must make your words good in deed.

The Indian must realize that the white man was coming as his neighbor. *Meliorem Lapsa Locavit*. But there was room for the Indian too, the children of the forest should have fair play. In the Virginia archives is Clark's appeal, in 1784, to begin the education of the Indians, in keeping with

NEW YORK CITY AT THE TIME OF THE REVOLUTION

his policy for preparing them to share the better in place of the fallen. Those Kentucky settlers still harassed by parties of roving and thieving bucks, and generally considering out of bitter experience that the only good Indian was a dead Indian, must have thought that their old defender had indeed turned to drink.

He had not profited by any opportunities while a member of the commission. Meanwhile some of his land patents in Kentucky, which he had taken out as a stripling before the war, were worth a small fortune so rapidly had prices risen. But he had sold many to get funds for his expeditions and garrisons. He was not looking out for the sections which were still in his name, but mortgaged.

Higher rose the tide of emigration to Kentucky which now had seven counties in place of three. In 1784 land office fees were five times the total of the previous year. The infection of expansion had become a hectic fever. The rich land was coming into its own in a generous yield of crops.

Log schoolhouses and churches were being "raised" among the clusters of cabins. A new seminary for higher education was established, Clark being named as one of the trustees. In all its pressure of enterprise in carrying its institutions forward, pushing, pulling, arguing, cursing, praying and quarreling in a riot of energy, resentful of governmental paternalism, the cult of the little valleys was acting true to form in the great valley.

There were all kinds in that migration to Kentucky; from boys with the down still on their cheeks to white-haired men; from criminals to clergymen; from illiterate to school teachers and college graduates and the best blood of the East; from town loafers, drunkards, family scapegraces to leading citizens whose loss was publicly deplored in their home communities; young lawyers looking to grow up with the country to political power; men of brawn and of guile; men who had given their fortunes to the Revolution and would begin the battle afresh for another competence; former Continental officers and privates and loyalist sympathizers; and those who would inveigle from the hives the honey which others had gathered.

Among the newcomers was young James Wilkinson, a carpet general on the Continental side who said he represented a group of Eastern capitalists. Biographers looking for a complete villain, who has the attractive without the vigorous Mephistophelian qualities, will find in him a perfect subject. In studying Wilkinson's career, historians, who would hold the balance of discrimination nicely in rectifying bad reputations by discovering some compensating virtues, have found that the point of a camel's hair brush would carry all the necessary whitewash.

He was in the Gates cabal against Washington. This failing, he fawned on Washington who privately took his measure. But he was a leech that had to be borne. Leaders feared openly to offend him as they passed him on lest their plans should be hobbled by his facile and plausible duplicity. The impressionable people of the settlements were fair game for one who had refined his remarkable natural gifts for intrigue by keeping close to the lobbies of Congress in his military career. He would develop the art of politics as his part in the future of Kentucky. Handsome, small of stature, indefatigable, a brilliant expert in the whispered confidence of all things to all men, he was soon busy in chicane which was the breath of life to him.

Clark, who was then absent on his missions, was the big name in Kentucky. But there were men whom his discipline had offended. Many of the late arrivals had never seen him.

There could be no striking hands in a political cabal with this imperious soldier who rarely wrote letters. Busy in gossip on the spot, writing many letters to the East, Wilkinson, who had tried to enmesh Washington, now began spinning his web around Clark. He spread the tale of Clark's drinking habits. The hero of Illinois was finished; he had become a sot.

With the seaboard so far away and Kentucky growing so fast, Wilkinson pretended to side with the growing local sentiment to make Kentucky a separate state. Kentuckians were told they might depend on the aid of his powerful influence in the East, when, as it was later learned, he was secretly blocking the plan.

And the Clark who had been seen so often on the trails in the old days was not moving about Kentucky settlements, but had turned Cincinnatus after his duties with the Indian commission were over. He was interested in a smaller patriarchy in which his father was patriarch. He had not in mind being a Governor or Senator; he was Clark, the planter, again.

On Mulberry Hill, looking out over the river and the town George had founded, John and Ann were building a new homestead in an estate of many virgin acres. Around them, in Scotch clan fashion, were the sons and the in-laws who, with the help of their negroes, were lumbering and plowing and planting and setting up a grist mill.

George was knowing what it meant to sleep in the same bed night after night in the joy of a permanent rest billet. Instead of thinking of "things in general" he was finding that it was very "agreeable to human nature" that creditors wanted their debts paid by him when there was no money in the Virginian treasury and Virginian statesmen were thinking that Kentucky as well as the Illinois country was lost to them. And all they were saying about George in the Kentucky valleys was in keeping with the way his soldiers had of "passing from one extreme to another." He liked his hill in sight of the great river better than living in a valley. His services were not needed when Congress had authority over the Illinois country and the Kentuckians were numerous and strong enough to protect themselves.

But Congress was finding no land purchasers to bring revenue from the North West Territory, which it could not afford to garrison. Trouble was brewing. If no Indians were attacking Louisville their depredations were increasing in the Licking region. Events were taking the course anticipated.

Restless ex-soldiers and pioneers were ranging through the North West Territory blazing tomahawk claims. They were quarreling with the French inhabitants in Vincennes where the Spanish were busy in intrigue. More and more braves were on the warpath which led them across the Ohio against the Kentucky villages. The tiny regular garrison on the Ohio could think only in terms of defending itself.

County lieutenants saw that it was time to give the Indians another licking which would make them "good for a spell" at least. Clark might have become a drunkard, but in the rivalry for leadership his was the name that occurred to all. Cincinnatus was called from the plow.

He was hesitant, now, the man of quick decision and swift action. To march out and march back again was only another error in the chain of errors in dealing with the problem as he looked into the future. There should be a permanent system with garrisons. He was doubtful if the Kentuckian militia had any legal right to cross the river into territory under the direct jurisdiction of Congress. Lawyers, who advised him, strained a point in an affirmative opinion to agree with popular sentiment.

Again he formed an army of volunteers when the regulars, which he asked for as a nucleus, were refused; again he was on the march; again he was in Vincennes, the Indians falling back before him. When he wanted to go on to the Wabash villages the two hundred militia of one county had had enough campaigning. They would be back to their farms and traps. He had lost his power over their imaginations. Refusing in a body to obey orders, they deserted.

Otherwise, Clark might keep them going until they reached Detroit, which was still held by the British despite the terms of the treaty. There were many pelts coming out of the Michigan woods. We had sent no garrison to relieve the British garrison.

The reports of the dissension of the states in their effort to form a permanent consitutional government, the growing antipathy of the Indians to the roving land hunters, when the war had left so many border ruffians without occupation, might well encourage British as well as Spanish anticipation that the break-up of the American confederation was inevitable. The sorely tried and penniless young nation of the little valleys had an addition of more territory in the great valley than it could salivate let alone digest. There was no government from Pittsburgh to the Mississippi, north of the Ohio, except of Indian chiefs, the French communities and land prospectors and adventurers.

Clark was the autocrat, again acting with a free hand and taking supplies to feed his soldiers, as he settled the differences between the Americans and French and confronted Spanish intrigues. Again he was holding councils with Indian chiefs; again he appeased them. They would be quiet for a time.

Long before his return the deserting soldiers were back in Kentucky spreading their tales of justification which found a ready listener in Wilkinson who was using the mails freely to his friends in Virginia and in Congress.

And indignation against Spain was rising among the Kentuckians. Despite all John Jay could do, when he turned to the task of settling differences with Madrid after he finished that of the treaty of peace with Britain, Spain held fast to her right to the exclusive navigation of the Mississippi. Thus she had a strangle hold on the passage of the Kentuckians' pelts, grain, flax and meat to market by the river route.

Wilkinson, making favor for himself by blaming Jay as a public enemy, would be the deliverer by a stroke of initiative as a private ambassador who would succeed where Jay had failed. Here was opportunity for a trading monopoly for himself. He took a cargo of Kentucky products and sold it at a profit to himself, in New Orleans, where he found a rich prospect for his talents in Spanish ambitions.

Now he could play both ends against the middle while he knew the minds of both ends and the middle. Never had a master of intrigue such muddy waters in which so many fish were ready to rise to his bait.

Meanwhile, in face of such cabals and the clash of personal and sectional interests, never were honest men deserving of more credit than those who were trying to put the new nation on a sound basis for the future. Washington might not have his wish to remain on his plantation. He was the rock, the foundation stone for all the building. He had to find a new stock of patience to carry him through the reconstruction period.

Congress was not pleased when it heard that haughty Virginia had sent an armed expedition across the Ohio territory beyond its jurisdiction; nor were the influences in the lobbies which looked to future land interests in the region. And the Kentuckians were asking Virginia for their independence as they berated her with neglect of their interests.

Wilkinson's sowing was bringing the harvest. He had been on the commission to investigate Clark's conduct of his campaign for which Clark had asked when he heard of the talk upon his return to Kentucky. Both in Philadelphia and in Richmond Clark was presented as a wild swashbuckler who had become a drunkard and was looking for another adventure of the same order as his dash into the Illinois country.

Spain protested that he had taken the property of Spanish subjects in Vincennes without authority; and Wilkinson added to this intrigue the climax that Clark had kept a garrison at Vincennes as a nucleus for organizing a freebooters' raid on New Orleans. This was not pleasing news to Congress in the course of delicate negotiations with Spain.

Upon his return to Kentucky, Clark had sent in a report explaining the value of maintaining a garrison of one-year militiamen for a time in Vincennes in good faith with the settlers and the Indians. But, in face of the uproar in Congress turned against Virginia, and of the accusations of Spain, Governor Randolph issued a proclamation repudiating Clark's actions and his supposed plan to attack New Orleans.

When Clark read this he had no Washingtonian second thoughts to restrain his temper from a public outburst. The giant had the privilege of telling the little Wilkinson what he thought of him; and Wilkinson laughed at him in triumph. Clark was not the diplomatist of Indian councils, or with the French in the Illinois country, in his message to the Governor.

"I respect the *State* of Virginia. The information you have received hath been stained with the blood of your country. Facts will prove themselves."

And so his public career closed. Cincinnatus returned to Mulberry Hill. He was thirty-five.

Wilkinson kept on climbing until he was commander of the United States Army. "Facts will prove themselves!" In time the truth caught up with the busy letter writer. American and Spanish archives divulged their merciless parallels.

It was Wilkinson who had engendered the charges against Clark; who had tried to prevent Jay's securing the navigation rights; who was on record as having complained that his loyalty to Spain was interfering with his influence in the States; who was receiving a Spanish pension while in the uniform of the United States Army. He was a genius of his kind.

CALL THE DRUMMER!

XXXIV

IN SIGHT OF HIS RIVER

FAMILY tradition tells us that Clark was "a changed man after that." This refers to the messages that a Major Williams, who lived at Natchez, brought up the Mississippi from Terese De Leyba. After her sister's death, and her brief glimpse of Clark in the stress of saving St. Louis from capture in the Spring of 1780, came the death of her brother, the Governor. She was left without blood kin in America. Any letter she sent might be months in reaching Clark if he ever received it; an answer months in returning. Her Cid was away facing manifold dangers. Word must have come across the river of the force that De Peyster was starting to overwhelm Clark.

Colonel Vigo, her brother's partner in business, was bankrupt from honoring Continental script, whose depreciation was bringing such hardship to the French settlements. Merchant Gabriel Cerré, who was in straits for the same reason and ill as well, must have given concurrence to the prophecies that Clark's empire was tottering; that he would soon be a refugee if he were not tomahawked. Spain was not an ally of the United States and was hoping to profit out of the war by further expansion of territory in the great valley.

That small and dark Spanish girl was in a very lonely position. If we accept the romance, then the influence of all the people in the garrison at St. Louis depreciated her infatuation with the Big Knife adventurer. What madness to think of him! She would never see him again. The cruel wilderness had closed in on her Cid.

A new governor was coming. The acting governor must see her on her way down the river in a convoy with a safe escort when the southern Indians were on the warpath.

She did not go to Spain, but remained with friends in New Orleans for more than a year. Was she waiting for word from Clark? He may not have known that she had left St. Louis until after his return from Virginia to raise troops. Then he may have had another cause for heartbreak than final failure to muster enough men to take to Detroit.

Creditors were already appearing with their claims. With his vouchers destroyed in Williamsburg, the old capital, or Richmond the new, he was uncertain of the total liability he might have incurred when he had hesitated at no cost to win and hold the Illinois country and protect the Kentucky settlements.

Such was the situation when Major Williams came with the message from Terese. The dreamer who had made some of his dreams come true had no white-pillared mansion to offer. The creditors would attach it as soon as he began to build it. He sent back her letters and she destroyed his letters. After her return to Spain, she entered a convent.

It was at this time that reports of his hard drinking became rife. It was a period, one repeats, when all men drank and were tempted to drink too much. Liquor was heat, after long exposure on the trail, promoting sleep in wet clothes when there was no sizzling steam radiator to welcome the traveler, and no hot coffee or chocolate at the corner drug store to take its place. It was a part of the ration of both the British and American armies; a way of combating malarial chills when there were no nets against the storms of mosquitoes; a tonic for debility; preventive medicine for all manner of ailments which have been brought under control since Pasteur's genius flashed light into the darkness.

When William Clark was married Dr. O'Fallon wrote a list of health rules for the bride which not only did not despise the use of strong liquor internally but advised a weekly sponge bath of the first run of whiskey, whose therapeutic value must have been equivalent to a modern alcohol rub. The decisive question in social efficiency was whether or not a man was able to "carry his liquor." When he reached a point where it was thought that he could not, that was reason for all his shortcomings and set him on the way to a sot's incompetency.

And men bolstered up flagging energies with drink. They used it to fight despondency. Clark had drawn more than the drafts which his creditors were presenting. He had drawn drafts on his future strength; burned up the fuel of a lifetime in ten years' effort; endured exposure on the trail for which, as every campaigner knows, he must pay in the end. One of the strains which he had repeated, without intervals of rest, was equal to a single forced march which veterans cherish as the supreme proof of their youthful virility.

It hurt him, as he struggled with his debts, that he was not able to lend a helping hand to Oliver Pollock, who found himself, soon after the close of the Revolution, imprisoned in Havana for his debts.

Pollock managed to get a parole to go to Philadelphia. There, when financier met financier, he had a sympathetic listener in Robert Morris, who had sacrificed his own fortune for the cause, as had Mason and Wythe and many others, while Washington's had been heavily impaired. Morris secured a sum in cash on account of the money due to Pollock. With this as capital the gallant Oliver gained time from his Havana creditors, returned to "mercantile pursuits," paid all his debts and made another fortune.

Pollock was a clever business man reinforced with vouchers. What was the use of Clark protesting that he had sent his in when Benedict Arnold had destroyed them? Words did not take the place of vouchers.

He looked after the little land he had left; he directed the laborers on his father's big plantation. Hunting was his sport; his luxury a good saddle horse; his pastime reading and studying the fauna and flora of the forests. When he felt extravagant he would send to Virginia for a book he wanted, and his friends scoured the country for books of biography or history for him.

When he was not reading as he sat on the porch of Mulberry Hill, looking out on the river, he was wrapped in an Indian silence. Probably he often had a glass of toddy at his elbow. People who saw that had confirmation of his vice. When the curious were present, perhaps he took another toddy in order to give scandal another leg.

His work was done. There was the record. Others must carry on when they did not need him. The taking of Vincennes had been his high water mark. There was no haling him forth in his uniform to strut as a hero of the past at public ceremonies; and his seclusion was further proof that John Barleycorn had him.

"I shall proceed on and rouse up George Rogers Clark," wrote John Pope in his diary in 1790, "who, Kentuckians say, hath actually been in a profound slumber for the last four years, without the least sign of awakening whatever." Possibly Pope expected to find him intoxicated. Whether Clark had had one toddy, or three or four, or none at all, Pope mentions that he was "highly pleased with the rare Atticism of his wit" and remarked on "the profundity of his judgment aided by reflection and matured by experience."

As he kept up the battle with his debts, settling some and compromising others, while more appeared, he was thinking of schemes for making a quick fortune. He would build a lock canal around the Falls of the Ohio, but could get no financial backing, which was not surprising when the missing vouchers had left him under suspicion as a business man. He invented a machine to save labor in propelling boats in rivers. Details about it are lacking, the plans lost, but he was confident of its practicability. Robert Fulton was at

WHEN THE STEAMBOAT REVOLUTIONIZED RIVER TRAFFIC.
ROBERT FULTON'S *"Clermont"* AT CORNWALL ON THE HUDSON, IN 1810

work on the same idea, and soon he was to build the first of the steamboats which were to speed the destiny of the rivers.

Meanwhile the letter from his old schoolmate James Madison, later President, had set Clark to writing the Memoir which he had not the heart to carry beyond Vincennes. It was found among his papers and with it a blast in answer to an article in the *American Museum* by Pelitiah Webster, which supported the view of archeologists of the time that the mounds scattered through the great valley could not have been built by a people of such low culture as the present aboriginal inhabitants. Pelitiah and other experts thought that they must have been built by the legendary Welsh prince Madoc in his search for Utopia, or by De Soto in his explorations.

"The back country has been my study for years," said Clark to Pelitiah who had not been west of Pittsburgh. He thought that Madoc and De Soto must have had a busy time if they had built all the mounds he had seen in his travels. He went into detail of the relation of their location to the water courses, told of a day spent studying the famous ones at Cahokia and explained his theory of the purpose and system of their construction.

Chief Baptiste had told Clark that the mounds were the palaces of his forefathers when his people had many large towns. Clark thought that this must been at least five hundred years ago and he saw no reason why Chief Baptiste's history was not "at least as good as part of ours." When the scientists ceased to speculate and began digging Clark's theory was proved to be correct and the astuteness of his deductions astounding.

In 1790 when Jefferson was in Washington's cabinet the Indian storm broke again. General Harmar, the regular commander in the West, with a nucleus of regulars in an army of militia, was badly defeated. Fear started panic on the frontier as many tribes set out to avenge their ancient wrongs. There was a call from his old veterans that Clark should be put in command of a retaliatory expedition.

"Rank and file fighting will not do against the Indians," Jefferson said, and he wrote to Judge Innes asking "if it would not be possible to bring Clark forward again."

But General St. Clair of the regulars was to take the field himself, while Clark appealed to his veterans to support him. St. Clair was also defeated and Clark's veterans were saying that the result would have been different if Clark, who had never been beaten, had been in command. After long and thorough preparation, General "Mad" Anthony Wayne, commander-in-chief of the regular army, took the field with a powerful, well-equipped force and beat the Indians in the battle of the Fallen Timbers near the Falls of the Maumee.

Nor was that the end. The British were still charged with encouraging the Indians to the warpath when General William Henry Harrison, in 1811, won his victory over Tecumseh which led to the hard cider "Tippecanoe and Tyler, too," campaign of 1840 that eventually made him President. There was political capital for the Indian fighters under the method which Clark thought was shortsighted.

Clark was surprised at Jefferson's friendliness when he had thought that Jefferson had lost faith in him after Randolph's proclamation denouncing him. He wrote to Jefferson that he had been in seclusion because he would keep clear of "the little faction of the western countries so incident to all infant settlements." They would work out their own salvation to maturity. He was glad to serve when called.

An old man before his time, he dreamed of action, but the fire of action was out of him and his faculties impaired. He toyed with a plan to recuperate his fortunes by establishing a settlement under a Spanish land grant, but his conditions, which would have meant spreading American sovereignty, were unacceptable. At the time of the Citizen Genet affair, when it looked as if we might go to war, he issued a call for volunteers. It was the surge of memory whipping his blood for a while with promise of another adventure.

Time wore on as he read and coursed the woods and satisfied a few more creditors. In 1799, the year of Washington's death—Mason and Wythe were already gone—came his father's death three months after that of his mother. Father John left George's estate to William, for he knew that all the unpaid creditors would be on George's back as soon as it was known that he inherited some property. And the father had been bitter and Jonathan bitter that George should be held liable for debts of the State now that the United States was satisfying so many other claims.

William had become an officer of the army. In the battle of the Fallen Timbers young Meriwether Lewis, four years his junior, had served under him. Lewis became the private secretary of President Jefferson.

Lewis and Clark! Little brother William was to be the Clark known to every schoolboy and girl. A note from George Rogers to Jefferson, the only request he made through many years, had called the attention of the old neighbor at Shadwell to another engaging member of the Clark family, which led to William's assignment to explore a new back country, that of the new Louisiana Purchase.

If George Rogers had not defended the Kentucky settlements and taken the Northwest, and the British boundary line had been on the Ohio or even on the Appalachian ridges, then we should have gained the latest annexation only by a war with Britain and Spain. The outcome of that, in view of the results of our amateur campaign in 1812–'14 when the British burned Washington, would have been quite problematical.

Federalist Alexander Hamilton, challenged with being an imperialist, had established a sound financial system which was the support of his political opponent, Thomas Jefferson, the father of democracy, in an imperialist part. Now our treasury was not empty. The young nation was on its feet.

New England's clipper ships were taking their toll on the seas and new factories were rising on her streams. The settlers' produce was flowing freely down the Mississippi. The real estate of former royalists and rebels in New York was rising in value as trade increased. Virgin soil, in the region which Jay insisted should be also American, was being spattered with the snowballs of a new crop which the spinners of the world were demanding in making a new cheap kind of cloth. Cotton was on its way to be king in place of King Tobacco as an export. Currency sound and people making money, with large families of children still the rule and immigrant labor pouring in, Congress was successfully laying taxes.

Something more substantial than twelve hundred pounds in depreciated paper money and authority to raise volunteers, who must fight in rags without pay, was behind that well-equipped Lewis and Clark expedition. It was under Jefferson's personal care as the Louisiana Purchase was his own child. It had all the army list from which to choose the fittest personnel as eager to go as a Boy Scout of today with an exploring expedition under Commander Byrd.

Brother William bore a letter in Jefferson's own hand, a very masterful inclusive Jeffersonian official blanket letter. As President of the United States he commanded all consuls, agents and other officials of the United States, and requested all bankers and commercial interests, home and foreign, to honor the drafts of Lewis and Clark. "I solemnly pledge the faith of the United States that these drafts shall be paid punctually on the date they are made payable."

So the Clark name was to be blazed on the breadth of the continent from the Alleghenies to the Pacific; so the second son of the majestic Ann had supplied her youngest son with his starting point in the wilds beyond Lake Michigan.

Through unknown territory, where the boundary line between Britain and the United States had not been settled, William was to be George's relay. He was to carry on past the Black Hills, on by the route of Hill's railroads over the Rockies, to Puget Sound. But there was no John Jay on hand when the "fifty-four forty" issue was inflaming Oregon settlers forty years later.

Before starting on his own adventure, in 1803, William visited George. It must have been a most brotherly meeting. Out of the maturity of his experience the elder could give the younger much advice.

William did not have to make war, or risk all on desperate strokes. His part was to explore and take notes, the joyful business of studying natural history and tribal customs. Perhaps he would see some remains of mammoths. These interested both George and neighbor Jefferson very much. George had sent some to Jefferson for his museum long ago.

And George remembered the braves who had come to see him at Cahokia all the way from the sources of the mysterious Missouri which William might now map. There were many questions which interested George and for which William might learn the answer. And William would find that the nature of the plains Indians was much the same as of the forest Indians with whom George had made his treaties. They would be now seeing for the first time the palefaces of whom they had heard. They would be hospitable and courteous to a small, well-mannered group of palefaces, who were only travelers and did not stop to raid their game preserves and build cabins.

William should be as ceremonious as they, and bear himself as a great chief, and have his men bear themselves as chiefs serving under him. And, despite that letter from

President Jefferson, William had better take care about his vouchers, for politics and government sometimes became very mixed. Even as George was the disciple of George Mason, so was William the disciple of that elder brother to whom he had listened long ago in round-eyed boyish wonder.

It was at Clarksville, it seems, that the spent elder brother bade good luck to the younger brother who was taking his place on the trail. There George had built a little house on a hill, across the river from Louisville, where he was in sight of the panorama of the falls and the town.

At last the promise of land by the "select gentlemen," which he had revealed to his soldiers on Corn Island to inspire them for the march to Kaskaskia, was being kept. Through the intercession of Senator Breckenridge he had been given a grant six miles square which he was surveying and dividing into sections. As soon as his part became of any value some creditor would turn to him asking for an installment on account; but, no matter, he was used to that.

He had to live. There were many shelves filled with his books in the new house. Three blacks, Cupid, Kit and Venus, who had been with his father and mother, looked after him and helped till his land. He had to ask the man who built his bathroom to wait a little for his pay.

Here he was when William, more famous now through the length of the land than himself, returned to tell of the Indians he had met; of the vast dry plateau he had crossed and the mighty mountains he had scaled; of the great bears and elk and the trout in the streams, and of the rich virgin soil in a moist soft climate sloping down to the sea where there were wondrous harbors—which in the East they were saying, as they were once of the Ohio valley, would always be a worthless wilderness and, therefore, would better be left to the Indians and the panthers.

And here it was that George and a visitor after his own

heart had their talks. Audubon, the pioneer naturalist, was not speculating on second-hand information in the fashion of those fellows who wrote in the *American Museum*. He was seeing the life of the forests for himself; he, too, was fascinated by the habits of wild creatures. Audubon's notes of their talks were lost. Clark made none.

"General Clark has become frail and rather helpless," Josiah Espey wrote in 1805, "but there are the remains of great dignity and manliness in his countenance, person and deportment." Espey was struck with what he calls "perhaps a fancied likeness" to Washington.

Fellow farmers from the quarter sections dropped in to see him. He had in them another patriarchy as president of the commission which governed the grant. His old officers and soldiers came out of their way to pay their respects.

Farther still came the Indian chiefs he had known. They had done battle against other Big Knives in the meantime and beaten them, too; but Clark was still their brother, fellow to the Great Spirit, the unbeaten miracle warrior. When they lighted the peace pipe again he must take the first puff. In understanding Indian silences, forest silences, they sat in sight of the river's flow with the ghosts of their memories of the days when they were young and their sinews springy on the trail.

And so on until 1808 when, one day, Clark's right side went dead from a stroke of paralysis. Soon afterward he had an infection of the foot which spread until the surgeons decided that an amputation halfway between the knee and hip was the only way of saving him. It did not seem to him that life mattered much when his race was so far run; but it did to all the brothers and sisters and in-laws of the Clark clan and to his old veterans.

There were no anesthetics in those days to relieve pain. When he asked for a drummer to play during the operation, a canvass brought two drummers and two fifers, too. During the hour the surgeons were at work they circled the house. Without a tremor in his face Clark was beating time to the marching music with the fingers of his live hand. Saw, saw on the bone—ripple the fifes—we'll reach Vincennes yet! Sew the flaps of skin together—roll the drum—Helm's flag is up again!

Soon after this brother Jonathan died. George thought this unfair when Jonathan had a family and he was prospering; while he, himself, was only waiting to die, as he said. It was some time afterward that he wrote to Colonel Vigo that "life's tenderest string" had been broken. This might have referred to Jonathan or to Terese; for the Colonel must have known of the love affair.

Then a member of the Virginia legislature heard that George Rogers Clark was in a wheel chair. He offered a resolution which passed. A delegation was bringing the veteran a sword which had an inscription this time. He received the "select gentlemen" courteously. We may see him in his wheel chair with the sword across his lap as they felicitated him.

He had made no public complaints. But memories came back. A sword, now! He was said to have remarked that when Virginia needed a sword he had served her with his own. Bread was more in order. That proclamation of Governor Randolph's posting him as a marauder and a cheat! This had not been repudiated.

And those vouchers? He knew he had sent them in! Vouchers! Yet, as he had written, "but a country was at stake, and if it was imprudence, I suppose that I would do the same again, should I have a similar field to pass through."

"Facts will prove themselves!"

Those vouchers? If, instead of the sword, Virginia had only sent him the testimonial which I saw in the Virginia archives. What scenes of his youth it would have revived!

It tells the story of the pressure upon him in his battle against odds. If his father had seen it he would have known that his training of young George in business-like methods had not been in vain.

It was not until 1913, in the days of manifold sheets and card indexes, that seventy bundles of old documents in the State Auditor's office at Richmond were brought over to the State Library and opened. Clark's vouchers had not been destroyed by Benedict Arnold. Here they were, to the number of more than two thousand, close-written by his scattered commanders and quartermasters to save paper, and some even on sand paper and the backs of old playing cards.

Many times Clark's signature appears in making or countersigning a requisition. There is a warning from him to subordinates to keep expenditures down. His garrison commanders asked frequently for rations of rum for their men and themselves, but Clark made not a single requisition for any kind of alcoholic beverage for himself.

No item was too small to be accounted for by a written order, not even two candles, a ramrod or three sheets of precious writing paper, in the list which includes calking hemp and calking irons for boats, axes, grindstones, scythes, whipsaws, Peruvian bark (quinine), hats, winter underclothes, awls, files, augers and fishhooks as well as meat, flour and corn and lead and ball.

From far and near, in that wilderness patriarchy, came appeals for all manner of supplies; of soldiers on starvation rations, or ill from eating buffalo meat that was becoming wormy for want of salt to preserve it; for some kind of dependable credit when all traders had ceased to honor drafts in Continental script. Yet, through these tales of misery brought to the patriarch, ran the spirit of loyalty to him, which had determined Helm "to act brave."

XXXV

THE VISION FULFILLED

IT was 1818. Clark had become so frail that his sister Lucy, Mrs. Croghan, had persuaded him to be brought across the river to her home in Locust Grove. Only the great head with its wisps of greyish hair, and the high nose with the skin parchment over the cartilage, and the big bony shoulders, remained of youth in its power. Another stroke of paralysis had left him speechless.

Niece Diana Gwathmey, "she was very lovely" the accounts say, came often to the side of his chair. He tried in vain to make his tongue carry his greeting to her. He patted her hair and a smile came into the deep-set eyes, such very old eyes, now.

There was an understanding between the two. Before his stroke he liked to talk with her. Sometimes he would break out saying that she might have had a charming woman for an aunt if—and then the Indian silence. Why explain even to dear Diana? One secret even she might not share.

And years before he liked to talk to his cousin, Mrs. Semple, who wrote to Dr. Draper that her aunt, Ann Clark, "said she had heard that George had seen a Spanish nun somewhere and fallen very deeply in love with her. Why he could not get her, or what became of her, she did not or could not tell. She said that was the reason why he took no notice of ladies and was surprised to see him pay me so much attention." It was his impoverishment, brother William said, that broke the engagement.

When still young, soon after the Revolution was over, he had given up dances and parties of which he was so fond. He may have taken too many toddies, but no whisper of any scandal about women in his career has come down to us. Either he had loved Terese or he had loved not at all; and the soldier who fought and marched with all the power in him would have loved with all the power in him. It takes a great overmastering love between a man and a woman, of two widely differing races and cultures, to defy all the countering inhibitions which were more pronounced in the seventeen eighties than to-day.

Some veterans and an occasional Indian chief came to call; but these survivors who had been Clark's friends when he was young were now old, too. To the younger generation of the flourishing state of Kentucky the man in the wheel chair was as good as dead, a figure of romantic yesterdays of which their elders talked.

Much had passed since he first came down the Ohio. In Europe Napoleon had risen and fallen and was dying in exile in St. Helena. In the United States James Monroe was President in the era of peace and plenty.

Thomas Lincoln, who had moved over the divide from Virginia, had now crossed the river to take up a quarter section in Indiana. His son Abraham was nine years old. Four years later Ulysses S. Grant was to be born near the site of the Indian battle at Point Pleasant. He was also to be charged with taking too many toddies, which led to Lincoln's famous inquiry as to what brand he drank in order to keep other generals supplied.

General Andrew Jackson was championing a new style of democracy which was not altogether a welcome offspring to that intellectual aristocrat, Thomas Jefferson, the father of democracy, who, at seventy-five, was busy building his new university in what had been the back country of Albemarle county of his youth.

Henry Clay, who had migrated to Kentucky as a young Virginia lawyer, was now in his third term as Speaker of the House of Representatives in the new capital city which was named after the man who was now called the "immortal father of his country" although he had been so much abused in his time. Daniel Webster, who had been unseated in Congress for his opposition to rechartering the United States Bank, was arguing the Dartmouth College case before Chief Justice John Marshall.

John Jacob Astor was looking after the nation's fur business; and his "Oll Korrect" on bills, which was to endure in the language as "O.K.," did not interfere with the flow of profits which he was boldly investing in farms in the Union Square region and even beyond it on Manhattan Island.

The new steamboat was appearing on western rivers to speed the growth of Cincinnati, St. Louis, Louisville, Memphis and New Orleans and the rise of other towns on their banks. Young Cornelius Vanderbilt, who was abreast of the mechanical progress of the time with his new steam ferry in New York harbor, was to see a richer prospect for fortune in the railroads which were to cut across the river courses and speed the growth of "Chicagou" and give rise to cities beside steel tracks. But long afterward, in the era of "white coal" their water power was to make the rivers mighty again.

Governor De Witt Clinton of New York had well under way the daring project of the Erie Canal which was to be the channel of the migration from the Hudson and New England valleys westward; and this was eminently gratifying to those interested in the future of Buffalo and of the Ohio Reserve and the new town at the old Cuyahoga portage which was named after pioneer Moses Cleveland.

There was a new Northwest. The old North West Territory had been partitioned. Ohio had been admitted as a State in 1803, Indiana in 1816 and Illinois was to be admitted in 1818. Michigan was a Territory looking forward to admission, and Detroit was on the way to be more than a fur trading and garrison post.

Meliorem Lapsa Locavit! A better thing had come. The vision was being fulfilled, if not in just the way that Clark had planned, yet in desired result through the peculiar cohesion of the mass energy of individualism, "tomahawk claim" and "corn title," according to the cult of the little valleys.

That peaceful Monroe era, when big men were turning to private enterprises to the neglect of politics, was beginning to bless the sturdy founding fathers as their earthly reward, after the majority of them had already gone to their heavenly reward or were too feeble to stand in the way of youthful political ambition.

The speechless and helpless old man could watch the flow of his river and look across it to the land of his daring do, and recall, perhaps, as his most secure secret, the day when he had met a Spanish governor's sister. Terese was to die in a convent in Spain two years after he went to sleep quietly, on a February day in 1818, in his wheel chair on the porch at Locust Grove.

THE END

INDEX

Date Due

	PRINTED IN U. S. A.		

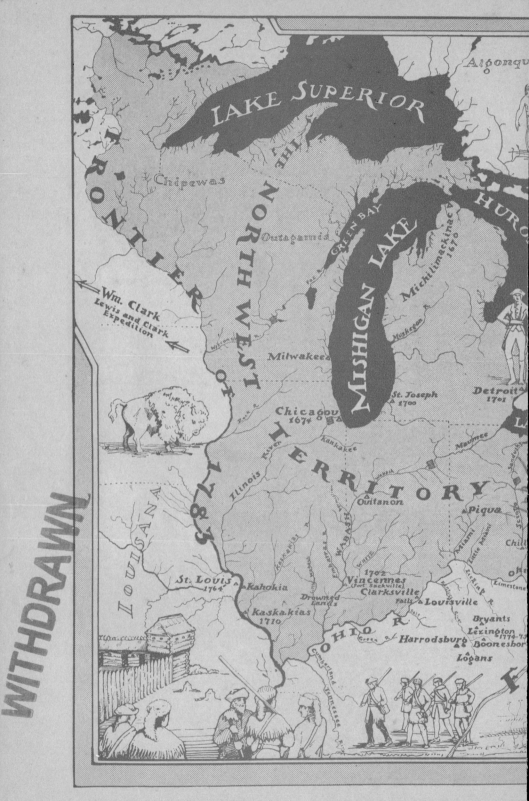

This MAP IS BASED in ESSENTIALS on the FIRST PUBLISHED MAP of the UNI